ENGLISH PLACE-NAME SOCIETY. VOLUME XXIV
FOR 1946–47

GENERAL EDITOR
A. H. SMITH

THE PLACE-NAMES OF OXFORDSHIRE

PART II

THE PLACE-NAMES OF OXFORDSHIRE

By

MARGARET GELLING

BASED ON MATERIAL COLLECTED BY

DORIS MARY STENTON

PART II

CAMBRIDGE

AT THE UNIVERSITY PRESS

1954

PUBLISHED BY
THE SYNDICS OF THE CAMBRIDGE UNIVERSITY PRESS

London Office: Bentley House, N.W. 1
American Branch: New York

Agents for Canada, India, and Pakistan: Macmillan

Printed in Great Britain at the University Press, Cambridge
(Brooke Crutchley, University Printer)

CONTENTS

MAPS

X. WOOTTON HUNDRED

Wutton' 1168–9 P *et passim* with variant spellings *Wuttun(a)*,
Wuttun, Wuttun' to 1428 FA
Witton' 1169–70, 1187–8 P
Wotton' 1193 P *et passim* with variant spellings *Wotton(e)* to
1441–2 Eynsh
Wootone 1285 *Ass*

v. Wootton *infra* 293. It is stated in DB that three hundreds belong
to the royal manor of *Optone*, and this statement can only be explained
by assuming that *Optone* is a very poor form of the name of Wootton:
there is no Upton within reach, and the "three hundreds of Wootton"
are mentioned 1175 and 1182 P.

1. Middle Aston

MIDDLE ASTON

Estone 1086 DB, *Estona* 1219 Fees, *Midelestun'* 1220 Fees,
Mid(d)eleston' 1240–1 *Ass*, *Eston'* 1242–3 Fees, *Middeleston'*
1242–3 Fees, 1268 *Ass*, *Midelest'* 1275 Ipm
Midelaston' 1273–4 RH *et freq* with variant spellings *Middelaston'*,
Middalaston' to 1336 Cl, *Midlaston* 1316 FA, 1392 Cl, *Middel
Aston* 1428 FA
Middilhaston' 1284–5 FA, *Meddel Haston* 1320 Ch, *Middel Haston*
1346 FA

'East tūn.' It is between North and Steeple Aston.

GARDEN COPSE (6″) is so named 1896 Brookes: cf. *the Gardens* 1763
Brookes. GRANGE FARM is *The Grainge Farm* 1763 Brookes.
HORSE WELL, RASPBERRY BRAKE, THREE CORNER CLUMP and WARREN
COPSE (all 6″) are so named 1896 Brookes. MILLBROOK SPINNEY is so
named 1896 Brookes.

FIELD-NAMES[1]

(*a*) In 1896 Badger Close (so named 1763), Barn Ground (so named 1763),
Boldhams (*Ballum Meadow* 1763), The Close, Copse Close, Daffydowndilly
Clump, The Dairy Ground (so named 1763), Dove-house Orchard, Dun-
stable, Great Meadow (so named 1763), Hall Common, Hanglands Brake
(*Hanglands* 1763, *v.* hangende), High Ridges (so named 1763), Lawn, Many

[1] Except where otherwise stated, the forms are from Brookes.

Wells (*Maney Wells* 1763), Nethercote Meadow (*Nethercroft Meadow* 1763), Nine Elms, Nut Orchard, Oak Lane, Old Orchard, Upper Ponds, Large and Lower Pond (all so named 1763), Puddle Pits (*Pudle Pit* 1763), First and Far Sandhill, The Sandy Ground, Sandy Way (so named 1763), The Seech (probably the dialect word *sich(e)*, 'brook, ditch'), Sheep Walk, The Slack (*slack* is a dialect term for a hollow), Stone Green (so named 1763), Tooley Hill (*Tuley Piece* 1763, *Tuley Tree Quarter* 1793 *EnclA*, *Tewley Bush* 1797 Davis, the first element is probably 'Tew' from Duns Tew), Town End Close, Wheel Furrow.

(*b*) In 1763 *Brook Acres, Burgate, Church Piece, Clay Furlong, Old Cow Pasture, The Crofts, Long Ditch, Holey Well, Home Close* (*v.* home), *Honey Mead* (*v.* honey), *Lime-kiln Ground, The Moore, The New Spinney, The Park, Pleasure Grounds, Puden hedge piece, East and West Ratnells, Old St. foin Ground, Stone Style piece, Town Piece, The Walks.* In 1278–9 (RH) *Lybetesham, Sarpenham* (*v.* hamm; the first elements are probably personal names).

2. North Aston

NORTH ASTON

Estone 1086 DB *et freq* with variant spellings *Eston(a)* to 1217 Cl, *Nort' Eston* 1200 Cur, *Norhestun'* 1220 Fees, *Nord Eston* 1232 Cl, *Norzeston* 1235–6 Fees, *Norteston'* 1242–3 Fees, *Northeston'* 1242–3 Fees, 1268 *Ass*

North Aston' (bis) 1246–7 *Ass, Northaston'* 1278–9 RH *et freq* with variant spelling *Northaston* to 1373 Cl, *Noraston* 1284–5 FA, *North Aston* 1428 FA

Nord Haston 1346 FA

'East tūn.' It is north of the other two Astons.

COLDHARBOUR FM: *v.* Fan. DANE HILL is *Dean Hill* 1797 Davis; cf. *Dean Hill Farm* c. 1840 *TA, v.* denu. THE FOLLY (6″) is so named c. 1840 *TA, v.* folly. FOX AND CROWN INN (6″) is *Fox Hall* 1797 Davis. THE GREEN. Cf. *The Town Green* c. 1840 *TA*.

FIELD-NAMES

(*a*) In c. 1840 (*TA*) The Bestmoor (Bessmore 1591 *Survey*, Beastmoor 1685 (c. 1700) *BodlT, v.* mōr), Bustard Hill Spinney, Bushwell Ground, Cross Meadow, Dairy Ground, Fox Close, Horse Moor, Job's Close, Lime Kiln Ground, Mayors Close, Ney Meadow, Picked Close Slade (*v.* picked), Pound Orchard, Rice Ham, Rush Bed Cover, The Slade (*v.* slæd), Side Land (*v.* sideland), Town Leys, Upper and Lower Wins Ground.

3. Steeple Aston

STEEPLE ASTON [sti·pl a·stən]

Estone 1086 DB, c. 1260 Os (p), *Estona* c. 1186–92 Eynsh,
Stipelestun' 1220 Fees, *Stepel Eston'* 1224 Cl, *Stepeleston'* 1242–3
Fees *et freq* with variant spelling *Stepeleston* to c. 1265 Os,
Stepulestone c. 1265 Os, *Stepileston* 1428 FA

Stepelaston' 1278–9 RH, *Stupelaston* 1307 Ipm, *Stepel Aston* 1316
FA, 1330 Cl, *Stepelaston, Stepil Aston* 1362 Cl, *Stapelaston* 1368
Cl, *Stepulaston* 1384 Cl, *Stepull Aston* 1428 FA

Stepelhaston 1284–5, 1346 FA, *Stepulhaston* (bis) 1366 (c. 1444)
BC, *Stepilhaston* 1389 Cl

'East **tūn**,' to which 'steeple' has been prefixed.

NOTE. TUER LANE. *Tewer* is a word used in this part of the country for
a narrow passage; it occurs also in the field-names of Hook Norton 355.

DEAN CLUMP (6″), PLANTATION. Cf. *Denelac* 1278–9 RH, *Deneswey*
late hand Os. 'Stream and way in a valley,' *v.* **denu, lacu, weg.**

BRASENOSE FM is so named 1806 Brookes. DUCKWORTH'S WELL (6″)
and HOPCROFT'S HOLT are *Duckets Well* and *Hopcrafts Holt* 1767
EnclA: a family named *Hopcraft* appears in 18th century records
mentioned by Brookes.

FIELD-NAMES

(*a*) In 1896 and 1929[1] (Brookes) Barn Ground, Big Field, The Big
Meadow, Brackley Leys (Brackley is about nine miles away in Nth), Can-
nigers Meadow, Conegar (*Coney Gears* 1767 *EnclA*, *v.* conygree), Church
Gardens, Creek's Field (*Creek's Close* 1806 Brookes), Dairy Ground,
Dickeridge Meadow (*Dickredges* 1767 *EnclA*), Dry Well (*Dry Well Furlong*
1767 *EnclA*), Fir Lane, Fishpool Spinney and Meadow, The Folly Field
(the 'folly' is a mock ruin built in the 18th century, *v.* folly), Fox-holes
(*v.* fox-hole), The Goggs (so named 1767 *EnclA*, *v.* gogg), The Grange,
Great Ground, Little and Big and South Heydon (*Hayden* 1634 (c. 1700)
BodlT, *Heydon Way*, *Sandy Haydon*, *Haydon Upper Furlong* 1767 *EnclA*),
The Home Ground (*v.* home), Miller's Close, Otley Hill, Pest-house Field
(*v.* pest-house), Pump Ground, Rectory Field, Rush Close, Sand-hill (*Great
Sandhill* 1806 Brookes), Sixty Foot Field, Lower and Upper Spurway, Still
Close Meadow, Stone Pit Ground and Field (both so named 1806 Brookes),
Wincote.

(*b*) In 1806 (Brookes) *Church-yard Close, Furze Dean, Plough Dean, The
Hanging Field* (*v.* hangende), *Honey Ham Way Ground* (*Honey Ham* 1767

[1] C. C. Brookes states that some of these are taken from a map of 1896, and
some collected in his own time.

EnclA, *v.* honey), *Lane Hill* (so named 1767 *EnclA*), *Lockwell* (so named 1767 *EnclA*), *The Mantle with Strings* (*Mantle Acre, Strings* 1767 *EnclA*, for the latter *v.* strings), *Parson's Hook, Slad Hill Furlong* (*Slade Hill Furlong, River Slade* 1767 *EnclA*, *v.* slæd), *Walnut Tree Close, West Green, the Youlings*. In 1767 (*EnclA*) *Baliol Meadow, Beech Walk, Church Way Furlong, Long Clay Furlong, Short Clay Pit Furlong, College Close, Cut* (*v.* cut), *Dairy-ground Road, Doctor's Block, Fiddle Butts* (*v.* butts, *fiddle* is used in dialect for various plants), *Fill Barn Furlong, Kings Bushes, the Milking Place, Nizewell Head* (*Nine Wells* 1720 Brookes), *Sands shooting North and South, Sands shooting East and West, Shepherds Hill, Slatter Ford* (*Sloterford', Sloteruuelle* c. 1210 Bodl, *Slotresford* c. 1215 Os, this might be identical with Slaughterford near Slaughter in Gl, for which Ekwall (DEPN) assumes an OE *slōhtre, 'muddy place,' corresponding to the word found in the German name *Schlüchtern*, though some sign of the -*h*- might have been expected), *Spoil Bank*[1], *Ten Score Baulk, Turk Hedg Furlong, The Warren, Water House, Watery Lane, Wootton Yerds*. In 1278–9 (RH) *Sitarescleve* (this is another occurrence of the name *Sciteres clif* found in BCS 932 in Sunningwell Berks: probably the two forms are equivalent to the name Shooters Hill, which occurs in Nth and K, possibly meaning 'hill used for archery practice'; here the second element is clif, cf. the field-names of Wychwood 390, where this first element appears compounded with hōh).

4. Steeple Barton

Steeple Barton

> *Bertone* 1086 DB, *Bertona* 1186–90 Os, *Berton* c. 1195 (c. 1425) Frid, 1265 Ch, *Bertun' Johan* 1220 Fees, *Magna Berton'* 1242–3 Fees, *Berton', Berton Major* 1246 Ch, *Stepelbertone* 1247 FF, *magna Bertone* 1285 *Ass*, *Berton Seint Johan* 1398 Cl, *Magna Berton* 1428 FA
>
> *Barton'* 1235–6 Fees, *Magna Barton'* 1240–1, 1268 *Ass*, *Magna Barthon* 1246–7 *Ass*, *Stepel Bartona* 1247 Os, *Stepelbartona* 1247 FF, *Barton' Magna* 1278–9 RH, *magna Bartone* 1285 *Ass*, 1316 FA, *Barton Seynt Jehan* 1349 Ipm, *Barton Seint Johan* 1349 Cl, 1356 Ch, *Barton Sci Johannis* 1376 Cl, *Magna Barton* 1428 FA, *Steple Barton* 1584 AD

Middle Barton

> *Mydell Barton* 1449 Cl, *Middilbarton* 1509–10 Os

Sesswell's Barton (6″)

> *Bertone* 1086 DB, *Bertona* c. 1210 Bodl, *Bertun' Odun* 1220 Fees, *Berton' Odonis, Berton' Ede* 1242–3 Fees, *Berton Goede* 1273–4 RH, *Berton Roede* 1275–6 RH, *Berton Rede* 1428 FA

---

[1] This is a term for a bank or mound of refuse earth or similar material.

Bartona c. 1215, 1245 Os, *Bartona Odonis* 1245 Os, *Odebartona* 1247 FF, Os, *Barton Ede* 1278–9 RH, 1316 FA, 1334 Ch, *Barthone Odonis* 1280 Os, *Ode Bartone* 1293–4 St John, *Ode Barton* 1320 Ch, *Barton Oede* 1337 Cl, *Barton Odonis* 1338 Cl, 1389 Os, *Barton Eudonis* 1350 Cl, *Barthona O(u)donis* 1350 Os, *Barton Sharshill* 1517 D Inc, *Seswell Barton* 1797 Davis

v. beretūn: the earliest form for Westcot Barton (250) suggests that this group of names contains *bærtūn, with the same meaning.

The parish of Steeple Barton contains the two manors of *Great Barton* and Sesswell Barton formerly *Barton Odonis*. *Great Barton* is so called in distinction to Westcot or *Little Barton*, and was sometimes called *Barton St John* from the family *de Sancto Johanne*, who had land there in the 12th, 13th and 14th centuries. *Barton Odonis* takes its suffix from *Odo* de Bertona, who grants land there c. 1210 *Bodl*. It became Sesswell Barton from William de *Shareshull*, who is given free warren there 1334 Ch and land 1350 Cl. An early stage in the transformation of the last name is seen in a letter of Sir Thomas More dated 1530[1], where it is called "the manor of Sharshelberton in the parishe of Stepleberton."

BARTON GROVE, LITTLE GROVE (both 6"). Cf. *la Graue* 1230 Os, 1270 Ch, *Grave* 1354 Ipm. *v.* grāf(a).

DADDLES CLOSE SPINNEY (6"). Cf. *Dodewelle* c. 1200, c. 1240 Os. '*Dod(d)a*'s spring or stream,' *v.* w(i)elle.

MAIDEN BOWER is so named c. 1840 *TA*. *v.* PN Cu 255–6.

RAYFORD LANE (6"). Cf. *Ragheford* c. 1220 *Bodl*, (*pontem de*) *Raureford* 1278–9 RH, *Raford Medowe* 1658 *Bodl*, *Rairford Lane* 1795 *EnclA*. 'Ford frequented by herons,' first element hrāgra, 'heron,' second element ford.

SHOWELL COVERT (6"). Cf. *Seuelle* c. 1210 *Bodl*, *Seuewellestlade* c. 1210, c. 1240 Os, *Sewelle* late 13th Os. 'Seven springs,' identical with Showell Fm in Little Tew 291. The final element of *Seuewellestlade* is (ge)lād, 'track, watercourse.'

BUSWELL'S THICKET (6") and LEYS FM. Cf. *Buswell's Thicket wood* and *The Leyes* c. 1840 *TA*. HOAR STONE (there are two on the 6" map). Cf. *Whorston* c. 1840 *TA*, *v.* hār, stān. PURGATORY is so named 1797 Davis, *v.* Fan. STEEP HILL is so named c. 1840 *TA*.

---

[1] *The Correspondence of Sir Thomas More*, ed. Elizabeth Frances Rogers, Princeton 1947, p. 430.

WHISTLOW. Cf. *Westalow way and hedge* 1634 (c. 1700) *BodlT*, *Whisterlow* 1685 (c. 1700) *BodlT*, *Whistelow Farm* 1795 *EnclA*.

FIELD-NAMES

(*a*) In c. 1840 (*TA*) Beech field, Briar Land (*Brierland* 1658 *Bodl*, *Brierlands* 1666 *Bodl*: cf. *Brerforlong* c. 1200 Os, *Brerfurlong* c. 1240 Os, 1247 FF, with first element OE *brǣr*, 'briar'), Burnt field, Dove House Close, Fox Cover, Handy ground, Little and Great Holt ground, Little Moors, Great and Little parsons ground, Parsons meadow, Little pittins, Sandy meadow, Shew Hill, Warren piece, Lower and Upper Westerly, Woodfield.

(*b*) In 1685 (c. 1700) (*BodlT*) *the Calves Close, Church Field, Elm gap, Fern slade, horns way, Ingrahams furze, Lettam leyes, longe meere, Maple Bush hill, Marches Quarre, the Slatt furlonge, the vicaridge peece, Vicars Cross, the wool furlonge*. In 1634 (c. 1700) (*BodlT*) *the Great Stone, Leinwell way, Ramford way* ((*oþ*) *ramma ford* 958 (12th) BCS 1042, *Ramford* c. 1192 Os, c. 1210 *Bodl*, the literal interpretation is correct: there are places called (*and lang*) *ramma dæne* 958 (12th) BCS 1042, and *Rammedenesheuede, Rammeswelle* c. 1210 Os in the neighbouring parish of Wootton, with final elements denu, hēafod and w(i)elle), *Redhill, Rosely furlong, Saltpitts, the Sandy furlong*. In c. 1240 (Os) *Crofteslondesende* (cf. *Croftland* c. 1210 Os, *Croftlande* c. 1210 *Bodl*, v. croft, land, ende), *Dodendene* (*Doddendene* c. 1200 Os, '*Dod(d)a*'s valley,' v. denu, evidently named from the same man as Daddles Close Spinney in this parish: cf. *Doddendeneshelde* c. 1270 Os under Westcot Barton, to which h(i)elde has been added), *Halfurlong* (v. h(e)alh), *Hurstanesfurlung* (the first elements may be hyrst and stān), *le Slade* (v. slæd, *Stladda* (? for *Scl-*) c. 1210 Os is probably a poor spelling of this), *Stanlow* (v. stān, hlāw), *Wadbreche* ('breche where woad is grown'), *Utfurlunge, Hutfurlong* (*Utfurlang* c. 1210 Os, first element ūt, 'out'). In c. 1233 (Os) *Brodeweisende* (v. brād, weg, ende), *Cagelesmere* (also c. 1210 Os, v. mere), *Grenesdic* (v. grēne, dīc), *Langelowe* (cf. *Nordlangelawe* c. 1210 Os, *Langelaue* c. 1210 *Bodl*, 'long barrow,' v. hlāw; 'north' has been prefixed to one form), *Socheslowe* (*Succhelaue* c. 1210 *Bodl*, *Shuckelawe* c. 1215 Os, first element scucca, 'goblin,' second element hlāw). In c. 1215 (Os) *Demnesweye* (the word *demon* is not recorded till the late 14th century, but in view of the reference to goblins *supra*, and the presence of the burial ground commemorated in the name of Berrings Wood in Glympton, it is reasonable to assume it as the first element of this name: second element weg), *Etfurlong* (*Ethfurlong* c. 1210 *Bodl*, first element may be hǣþ), *Langlawe Slade* (*Langelausslade* c. 1210 *Bodl*, 'valley by the long barrow,' v. slæd), *Langehale* ('long h(e)alh'), *Wylauesdene* (*Wilausdene* c. 1210 *Bodl*, '*Wīglāf*'s valley,' v. denu). In c. 1210 (Os) *Bremhell* (v. hyll), *Grascrofte* (v. gærs, croft), *Netherwdel, Putta* (v. pytt), *Sudlangebreche* ('south long breche'), *Tunga* ('tongue of land'), *Wyrstaneslawe* (v. hlāw; first element a personal name). In c. 1210 (*Bodl*) *Angedelande* (this is perhaps a poor form of the common name 'hanging land,' for which v. hangende), *Sauuinesueie* ('*Sǣwine*'s weg').

5. Westcot Barton

WESTCOT BARTON

Bærtune 1050–2 (13th) KCD 950 (p)
Bertone 1086 DB, *Bertona* c. 1180–9, 1186–92, 1193–1200 Eynsh,
  Berthone 1203–6 Eynsh, *Bertun'* 1220 Fees, *Parva Berthona* 1239
  Eynsh, *Westcote Berton'* (bis) 1242–3 Fees, *West Berton* 1428 FA
Parua Bartona 1221 Os *et freq* with variant spellings *Parva Barton'*,
  Parva Bart(h)on, *Parua Barthona* to 1428 FA, *Westkote Barthona*
  c. 1260 Os, *West Barton* 1268 *Ass*, 1346 FA, *Westkote Barton'*
  c. 1270 Os, *Westbarton* 1283 Cl, *Bartone* 1285 *Ass*, *Westbardon*
  1290 FF, *Barton' Parua* 1291 Eynsh, *Barthone Parua* 1320
  Eynsh, *Bartona Parua* 1414–31 Eynsh, *Westcotebarton* 1509–10
  Os, *Westcote Barton* 1539 Eynsh
Westcot 1246 Ch, *Wescote* 1382 Cl

v. beretūn. Westcot means 'west cottage(s),' *v.* cot(e).

DOWNHILL FM and HORSEHAY FM. Cf. *Down hill* and *Horsehay* 1634
(c. 1700) *BodlT*, *Down Hill Field* and *Horse Hay* 1795 *EnclA*.

FIELD-NAMES

(*a*) In 1795 (*EnclA*) the Barnhills (*Barnhill* 1685 (c. 1700) *BodlT*), Brid-
bury Close, Burnthouse Meadow, Clay Hill, Corfley Meadow, Goose Acre,
Green Way, Long Holborn furlong, Herd's Way (*herds way* 1685 (c. 1700)
BodlT), Hollow Way, Mill Pike (*v.* picked), Pittire Meadow, Pound Lane,
Sandy Way (*Sondiwey* c. 1270 Os), Setholm, Sleyford Bridge, Snipemoor
Furlong (*Snitemore* 1634 (c. 1700) *BodlT*), Stone Hill (so named 1634
(c. 1700) *BodlT*), Three Bush Hill, Wood Way, Woolpack Lane.

(*b*) In c. 1270 (Os) *Wowelonde* (*v.* wōh, land). In c. 1180–9 (Eynsh)
Morhei (*v.* mōr, (ge)hæg).

6. Begbroke

BEGBROKE

Bechebroc 1086 DB, *Bechebrok* 1268 Cl
Bekebroch' 1188 P *et passim* with variant spellings *Bekebroc*,
  Bekebroc', *Bekebrok(e)*, *Bekebrok'*, *Bekebruk*, *Bekebrokes* to 1476
  AD, *Beckebroc* 1220 Fees, *Bekkebrok* 1242–3 Fees, *Beckebrok*
  1247 FF, 1335 Ch, *Beckebrok* (bis) 1285 *Ass*
Bikebroc 1233 Bract
Beckbroc 1235–6 Fees, *Bekbrok* 1297 Cl, *Bekbroke* 1526 LS
Brockebrok 1284–5 FA
Begbroke 1551–2 *Survey*

'*Becca*'s stream,' *v.* brōc and cf. Beckley 165.

FIELD-NAMES

(a) In c. 1840 (*TA*) Culls Heath Wood, Dill ground (*dill* is a dialect word for the vetch or tare, especially *Vicia hirsuta, sativa* and *sepium*), Hussey Ground, Image ground, Parsons Copse, Rum Close, Sidd Marsh, Watering ground.

7. Bladon

BLADON [bleidən]

> *Blade* 1086 DB
> *Bladene* 1141 OxonCh *et passim* with variant spellings *Bladen(a)*, *Bladen'* to 1797 Davis
> *Bladon'* 1208 OblR, 1254–5 RH, *Bladone* 1285 *Ass*
> *Bledon'* 1268 *Ass*

> *Bladon* is the old name of the river Evenlode, *v. supra* 7.

THE LINCE (6″) is *Dene Linche* 1258 Os. First element denu, 'valley,' second hlinc, 'hill.'

8. Cassington

CASSINGTON

> *Cersetone, C(h)ersitone* 1086 DB
> *Chersintone* a. 1123 Eynsh *et freq* with variant spelling *Chersintona* to 1197–8 Eynsh
> *Kersint'* 1123–33 OxonCh *et passim* with variant spellings *Kersinton', Kersint(h)ona, Kersinton(e), Kersintune, Kersynton'* to 1252 FF, *Cersintun'* 1220 Fees
> *Chersington'* 1169, 70 P
> *Chersentune* (bis) c. 1200 Belvoir
> *Karsintone* 1197–1208 Eynsh *et passim* with variant spellings *Carsintone, Karssinton', Karsinton, Karsintona, Carsynton* to 1320 Ipm
> *Kersington'* c. 1219 (c. 1280) S (p), *Kersyngtone* 1228, 30 Eynsh (p), *Cersington* 1246–7 *Ass, Kersingtone* 1285 *Ass, Kersington* 1290 Ch, *Kersyngton'* 1297 CornAcc
> *Cassington'* 1246–7 *Ass, Cassingtone* 1526 LS
> *Carsiton'* 1246–7 *Ass*
> *Karsington* 1275 FF *et freq* with variant spellings *Carsington', Carsingtone, Carsyngton, Karsyngton* to 1450 Cl

'tūn where cress grows,' *v.* cærse. Ekwall (DEPN) assumes an adjective **cærsen* as the first element of this and of Carsington Db.

BURLEIGH FM, WOOD take name from (*hyða* of) *Burgesia* (? *Burgelia*) c. 1200 Belvoir, *Buroule, Beroule* 1254–5 RH, (*bosco de*) *Burgwele*

1266 Ch, *Burleghe* 1271–2 *For*, (*bosco de*) *Borgelegh* 1273–4 RH, *Boroule* 1278–9 RH, (*bosco de*) *Burghwele* 1306 Cl, (*bosco de*) *Burghle* 1310 Cl, *Burghwell* 1320 Cl, *Burgwole* 1330 Ch. Cf. *Burleigh feld* 1606–7 *Survey*, *Burley Wood and meadow* 1608–9 *Survey*. 'Wood by a burh,' *v.* lē(a)h. The burh is doubtless the earthwork on Bladon Heath. There is confusion between lē(a)h and w(i)elle in the second element, possibly due to the proximity of Purwell Fm. The early spellings for Burleigh PN Herts 131 show some similarity to these, without the confusion with w(i)elle.

PURWELL FM is *Pyrwelle* 1551–2 *Survey*, *Peril Farm* 1821 O.S. Possibly 'pear-tree stream,' *v.* pirige, w(i)elle. Chambers (55) says that the name preserves that of some purlieus of Wychwood Forest, but the forms do not support this conjecture.

SOMERFORD (lost) is *Somerforde* c. 1230 Eynsh, 1316 FA, 1551–2 *Survey*, *Sumerford* 1241–64 Eynsh, *Somerford* 1297 CornAcc, 1300 Ipm. 'Ford used in summer.' The same name occurs in Ch, Gl and W.

WORTON

Vvrtone 1086 DB

Wrtona a. 1123 Eynsh *et freq* with variant spellings *Wrtun'*, *Wrthona* to 1222 Eynsh

Wurtton' 1194 P, *Wurton* 1237 (c. 1300) Fees

Worthona 1199, 1259 Os, *Worton'* 1242–3 Fees

Wourton' 1297 CornAcc

'Herb or vegetable enclosure,' *v.* wyrt, tūn, and cf. PN Mx 28, PN W 248, PN NRY 265.

JERICHO FM is so named 1822 O.S.

FIELD-NAMES[1]

(*a*) In 1804 (*EnclA*) Batmoor Lot Meadow or Batemoor Lotmead (*Batemore*, *Batemora* a. 1152 Eynsh *et freq* to c. 1285 (c. 1450), *Battemore* c. 1220, c. 1230, c. 1240 (all c. 1450), '*Bata*'s marsh,' *v.* mōr, lot)[2], Brimsgrove Field, Flexy, Godshill Field, Gravel Pits, Heath Field, Horse Common, Lammas Closes (*v.* Lammas), Lands Field, Little Limpton Meadow, Great Lympton Meadow (*lynton'* c. 1270 (c. 1450), *litell' lynton'* c. 1280 (c. 1450), *v.* lĭn, tūn), Moorlands Common (*the morelond'* c. 1280 (c. 1450)), Nine Lands Field, Pluck Patch, The Slade (*the slad* 1701 Bodl, *v.* slæd), Town Close, Worsey Meadow (*Wareseye* 1229 FF, *Wyresh(e)y* 1228–39 (14th) Chambers, *Wyrsseia* 1281 Eynsh, *Wyresheye* 1328 Eynsh, '*Wīghere*'s island,' *v.* (ī)eg).

[1] Except where otherwise stated, the forms are from Godstow.
[2] *Bata* occurs in *Batan cumb* BCS 1174.

(*b*) In 1701 (*Bodl*) *astladds* (possibly 'east slæd'), *bearlands* (*Berland*'
c. 1275 (c. 1450), 'barley land,' *v.* bere), *bandlands* (*Banlond*' c. 1280
(c. 1450), *v.* bēan, land), *Kingsway* (*kyngeweyesende* c. 1280 (c. 1450), *kyngis-
weye* c. 1285 (c. 1450), 'king's way'), *new parke, red lime furlong*. In c. 1350
(c. 1450) *Bolenham* (*Boleham* c. 1220 (c. 1450), *Bulnehamhoke, Bolenham*
c. 1270 (c. 1450), 'bull's or *Bula's hamm,' hōc has been added to one form),
Borowgham (*Borowham* c. 1270 (c. 1450), *Borengham, Borneham, Boronham*
c. 1285 (c. 1450), *v.* burh, hamm: the former is probably the earthwork on
Bladon Heath), *Heymede* (*v.* hēg, mǣd). In c. 1300 (c. 1450) *adgarston*
(*v.* gærs-tūn), *Corneheyte* (*Sornheyte* c. 1244 (c. 1450), *v.* corn, eyt), *lambecote*
(*lambcupe* c. 1270 (c. 1450), 'lamb shelter'), *Ophul* ('up hill'), *Storthebreth*
(probably a variant of the common field-name 'short broad,' with 'breadth'
as second element). In c. 1285 (c. 1450) *Bradforde* (*Bradeford*' c. 1270
(c. 1450), *v.* brād, ford), *Curtoforlonge, dedecherle* ('dead man,' *v.* ceorl; the
same name occurs PN Nth 275), *Ferthehulle* (*v.* fyrhþ(e), hyll), *Hay*(*a*), *the
haye* (*v.* (ge)hæg), *Hidacre* (*the hideacre* c. 1220, c. 1276 (both c. 1450),
v. hīd), *Hureleye* (possibly identical with Hurley Wa (PN Wa 18), of which
the elements are hyrne and lē(a)h), *polfurlonge* (*porforlonge* c. 1270 (c. 1450),
polfurlonge c. 1275 (c. 1450), 'pool furlong'), *Ruforlong*', *Rousfurlonge, Row-
furlonge, Rouforlonge* (*v.* rūh), *Shortforlonge*. In c. 1280 (c. 1450) *framcorde,
the haldefeld*' (*oldefeld*' c. 1270 (c. 1450), *v.* (e)ald, feld), *the hanginlond*
(*Hangindelond* c. 1213–28 AD, *hangyndelond*' c. 1270 (c. 1450), *v.* hangende),
Mochelforlonde (first element mycel, 'great'), *putlesdenesforlonge* (*putlesden*'
c. 1270 (c. 1450), *puthlesden*' c. 1275 (c. 1450), *v.* denu, first element pyttel,
'kite'), *rede hegge* (*v.* hrēod, rēad, hecg), *Sarnildeshoke* (*v.* hōc, the first
element is probably a personal name), *Surrelond* (*Surelond*' c. 1270 (c. 1450),
'sour land,' *v.* sūr). In c. 1276 (c. 1450) *farenhulle* (*farnehull*' c. 1190 (c. 1450),
Farnhull' c. 1270 (c. 1450), *v.* fearn, hyll), *the grenewey* (*v.* grēne, weg),
Rewneye (*Rouueneye* c. 1275 (c. 1450), *v.* rūh, (ī)eg). In 1275–6 (c. 1450)
Thoryndon' (*v.* þorn, dūn). In c. 1275 (c. 1450) *Cogchesham* (*v.* hamm),
Halradesclade (*Aldradeslade* c. 1270 (c. 1450), 'Ealdrǣd's valley,' *v.* slæd).
In c. 1270 (c. 1450) *Francwordy or francherdie* (second element worðig, the
expanded form of worþ: first the personal name *Franca*), *the grene downe*
(*v.* grēne, dūn), *fuleslo* (*v.* fūl, slōh, the name occurs also in Bensington and
Shirburn), *morelakefurlonge* (*v.* mōr, lacu), *shortiscome or shortescome* (*v.*
cumb, first element probably 'short'), *snitemore* (*v.* mōr, first element snīte,
'snipe'), *longewowe* (*v.* wōh). In c. 1244 (c. 1450) *Barkecrofte* (*v.* croft; first
element beorc, 'birch-tree'), *harestane* (*v.* hār, stān), *Withele, wythele*
('willow wood'), *wythibedde* (*v.* wīðig). In c. 1220 (c. 1450) *chenosche, New-
crofte* (*v.* nīwe, croft). In c. 1200 (Belvoir) *Foxwere* ('fox weir'). In c. 1190
(c. 1450) *the heyte* (*v.* eyt).

9. Combe

COMBE

Cvmbe 1086 DB, *Cumba* 1141–2 Eynsh *et passim* to 1270 Eynsh,
Cumba Regis 1163 P, *Cumbe* 1231 Ch *et passim* to 1293 Cl, *Cumb*
1251 Cl

Cumbes 1201, 6 Cur (p), 1242–3 Fees
Comba 1220 RoyLet, *Longa Combe* 1357 Pat, *Combe* (bis) 1399,
  1406, 1413 Eynsh, *Longecombe* 1446, 51 Eynsh, *Longcombe* 1464,
  75, 83 Eynsh, *Longe Combe* 1534 Eynsh
Coumb' 1273–4, 1275–6 RH, *Coumbe* 1291, 1320, 1399 Eynsh
COMBE BRIDGE (6″) is *Comb bridge* 1606–7 *Survey*.

'Valley,' *v*. cumb. It was evidently known as 'Long Combe' in
the 14th, 15th and 16th centuries. Mr C. S. Emden informs us that
the site of the village was moved to where it now is on the hill-side
from a position down in the river-valley, half a mile away, about 1350.

BOLTON'S LANE (6″) is *Bolton's lane* 1606–7 *Survey*. COMBE CLIFF
(6″) is on the river-bank, *v*. clif. FROGDEN WOOD (6″): cf. *Froggen
closes* 1606–7 *Survey*, *Frogden* 1606–7, 1608–9 *Survey*. NOTOAKS
WOOD is *Nottoakes* 1608–9 *Survey*, *Nattockes Wood* 1778 *Tithe
Survey* in Lincoln College, *Knot Oakes Wood* 1863 *Terrier* at Blenheim. *v*. nattock. WEDGEHOOK WOOD (6″) is so named 1822 O.S.:
possibly identical with *Wirges hooke(s)* 1606–7 *Survey*. WESTFIELD FM
takes name from *Westfeld* 1273–4 Imp, *Westfield als Coome Homefield*
1608–9 *Survey*.

FIELD-NAMES[1]

(*a*) Modern: Binwell Field and Bank (*Binwell Meadow* 1863), Chatterpie
(this is a dialect term for a magpie), Collins Ground, Goulden's Close (also
1863), Horn's Close, House Ground, Ramfield, Tag Green (*tag* is a dialect
term for a young sheep), Tinkers Close, Wellfield. In 1863 (*Terrier* at
Blenheim) Barn Ground, Coalman Meadow (*Colnham* 1278–9 RH, *Colneham*
1300 Wych, *Coln(e)ham* 1606–7 *Survey*, *Colenam als. Coome meadow* 1608–9
Survey, '*Cola*'s hamm'), Cow Common, Fairy Ground, Mill Meadow, New
Park End (New Park is on the 6″ map in Blenheim Park), Puddle Piece,
Rough Piece, Shepherds acre, Transport ground, White Hill Ground.

(*b*) In 1793 (Estate Act) *Berry Field* (cf. *Berryland, Bury orchard, Buryfeld,
Burymeade* 1606–7 *Survey*, *Berry field* 1608–9 *Survey*, *v*. burh), *Upper and
Lower Church Close, Clayham Meadow* (*Cleyham, Clayham* 1606–7 *Survey*,
Clayne meadow 1608–9 *Survey*, *v*. clǣg, mǣd), *The Parsonage Close*. In 1778
(*Tithe Survey* at Lincoln College) *Chain Meadow, Chalgrove Meadow,
Furzey Leys, Long Northall Furlong, Old and New Sate Furlong* (*Old Assart,
Newe Assart* 1606–7 *Survey*, *v*. sart). In 1608–9 (*Survey*) *Coome green,
Coome Towne Meade, Hartesore* (*Hartsole* 1606–7 *Survey*, possibly 'hart's
soil': *soil* NED sb[3] 2 means 'a pool or stretch of water, used as a refuge by
a hunted deer or other animal'), *Homefield* (*v*. home), *Perfumes, Robertes
foord, Wignam meadow* (*Wigenham* 1278–9 RH, *Wignham, Wignem, Wyg-
(g)enham* 1606–7 *Survey*, '*Wicga*'s hamm'), *Wyer close*. In 1606–7 (*Survey*)

---

[1] For the modern list and the lists for 1863 and 1778 we are indebted to Mr C. S.
Emden.

Bredecroft (first element *brǣdu*, 'breadth'), *Bridgmead*, *Brockhole* ('badger set'), *Cawsey* ('causeway'), *Colnoe*, *Corwell*, *Francden*, *Gallies wood*, *Gallowes wood*, *Galloes*, *Gorrell heath*, *the Grove*, *Hawkhurst Tey*, *le free Hichen* (*v.* hechinge), *Horsehole*, *Island wood*, *Landfield*, *Masterland Hill*, *Mattocke close* (*Mattockes Close* t. Hy 8 *AugmOff*), *Meadclose*, *Overthwart*, *Shepehouse close*, *Shortenorthe*, *Schornethorne*, *Slackpittes*, *Sneacre*, *Standelles* (*v.* stān-(ge)delf), *Ten acres*, *Whit waye*, *Wonacre*, *Wonhaker*, *One acre* (*Onacre* 1278–9 RH, 'one acre'). In 1285 (*Ass*) *Howacre*. In 1278–9 (RH) *Oxenemed* ('oxen's mead'), *Widege*. In 1273–4 (Ipm) *Estfeld* ('east field'), *Morfeld* (*v.* mōr), *Radewell*, *Sulham*.

10. Deddington

DEDDINGTON

Dædintun 1050–2 (13th) KCD 950 (p)

Dadintone 1086 DB *et passim* with variant spellings *Dadinton'*, *Dadinton(a)*, *Dadintun'*, *Dadynton'*, *Dadinthone*, *Dadyntone* to 1428 FA, *Daddinton'* 1242–3 Fees

Dedinton' c. 1160 Eynsh, 1195 P

Dadingtone 1227 FF *et freq* with variant spellings *Dadington'*, *Dadington*, *Dadyngtone* to 1526 LS

Datinton' 1235–6 Fees, 1246–7 *Ass*

Deydyngton 1580 AD

DEDDINGTON CASTLE. Cf. "Willelmus le Diue miles et dominus castelli de Dadinton" c. 1230, *Report on Manuscripts in Various Collections*, vol. vii, p. 40, Historical Manuscripts Commission, 1914. CASTLE STREET (6″). Cf. *Castell Side Street* 1588 *Bodl*.

'*Dæda*'s farm,' *v.* ingtūn. *Dæda* is the same name as that which appears as *Deda* in Bede's Ecclesiastical History.

NOTE. EARL'S LANE. Cf. *Earl's Closes or Pieces* 1808 *EnclA*, and possibly *le Yerles* 1550–1 *CourtR*. NEW STREET may be *New Street* 1413 *Windsor*, *le Newestrete* 1423–4 *CourtR*, *New street* 1591 *Survey*, 1612 *Bodl*[1]. PHILCOTE STREET (not on map) is *Pilcock Street* 1612 *Bodl*, *Pilcoke Street* 1625 *Bodl*.

Lost street-names are *Chepyngstret* 1365–6 *CourtR* (*v.* cīeping) and *Markett streete* 1591 *Survey*, the latter name being a later version of the former, and *Fylkyngstrete* 1416–17 *CourtR*.

CLIFTON

Cliftona c. 1170 OxonCh *et passim* with variant spellings *Clifton(e)*, *Cliffton*, *Clyfton(e)*

'tūn on the river bank'; *v.* clif and cf. Clifton Hampden 149.

---

[1] The identification is far from certain. Miss Helen Loveday informs us that the modern name is thought to date from the making of a turnpike here, but that on the other hand several of the oldest houses stand in this street.

HEMPTON

> *Hentone* 1086 DB, 1254 Eynsh *et passim* with variant spellings
> *Henton, Henton', Henthone* to 1346 FA
> *Haitona* c. 1210–18 Eynsh
> *Hyantona* 1218–28 Eynsh
> *Heenton* c. 1230 AD, 1300 Ipm
> *Emptone* 1285 *Ass*
> *Hemptone* 1285 *Ass et passim* with variant spelling *Hempton*
> *Hemton* 1675 Ogilby
> *Hampton* early 18th ParColl

'(At the) high tūn.' Cf. Henton in Chinnor (107).

ILBURY FM takes name from *Galoberie* 1086 DB, *Wolebire, Welebire, Wellebir'* 1192, 4, 6 *et seq* P, *Jellebire* 1205 Cur, *Jelebiri* 1208 OblR, *Elebere* 1220 Fees, *Yeleberi, Ielebur'* 1242–3 Fees, *Ielebir'* 1235 FF, *Yholebur* 1246 Ch, *Galburghyre* c. 1270 (c. 1450) Godstow (p), *Youleburie* 1278–9 RH, *Iollebury* 1289 FF, *Yelebyre* 1285 *Ass*, *Yol(u)ghbury* 1328, 9 Ch, *Yoleghbury* 1349 Ipm, *Elbury* early 18th ParColl. 'Yellow fort,' OE *geolu burh*. The burh of the second element is obviously the nearby prehistoric camp, and the Vicar informs us that this is situated at the end of a ridge which yields markedly yellow ironstone. Cf. Iron Down (394), about a mile away.

THE FISHERS is *The Fishers* 1793 *EnclA*, *Fishers* 1808 *EnclA*. This was the great fish pond surrounded by small stews which supplied fish for the castle. HAZELHEDGE FM takes name from *Hazel Hedge* 1808 *EnclA*. LEADENPORCH FM is *Ledynporche* 1463 Windsor, *Leeden porche* 1534 Windsor, *farm called the Leaden porche* 1591 *Survey*. THE WINDMILL (6″). Cf. *le Windmill* 1580 AD: this may be identical with *Westmulne* ? 1154–63, 1194 Eynsh, *Westmulle* 1163–80 Eynsh, *v.* **myln**.

FIELD-NAMES

(a) In 1933 (from *The Story of Deddington* by Mary Vane Turner) Barn Ground, Barson Hill (*Basord Hill* 1808 *EnclA*, cf. *Baston hole* 1591 *Survey*), Basil, Battle Thorn, Breach, Lower Breach Furlong (*Lower Breath Furlong* 1808 *EnclA*, cf. *le brech* 1333 Windsor, *v.* **breche**), The Butts (*v.* **butts**), Castle Side, Chapman's Leys, Dairy Ground, Eyford Hill, Hill Ground, Hoyle Hill (*Oil Hill* 1808 *EnclA*), Kite Moor, The Lake, Malinger, Oak Tree Ground, Pest House (*v.* **pest-house**), Picked Ground (*v.* **picked**), Plank Meadow (so named 1808 *EnclA*, *v.* **plank**), Round Hill, School Ground, Tank Ground, Little Thistle, Thistle Hill, Town's End, Wand Brook, Westmore Hill (so named 1808 *EnclA*), Wet Lands, Windmill Field. In 1808 (*EnclA*) Astall

Furlong, Barnhill Furlong, Batoss Orchard, Berryfield Tavern Close, Bimley Acres, Bowling Alley Close, Briar Furlong, Bugbrook Butts and Slade (*Bockebroc* 1320 *Windsor*), Bullen Withies, Cats Tail, Cave, Cherwell Moors, Church Pits Ground (Miss Helen Loveday informs us that this is believed to be the place where stone was quarried to rebuild the church tower in the 17th century), Clay pits (*le Cleyputtes* 1306 *Windsor*), Coloss Paddock and Garden, Great Coomb(e) (cf. *Coumbeforlong* 1422 *Rental*, v. cumb), Cow Food Butts (*v.* butts), Elder Stump, Fernhill, Fillbrook Leys, Fox Holes (*v.* fox-hole), Grove Ash, Guinea Furlong, Hanwells Hook, Harbours Hill, Hill Bourne Furlong, Hill way water Furlong, Hollwell Furlong (*Holewell* 1341 *Windsor*, *v.* holh, w(i)elle), Lank Furlong (*v.* lang), Marsh Hole Leys, Nuttings Grave, Nuttree Lane Close, Parsons Close, Pound Close, Sands Hill, Deep Slade(s), Slade Lane Close (*v.* slæd), Tatehills (*Teytell* 1550–1 *CourtR*), Three Thorn, Wall close, White Way.

(*b*) In 1591 (*Survey*) *Bamons bridge*, *Bere mouthe* (said to be where a brook enters the Cherwell), *Drunken billam*, *Fishwere*, *Lay Shere*, *Lyme pittes* (*Lyme pytte close* 1550–1 *CourtR*), *Vallesham*. In 1508–9 (*Rental*) *Chepacre* (*Chepacrestede* 1368–9 *CourtR*, *chepacreplace* 1416–17 *CourtR*, first element *cēap*, 'market'; stede, 'place,' has been added to the 1368–9 form). In 1422 (*Rental*) *Bordlond*, *Ouerbordleyn*, *Midelbrodleyne*, *Nethirbrodleyn* (*v.* lain), *Byggeforlang* (first element 'big'), *Fyueredes*, *Goldhornforlong*, *Haseleste*, *Bewesthasilstrete* (the second name means 'west of hazel street'), *Hedeforlang*, *Hiebodeshalle*, *Pokemedyforlong*, *Pouchereshalle*, *Ryehulle*, *Rytheham*, *Standelf* (stān-(ge)delf, 'quarry'), *Stonycroftforlong*. In 1423–4 (*CourtR*) *Boleland*, *Langagefurlong*, *Myddenhull* (the first element may be *midden*, 'dung-hill,' though the word is only recorded in ME with the suffix *-ing*), *Reekyerde*. ('rick-yard'). In 1408–9 (AD) *Beresy*, *Gardynereshegge* (*v.* hecg), *Hascumbe* (second element cumb). In 1379–80 (*CourtR*) *Astropyngmede* (cf. *Estrop* 1306, 1324, *Westhrop* 1325 in *Windsor*, apparently lost places in Deddington, *v.* þrop). In 1374–6 (*CourtR*) *Furthull*. In 1368–9 (*CourtR*) *Alhull* (*Alhul* 1320, 4 *Windsor*). In 1365–6 (*CourtR*) *le Landew* (*v.* landew), *Thedrych*. In 1289–90 (*CourtR*) *Littlemers* (*v.* mersc).

11. Eynsham

EYNSHAM [enʃəm]

(*ad*) *Egenes homme* 864 (11th) BCS 509, *Egenessam* 1130–50 OxonCh, *Egenesham* 1163, 85 P, c. 1270 Gervase, *Egeneisham* 1190 P

Egonesham c. 925 (s.a. 571) ASC A

Egnesham 1005 (late 12th) Eynsh, *Egneshammensem* c. 1080–7 (late 12th) Eynsh, *Egnesham* 1093–1100 Eynsh *et passim* with variant spellings *Egnesham(i)e* to 1385 Eynsh

Eglesham 1086 DB, *Eglessam* 1100–7 (1377–8) Eynsh

Eghenesham 1136–9 OxonCh

Einegsham c. 1160 RegAntiquiss

Einesham 1185 RotDom *et passim* with variant spelling *Eynesham*
to 1471 Eynsh, *Aynesham* 1230 P, 1428 FA, *Einnesham* 1311 Cl
Eisneham 1193–1200 Eynsh
Eignesham 1197–1200 Eynsh *et freq* with variant spellings *Eygnes-
ham(ie)*, *Eygnesham*' to 1320 Eynsh
Enesham c. 1200 Belvoir, 1205 Fine, 1220 Fees, 1275–6 RH,
Enesh' 1203 Cur
Hegnesham 1241–64 Eynsh
Eyneham 1242 Fees
Eynsham 1428 FA, 1585 AD, *Eynsam* 1517 D Inc
Ensham 1821 O.S.
EYNSHAM MILLS. Cf. *Egnesham Mulne* 1298 Eynsh.

Second element hamm. The first is probably the personal name
*Ægen, which is found also in Eynsford K (*v.* PN Ess 517). Ekwall
(DEPN) is unwilling to adopt this etymology in view of the ASC
form in *Egones-*.

NOTE. ABBEY ST, according to Chambers (68) is part of what was called
Mullhende (1342 Eynsh) and *Mill Street* in 1650, *v.* myln, ende. ACRE
END ST is *Acre End* 1518 Chambers. COWLEAZE LANE (not on map) and
CUCKOO LANE are so named 1802 *EnclA*: the latter name occurs also 1782
Chambers. HIGH ST is *via regalis* 1299 Chambers, *Temesestre(e)t, Temestret,
Temstreete* 1414 (c. 1630) *Corpus* (i.e. 'Thames Street'): there is a *Hyghestrete
Furlong* 1483 *CourtR*, which may contain an early occurrence of the modern
name. MEAD LANE is *Bitteralls Lane* 1782 Chambers, *v.* 261; *Biterall Lane*
occurs also in the 1802 *EnclA*. MILL ST is so named 1650 Chambers,
cf. *myll-lane* 1607 (c. 1630) *Corpus*. QUEEN ST was *Puck Lane* 1615, 50
Chambers; Chambers (68) says this name has been transferred to *Pug Lane*,
which was *Love Lane* in 1650. SPARACRE LANE takes name from *Sparewacre*
1484–5 *CourtR*, 'sparrow acre'; Chambers identifies it with *Town End* 1615.
    The point where Acre End St and High St meet Mill St was called *Carfaxe*
1527 NED, *Carfolks* 1650 Chambers, probably from Carfax in Oxford, *v.* 38.

BOWLES FM takes name from *Boweles* 1282 Fine (p), *Boules* 1285
Ass (p).

CHILMORE BRIDGE (6″) is *Chelmore Bridge* 1822 O.S. The same first
element is found in *Chelbreade furlonge, chelbred Yate* 1615 *CorpusMap*,
Chillbridge Gate and Furlong 1802 *EnclA*, and in the modern name
of the stream in question, Chil Brook. The element is presumably
OE ceole, 'gully.' *-breade, -bred* is brǣdu, 'broad piece of land,' and
Yate is geat. For the suffix of the present bridge name, *v.* mōr.

DERRYMERRYS BARN (6″). Cf. *Diamorris Close* 1615 Chambers, *Davy-
Mary Close* 1650 Chambers. Chambers (70) suggests that the original

name was *Ave Maria Close*, and that there was a shrine of the Virgin here.

FOXLEY FM may take name from *Foxle* 1247–8 AD (p), 1346 FA (p). 'Fox wood,' *v.* lē(a)h.

HIGHCROFT LODGE (6″) takes name from *Huythecroft* 1328, 63 Eynsh, *Huthecroft* 1363 Eynsh, *Highcroft* 1473–4 *CourtR*, *Hyghecroft* 1481–2 *CourtR*. The first element is hȳþ, 'landing place,' second element croft. Chambers (87) says that the croft was to the east, which would be between the house and the river Evenlode, and that he has eliminated the corruption to 'high croft' in the modern name.

MONK'S WOOD (6″) is *Munkeshode* 1363 Eynsh, *Monkeshode, Mongeshode* 1473–4 *CourtR*. For the second element *v.* PN ERY 226. An unrecorded OE *hōd*, related to *hēdan*, 'to protect,' and meaning 'shelter,' would give good sense here, the name meaning 'monk's hut.' It is very near the site of the Abbey.

NEWLAND HO (6″) takes name from *Niueland* 1229 FF, *v.* nīwe, land. Chambers (8) says that this was a new borough created to the north of the old one because the latter was inadequate for the influx of settlers attracted by the market. The charter of this *Nova Terra* was witnessed by the abbey chapter and delivered to the communa of burgesses in 1215.

SWINFORD BRIDGE (6″) is (*passagium de*) *Swyneforde* 1299 Eynsh, *Swynefordehythe* 1362 Eynsh, *Swynfordhuythe* 1481–3 *CourtR*. 'Swine ford': -*h(u)ythe* means 'landing place,' *v.* hȳþ. The village of Swinford is over the boundary in Berks.

THE THRIFT (6″) is *le Frith* 1268–81 Eynsh, 1300 Wych, *Leffrth* 1280 Eynsh, *le Fryth* 1481–2 *CourtR*. 'The wood,' *v.* fyrhþ(e).

TILGARSLEY (lost, on site of Britannia Inn (6″))

> *Tilgaresle* 1200 FF *et passim* with variant spellings *Tilgaresl'*, *Tylgaresle(ye)*, *Tilgaresley(e)* to 1383 Eynsh, *Tilgarisle* 1316 FA
> *Tilderesleg'* 1246–7 *Ass*
> *Tilgarsle* 1264–8 Eynsh *et passim* with variant spellings *Tylgarsleges, Tilgarsley(e)*, *Tylgarsle(e)*, *Tylgarsley(e)*, *Tylgarslegh'* to 1797 Davis
> *Tilgardesle(ke)* 1278–9 RH, *Tilgerdesle* 1370 Eynsh, 1371 Cl
> *Tylgarle, Tylgarsele* 1285 *Ass*
> *Tilgersleye* (bis) 1378 Eynsh, 1473–4 *CourtR*

'*Tilgār's wood or clearing,' v. lē(a)h. Tilgares dic, obviously containing the name of the same man, appears in the boundaries of Eynsham 1005 KCD 714. *Tilgār is not recorded elsewhere, but both elements occur in personal names. All the inhabitants of the hamlet died in the Black Death, and the Abbot of Eynsham was obliged to take the holdings into his own land (Chambers 34).

BARNARD GATE is Barnard Yate 1725 Bodl, v. geat. BELL BRIDGE (6"). Cf. Bell Closes 1807 EnclA. BLINDWELL FM AND GORSE (both 6"). Cf. Blindwell Coppice 1650, 1781 Chambers, 'spring hidden by vegetation.' CASTLES COPSE and PARTLOWS COPSE (6") are Castle's or Castell's Coppice and Partlow's Coppice 1802 EnclA. CITY FM and LITTLEGREEN FM are so named 1822 O.S. CLAYPIT CLUMP and EYNSHAM WHARF (both 6"). Cf. Claypits furlong and Wharf Stream and Water 1802 EnclA. NEWFIELD COTTAGES (6"). Cf. Newfield 1650 Chambers. SOUTHFIELD BARN (6"). Cf. Southefelde 1363 Eynsh. TWELVE ACRE FM. Cf. Twelueacre 1363 Eynsh, Twelvacres 1483–4 CourtR. WOODLEYS COPSE (6") is Woodleys Coppice 1650 Chambers, Wood leace Coppice 1802 EnclA.

FIELD-NAMES[1]

(a) In 1934 (from a Redemption of Corn Rents in the County Record Office) Black Pit Head, Chatter Holt (Charterhold 1650, 1708 Chambers; the term charter-hold is first recorded in 1710 for 'land held by charter'), Clattin's Ground (Claydens, Cladins 1650 Chambers), Double Mound, Great Greensward Ground, Hopjoys Close (Hob Jonys 1570 Chambers, Hobirons 1650 Chambers, Hop Jones 1782 Chambers), The Langcott, Lanket (v. lanket), North and South Lawn, Pebly Hill, Perch Close (Pearts Close 1517 Chambers, Perch Close Green 1802 EnclA, named from a family called Pierte, mentioned 1443 Chambers 117), First and Second Rumoor (Rumoors 1802 EnclA), The Tiffens (cf. Tybbyns croftes 1443 Chambers), Wrothy (Wrougthey 1228–39 (14th) Chambers, Wrotheye 1284 Chambers, Wroghechhey, Wroghethey, Wroghtehey 1363; no alternative can be offered to the etymology 'island of debate,' second element (ī)eg, first OE wrōht, suggested by Ekwall, Chambers 126, cf. Wrautam PN Wa 189). In 1858 Bear Meadow (Baremede 1363, v. mǣd; first element bearu, 'grove'). In 1841 (Bodl) What's Blake (wattes blacke 1615 CorpusMap, Watt's Lake 1802 EnclA). In 1802 (EnclA) Ake Hill (Hekehulle 1241–64, Þekehulle 1268–81, le Ekehull(e) 1481–3 CourtR, Eake hill 1615 CorpusMap), Ambury Green and Close (Almery Close 1545 Chambers, Ambery Close 1569 Chambers), Common Ayott, Several Ayott, The Ayott or Nait (v. eyt), one form has N- from ME atten, 'at the'; v. several), Berry Close, Bitterall Lane (Betterhale 1228–39, Bitterhale 1241–64, Biterhale, Byterhale 1363, Bytterhal 1481–3 CourtR, Bitterolls 1656 Bodl, second element h(e)alh; Chambers (109) says that the locality favours the

---

[1] Except where otherwise stated, the forms are from Eynsh.

interpretation of the first as 'bittern': *botor* is the only spelling of this word on record before 1388, when it appears with an *-i-* in Chaucer—"as a Bitore bombleth in the Myre"—but the word is not well recorded in ME, and this name may contain a form of it), Blowings Lands (*la Blowende* 1267–84 Os (p), *Blowend* 1300 Wych, *Blowen* 1608–9 *Survey*, probably 'windy district,' *v.* ende)[1], Bungay's Meadow (*Benengey, Benyngey* 1363, *Bannynges croft* 1443 Chambers, *Bungie* 1650 Chambers, second element (i)eg), Catsbrane Brook (*Cattesbrayn* 1328, *v.* catsbrain), Great Collett (Chambers (111) identifies this with *Colewrþe* 1268–81, *Collwurth lane* 1481–3 CourtR, *Coulworthe Closes, Couleworthe slade* 1615 *CorpusMap*, 'Cola's enclosure,' *v.* worþ; identical with Colworth PN Sx 75 and a field-name in Hampton 214: slæd has been added to one form), Conduit Corner (*Conduite Field and Furlong* 1615 *CorpusMap*), Cuckoo Pens and Closes (cf. *Cookoyate* 1481–3 CourtR[2]), Deadland Corner (*Dedlond* 1442 Chambers), Dovehouse Close (so named 1788), Fordsham Lane, Gossard Furlong, Ham (*v.* hamm), Hillands (so named 1650 Chambers, cf. *Hillandmeade furlong* 1605 *CorpusMap*), Howland Cross (*Hony(e) Crosse* 1615 *CorpusMap, Haume Cross* 1650 Chambers, *Howling Cross* 1697, 1788 Chambers, 1822 O.S.: Chambers (70–1) suggests that *Howling Cross* is the original form, and that it is a variant of the name Weeping Cross, for which see 396: the *CorpusMap* has a drawing of an actual cross), Kingston Green (*Kyngesdone* 1363, 1473–4 CourtR, *Kingstone Green* 1697 Bodl, 'king's hill,' *v.* dūn), Linton Piece (*Lintune* 1261, *Lyntons* 1481–3 CourtR, 'flax enclosure,' *v.* līn, tūn), Litchfield (*Lieche fielde* 1615 *CorpusMap*), Ludmoor (*Lodemere, Ludemere* 1241–64, *Ludemere* 1268–81, *Lodemere* 1363, *Ludmeare* 1484–5 CourtR, 'Luda's pool,' *v.* mere), Means Close (*meane close* 1615 *CorpusMap, v.* (ge)mǣne), Mill Moors (*Mulemora* 1229 FF, *v.* myln, mōr), Moorsey Meadow, Oathursts (*Otehurst* 1363 Eynsh, 1483–4 CourtR, *v.* āte, hyrst), Oldlands (*Oldeland* 1545, 1650 Chambers), Pentecroft Green, Pentecrofts (*Penycroft* 1481–3 CourtR, *Penycroft Close, Pennticraft Close* 1650 Chambers, *v.* penny), Pinkcroft (Chambers (117) identifies this with the preceding name), Pound Gate (*Pound* 1601 Chambers), Ram Close (so named 1650 Chambers, *Rames close* 1679 Bodl), Red Lands Furlong (*Redlandes furlong* 1615 *CorpusMap*), Ring Fence, Rod Ham (*v.* rod), Saywell, Stump Stile, Toll Acre[3], Trumpet's Meadow (*Trumpermede* 1363, *v.* mǣd; first element 'trumpeter,' probably, as Chambers (119) suggests, a local name for some bird), Withy Slade (so named 1697 Chambers, *v.* wīðig, slæd), Wrestling Grounds.

(b) In 1788 (Chambers) *Cheese Cake* (cf. 376), *Golden Furlong* (*Golding Furlong* 1782 Chambers), *Skrub*. In 1782 (Chambers) *Lark Slad* (cf. *Larke dale* 1615 *CorpusMap, v.* slæd), *Mean Croft* (*Menecroft* 1443 Chambers, *v.* (ge)mǣne, croft). In 1708 (Chambers) *Claywire* (*Clay-wyre* 1650

[1] Part at least of this was in Handborough.

[2] *v.* cuckoo-pen: this is recorded in EDD as an alternative term to *cuckoo-gate*, used of a swing gate in a V-shaped enclosure.

[3] "which for time immemorial has freed and exempted the inhabitants of the parish of Ensham from toll of all cattle corn grain and all other goods wares merchandizes whatsoever sold or offered to sale within the said City"—the "said City" is Oxford.

Chambers, *v.* **clæg, wer**). In 1650 (Chambers) *Bole Wyre, Bowlwyre* (*Bowlwere* 1302, *v.* **wer**), *Breach* (*Brech* 1389 Chambers, *v.* **breche**), *Dasie Furlong, Green Dragon, Haymarch Furlong* (*Heymersh furlong* 1473–4 *CourtR, Hyemate* 1615 *CorpusMap*, second element **mersc**), *Lammas Close* (*v.* **Lammas**), *Lilly Wyre* (*v.* **wer**), *Lintbrow Lane, Longleigh* (*le Longelete* 1363, the second element might be an early occurrence of *leat*, 'watercourse,' which is first recorded 1590–1), *Lot Furlong* (cf. *Lotte meadowe* 1605 *CorpusMap, v.* **lot**), *Meerstone Hill, Noble Furlong, Partridge Mead* (*Patrichesmede* 1363, 'Patrick's meadow'), *Reeke Close* (**reek** is a well-recorded form of the word *rick*), *Shut-lock Ham* (*Sidelakesham* 1213–28, *Sudelakesham* 1268–81, *Sydelakesham, Sedelakesham* 1363, *Shutlockes Ham* 1615 *CorpusMap*, '*Sidelāc*'s **hamm**'; a name *Sideloc* is recorded once, and both elements are common in personal names), *Strond Wyre, Stubbefurlong* (so named 1360, 1650 Chambers, *Stubelfurlong* 1360 Chambers, first element 'stubble'), *Swench Hill, Waymbut.* In 1615 (*CorpusMap*) *Barrowe Hill* (*v.* **be(o)rg**), *Belgrave acre* (*Belegrave* 1363, 6, probably as Chambers suggests (79) named from the *Belegrave* family mentioned in the 13th), *Bitter Dale* (*Bedredeie* 1213–28, *Beterdeye* 1363, *Bitterdie* 1483–4 *CourtR*, second element (ī)**eg**), *Black bushe furlong, Butte lande* (*v.* **butts**), *Calke crofte slade* (Chambers identifies this with *Caluecrofte* 1213–28, *Caldecroft, le Calvecroft* 1363, 'calves' croft'), *Crabtree furlong, Deadmanes buriall, Elder stump furlong, Fallowe Close, Parker peece, A Slade* (*v.* **slæd**), *Stewerde bushe furlong* (cf. *Stywardispathe* 1363; Chambers (47) says there was a villein John *Stiward* in 1279), *Stonende Bridge, Toune Close, Short and Long wales, short walles* (Chambers identifies this with *Waltoneforlong* 1281), *white pittes, widowes ham* (*v.* **hamm**). In 1605 (*CorpusMap*) *Banlandes* (*v.* **bēan, land**), *Broade Leaes* (*v.* **lǣs**), *Bye southe meadowe, Cotteman Meade* (*v.* **cotman**), *Creste furlong, Short and Long Downe* (*v.* **dūn**), *Ensh'me Stone, The farme grounde, The Gleebe, Holte meade, Mead way balke, the Millne Fielde* (*v.* **myln**), *Ouer Welbrook, The Parke* (*v.* **pearroc**), *Pigeon poole, Stande hilles* (possibly **stān-gedelf**), *welheade, wooe landes* (*v.* **wōh, land**). In 1545 (Chambers) *Highwood* (*le Heyewode* 1363, probably 'high wood'), *Owtwood* (*v.* **in**). In 1517 (c. 1630) (*Corpus*) *Choppers Acre* (*Chopperacr'* 1363; Chambers (91) suggests that this name is derived from *chop* in the sense 'exchange'—it was applied to holdings subject to rotation: the term is not recorded elsewhere). In 1485 (*CourtR*) *Hyndebest.* In 1484–5 (*CourtR*) *Whytecrofte Parrock* (cf. *Wytecroft* 1443 Chambers, *v.* **hwīt, croft, pearroc**). In 1483–4 (*CourtR*) *le Brodclos* ('broad close'), *Burslade* (*v.* **slæd**), *Cloddynges* (this might be a derivative of the verb *clod*, 'to clear land from lumps of earth,' or of the noun *clod*), *Zony.* In 1483 (*CourtR*) *Nonacra.* In 1481–3 (*CourtR*) *Bagbrygge* (*v.* **brycg**), *Howbrygge* (*v.* **brycg**), *Howndeyiend, Roketacre*[1]. In 1473–4 (*CourtR*) *Hochyngfurlong* (*v.* **hechinge**, the *-o-* should doubtless be *-e-*), *Longdale* (*Langedale* 1213–28, *Langdale* 1363, 'long valley'). In 1470 (Chambers) *Poukebrige* (*Poukebrugge* 1406 Chambers, 'goblin bridge,' *v.* **pūca, brycg**). In 1443 (Chambers) *Charescroft, Docerscroft, Fallerscroft, Foxooles* (*v.* **fox-hole**), *Oxenpenie* (*v.* **penny**), *Pulleserscrofts, Waterpeces Crofts, Whyteknaysterscroft* (*v.* **hwīt, croft**), *Wytecroft* (*v.* **hwīt**,

[1] *rocket* is first recorded in 1548 as a name for hedge mustard, *Sisymbrium officinale.*

croft). In 1442 (Chambers) *Boldecroftes* (*v.* croft, first element bold, 'building'). In 1366 *Goseford* ('goose ford'). In 1363 *Acheley, Achey* (the first name means 'oak wood,' *v.* āc, lē(a)h; the second is either a mistake for this or 'oak island,' *v.* (i)eg), *Apestede* ('aspen place,' *v.* stede), *Bulput* (*v.* pytt; the first element could be 'bull' or a personal name), *Claxhurst* (*v.* hyrst; first element probably the personal name *Clac*[1]), *Clayhuch'*, *Clayhuthe, Cleyhuthe* (*Cleihute* 1213–28, *v.* clæg, hȳþ), *Costloteit, Costloneit* (*Cotsetneyde* 1268–81; Chambers (111) suggests that the 1363 names are errors for the earlier one, but they might have *cotsetle* as first element instead of *cotset*, both words meaning 'cottager'; second element eyt), *Culuyrmede* ('wood pigeon mead'), *Ouereyt, Neþereyt* ('over and nether eyt'), *Forner, Froggenhale* ('h(e)alh frequented by frogs'), *Landemede* (*Lanmede* 1213–28, *Landmede* 1268–81, *la Landmede* 1312, *Landmed'* 1328, *v.* mǣd), *Lodemede* (*v.* (ge)lād, mǣd), *Longemede* (*Langemede* 1281, *v.* lang, mǣd), *Loteshull, Lutteshulle* (*Luttershulle* 1241–64, *v.* hyll; there is some evidence for the existence of a stream-name from OE *hlūtor*, 'clear,' which would be a possible first element, *v. supra* 6: Chambers identifies this with Litchfield in the *EnclA*), *Stonyham* ('stony hamm,' *Stoweham* in the same source is probably another form of this), *le Westyrtte* ('west steort'), *Weymore* (*le Weymora* c. 1220, *v.* mōr). In 1302 *Forthwere* (*v.* wer), *Godycrofteshamme* (*v.* croft, hamm), *Halkwere* (*v.* h(e)alh, wer), *Wythegeneham* (*v. Wygon Mill* in Benson 118). In 1281 *Hemehurst* (*v.* heme), *le Hurst* (*v.* hyrst). In 1268–81 *le Berewes* (the plural of *bearu*, 'grove'), *Breriforlong* ('briary furlong'), *Cherebrugge* (*v.* brycg), *Holewellehulle* (*v.* holh, w(i)elle, hyll), *Refham* (*v.* refham), *Scipforde* ('sheep ford'), *Scorthegrene, Sortegrove* (also 1241–64, 'short green and grove'), *Strandputtes* ('pits by the river bank'), *Wakwed, Wdecroft* (*Wodecroft* 1241–64, *v.* wudu, croft), *Wdelongemannecroft, Yethulle* (*v.* hyll). In 1241–64 *Kitterichhurst* (first element 'kite,' other elements *ric*, 'stream,' and hyrst; *pyttel*, 'kite,' appears in the field-names of the neighbouring parish of Cassington), *Mikelforlong* (first element mycel, 'great'), *Wudemanne Muleweye* (apparently 'woodman mill-way'). In 1229 (FF) *Binthale* (second element h(e)alh, first beonet, 'bent grass'). In 1213–28 *la Barre, Horcleye* (*Horsley Mede* in margin in late hand, 'horse pasture,' *v.* lē(a)h), *Wethemore* (*v.* wiðig, mōr). In 1005 (late 12th) (Eynsh) (*on þa*) *ealdan dic* (*v.* (e)ald, dīc), (*on þær*) *gemær treow* ('boundary tree'), (*on*) *hæðfeld* (*v.* hæþ, feld), (*on*) *swana croft* ('herdsmen's croft'), (*to*) *þrim acon* ('three oak trees'), (*on*) *weardstige* (the elements are *weard*, 'watch, guard,' and *stīg*, 'path'; the sense of the compound is uncertain), (*on*) *Winburge stoc* (the second element is shown to be stocc by the following phrase *of þam stocce*; *wīnburh* is a poetical compound in OE, except once in the Paris Psalter when it seems to mean a walled vineyard).

12. Glympton

GLYMPTON [glimtən]

Glimtuna 1050–2 (13th) KCD 950[2] *et freq* with variant spellings *Glimton', Glimtun', Glymton, Glimton* to 1664 Eynsh

[1] The same name occurs in Shifford (328).   [2] v.r. Paris *Gluntune*.

Glintone 1086 DB *et freq* with variant spellings *Glintona, Glinton'*,
    Glynton(e) to 1689 Glymp
Clinton' 1199 P *et freq* with variant spellings *Clinton(e), Clyntone*
    to 1314 Ch
Clinctona 1231 Bract
Clantona 1235–6 Bract
Glimpton 1252 Cl *et freq* with variant spellings *Glimpton', Glympton*
Climpton 1268 *Ass*
Ghimpton 1284–5 FA
Clymton 1362 Ipm

'tūn on the river Glyme' (*v. supra* 7). For the forms *Glinton(e)*
and *Clinton(e)* cf. the quotation from Dugdale (1656) in PN Wa 173:
"Clinton (now vulgarly called *Glinton*) in Oxfordshire."

BERRING'S WOOD (6″) takes name from *Buriens, Boryens* 1245–6 *For*
(p), (*Hamelet' de*) *Boriens* 1278–9 RH, *Bor(i)ens* 1278–9 RH (p), *Bononz*
(? for *Borienz*) 1316 FA, *Beryams, Boryams* 1610 Glymp. Cf. *Berins
Lane, Berins closes, Beryns Lane end* 1608–9 *Survey, Boriams hill* 1653
Glymp. The plural of OE **byrgen**, 'burial place.' The early field-
names of the neighbouring parish of Steeple Barton are interesting
in this connection. There are four names which contain hlāw,
'tumulus,' and two which refer respectively to goblins and to a
demon. No medieval field-names have been found for Glympton
itself. *v.* Addenda liii.

GLYMPTON WOOD is *Glimhemwode* 1278–9 RH, *Glympton Wood*
1608–9 *Survey, Glym Wood* c. 1840 *TA*. 'Wood of the people of
Glympton,' *v.* hǣme.

HOBBARD'S HILL is *the hopyard hill* 1685 Glymp.

SLAPE BRIDGE (6″) is so named 1608–9 *Survey*. This and SLAPE
BOTTOM (6″) etc. take name from *Slepe* 1225 FF, 1246 Ch, *Slape*
1278–9 RH (p) *et freq, Slap* c. 1298 Eynsh (p). Cf. *Slape hill* 1653
Glymp. OE slǣp, 'slippery place.'

CALLOWHILL BRAKE (6″). Cf. *Callow Hill* 1822 O.S., c. 1840 *TA*,
v. 284. CUCKOO PATCH, DEADMOOR BRAKE and SWANS NEST (all 6″).
Cf. *Cuckow Patch Copse, Dead Moor* and *Swans Nest Copse* c. 1840
TA. GLYMPTON ASSARTS FM. Cf. *Glympton Sartes* 1608–9 *Survey*,
Sarts Farm c. 1840 *TA, v.* sart. HARK WOOD (6″) is *Harkwood,
Harcottes* 1608–9 *Survey, Harcottes or Hark Wood* 1610 Glymp.

Pool Bottom (6″) is so named c. 1840 *TA*. Sideland Wood (6″).
Cf. *Sidelands, Sidelands Wood* c. 1840 *TA, v.* sideland.

FIELD-NAMES

(a) In c. 1840 (*TA*) Ash Pieces, Bank foot, Little and Great Bassett, Berry
Close, The Bir, Bottham, Bottoms Copse, Broken Cross, East and West
Dirty Furlong, Fox Cover, Gallows Furlong, Gamidge Close, Gravel Pit
Field, Hunting Ground, Great Leazows (*Le Leasowes* 1606–7 *Survey, v.* lǣs),
Single Oak, Slip (*v.* slipe), Water Lane Meadows.

(b) In 1608–9 (*Survey*) *The Bound, Green Sarts* (*v.* sart). In 1233 (FF)
Frid (*v.* fyrhþ(e)), *Redemere* (*v.* hrēod, mere), *Thaclum.*

13. Gosford and Water Eaton

GOSFORD

> *Goseford* c. 1242–6 AD *et passim* with variant spelling *Goseforde*
> to 1316 FA
> *Gosford* 1509–10 Os

GOSFORD BRIDGE (6″) is *Gosefordebrugge* 1395 *Bodl.* GOSFORDHILL
FM (6″) is so named c. 1840 *TA*.

'Geese ford,' *v.* gōs. For other occurrences of this name *v.* PN Wa
166, PN D 608, PN Cu 393, PN NbDu 95.

WATER EATON

> *Eatun* 864, 904 (both 11th) BCS 509, 607[1], *Eaton*' c. 1130–40
> (c. 1425) Frid *et freq* with variant spellings *Eaton(a)* to 1376
> (c. 1425) Frid, *Watereaton*' c. 1220–30, 1227–8 (both c. 1425)
> Frid
> *Etone* 1086 DB *et freq* with variant spellings *Et(h)ona, Eton*', *Etun*'
> to 1376 (c. 1425) Frid, *Ettonam* 1129–33 OxonCh, *Etthon*' c. 1135
> OxonCh, *Ettona* 1154–68 Os, *Water Eton*' 1227 (c. 1425) Frid
> *et passim* with variant spellings *Water Etona, Watereton(e)* to
> 1509–10 Os, *Watertone* 1285 *Ass, Eton Aquarum* 1509–10 Os
> *Hetune* 1157–8 (c. 1320) Frid
> *Ætona* c. 1160 OxonCh
> *Eutun Roberti* 1220 Fees

OE ēa-tūn, 'tūn by a river,' to which 'water' has been prefixed to
distinguish it from Woodeaton 194–5.

---

[1] The identification with Water, rather than Wood, Eaton is proved by the
occurrence of *Wifeleslace* in the boundaries given in BCS 607 and also in those of
Cutslow adjoining Water Eaton, *v.* the field-names of Marston 181.

CUTSLOW

    (*into*) *Cuðues hlaye* (*sic* for *Cuðnes hlawe*) 1004 (t. Ed 2) Frid

    Codeslam, Codeslave 1086 DB, *Codeslowe* c. 1142, 1376 (both
        c. 1425) Frid, 1280 Os, 1316 FA, *Kodeslawe* c. 1220 Os, *Codes-
        lawe* 1246–7 *Ass*

    Cudeslawe 1123–33 OxonCh *et passim* with variant spellings *Cudes-
        lawia, Cudeslowe, Cudeslauya* and *Cuddeslawe* to 1259 Os

    Culdeslauia (bis) 1320 Ch

    Coteslowe 1480 Frid

    Cutslow, Old Cutslow 1797 Davis

'*Cūþen*'s or *Cūþwine*'s burial mound,' *v.* hlāw. It is not impossible
that the man buried here is the one who gave his name to Cuddesdon
(167–8) about eight miles south-east. The barrow was destroyed in the
13th century: *v. Antiquity* 1935, where Professor H. M. Cam draws
attention to an entry in the Assize Roll for 1261 which she translates
"Two strangers were found killed under the how (Latin *hoga*) of
Cutteslowe. The hundred jury testify that evil doers are wont to lurk
in the hollow of the how, and that many robberies and homicides
have been committed there. Therefore the sheriff was commanded
to level the how."

FRIEZE FM (6") takes name from (*capella de*) *Fres, Fries* c. 1200 Os,
Fres c. 1220 Os *et freq* to late 13th Os, *Frees* 1389 Os, *Frice* 1509–10
Os, *Friece Fm* 1822 Os. MINNIS FM in Yarnton is called *Old Frice*
1797 Davis. According to Os iv, 105, the name belonged originally
to a wayside chapel in Yarnton parish founded by a bridge hermit:
there is a *ponte de Fres* 1271 Os. The chapel is not mentioned in *Valor
Ecclesiasticus*, and Wood could find no trace of it. Adam *Fres* and
Alice *Frees* are mentioned c. 1270 (c. 1450) and 1275 (c. 1450)
Godstow as landowners in St Giles Parish, Oxford, which is very
close. It is impossible to say whether the family gave name to the
place or vice versa.

PIXEY MEAD takes name from *Pechesia* 1171–3 Kennett, *Pyxey* c. 1180
(c. 1450) Godstow, *Pekeseye* c. 1182 (c. 1450) Godstow, *Pechesie*
c. 1185 CartAntiq, *Pyxseye* t. Hy 8 *Valor*, *Pixey* 1774 Stapleton.
'*Pīc*'s island,' *v.* (ī)eg.

HULK MILL (lost) is *molendino…quo Hulc vocatur* c. 1220 (c. 1425)
Frid, *molendinum Hulc* 1220–1, late 13th Os, *Hulkesmulle* 1359, 88 Os:
the owner, Robert *Hulc*, is mentioned 1225 Os.

SPARSEY BRIDGE (6″) is so named 1797 Davis. It takes name from *Spareweseyam* c. 1130–50 Os, *Sperueseiam* 1143 OxonCh, *Spareweseie* c. 1160 OxonCh, *Sparesweseye* 1154–63 Os, *Spareweseya* 1145–7 (late 13th) Os, *Spareweseye* 1183–5 Os. The meaning may be 'island frequented by sparrows' (*v.* (ĭ)eg), but the first element is probably in the genitive singular, and may be a personal name. The synonymous *pinnock* occurs several times in field-names as a personal name or a surname, *v.* 64.

SOUTHFIELD FM is so named 1822 O.S.

FIELD-NAMES

(*a*) In c. 1840 (*TA*) Louse Hall Field (*Loose-Hall* 1685 Stapleton, *Lowse Hall* 1675 Ogilby ("so called by the scholars"), *Louse Hall* 1795 Stapleton, *v.* Fan).

(*b*) In 1647 (*Bodl*) *Caunum* (*Canhame* 1634 Stapleton[1]). In 1582 (*Bodl*) *Greate Acham* (*Akhamweer* 1509–10 Os, *v.* āc, hamm, wer), *Calves close*, *Toddenham* (*v.* hamm). In 1509–10 (Os) *Dokisweer* (perhaps 'duck's weir'), *Holtisweer*. In 1388 (Os) *Haywardeshalfacre* (the *hayward* was the officer having charge of fences and enclosures), *Kyngesyate* (*v.* geat). In 1359 (*Bodl*) *frere Rogeres croys* ('brother Roger's cross'). In 1359 (Os) *Gyberichs* (*Giberis* 1225 Os). In c. 1300 (Os) *le Mulewardes acres* (*millward* was used as a synonym for 'miller'), *Stotforlung*, *Stotmede* (*v.* mǣd; first element *stott*, 'horse, bullock'). In 1280 (Os) *Bodesle* ('*Bode*'s wood or clearing,' *v.* lē(a)h). In 1154–68 (Os) *Benacre* ('bean acre'), *Breche* (*v.* breche). In 1004 (t. Ed 2) (Frid) (*to þes*) *biscopesge meron* ('bishop's boundary'). In 904 (11th) (BCS 607) (*to*) *fagan floran* (*v.* Fawler 421), *mycla þorn* ('great thorn tree'), (*on þa*) *þyrnan* ('thorn tree'), (*to*) *wulfunes treow stealle will* (first element the personal name *Wulfhūn*, to which have been added trēo(w), *steall*, 'place, cattle-stall,' and w(i)elle).

14. Handborough

HANDBOROUGH, CHURCH AND LONG [hænbərə]

> *Haneberge* 1086 DB *et passim* with variant spellings *Haneberga(m)*, *Haneberg', Haneberg, Haneburgh, Haneberwe, Hanebrew, Haneborg, Haneburne, Hanebor', Hanebergh(e)* to 1370 Eynsh, *Hannebergh'* 1240–1 *Ass*, *Hanneberge* 1251 Cl, *Hanneberg* 1280 Eynsh, *Hanneburghe* 1370 Eynsh
> *Hageneb'ga* 1156 P
> *Hauerberga* 1194, 1204 P, *Hanerberge* 1205 P
> *Heneberg'* 1200 P, *Henebrewe* 1242 P, *Henneberg'* 1251 Cl

[1] This is said in Stapleton (19) to survive as Canaham.

Hanberge c. 1200 Eynsh, *Hanburghe* 1246 Eynsh, *Hanboroughe*,
   Hanborowe 1428 FA
Hameburg' 1224 Cl
Harebergh' 1240–1 *Ass, Horneberghe, Hurneburghe* 1285 *Ass*
Haunneberg' 1268 *Ass*

The forms in 1156 P and 1268 *Ass* point to the etymology '*Hagena*'s
hill,' *v.* be(o)rg.

DOWNHILL FM (6″) may be *la Dunhall'* 1267–84 Os (p), *Dunhalle*
1267–84 Os (p) *et freq* with variant spelling *Dunhall* to 1428 FA (p),
la Dunhalle 1268–81, 1294 (p) Eynsh, *Dunhale* 1273–4 RH (p), *la
Dounhall* 1277 Ipm (p), *Dounhalle* 1280 Eynsh (p), *Downhalle* 1290
Eynsh (p), 1309 Fine (p), *Dounhale* 1309 Eynsh (p). 'Hall on a hill,'
v. h(e)all. The first element is dūn. The modern name is due to
popular etymology.

GOOSE EYE COTTAGE (6″) takes name from *Goseye* 1278–9 RH, *Goosey*
1606–7 *Survey, Goose Eye Close* 1773 *EnclA. v.* gōs, (ī)eg.

PINSLEY WOOD is *Pinnesle* 1254–5 RH, *Pinsley Coppice* 1606–7 *Survey*,
Pynsley Wood 1608–9 *Survey*. 'Pin's wood,' *v.* lē(a)h [1].

ABEL WOOD (6″). Cf. *Abwell* 1606–7 *Survey, Abel Meadow and Close*,
Avel Wood 1773 *EnclA.* COOK'S CORNER. Cf. *Cookes croft* 1606–7
Survey. MILL WOOD is *Mill Wood, Myll wood* 1608–9 *Survey*. THE
ROW may be *Comborow meadowe* 1605 *CorpusMap, Cumbrow mead*
1606–7 *Survey, Coombrowe meadow* 1608–9 *Survey*: apparently
'Combe Row,' Combe (254) being an adjacent parish.

FIELD-NAMES

(*a*) In 1773 (*EnclA*) The Assart (*The Asserte* 1605 *CorpusMap, le Sarte*
1606–7 *Survey, v.* sart), Berry Close (so named 1605 *CorpusMap, v.* burh),
Blind Lane, Middle Breach (*le Brech* 1267–84 Os, *Breach or The Breache*
1605 *CorpusMap, v.* breche), Bull Close, Chalcroft Meadow (*Chawcrofte*
1606–7, 1608–9 *Survey*), Chalgrove, The Chaswells (*Chasewell close* 1605
CorpusMap), China Weir (*Chanye were* 1605 *CorpusMap, Che(y)nie Weare*
1606–7 *Survey*), Cocklecroft (so named 1606–7 *Survey*), Crease Furlong,
Long Down Furlong, Fenlake Meadow (*Fen lake lot meadowe* 1605 *Corpus-
Map, Fenlake* 1606–7 *Survey, v.* fenn, lacu), Fishery Road, Frog Lane,
Furley Close, Gallows Close, Heath Lane and Close (*Heath fielde lane and
close* 1605 *CorpusMap, King's Heath, The Great Heath* 1608–9 *Survey*),
Hencroft Butts (*Hen crofte* 1605 *CorpusMap, v.* henn, croft, butts), Hide Close,
Hyde Lane (*le Cornehide, le Busshie hide* 1606–7 *Survey, Bushy Hide* 1608–9

---

[1] Mr Gover informs us that Pinsley in Cosham, Ha, is *Pynnesle* 1353 FF.

Survey, v. hīd), Holland Furlong (*Hollande Close* 1605 *CorpusMap*), Iron-monger's Close (*Ironmongers* 1606–7 *Survey*), Leys Lower Breach (*v.* breche), Marking Piece Style, Murzeley Closes (*Mosele* 1268–81 Eynsh, *Mouslee* 1300 Wych, *Musley close* 1605 *CorpusMap, Musley, Mowsley Corner* 1608–9 *Survey*, identical with Moseley Wo (PN Wo 356), with second element lē(a)h and first either *mūs*, 'mouse,' or a personal name *Mūsa*), Nye Meadow (*Nye meade* 1606–7 *Survey, Hanborowe Nye Meadow* 1608–9 *Survey*), The Paddock, Pidgeon House Lane, Priest Close, The Ridings (*le Ridinges* 1606–7 *Survey, v.* ryding), Silk Hill, The Smarts (*Smartes* 1606–7 *Survey*), Snap Style, Stone Acre Meadow (*Stone Acres* 1606–7, 1608–9 *Survey*).

(b) In 1608–9 (*Survey*) *Great Burham, Foule* or *Fowle Lane, Gospell oke* (*v.* gospel), *Spratsham* (*Sprattsham, Spratsom meade* 1606–7 *Survey*). In 1606–7 (*Survey*) *Benley, Blacknoll* (*Blacknell furlong* 1605 *CorpusMap*), *Bury Norton, Camber mead, Cotland mead* (*Cotlands* 1606–7 *Survey*), *Cowmore, Furfield, le Furties field* (*v.* forþ), *Hasell Parrett, le Hatchfurlong* (cf. *Hache waye* 1605 *CorpusMap, v.* hæcc), *Hey meade* (*v.* mǣd), *Millham* (*v.* myln, hamm), *Meadhey* (*v.* mǣd, (ge)hæg), *Peake Hill, Savage Pool, Stone meadow, Town Walls Farm, Warnesford, Wirdesden* (*weresden furlong* 1605 *CorpusMap*). In 1605 (*CorpusMap*) *Aberye Crofte, All landes, Badmans hill, Bruton hill, Churchtowne close, Clay(e) crofte, Cockes stile, Conyegree pittes* (*v.* conygree), *Deane* (*v.* denu), *The Gleebe, Shorte* and *Longe Hale* (*v.* h(e)alh), *Hey fielde Moore, Ludcrofte, Milne hill* and *fielde* (*v.* myln), *parsonage lane, Quarrey pitte waye, Rose well gutter, Speare sharpe, Stonepitte furlong, Stonyehill, Towne close, Shorte wimmore, Longe winmore, wood end waye, woode waye, woolbitten furlong*. In 1300 (Wych) *Bladenebrugg* (*v.* brycg; *Bladon* is the old name of the Evenlode, *v. supra* 7), *Kavereshull* (*Chavereshull* 1231 Ch, *Chevereshull* 1278–9 RH, *v.* hyll; the first element is the personal name *Cāfhere*, probably found in Caversfield 204 and in Caversham Berks, which appears to have been fairly common in this part of the country: a *Caveres-wellebrok* is also mentioned 1300 Wych, *v.* w(i)elle, brōc), *Roweleye* (*v.* rūh, lē(a)h). In 1278–9 (RH) *la Rude* (this might be the unrecorded OE word *rȳ(h)ð*, which is the source of Reed Herts (PN Herts 161): it means 'rough land'). In 1267–84 (Os) *Cumede* ('cow meadow'). In 1232 (Cl) *Thurkeldes-hide* (*v.* hīd: the first element looks like the Anglo-Scandinavian personal name *Thurcytel*).

15. Hensington Within and Without

HENSINGTON

Hansitone 1086 DB
Hensint' c. 1130 OxonCh *et passim* with variant spellings *Hensinton', Hensintone, Hensinton(a), Hensintun, Hensyntone* to 1278–9 RH, *Hensentun* 1185 Templars, *Hencinton'* 1196 FF, Cur, 1234 Cl
Heincintone, Heinsintone 1218 FF
Enstintun' 1220 Fees

Hescinton' 1240–1 *Ass*
Hensington 1268 Cl, *Hensingtone, Hensyngtone* 1285 *Ass*
Hansington, Hengsyngtone 1285 *Ass*

The same first element is found in (*of ealdon*) *Hensing'lade*, (*into*) *Hensing lade* 1004 (t. Ed 2) Frid, a stream in Whitehill in the neighbouring parish of Tackley, and in *Hensegrave, Hessingrave* 1276 Cl, a wood in Hensington. The second elements of the three names are tūn, (ge)lād and grāf(a). Ekwall (DEPN) says "*Hensing* may be the name of a wood or stream derived from OE *hēns*, 'hens,' found in *hensbroc* 770 BCS 204 Wo."

SANSOM'S FM (6″) is *Sansomes Farm* 1822 O.S.

FIELD-NAMES

(*a*) In 1769 (Estate Act) The Grove (cf. *Gravesfurlong* c. 1190–1200 (c. 1280) S, *v.* grāf(a)), The Home Ground (*v.* home), Long Close, Morter Pit Furlong (*Morter pyttes* 1606–7 *Survey*).

(*b*) In 1606–7 (*Survey*) *Brode green, le Deane* (*v.* denu), *Lamplet close, Myddle mead, Wottonsartefield* (*v.* sart). In c. 1190–1200 (c. 1280) (S) *Benefurlang'* (*v.* bēan), *Blademore* (*v.* mōr; first element the old name of the River Evenlode, *v.* 7), *Catesfurlong, Chalfberggeweye* ('calf hill,' to which *weg* has been added), *Clayfurlang, Inmed'* (*v.* in), *Grenneput, Grenewey(e)* (*v.* grēne, pytt, weg), *Hefurlang* (*v.* ēa), *Horckeiayrfurlang', Milnepat* (*v.* myln), *Northmale, Pesfurlang* (*v.* peose), *Scortefurlang* ('short furlong'), *Wulhisehengfurlang.*

16. Heythrop

HEYTHROP [hiˑθrʌp]

Edrope 1086 DB
Heðrop 11th Heming[1], *Hethrope* 1223–4 RH *et passim* with variant
    spellings *Hethrop(p), Hethorp(e), Hetrop, Hetrop'* to 1381 Dean,
    Hettrop 1235–6 Fees, 1286 FF, *Heththrop* 1346 Dean
Hatorp 1166 (c. 1203) LN, *Hattrope* 1166 (c. 1230) RBE
Estropa 1191 (p), 1193 P
Etchrop' 1220 Fees
Hestrop 1223–4 RH, *Hesthtrop* 1307 Winchcombe
Ethrope 1235–6 Fees, 1326 (c. 1425) Frid (p), *Ethorp* 1285 *Ass*
Heythrop 1259 Ch, *Heithrop* 1286 Cl, *Heithrup* early 18th ParColl,
    Heythorp 1797 Davis
Eyrop, Eytrop 1261 Ipm
Hegtrop 1268 *Ass, Heghrop* 1285 *Ass*

[1] The initial *H* is interlined.

Hedrop 1319 (c. 1425) Frid (p)
Hatherope 1369 Dean

'High village,' *v.* hē(a)h, þrop.

DUNTHORP

Dvnetorp 1086 DB, *Dunitrop* 1175 P (p), *Dunetrope* 1182 P (p)
Dunestorp 1193 P (p), *Dunestrop* 1208 P (p), *Dunsrop'* 1238 Cl
Duntrop 1194 P *et passim* with variant spelling *Dunthrop(pe)*,
    Dunrop' 1238 Cl
Donþrop c. 1225 Os (p), *Donthorp* 1285 *Ass*
Dundrop 1247 (p), 1249 FF, *Dundrup* early 18th ParColl
Dounthorp 1334 Ch

'Village on the hill,' *v.* dūn, þrop, or '*Dunna*'s village.'

FIELD-NAMES

(a) In c. 1840 (*TA*) Castle Farm, Cold Comfort Farm, Kilney Closes.

17. Kidlington

KIDLINGTON

Chedelintone 1086 DB, *Chedelinton'* 1163 P
Kedelint', *Kederintona* c. 1130 OxonCh, *Kedelintona* 1183–5 Os,
    Kedelintone 1221–9, c. 1228 Os, 1261 FF (p), *Kedelinton* 1263
    Ipm
Cudelintona c. 1130–5 Os *et freq* with variant spellings *Cudelinton'*,
    Kudelinton, Kudelintun', Kudelinton', Cudelinton(e), Cudelynton(e)
    to 1380 Cl, *Cudelenton'* 1143 OxonCh, *Cudelentona* c. 1143 Os
Gudilintona c. 1150 *MertR*
Qudilintona c. 1160 OxonCh
Chidelintona c. 1165 OxonCh
Ketelinton' 1173 P
Kydelinthune 1203–6 (13th) Os, *Kidelintune* 1221–9 Os, *Kyde-
    linton'* 1261 Fine
Kudelingtone 1206 Os *et freq* with variant spellings *Kudelington'*,
    *Cudelingtune, Cudelington', Cudelyngtone, Cudelington, Cude-
    lyngton, Kudelyngtone* to 1389 Os, *Cuddelington* 1428 FA
Kedelington' 1251 FF
Kelelingtone 1262 FF
Kydelingtone 1263 Fine
Codelington 1268 *Ass*

Quedelinton' 1273–4 RH
Cudeligton 1278–9 RH (p)
Cudlyntone 1285 *Ass*, *Cudlynton* 1379 Cl
(*Neder*) *Kidlyngton, Nether Kydlyngton* 1428 FA, *Ciddlington* 1624
  Stapleton

'*Cydela's farm,' *v.* ingtūn. The personal name is a derivative of
Cyd(d)a.

CAMPSFIELD is *Campesfeld* 1221–6 Os (p), *Campesfelde* c. 1276 Os,
Campsfield 1765 *Bodl.* Cf. *Campfield close* 1606–7 *Survey*. Probably
'feld of the enclosure,' *v.* camp.

COTE (lost) is *Cota* 1164–6 OxonCh, *Cote* 1221–6 (ter) Os (p), *Cotes*
1251 FF, 1341 Cl (p). *v.* cot(e).

KING'S ARMS (6″) is *Kings Arms Inn* c. 1840 *TA*. LANGFORD LANE
(6″) is so named 1822 O.S.[1] STRATFIELD FM AND BRAKE (latter 6″)
are so named 1822 O.S. There is also a *stodfolde* c. 1276 Os, *Stadfold
hill, lane and field* 1634 Stapleton, *Statfold* 1647 *Bodl, Statfield* c. 1840
TA, from OE stōdfald, 'horse paddock,' and the farm name may be
a corruption of this.

FIELD-NAMES

(*a*) In c. 1840 (*TA*) Cromish field, Goozey Mead, Spindle Ground.

(*b*) In 1647 (*Bodl*) *Great and Little berry meadow, Berry more* (*Bury More*
1587 Stapleton, *v.* burh), *Chewer* (*Choare field* 1634 Stapleton), *Copthorne
field* (*v.* coppede), *Fernehill* (*Fernhull* c. 1276 Os, *v.* fearn, hyll), *Hardwick*
(*v.* heordewīc), *Lincrofte* (*v.* lin, croft), *Sandy furlong, Staple land* (cf. *Stapel-
forlonge* c. 1225 Os, *Staple furlong* 1634 Stapleton, first element possibly
stapol, 'post'), *Summer Leaze, Tenne penny leaze* (*v.* penny), *Wallett moore,
Wheatington* (first element probably *hwǣten*, 'of wheat'). In 1634 (Stapleton)
Burnt Crosse, Cleyfield, Sandy furlong, Lower Slad (*v.* slæd), *Strisehedge*. In
1587 (Stapleton) *Bentley*. In 1395 (*Bodl*) *Prykemonneswer'* (*Prikemanneswere*
c. 1240 Os, second element wer). In 1337 (Ipm) *la More* (*v.* mōr), *le Renegore*
(second element gāra). In c. 1276 (Os) *Dreytonesmore* (*v.* mōr: the first
element might be a surname: the nearest Drayton is over ten miles away),
Hangynde Londe (*v.* hangende), *Lambescote* ('lambs' shelter'), *Portforze*
(perhaps 'furzy ground near the town,' *v.* port), *Shaldestrete, Schalt Euel,*
(*cultura q.v.*) *le Schelde* (cf. the field-names of Hook Norton 357; the second
element of the second of the three names may be w(i)elle), *Were Forlonge*
(*Werefurlong* 1221–6 Os, *v.* wer). In c. 1270 (Os) *le Hechinge* (*v.* hechinge),
le Hulwey (*v.* hyll, weg), *Instanscrofte, Thorndone* (*v.* þorn, dūn). In 1221–6
(Os) *Rawenhurfle* (second element hwyrfel, 'circle').

[1] Cf. Plot (1676) p. 65, "a Quarry called Langford-pits, in the Parish of
Kidlington."

18. North Leigh

NORTH LEIGH

Lege 1086 DB, *Leg'* 1163 P, *Lega* 1167, 1192, 4, 5 P, *Nordleg alias Nordelegh* 1233 Ch, *Northleg'* 1237 (c. 1300) Fees *et freq* with variant spellings *Nort(h)leg'*, *Nordleg*, *Northlegh(e)* to 1314 Os

Leges 1130–50 OxonCh *et passim* with variant spelling *Legis* to 1259 Os, *Leghes* 1193–1200 Eynsh

Leies c. 1150 Eynsh

Leiga c. 1185 CartAntiq

Lea Bernardi 1190 P, *Northle* 1285 *Ass*, *Northlee* 1316 FA, 1526 LS

Northleya c. 1250 AD *et freq* with variant spellings *Northley(e)*, *Nor(h)tleye* to 1389 Os, *Leye* 1264–8 Eynsh

North Cleye 1284–5 FA

Northlye 1355 Ch, 1449 Eynsh, *North Lye* 1428 FA

'North lē(a)h.' *Bernard* is *Bernard* de St Walerico, mentioned 1167 P. Cf. South Leigh (276).

ASHFORD BRIDGE, MILL (both 6″) take name from *Aissour'* 1176 P, *Aissoura* 1177 P, *Assoura* 1179 P, *Assouere* 1278–9 RH (p), *Ashford* early 18th ParColl. The mill is *molendinum de Asshore* 1297 CornAcc, and William *molend.* is the person concerned in the 1176 reference. 'Ash tree bank,' *v.* æsc, ōfer. 'Ford' has been substituted for the original second element.

OSNEY HILL (6″) is so named 1650 Chambers, 1802 *EnclA*. Cf. *Oseneyslond* 1389 Chambers, *Osney Leaes* 1615 *CorpusMap*, both in Eynsham. The reference is to Osney Abbey.

STURT COPSE (6″) is so named 1822 O.S. Cf. *Stirte* 1526–7 *CourtR*. *v.* steort, 'tongue of land.'

WHITEHILL BRIDGE, WOOD (both 6″) take name from *Witenhull*, *Wytenhull'*, *Witenhull'* 1278–9 RH (p). '(At the) white hill,' *v.* hwīt, hyll.

WILCOTE

Widelicote 1086 DB

Wiuelicota 1151 (late 12th) Os *et passim* with variant spellings *Wyvelicote*, *Wiuelecote*, *Wivelecote*, *Wyvelecot'*, *Wivelicot'*, *Wyuelecot(e)*, *Wyvelekote* to 1320 Eynsh

Wyvilcot 1216 Cl, *Wyvelcote* 1316 FA, 1367 Cl, Ipm

Wyuli'gcote 1230 P

Wivelton 1235 Cl
Wevelkot c. 1246 AD
Wiuelescote 1247 FF, *Wyuelescote* 1285 *Ass*
Cf. *Wilcott greene, field* 1608–9 *Survey*

'**Wifel*'s cot(e),' with connective ing. For the personal name cf.
PN W 326.

PERROTTSHILL FM is so named 1822 O.S. James *Perrott*, Esq., is
mentioned early 18th ParColl as lord of the manor built by his family
seventy years before.

BRIDEWELL FM is so named 1797 Davis. BRIDGEFIELD BRIDGE AND
BRAKE (both 6″) and HOLLY COURT FM. Cf. *Bridgefield Farm* and
Holy Court 1822 O.S. CONEYGAR COPSE (6″) is *Coney Gree Wood*
c. 1840 *TA*; *v.* conygree. EASTEND is *le Estend* 1529–30 *CourtR*.
HEATH FM (6″). Cf. *le Hethe* 1524–5 *CourtR*. HOLLY GROVE. *Hoby
Grove* c. 1840 *TA* may be a mistake for this. LOWER RIDING FM
(6″). Cf. *Nether-riding* 1626 *Bodl*, *v.* ryding. SUMTETHS COPSE (6″)
may be connected with *Great and Little Sumptier* c. 1840 *TA*.

FIELD-NAMES

(a) In c. 1840 (*TA*)[1] Great and Little Balkes Close, Balkes Copse, Brierly
Close, Chapel Yard, Grimsole field, Parsons piece.

(b) In 1682–3 (*Bodl*) *the little paddock*. In 1682 (*Bodl*) *Mockmer's Close*
(*Mokemers* 1526–7 *CourtR*), *Rickyard Close*. In 1676 (Plot) *Smithen green*
(the first element might be *smeðe*, 'smooth'). In 1652 (*Bodl*) *Kyteslane*. In
1626 (*Bodl*) *Close Meade, Hills-peece, Newell end* (*Newelyende* 1499–1500
CourtR). In 1608–9 (*Survey*) *Cadwell field, Hey Crofte, Town closes*. In
1529–30 (*CourtR*) *le Whetefeld* (*v.* hwǣte, feld), *Wodemerkes* (*Wodmerke
hegge* 1524–5 *CourtR*, *le Wodmarkes* 1526–7 *CourtR*). In 1527–8 (*CourtR*)
Duddewell crosse, Strode Yatte (*v.* geat; the first element might be *strōd*,
'marshy land'). In 1526–7 (*CourtR*) *White Forde*. In 1525–6 (*CourtR*)
Grysemore (*v.* mōr). In 1524–5 (*CourtR*) *Eggyns more broke, Estmond yate*
(*v.* geat). In 1512–13 (*CourtR*) *Kenestrete* (*Kynnestrete* 1349 *Bodl*), *Sparous-
close*. In 1499–1500 (*CourtR*) *Achampese, Reuelle*. In 1300 (Wych)
Bisschopesden' ('bishop's valley,' *v.* denu), *Mirabelescroft* ('Mirabel's croft'),
Nethergate, Sawrode (second element *rod*, 'clearing'; the first might be
s(e)alh, 'willow,' but it is very early for the *Saw-* spelling), *Scharpesterte*
(*v.* steort; first element 'sharp'), *Sigardesthorn*' ('Sigerēd's or Sigeweard's
thorn tree'), *Sullesleye* (second element lē(a)h; the first is uncertain), *Tre-
maunemere*. In 1298 (Eynsh) *Grundesweleye* (the elements are probably
groundsel NED sb[1] and (ī)eg). In 1278–9 (RH) *Grasacr', Grasham* (*v.* gærs,
hamm), *Refham* (*v.* refham), *Thacham* (*v.* þæc-hamm). In c. 1250 (AD) *le
Forehey* (second element probably (ge)hæg; the first is *fore*, 'in front of').

[1] Only the Tithe Award for Wilcote is available.

19. South Leigh

Stanton'lega 1190 *et seq* P, *Stantonlega* 1197 P

Sothleye, Suthleye early 13th *Bodl, Sudleye* 1250 Cl, *Suley(e)*
1278–9 RH, *Suthleye* 1310 Cl

Sutlega early 13th *Bodl, Suhtleg'* (bis) 1246–7 *Ass, Suthlege* 1247
FF, *Suthlegh* 1285 FF, *Suthleghe* 1315 Ipm, *Suhtlegh* 1316 *Bodl,
Southlegh* 1327 *Bodl*

South Lee 1316 FA

'South lē(a)h.' *Stanton-* from its proximity to Stanton Harcourt,
as an alternative way of distinguishing it from North Leigh.

HOMAN'S FM (6") and TAR FM etc. may be connected with Henry
Home, who has land here 1278–9 RH, and Thomas *T'ry*, whose
widow appears in the same connection ib. TAR FM AND WOOD are
so named 1822 O.S.

FURZY BREACH is *Firzie breach* 1654 *Bodl, Furzey Breach* c. 1840 *TA*:
v. breche. HILL FM (6") AND HOUSES. Cf. *Hill Ground* c. 1840 *TA*.
KIMBER'S BARN and MOOR LANE (both 6") are so named c. 1840 *TA*.
NORTHFIELD FM (6") is so named 1822 O.S., cf. *Northflede* 1242 FF.

FIELD-NAMES[1]

(a) In c. 1840 (*TA*) Barefoot Close, Barn Paddock, Birds Hay (*Bird's
Haye* 1693, *v.* (ge)hæg), Great and Upper Dean (*v.* denu), The Down, Hill
Street Lane, Great and Little Kitchen Closes (*v.* kitchen), Lady's Sait (*v.*
Lady, *sait* in these names is probably an error for sart, *q.v.*), The Lawn, Lies
Field (*Lyesfeilde, Lyesdowne* 1617), Mad Croft (*Madcrofte* 1619, *v.* mǣd),
Parsons Breach (*Parson's Breache* 1628, *Parsons Breach* 1658, *v.* breche),
Pasture Plat (*v.* plat), The Patch, Peas Breach (*Perse Breche* 1438, *Pease
Breache* 1608–9 *Survey*), the Pen, Upper and Lower Rushley (cf. *Rushney
Breche* 1702), Little and Upper and Long Sait, Ship Close (cf. *Sheepehouse
Close* 1619), Snakes Hole Corner, Stockwell Piece (*Stockwell* 1603), Tom
Acre, Stubble and Great Warren (cf. *the Warren* 1605), Hither and Long
Ward Wood (*Wardwood* 1654, 8), Wastings, Great and Little Weights, Long
Weses.

(b) No date *Silverpeece*. In 1706 *Firecroft*. In 1702 *little Redd Moore,
Greate Sart* (*v.* sart). In 1670 *Bourne hamme* ('hamm by the stream,' first
element burna), *the Lott meade* (*v.* lot), *Rose paddock*. In 1621 *a Lammas
ground called Budcrofte* (*v.* Lammas, *bud* is a dialect term for a yearling calf).
In 1603 *Faire meare bushe, Leame Furlong*. In 1556 *Shilcotsale*. In 1555
Tylcrofte. In 1226–7 *Thornehill*. In early 13th *Eefurlong* (first element ēa,
'river').

[1] Except where otherwise stated, the forms are from *Bodl*.

20. South Newington

SOUTH NEWINGTON [nuˑtən]

Niwetone 1086 DB, 1208 FF, *Niweton'* 1181 P

Nevtone 1086 DB, *Neuton'* 1204 P, 1205, 6 Cur, *Neutona* 1219 FF, 1234–5 Bract, *Neutone* c. 1224 Os, *Newtone Iuel* 1399 Eynsh, *Southnewtone* 1526 LS, *South Newton* 1675 Ogilby

Neuuentone 1163–6, 1194 Eynsh, *Newenton'* 1163–6 Eynsh *et passim* with variant spellings *Newent(h)one, Newentun', Newentona* to 1428 FA, *Neuwenton* (bis) 1204 Fine, *Newnton'* 1227 Ch, *Suthnewentone* 1285 *Ass, Suth Newenton'* 1302 Ipm, *Suth Newentone* 1320 Eynsh, *South Newenton'* 1341 AD, 1368 Cl, *Southnewenton'* 1378 Cl, *Newenton Jewell* 1395 Cl, *Newentone Iewelle* 1399 Eynsh, *Newentone Iewell* 1413 Eynsh, *Newnton* 1428 FA

Niwinton' 1179 P, *Nywyntone* 1285 *Ass*

Niwentune 1201 Eynsh *et freq* with variant spellings *Niwenton(a), Nywentona, Nywentone, Niwenton'* to 1401–2 FA, *Niewenton', Niew'ton* 1204 P, *Niventon Juel* 1278–9 RH

Newintone 1201, 19 Eynsh, *Newinton'* 1224 Cl, *Neuinton'* 1238 (c. 1300) Fees, *Neuynton'* c. 1245 AD, *Neuwynton'* 1300 Ipm, *Newynton'* 1316 FA, 1346 Ipm, *Newyntone* 1390 Eynsh, *Newynton Jowel* 1369 Ipm, *South Nuynton* 1539 Eynsh

Neweton' 1205 Cur, 1224, 7 Cl, *Newetun'* 1222 Cl, *Newetona* 1234–5 Bract, *Neweton' Iuel* 1269 FF

Newigton 1401–2 FA, *Southnewington* 1537 Eynsh

'(At the) new tūn,' *v.* nīwe. The suffix *Juel* is explained by D. Royce (Oxfordshire Archæological Society Transactions for 1875), as from a family named *Ivaus* (Ralph Ivaus is mentioned 43 Hy 3) or *Ivals*, whose name appears as *Jewell* in Harl. MSS 1187, f. 93b.

HYDE FM (6″) is *Hida* 1192 Eynsh (p), 1205 Cur (p), 1208 Fine (p), *la Hida* 1236–7 Bract (p), *la Hyde* 1278–9 RH (p). *v.* hīd.

PETER'S PIECE (6″) is so named c. 1840 *TA*.

FIELD-NAMES

(a) In 1795 (*EnclA*) Adwell furlong, boggy mead, Brookmor(e) leys, Carrion lane, Close furlong, the Cowpasture, dry leys, Flax mead, Foxgate furlong, Fox lane, the Furzes (*the Fyrsyn* 1506–7 *Valor*, the early name is a dialect term for *furze*), Garden Furlong, the great and little hills, Great

Hill, home close (*v.* home), homehill (possibly identical with *Hamhille* late 12th Berkeley[1], *Honhulle* c. 1250 Os; the forms are not consistent enough for an etymology to be suggested), the hooks, Lakes meadow (*the Lytyll Lake, Bannynges* or *Bannegers lake* 1506–7 *Valor*, *v.* lacu), Langdon (*Lytyll Longedone* 1506–7 *Valor*, 'long hill,' *v.* dūn), Langley leys, Mare leys, meagre hill (*v.* Fan), Merelake, Mill Acre(s), Moor meadow, mouse hill (*Mowsewelle leyne and Hill* 1506–7 *Valor*, *v.* w(i)elle and lain, first element apparently 'mouse'), picked close (*v.* picked), Road Furlong, Rushbed furlong and leys, small mead, South side, Swinehill Pitts, Swinehill path furlong, Townsend leys, tythe platt (*v.* plat), Wamborough, Wamborough Slade (*v.* slæd), Whiteland brook mead, Whiteland meadow (*Whitelond mede* 1506–7 *Valor*), Wildern (possibly *Wharledone* 1506–7 *Valor*, which might mean 'round hill,' with second element dūn, and first *whorl*, 'circle,' from OE *hwyrfel*), Windmill furlong.

(*b*) In 1506–7 (*Valor*) *Brode forlong* (*v.* brād), *the Broke mede, Creve* (? *Greve*) *forlong* (the first element could be *græfe*, 'brushwood'), *Falwell wey and Hill, Harepytt forlong, Heye way, Howmylle forlong and Forde, Howemylle cope, More place, Oxe gate, Parsons Pytte, Parsonage yard, Pece Breche* (*Pesebrechys* 1436 Os, 'breche where peas grow'), *Pytte forlong, Redcleffe* ('red clif'), *Smythene hille* ('smooth hill'), *Stonbryge* ('stone bridge'), *Tew crosse* (Great Tew adjoins this parish). In c. 1250 (Os) *Wycham* (*v.* wichām).

21. Rousham

ROUSHAM [rauʃəm]

Rowesham, Rovesham 1086 DB

Roduluesham c. 1130 OxonCh, *Rodulfesham* c. 1181 Gor, *Rodolvesham* c. 1200 Os

Roulesham 1202 P *et passim* from 1285 *Ass* to 1428 FA, *Rowlesham* 1350 Os, *Roulisham* 1428 FA

Rotlouisor' (bis) 1204 FF

Rouelesham 1214, 16, 17, 1350 Os

Rolesham (bis) 1220 Fees *et freq* to 1334 Ch, *Rollesham* 1227 FF *et passim* to 1401 Ch, *Rolleshame* 1227–8 WellsR, *Rolusham* 1346 FA

Rolfesham c. 1240 Os, *Rolvesham* 1278–9 RH

Rodlesham 1259 Os

Roghelesham 1308 Cl

Rullesham 1526 LS

'*Hrōþwulf*'s hām.' Identical with Rowsham PN Bk 89–90.

[1] F. W. FitzHardinge, *Descriptive Catalogue of the Charters and Muniments...at Berkeley Castle,* Bristol 1892.

HEYFORD BRIDGE (6″) is *ponte(m) de Heyford* 1278–9 RH, *Hayford-brygge* late hand Os. *v.* Heyford 218–20.

WATERLEYS COPSE (6″) takes name from *Watrey Leys* 1729 *Terrier*, *Watery Leys* c. 1840 *TA*.

FIELD-NAMES

(b) In 1776 (*EnclA*) *Berry Close, East Dry Close* (this and *West Dry Close* appear 1729 *Terrier*), *Plow Close* (also 1729 *Terrier*), *Turnip Close* (also 1729 *Terrier*). In 1729 (*Terrier* in the possession of Mr Cottrell Dormer) *Bandledown piece, Beeching Tree Leys, Black acre, Boggs, Breach* (*v.* breche), *Bridge Close, Bunkus close, Butts, Clay Butts* (*v.* butts), *Calves Close, Church furlong, Clerks Bitts, Cliffehull, Common Wast, Constables Ham* (*v.* hamm), *Copid Bush Furlong* (*v.* coppede), *Coppins Close, Corn ground, Costers Close* (*v.* cot-stōw), *Culverwell Furlong, Deepham, Deporage Ham* (*v.* hamm), *Eldorn Stump* (*eldern* is a common dialect form of *elder*), *Foxholes* (*v.* fox-hole), *gallows piece, Hades* (*v.* hades), *North Hay Corner, Hay mead slade* (*v.* (ge)hæg, slæd), *Hemnell, Lang Furlong* (*v.* lang), *Broadway Leets, Lime Kill Leets, Leets Hanging on the Hill* (*v.* leet), *Mitchel Mead, Mortar Pits, Parsonage Close, Picks at Horspool* (*v.* picked), *Play Close, Rye Furlong, Sandy Piece, Shambles Cross, Stambrook Furlong, Staples Close, A Stripe, Wheelbarrow Piece, Long Yards.* Late hand (Os) *the Heywey* (*v.* hēg, weg), *Wyllghgore* (*v.* gāra, first element *welig*, 'willow').

22. Sandford St Martin

SANDFORD ST MARTIN

> *Sanford* 1086 DB *et passim* with variant spelling *Sanforde* to 1273 Os
> *Saunforde* 1225–6 WellsR, *Saunford* 1246–7 *Ass*, 1278–9 RH, *Saunford, Sanford* 1258 Os, *Saunford'* 1268 *Ass*
> *Sandford* (bis) 1240 Os, 1316 FA, 1320 Ch, 1350 Cl
> *Samford* 1270 Ch
> *Santford* 1341 Cl, 1389, 1413 Os

'Sandy ford.' St Martin from the church dedication. Cf. Sandford on Thames.

GROVE ASH FMS. Cf. *Grava* 1225–6 WellsR *et freq* with variant spelling *Grave* to 1401–2 FA, *la Grave* 1270 Ch, *Grove Asshe* 1590 Bodl, *Grove Ash* 1797 Davis. *v.* grāf(a).

LEDWELL

> *Ledewelle* 1086 DB, *Ledewell* 1316 FA
> *Ledwell* 1186–91 Os *et freq* with variant spelling *Ledwelle* to 1413 Os
> *Lodwell'* 1268 *Ass*
> *Lydewell* 1270 Ch
> *Ludewell'* 1273–4, 1275–6 RH, *Ludewella* 1314 Ch
> *Lodewelle* (freq) 1285 *Ass*

The first element is the common OE river-name *Hlȳde*, meaning 'loud stream,' *v.* RN 273. *v.* w(i)elle, and cf. Ludwell Fm (294).

HANGMAN'S HILL (6") and RAVEN HILL are so named 1706 *Bodl* and c. 1840 *TA* respectively. HOOPER'S COPSE (6"). Cf. *Hoopers Meadow* c. 1840 *TA*.

FIELD-NAMES

(*a*) In c. 1840 (*TA*) Apple Tree Mead, Bull Meadow, Crab Tree Meadow, Dials Close (the reference might be to a sundial cut in turf, *v.* PN Cu 469), Fox Earth ground, Huck Hill, Parsons Meadow, Picked Meadow (*v.* picked), Pool Close, Ram Close, Ryeland, Sidling or Middle Hill ground (*v.* sideling).

(*b*) In 1706 (*Bodl*) *the Berry field, Berry Land* (*the Bery lande* 1602 *Bodl*, *Bury land* 1617 *Bodl*, *v.* burh), *Boywell, Caphill, Collyham, Deadsands, the Dean furlong* (*v.* denu), *Drawfurlong, Fausthill, green sward, Groveway, the hade acre* (*v.* hades), *Hashooks Hedg, Hemins, Hollow hill, the Horse Lays* (*v.* lē(a)h), *Lanck furlong* (*v.* lang), *Latterdine, Limps banks and hill, Ockerbridg, Paddlefords Bush, Long Read Furlong, the Sale, the Sands, Sinkmore, the Slid* (this looks like the word *slid*, 'valley' recorded in EDD for Yorkshire), *Little and Great Stockwells, Stockwell way, Stonehill, Stry Lees, Varnhill Slad* ('fern-hill valley,' *v.* slæd), *Wathill, Whitlum lees.* In 1413 (Os) *la Hethe* (*v.* hæþ), *Linlond* (*v.* lin, land).

23. Shipton on Cherwell

SHIPTON ON CHERWELL

> *Sceaptun,* (*to*) *Sceaptune* 1005 (late 12th) KCD 714
> *Sciptone* 1086 DB, c. 1220 Os, *Sciptune* 1086 DB, *Sciptune super Charewell* 1213–28 Eynsh, *Scipton'* 1235–6 Fees, *Scipton* 1278–9 RH
> *Shiptone* 1201 FF, *Shypton* 1280 Os, *Shyptone* (ter) 1285 *Ass*, *Shipton* (bis) 1314 Ipm, 1428 FA, *Shipton-upon-Charwelle* 1332 Cl
> *Siptona* 1209–18 WellsR, *Siptun'* 1220 Fees, *Sipton'* 1230–1 WellsR, 1242–3 Fees, *Sypton* 1246 Ch, 1314 Ipm

Schipton' (bis) 1268 *Ass, Schypton on Charewill* 1311 Ipm

Shepton 1268 Ch, 1401–2 FA, *Shepton upon Charewell* 1341 Cl,
    Shepton juxta Charwell 1401–2 FA, *Shepton uppon Charwell*
    1510 AD

Schupton 1284–5 FA

Shoptone by Charewelle (bis) 1285 *Ass*

Shybton 1314 Cl

Shutton by Charwell 1361 Cl

Stypeton 1401–2 FA

'Sheep farm,' OE scē(a)p-tūn: cf. Shipton under Wychwood 375.

SHIPTON SLADE FM is so named 1822 O.S.

FIELD-NAMES[1]

(a) In 1862 (Sale Catalogue)[2] Little Wharton's or Adam's Shrub (*Adams Shrub* 1814), Bacons Weir (*Beacon's Wear* 1768 EnclAct), Bigberry ((*to*) *Bicanbyrig* 1005 (late 12th) Eynsh, *Long Bigberry* 1606–7 Survey, 'Bica's burh'; *Picked Bigbie*, which appears in a 1769 Estate Act for Hensington and c. 1840 *TA* in Bladon, may contain another form of this name), Blackman Lands, Briar Furlong or Bush Piece (*Bush Piece* 1814), Cliff Hill (cf. *the Cliff Close* 1685 (c. 1700), *v.* clif), The Common, Coplow Field, Cotman's Farm, Little and Big Cotman (*Cottman way and Hook* 1634 (c. 1700), *Cotnam way* 1685 (c. 1700), *v.* cotman), The Crosses (cf. *the Cross peece* 1685 (c. 1700)), Damping Slade, Dirt Hill (*Durthill Furlong* 1589 Stapleton, *Durt Hill* 1634 (c. 1700), *dirt* is used in dialect of loose earth or mold), Little Fern Piece (*The little fearne* 1634 (c. 1700), *Great and Little Fern* 1768 EnclAct), Furmity Piece, Half Stream, Harper's Close and Piece (*Harpur's Close* 1768 EnclAct), Hemp Plot, Great and Little Henyards, High Field (so named 1685 (c. 1700)), Hogstye Piece (*hogsty furlonge* 1685 (c. 1700), *Hog Stye Piece and Slade* 1814), The Hurst (so named 1634 (c. 1700), cf. *Hur(s)tdich* 1220–2 Os, *v.* hyrst, dīc), Lower and Middle Lake, Paper Lake (cf. *the upper and neither Lake* 1634 (c. 1700), *the Lakes* 1685 (c. 1700), *lake* is used in dialect of a stream), Leys Furlong (cf. *the Lee furse* 1634 (c. 1700), *the Lays Close* 1768 EnclAct), Oldfield Plain, Pear Tree Furlong, Picked Piece and Slade (cf. *The Picks* 1634 (c. 1700), *v.* picked), Pilford Meadow (*Pilwarde* c. 1260–70 ChCh, *Pilford mead* 1634 (c. 1700), *Pillford Meadow* 1685 (c. 1700), *v.* pyll; there is a Pill Meadow in the adjoining parish of Tackley), Poors Allotment, Sainfoin Piece (*Sainfoin Close* 1768 EnclAct), Short Measure, The Slade (*v.* slæd), Stone Pit Ground (so named 1814), The Straits (*v.* Des), Tackley Furlong (*Tackly furlong and way* 1634 (c. 1700)), Well Spring Ground (so named 1814). In 1768 (EnclAct) Little Eights (*v.* eyt), The Green, North Meadow (*North Mead* 1634 (c. 1700)), Pond Close, Sheep House Close, Tilcox.

---

[1] Except where otherwise stated, the forms are from *BodlT*.
[2] There is a copy of this in the Bodleian Library.

(*b*) In 1685 (c. 1700) *the furze furlonge* (*the furze furlong* 1634 (c. 1700)), *Oatehill, Stranbridge furlonge* (*Stambridge furlong* (bis) 1634 (c. 1700), possibly 'stone bridge'), *woolans* (*Woolland furlong* 1634 (c. 1700), *v.* wōh). In 1634 (c. 1700) *The Two bitterall Acres, Cappen bush*[1], *the hill way and piece, Marcham, New Colledge Farm, Walton furlong.* In c. 1230 (c. 1280) (S) *Grenediche* (*v.* grēne, dīc), *Langelowe* ((*on*) *langan hlawe* 1004 (t. Ed 2) Frid, (*on*) *langan hlǽw* 1005 (late 12th) Eynsh (*v.* lang, hlāw, hlǽw), *Sititrop* (also 1217–30 (c. 1280) S, *v.* þrop). In 1217–30 (c. 1280) (S) *Crowellemore* (*v.* crāwe, w(i)elle, mōr). In 1005 (late 12th) (Eynsh) (*to* þam) *ealdan Crystelmæle* ('the old crucifix'), (*on* þa) *ealdan dic* (*v.* (e)ald, dīc), (*on* þone) *ealdan garan* (*v.* (e)ald, gāra), (*on* þa) *heh strǽte* ('high street'), (*andlang* þæs) *wudu weges* (*v.* wudu, weg).

24. Stanton Harcourt

STANTON HARCOURT

> *Stantone* 1086 DB *et passim* with variant spellings *Stanton*(*a*), *Stantun*', *Stant*(*t*)*on*' to 1288 Ipm, *Stantone Harecurt* 1268–81 Eynsh *et freq* with variant spellings *Stanton' Harecurte, Stanton Harecurt, Stantone Harcourd* to 1346 FA
> *Staunton*' 1234 Cl *et freq* with variant spellings *Staunton*(*e*) to 1428 FA, *Stauntone Harecurt* 1285 Ass (p) *et passim* with variant spellings *Staunton Harec*(*o*)*urt, Staunton Harecourte, Stauntton Harecourth* to 1428 FA, *Stawnton Harcourt* 1519 AD

'Stone tūn,' *v.* stān, which in this name probably refers to the stones known as The Devil's Quoits[2]. Robert de *Harcourt* is the owner 1193 P.

ARMSTALLS (6″) is *Hamstall*' 1213–28 Eynsh (p) *et freq* with variant spellings *Hamstall*(*e*) to 1316 FA, *la Hamstalle* 1281–1307 Eynsh. *v.* hāmst(e)all.

BEARD MILL is *Berdemulne* early 13th Bodl, *Burdemulne* 1278–9 RH (p), *Berdedmille* 1375 Bodl (p). Cf. *Beardirull Stream* 1712 FF. The first element may be a mutated form of OE *bord*, such as occurs in ON *byrði*. The meaning would then be 'mill made of boards,' *v.* myln.

FLEXNEY FM (6″) is *Flexneye* 1278–9 RH. The first element looks like an OE **fleaxen* from fleax, 'flax': cf. **cærsen* in Cassington (252) and **gærsen* in Garsington (174). *flaxen* is first recorded in 1521. Second element (ī)eg, 'well-watered land,' or possibly (ge)hæg, 'enclosure.'

PINKHILL FM ETC. Cf. *Pincle* 1278–9 RH, *Pyncle* 1316 FA, *Pinkle* 1797 Davis: *v.* pightel.

---

[1] *v.* PN Cu 67–8. The meaning is unknown. [2] *v.* Hawkes, p. 172.

PIRIHO WOOD (lost) is (*forete de*) *P'iho* 1161 P, (*bosco...de*) *Piriho* 1235 FF. This may be *Pereio* 1086 DB, 'pear-tree hill,' *v.* pirige, hōh.

SUTTON

> *Sutton'* 1207 Cur *et freq* with variant spellings *Sutton(e)*, *Suttune*, *Sutthun*

'South tūn.'

BLACK DITCH is so named 1774 *EnclA*. LINCH HILL. Cf. *Upper and Lower Linch* c. 1840 *TA*, *v.* hlinc. WEST END is *Westende* 1278–9 RH (p), *West End Village* 1774 *EnclA*, *v.* ende.

FIELD-NAMES

(a) In 1774 (*EnclA*) Back Bridge, Bear or Bare Lane (*v.* bere), Black Balls Elms, Bow Gate, Butts (*v.* butts), Cabbage Closes, Chapel Bridge Bottom and Corner, Clay Street Way, Coneyshire Corner, Cross Tree, Edgleys, Friar Wood (*Frerwoode* 1544 All Souls), Grouse Close, Long Guy, Hatchel(l) Lane, Hatch Gate (*v.* hæcc-geat), The Holm(s) (*v.* holme), Inn Mead (*v.* in), Kings End Lane, Land Mead, Meadow Plot Furlong, The Neaps, Penny Piece Furlong (*v.* penny), Potley, The Slade (*v.* slæd), Spring Furlong, Till Close, Whitehall Bush.

(b) In 1244 (FF) *Aluinelond* ('*Ælfwynn*'s land'; *Ælfwynn* is a woman's name), *Chaluecroft* ('calf croft'), *Cutelesmore* (*Kutelesmore* 1235 FF, '*Cytel*'s marsh,' *v.* mōr), *Sortehangle*, *Westmere* (*Westmore* 1235 FF, *v.* mōr).

25. Stonesfield

STONESFIELD [stʌnzfiˑld or stounzfiˑld]

> *Stvntesfeld* 1086 DB, *Stuntesfeld'* 1167 P *et passim* with variant
> spellings *Stuntesfeld(a)*, *Stuntesfeud*, *Stuntesfelde* to 1406 Eynsh,
> *Stuntisfeld'* 1174 P
>
> *Stuntefelda* 1130 P *et freq* with variant spellings *Stuntef(f)eld'*,
> *Stuntefeld* to 1273–4 RH
>
> *Stutfeld'* 1192 P (p)
>
> *Stontesfeld* 1222–3 WellsR, 1224 Cl, 1278–9 RH, 1316 FA
>
> *Stundesfeld'* 1230 Eynsh, *Stundesfeld* 1246 Cl (p)
>
> *Stutesfeld* 1242 P
>
> *Stintesfeld'* 1268 Ass
>
> *Sottefeld* 1285 Ass
>
> *Scotesfeld*, *Sconte(s)feld* 1285 Ass
>
> *Duntesfeld* 1285 Ass
>
> *Stonysfelde* 1526 LS
>
> *Stunsfeld* 1676 Plot

'*Stunt's field,' v. feld. Stunt(a) would be a nickname from OE stunt, 'foolish.' The personal name occurs in a number of minor names in the parish, v. Stonesfield Ford infra. The weak name *Stunta may be the first element of Stuntney (PN Ca 220–1).

BLOXHAM WOOD (lost) is bosco...de Blockesham 1234 Cl, bosco de Bloxam 1254–5 RH, boscum de Bloxham 1298 Eynsh. Bloxham is about ten miles north, but this wood is clearly somewhere near the west boundary of Stonesfield. There is also an Erleswode de Bloxham 1298 Eynsh, probably a part of the above.

CALLOW BARN takes name from le Callowe 1606–7 Survey. STONES-FIELD RIDING (6″) is Stonesfield or Callow Riding 1804 EnclA, v. ryding. callow, 'bare,' is first recorded of land in 1677 in Plot's Natural History of Oxfordshire 243, but occurs much earlier in place-names, v. DEPN s.n. Callow.

RUDDY WELL is Ruthereswelle 1298 Eynsh, Rotherewell' 1300 Wych, Rudder Well 1608–9 Survey. 'Cattle stream,' v. hrȳðer, w(i)elle.

SPRATT'S BARN. The last shaft from which the famous Stonesfield slates were taken was closed in 1909 (Arkell, p. 139).

STOCKEY BOTTOM, PLANTATION (both 6″, latter in Fawler) take name from Stecheye 1298 Eynsh, Stokhey(e) 1300 Wych, Stakhey 1608–9 Survey. 'Log enclosure,' v. stocc, (ge)hæg.

STONESFIELD FORD (6″) is probably Stontesford 1278–9 RH, Stuntes-forde 1298 Eynsh, Stuntesford 1300 Wych, Stuntesfoord 1608–9 Survey, Stonesford 1804 EnclA. The first element is the personal name *Stunt, which appears in the name of the parish. A Stontesham is also mentioned in the 1278–9 reference, and there is a Stuntescumb' 1273–4 RH and a Stuntesdon 1246 Ch, v. hamm, cumb, dūn.

FIELD-NAMES

(a) In 1817 (BodlT) the Bottom, Church Field (Churchfeild 1606–7 Survey), the Coombe road (cf. Comb Lane and way 1634 (c. 1700) BodlT, the parish of Combe is adjacent), New Barn, Picked Close (v. picked), Poor's Furlong, Town-side-furlong (the Townside 1634 (c. 1700) BodlT), Well Furlong (so named 1634 (c. 1700) BodlT). In 1804 (EnclA) Akeman street furlong, Bayley's Cross, broad pit furlong (Broadpitt furlong 1634 (c. 1700) BodlT), Cockshute (v. cockshoot), Dean Close, the Dean (v. denu), Fewdell Wood (cf. Fewden 1608–9 Survey), Long Gore furlong (v. gāra), the green, Green furlong (Stuntsfield grene 1608–9 Survey), Hanger's furlong (Hangers 1634 (c. 1700) BodlT, v. hangra), Middle Hill furlong, the Hill, Holly Bush furlong, Jennet's Assarts (Gennisart, le Gennettes Sarte 1606–7 Survey,

Tennettes Sarte 1608–9 *Survey*, *v.* sart), Maplewell (cf. *Mapeldorwellehull* 1257 Os, *Maple peece* 1606–7 *Survey*; the early name has OE mapuldor, 'maple,' as first element, to which w(i)elle and hyll have been added), Long Northal(l) furlong (*Northole, Northawe* 1606–7 *Survey*), Pear tree furlong (cf. *peartree field* 1685 (c. 1700) *BodlT*), Port Hedge furlong (*v.* port), River Lane (so named 1634 (c. 1700) *BodlT*), Long Shirton, short Shirton furlong, the Sidelong (*v.* sideling), Middle Slade furlong (*v.* slæd), Stickle Rod furlong, Town furlong, the waste, Wootton Riding (*v.* ryding).

(b) In 1712 (VCH O 1, 315) *Chesthill Acres* or *Chestrenhill* (Romano-British remains were found here, *v.* ceaster). In 1685 (c. 1700) (*BodlT*) *the breach* (*v.* breche), *Church land or Towne Land, Giles wall, the Towne furlong.* In 1634 (c. 1700) (*BodlT*) *Crab Tree Butts, the Parsonage Close, Westlands.* In 1606–7 (*Survey*) *Home fields* (*v.* home), *le Ridclose, Symonesgroue.* In 1300 (Wych) *Gerneleswode* (*v.* wudu).

26. Tackley

TACKLEY

Tachelie 1086 DB, *Taccheleia* a. 1161, 1194–6 Eynsh, *Tacchele* 1170–95 Eynsh

Takkelea 1176 P (p), *Takelea* 1187 P *et freq* with variant spellings *Takele, Takeley(e)* to 1525 AD, *Tackele* 1196 FF *et passim* with variant spellings *Tackelegh', Tackel', Tackelege, Tackelee, Tackeley(e)* to 1346 Ipm, *Takkele* 1227 Ch *et freq* with variant spelling *Takkeley* from 1306 AD to 1476 AD

Thackele 1219–20 RH, *Thackeley* 1285 *Ass*

Tacle 1278–9 RH, 1397 Os, *Takley* 1383 Cl, 1442–4 Eynsh, 1510 AD, *Tackle* 1480 Frid, *Takla* 1517 D Inc, *Tackley, Tuckley* 1675 Ogilby

Identical with Takeley PN Ess 535: the meaning may be '**Tæcca*'s wood or clearing,' second element lē(a)h. Ekwall (DEPN) suggests that the group of names he discusses under Tackley have an earlier form of *teg, tag,* 'a young sheep,' as first element. *Tackewell'* (*v.* w(i)elle) is mentioned 1196 FF as a place in Tackley.

NETHERCOTT

Nidrecote 1086 DB

Nuthercott' 1220 Fees

Netherekot' 1235–6 Fees, *Nethercot'* 1242–3 Fees, *Nethercote* 1285 *Ass*, 1476 AD

Nithercot' 1278–9 RH

Nothercote 1346 Ipm

'Nether cot(e).'

POUND HILL is *Pauenhull'* 1139 (c. 1450) Godstow, *Pounhyll* c. 1250 (c. 1450) Godstow, *Pound Hill* c. 1840 *TA*. The first element could be *pāwa*, 'peacock,' perhaps used as a nickname. Icelandic *pá, pái* is so used. Cf. Poundon PN Bk 56.

SNAKESHALL CLUMP (6″) takes name from *Snokeshull'* 1268 *Ass*. '*Snoc*'s hill.' The personal name is only recorded in place-names. Snoxhall, PN Sr 231, has the same origin as this name.

WEAVELEY FM[1] takes name from (*to*) *wiðigleas* (*gemæro*) 1005 (late 12th) Eynsh, *Wideli* 1109 Eynsh, *Widel'* 1159–62 Eynsh, c. 1160 RegAntiquiss, *Wytteleya* 1239 Eynsh. Cf. *Weefleye fielde* 1605 MapsOx. 'Willow wood,' OE wīðig-lē(a)h.

WHITEHILL FM

> *Wihthille, Wythull'* 1004 (t. Ed 2) Frid, *Yihthille* 1004 (t. Ed 3) Frid
> *Wistelle* 1086 DB, *Visteull'* (bis) c. 1200 St John (p), *Wistull* 1210–30 (early 13th) Thame (p)
> *Wichthulla* c. 1130 OxonCh *et passim* with variant spellings *Wi(h)cthill, Wicthull(e), Wicthill', Wicthilla, Wyhthulle, Wycthille* to 1294 Cl (p)
> *Withulla* c. 1152–70 Eynsh (p) *et passim* with variant spellings *Withull(e), Withill(e), Wythhull(e)*, to 1389 Os
> *Wihulla* a. 1176 Eynsh (p)
> *Wecthull'* 1206 Cur (p)
> *Wuthell'* 1208 Fine (p)
> *Whithulla* 1219 Bract (p), *Whythulle* 1285 *Ass*, *Whithulle, Whithalle* 1306 AD, *Whithull* 1428 FA, *White Hill* 1797 Davis, *Whitehill Farm* 1822 O.S.[2]
> *Wihgthulle* 1285 Eynsh (p), *Wighthull'* 1297 CornAcc *et freq* with variant spellings *Wyghthull(e), Wighthull(e), Wyghthill(e)* to 1438 AD
> *Whygthulle* 1315 Eynsh

'Hill with a curved hollow,' first element OE wiht, 'bend,' second element hyll. *v.* PN Wo 183 and PN D lii.

KING'S ARMS PUBLIC HOUSE (6″) and STURDY'S CASTLE INN are so named c. 1840 *TA* and 1822 O.S. respectively.

---

[1] There are two farms with this name.
[2] Now Old Whitehill Fm.

FIELD-NAMES

(a) In c. 1840 (*TA*) Acrely, Allgrove Piece, Ashwell Meadow and Hill Piece, Ashwell Hill Butts, Barn Picks (*v.* picked), Blacklands Piece, Be(e)chmore Piece, Bondland Furlong (possibly 'bean land,' cf. 340), Brand Iron Piece, Brockley Piece, Butts close (*v.* butts), Costell Ground (*v.* cot-steall), Crab Tree Piece, Dean Piece (*v.* denu), Dibdane Furlong, Great and Little Dicks hill, Lower and Upper Dog Kennell Piece, Dove House Closes, Glover Leys, Greasy Hill Ground, Lower and Upper Hades Piece (*v.* hades), Handkerchief piece (*v.* Fan), Fieldharder, Homerharder (*v.* 453), North Hay (*v.* (ge)hæg), The Heat Piece, Hedge Row, High Wood, Hog Bottom, Holm Meadow (*v.* holme), Hop Yard Ground, Lower and Upper Hutt Field, Hybrink Hill and Spring, Jack Tar Ground, Jobs Balk Furlong (*v.* Fan), Juniper Hill, The Lays (cf. *Leaes acres* 1605 MapsOx, *v.* lǣs), The Lashor or Lasher, The Lezzer Ground and Piece (*v.* 142), The Lizard Ground (this may be identical with *the Lagshorde* 1605 MapsOx, or it may be simply another version of the preceding name), Long Liddard, The Lints, Lints Break (*lints* may be a development of hlinc; cf. *The Linche* 1605 MapsOx), Lodging Acre, Loves Alley, Mad Croft Close (*v.* mǣd), Moor Slade Piece (*v.* mōr, slæd and cf. *la More* 1278–9 RH), Long and Short Over or Hover (*Longe and Shorte over* 1605 MapsOx), Paint House Close, Parsons Picks and Close, Pigeon Ground, Pill Meadow (*v.* pyll), The Plain, The Pound, Pull Back Mill, Puppy's Parlour, Great Red Lands, Saddle Back Field (*v.* Des), The Sidling (*v.* sideling), Great and Little Sidnells, Sixty Low Field, The Slade (*v.* slæd), Snakes Tail Piece, Stoney close, Stone Pit Piece (cf. *Wyitstandelf, Wyiterstandelf* 1314 *Bodl*, which has stān-(ge)delf, 'quarry,' as second element, and possibly a garbled version of the name of Whitehill as first), Sweetin Tree Piece, Swe(e)tingtree (a *sweeting* is 'a small, sweet early apple'), Tacknell, Twynhams Spinney, Turfham or Twifham Furlong, The Warren, The Rabbit Warren, Watercourse Piece, White Lands, Winter Furlong Piece.

(b) In 1605 (MapsOx) *The Cliffe* (the land is on the bank of the Cherwell, and the use of 'cliff' to mean 'river-bank' is very rare except in place-names), *Foreshooters* (*v.* forthshetere), *Fursen Close* (furzen is a dialect word for 'furze'), *Glyden-horne*, *Lott mead* (*v.* lot), *piked acre* (*v.* picked), *Oxford stones*, *Woodstocke stones*, *Stonyborow*, *Whitson moore*. In 1306 (AD) *le longedole* (*v.* dole). In 1278–9 (RH) *la Breche* (*v.* breche), (*piscaria q.v.*) *The Hold* (the word *hold* is recorded in the sense 'lurking-place of animals' from the 13th to the 19th century: and specifically of fish in 1787, *v.* NED *hold* sb[1] 9).

27. Duns Tew

DUNS TEW

Teowe, Tewa(m), Tvvam 1086 DB
Tiwe 1192 P, 1204 Cur (ter), Tiwa 1193 P, 1204 Cur, 1215 Cl, Tywe 1208 Fine

Donestiua c. 1210 Os, *Dunnestywa* c. 1233 Os *et freq* with variant
   spellings *Dunnestiwa*, *Dun(n)estywe*, *Don(n)estiwe* to 1294–5 AD,
   Dunestyue 1242 P, *Bonestywe* 1278–9 RH, *Dunes Tywe* 1287 Cl
Dunnesthiwe 1220 Fees
Dunestyuwe 1242 P
Dunstiwe 1242–3 Fees, 1273–4 RH, *Dunstywe* 1246–7, 1268, 85
   Ass, *Domstywe* 1284–5 FA, *Donstiwe* 1349 Ipm, *Dunstywa* 1389
   Os
Dunstighel 1285 *Ass*
Dunstowe (bis) 1285 *Ass*, 1316 FA, *Dounestowe* 1327 Cl, *Dunsto*
   1675 Ogilby
Dunestwye 1321 AD
Dunstuwe (bis), *Dunstue* 1327 Ch
Dunsteue 1346 FA, *Dunstew(e)* 1428 FA, *Donstew* 1461–2 BM

Cf. Ekwall (DEPN): "The name seems to be cognate with the el.
-tǣwe, *-tīewe*, *-tēowe* found in *æltǣwe* 'in good health, excellent,'
manigtīewe 'skilful.' This el. appears to be related to OE *teohh* 'race,
generation, troop,' MHG *zeche* 'row, order.' The meaning of the
OE word (? *tīewe*) may have been 'row,' whence 'lengthy object.'
Tew may then have been the name of the long ridge at which the
places are." The prefix to Duns Tew is the personal name *Dunn*.

DANE HILL. Cf. *Deanhill Ground* 1735 *Bodl*. First element 'valley,'
v. denu.

FIELD-NAMES[1]

(a) In 1793 (*EnclA*) Barton Sharp Furlong and Gap, Bitter Lands Furlong,
Long Breach Leys (cf. *Long and Short Breach* 1634, *v.* breche), Brook
Meadow (*Brookmead* 1634), Buffets Leys (cf. *Buffitts acre* 1634), Churchway
furlong (*Churchway* 1634), Cow Lane Close, Cuckold's Holt, Down end
Common, the home Close (*v.* home), little Lang furlong (*v.* lang), Red Hill
quarter, Ridges quarter, Sands Quarter (cf. *The Sands* 1634), Townsend
Butts and Closes, the Vicars home Close, Wainbrook Furlong, Wall Furlong
(so named 1634), the west End, the West end Common, Whittington Quarter
(*Wheatenton* 1634, *Whettington Hill* 1685, possibly 'wheat hill,' OE *hwǣten
dūn*), Witney Stone ford (Witney is about fourteen miles away).

(b) In 1685 *Breadimore*, *Breadimore Hill* (*Bredimore* 1634, *v.* mōr), *Brin-
close* (*Brinkclose* 1634), *Broad Ends* (so named 1634), *Cannimasse* (*Cainmas*
1634), *Constables way* (so named 1634), *Coppen hill* (*Copnel* 1634), *Court Field*
(so named 1634, *v.* courte), *the Cowpasture* (so named 1634), *Ennock Hill*,
Goose slade (*Gooslad* 1634, *v.* slæd), *Gosse furlong Butts* (*Goffurlong* 1634),

---

[1] Except where otherwise stated, the forms are from *BodlT*, and are (c. 1700).

Hanging (*Little and Great Hanging, Hangings* 1634, *v.* hangende), *the Hedge furlonge, Leapgar furlonge* (*Lipyate* 1634, a *leap-gate* is a gate which keeps cattle and sheep from straying, but can be leapt by deer), *the Ley brooke slade* (*v.* slæd), *the loepend field, the Great Marches, betwixt marches* (*Eastmarch Westmarch, Between the Marches* 1634, *march* is a dialect form of *marsh*), *Short and Long pease breach* (*Peasbreach* 1634, *v.* breche[1]), *picked Ends* (so named 1634, *v.* picked), *plowland Bushes, Rush bed* (cf. *Rushpitt* 1634), *small mead* (so named 1634), *stephens hedge furlonge* (*Steevens hedge* 1634), *Vicars Willowes* (*Vicars Withies* 1634), *the Wester Well* (*Westerall* 1634). In 1634 *Between the Lakes* (*v.* lacu), *the far furlong, Fulwell hanging* (*Fullwelle Hangyng* 1436 Os, *v.* hangende), *The hither furlong, Lines-mill, Parsons hedge, Stonepitts furlong, Watrey-yards*.

28. Great Tew

GREAT TEW

(*æt*) *Tiwan* 1004 (c. 1200) ASWills, *Cyrictiwa* 1050–2 (13th) Paris[2], *Tiwa Magna* 1165 P *et freq* with variant spelling *Tiwe Magna* to 1194 P, *Tiwe* 1185 RR *et freq* with variant spellings *Tywe, Tywa* to 1251 Cl, *Magna Tywe* 1195 P *et passim* with variant spellings *Magna Tiwa, Magna Tiwe, Magna Tywa* to 1401–2 FA, *Great Tywe* 1336 Cl *et freq* with variant spelling *Great Tiwe* to 1340 Cl
Tewam 1086 DB, *Magna Tewe* 1428 FA
Tiewa 1167 P
Thywe 1241 Cl
Gywam 1268 *Ass*
Magna Tyuwe 1285 *Ass*
Great Tuwe 1333, 49 Ipm, 1334 Cl, 1428 FA, *Magna Tue* 1346 FA

For etymology *v.* Duns Tew (288). 'Church' has been prefixed to one form.

BEACONSFIELD FM. Cf. *Beacon quarter* 1706 *Bodl, Beacon Fields* 1767 *EnclA*, 1797 Davis. CHESCOOMBE CLUMP (6″), HOOKERSWELL FM, HOPTON'S ROUGH (6″), MILL LANE (6″) and GREAT TEW PARK. Cf. *Chescomb Hill, Huckerswell, Hopton's Grounds, Mil(l)way* and *The Parks* 1767 *EnclA*. CONYGREE WOOD (6″). Cf. *Conygree* 1706 *Bodl, v.* conygree. THE GROVE, LEDWELL LANE and POOR BRIDGE (all 6″) are so named 1767 *EnclA*.

[1] The same name occurs in South Leigh (276) and South Newington (278).
[2] The form is miscopied *Cyrictuna* in KCD 950.

FIELD-NAMES[1]

(a) In 1767 (*EnclA*) Barnwell (possibly connected with *Bernhulle* c. 1278 Winchcombe, *Bernehulle* c. 1280 Winchcombe, *Hyderbornehul, Yonderbornehul* 1436 Os and *Bernhullesford*' ? c. 1240, *Bernehulleforde* c. 1270, *v.* hyll; the first element could be *bern*, 'barn,' or the personal name *Beorna*; 'hither' and 'yonder' have been prefixed, and 'ford' added, to some of the forms), Church Way (*Chyrchwey* 1436 Os), The Dog Kennell, Farhill, Galley Thorns, Greenaway, Hollow Marsh, the Ling part of Old Hill, March Cow pasture, March Hedge, Little Tew Marsh Gap, New Pool, Little Tew Oxenden (*Oxenden, Oxendeneshulle* c. 1260 Os, 'Oxen valley,' *v.* denu; hyll has been added to one form), Pool Head, Priest Croft, Rudaway, Morton's Townsend, Wood Way. In 1761 (Gray) Alepath (this might be identical with the '*Ægel*'s pit' which occurs in the field-names of Little Tew 292), Between the Hedges, Broad and Picked Castors (possibly identical with *Costowa* 1268 Os, *Costow* 1287–8 Bodl, *v.* cot-stōw), the Great Pool, the old Hill, Park Hill, plank pitts (*v.* plank), ten Lands, Wheat Lands.

(b) In 1436 (Os) *Berycrosse, Blakthyrne* ('blackthorn'), *Shortbreche, le Langbrech* (*Brech*' ? c. 1240, *v.* breche), *Bradmor* (*v.* brād, mōr), *Brokforlong* (*v.* brōc), *Brokemed(e)* (*v.* brōc, mǣd), *Goosdych* (*v.* gōs, dīc), *Flexlond* (*v.* fleax, land), *Fulleacre* (*v.* fullock), *Gretehangyng* (*v.* hangende), *Overhaydon, Netterhaydon* (final element dūn), *Hyllydoles* (*v.* dole), *Inhoke* (land cultivated while the rest of the field is fallow: *v.* the field-names of Ducklington 318), *Kalyngmersh* (*v.* mersc), *Lamcote* ('lambs' shelter'), *Oxgynmed, Shortbrod* ('short broad'), *Hydersande, Oversond, le Sond* (*sonde* ? c. 1240, *v.* sand), *Swayneshegg* (*v.* hecg), *Sydelyng super Stanwellhul* (*v.* stān, w(i)elle, hyll and sideling), *Thyktherne* ('thick thorn'), *Townforlong, Westmersh* (*v.* mersc). In 1278–9 (RH) *Inmed* (*v.* in), *Mulelond* (*v.* myln, land), *Reveton*' ('reeve's tūn'). In c. 1270 *litelfaremmanysdone* (*v.* lŷtel, dūn; the middle element is the personal name *Fareman*), *the gore* (*the heldegore* ? c. 1240, *olde gore* 1256, *v.* gāra; (e)ald has been prefixed to the earlier forms), *heneforde* (*v.* ford), *holewey* (*v.* holh, weg), *myddelsladesholde* (*Middislade* ? c. 1240, *Middisladeheld*' 1256, *Middisladehold*' 1266, 'middle valley,' *v.* slæd, to which hi(e)lde, 'slope,' has been added), *serplond*' (*serpelond*' ? c. 1240, *v.* land; first element *scearp*, 'rugged, steep'), *sprotte* (apparently OE *sprot(a)*, 'sprout, twig,' perhaps used in a collective sense), *undir the crofte* (*v.* croft), *Vermfurlong, the wewes* (*the wowes* ? c. 1240, *wewes* c. 1260, this is another instance of the mysterious name *wewes*, which occurs PN Sx 392, PN Sr 269, PN W 455: NED quotes the earliest form under the obsolete *wough*, from OE *wāg*, 'partition,' but this is a mistake), *the wode rigge* (*the wodebrigge* c. 1260, 'wooden bridge'), *Wolmereham* (*Wolmersham* ? c. 1240, '*Wulfmǣr*'s hamm'). In ? c. 1260 *Shrobbes* (also ? c. 1240, 'shrubs'), *Swytewelhulle, Swytewelleslade* (*witewellehulle, witewelleslede* ? c. 1240, *v.* hwīt, w(i)elle, hyll, slæd), *Voxlewesforlonge* (the first elements look like 'fox' and 'hill,' *v.* hlǣw, under hlāw), *wastaneshulle* (*wasteynshulle* ? c. 1240, *v.* hyll). In c. 1260 *setteles*.

---

[1] Except where otherwise stated, the forms are from Godstow, and these are all (c. 1450).

In ? c. 1240 *Banlond'* (v. bēan, land), *Batesham* ('*Bætti*'s hamm': the name *Betti* is recorded), *Brekesme*, *dudemede* ('*Duda*'s mǣd'), *fordyngmere* (v. mere), *herpe* (perhaps 'salt-harp'), *heryngeborow* (v. b(e)org: the first element might be the personal name *Hering*), *Heyclyue* ('high bank'), *hurth' welfurlong*. (v. w(i)elle), *porledstaple* (second element *stapol*, 'post'), *Shulebrede* (v. shovelbrode), *smalecombe* (v. smæl, cumb), *Somersmore* ('summer marsh,' v. mōr), *spercever*, *strate* (v. strǣt), *Swynysty* ('swine-sty'; the word is not recorded till 1340), *wowclyue* ('crooked bank,' v. wōh, clif).

29. Little Tew

LITTLE TEW

> *Tewe, Teowe, Teova, Tewa* 1086 DB
> *Tiwa* 1123–33 OxonCh, *Tiw* 1130 P, 1130–42 OxonCh (p), *Tiwe* 1130 P, *parua Tywa* 1200 Os *et passim* with variant spellings *parua Tiwa, parua Tywa* to 1316 FA, *Little Tiwe* 1268 Ch, 1350 Cl, *Little Tywe* 1275 Cl
> *Parua Thiwa* 1211 FF
> *Parva Tue* 1346 FA, *Little Tue* 1362 Cl, *Parva Twe* 1428 FA
> *Little Tiewe* 1368 Cl

For etymology v. Duns Tew 288.

SHOWELL FM ETC.

> *Sevewelle* 1086 DB *et passim* with variant spellings *Seuewell(e)*, *Seuewell'* to 1268 *Ass*
> *Sivewelle* 1086 DB
> *Sefewella* c. 1154–63 Eynsh
> *Seuelle* 1207 Cur
> *Sewelle* 1241–64 Eynsh *et passim* with variant spelling *Sewell* to 1401–2 FA
> *Swelles* 1252 Cl
> *Sowelle* 1278–9 RH
> *Showel* early 18th ParColl

'Seven springs.' The name is a common one: v. PN Nth 40, where a number of examples are given from other counties. In O the OE name, from *seofon* and w(i)elle, occurs again in Showell Covert (249), and Seven Springs (cf. PN Sr xliv) appears as a modern name on the 6″ map in Swinbrook.

COLDHARBOUR FM and HAYES'S BARN (6″) are *Coldharbour* and *Hays Barn* 1797 Davis. COLTSCOOMBE FM. Cf. *Coldscomb* 1794 EnclA. THE LUNCHES (6″): v. lunch.

FIELD-NAMES

(a) In 1794 (*EnclA*) Ayleborough Leys, Barrow Hill Furlong, Bill Furlong, Broom Close Butts (*v.* butts), Chalk Furlong, Claybut or Clay Butt Furlong, Cliftbrook Leys, Cleftbrook Furlong, Clumperry Furlong, Cooll Spring Furlong, Cow Lane, Crabtree Furlong, Cross Furlong, Mead Driftway (*v.* drift), Glebe Piece, Globe Close, Hall Head Furlong, Hall Road Furlong, Hammocks Leys, Little Hammocks, Hanwell Close, Hoar Stone Furlong (cf. *Anestan* c. 1260 Os, 'one stone'), Horse Croft Leys, Lays Close (*v.* lē(a)h). Leasow (*v.* lǣs), The March, The Paddock, Pikes or Piked Meadow (*v.* picked), Pophill Furlong and Butts and Leys, Pound Close, Priory Mead, Radwell Leys and Close, Rick Yard, Shortland Highway (*Shortelonde* c. 1260 Os), Slad(e) Furlong (cf. *Bradeslade, Brode Slade, Lutle Slade, Lutleslede* c. 1260 Os, *v.* slǣd, 'broad' and 'little' have been prefixed to the early forms), Springwell Furlong, Stone Furlong, Teasland Furlong, Town Closes, Tunthorpe Ground and Lane, Water Slade Furlong (*v.* slǣd), Well Spring Furlong, Wheatland Furlong, Whorley Pit Furlong, Wickham Furlong, Yell Hill. In 1788 (*Loveday*) Friar Bacon's bridge (cf. *supra* 35).

(b) In c. 1260 (Os) *Ailespiteshille* (*v.* pytt, hyll, the first element looks like the personal name *Ægel*, only found in place-names), *Anelaw* ('one barrow,' *v.* hlāw), *Blacotenhille* (*v.* hyll), *Blokemundelonde* (*Blakmundelond*' ? c. 1240 (c. 1450) Godstow, *v.* land), *Bradewellehale* (*v.* brād, w(i)elle, h(e)alh), *Coppede more* (*v.* coppede), *Hangindelonde* (*v.* hangende), *Helille, Hemede* (*v.* heme), *Hole* (*v.* holh), *Depe Kathole* (*v.* dēop, holh, the middle element is 'wild cat'), *More* (*v.* mōr), *Nattok* (*Nectuke* c. 1240 (c. 1450) Godstow, *v.* nattock), *Saltereslede* (*v.* slǣd), *Seruddeswrthe* (*v.* worþ), *Shendegiste Stanidelf* (*v.* stān-gedelf; the first word is obscure), *Wyt Othulle* ('oat hill,' to which 'white' has been prefixed).

30. Thrupp

THRUPP

> *Trop* 1086 DB *et freq* to 1297 CornAcc, *Tropa* c. 1130 OxonCh *et freq* to 1267 Ch, *Trope* 1219 Eynsh, *Trop*' 1221 FF, *Troph* 1278–9 RH
>
> *Throp* 1247 FF *et freq* to 1428 FA, *Throp alias Thrope* 1306 Ipm
>
> *Thorp* 1284–5, 1316, 1346 FA, 1300, 1306 Ipm, 1797 Davis
>
> *v.* þrop, 'farm, hamlet.'

31. Woodstock

WOODSTOCK

> *Wudestoce* c. 1000 F. Liebermann, *Gesetze der Angelsachsen*, I, 216
> *Wodestoch* 1086 DB *et passim* with variant spellings *Wudestoch*', *Wudestoc(ha), Woudestocham, Wodestoc, Wodestok*', *Wodestoke, Wudestok, Wudestok*' to 1464 AD, *Novam Wodestoke* 1500 Os

Odestoca c. 1115 AD

Vdestoc' 1130 P

Wdestoc c. 1150 SD *et freq* with variant spellings *Wdestoch'*,
  Wdestoch(e), *Wdestokes*, *Wdestok'* to 1220 Fees

OLD WOODSTOCK. Cf. *Oldwoodstock meade* 1606–7 *Survey*, *Old
Woodstock meade* 1608–9 *Survey*.

'Place in the woods,' *v.* stoc, **wudu**. The name is translated
silvarum locus by Symeon of Durham.

BLENHEIM PALACE. Called after the Duke of Marlborough's victory
in 1704.

32. Wootton

WOOTTON

(*æt*) *Wudutune* 958 (12th) BCS 1042

Oitone, Optone 1086 DB

Wuttona 1163 P *et freq* with variant spellings *Wutton'*, *Wuttone* to
  1285 *Ass*

Wotton' c. 1180–90 (c. 1425) Frid *et passim* with variant spellings
  Wotton(e), *Wotthone*, *Wottun* to 1277 Ch, *Wotone* 1526 LS

Wttona 1186–96 Eynsh *et freq* with variant spellings *Wtton'*,
  Wttun' to 1246–7 *Ass*

Wittona c. 1190–6 Eynsh (p), *Witon'* 1216 Cl

'tūn in a wood,' *v.* **wudu**. *widu*, an earlier form of the word, occurs
occasionally in OE, and frequently in place-names. On the second
of the DB forms *v.* the hundred-name *supra* 244.

UPPER AND LOWER DORNFORD FMS

Deorneford '777' (12th) BCS 222

Derneford' c. 1100 (late 12th) EHR xlviii *et passim* with variant
  spellings *Derneford(e)* to 1401 Cl, *Dernford* 1428 FA

Daerneford 1109 Eynsh

Darneford 1159–62 Eynsh, *Darneford'* c. 1160 RegAntiquiss,
  Darnefford 1471 Eynsh, *Darnford* 1676 Plot

Denneford 1220 Fees, *Deneford* 1368 Cl

Durneford' 1268 *Ass*

Danford 1606–7 *Survey*

'Hidden ford,' *v.* d(i)erne. The change to -*o*- is evidently a late one.
The river-name Dorn is a back-formation. The name occurs also in
Finstock (422) and Sandford on Thames (187).

HORDLEY FM

Hordlega 1194 P *et passim* with variant spellings *Hordleia, Hord-leg(h)', Hordleyg', Hordle(y), Hordlegh, Hordele* 1230 P *et freq* with variant spelling *Hordeleye* to 1316 FA
Horlega 1197, 8 P
Hordesleg' 1242 P, *Hordesleye* 1283 Fine
Ordlegh 1268 *Ass*
Hoddeleghe 1285 *Ass*

'Treasure lē(a)h,' *v.* hord. The farm is very near Akeman Street: *v.* PN Sr xviii for the possible reference in such names as this to treasure buried in Romano-British times and found by Saxons.

LUDWELL FM

Lvdewelle 1086 DB, *Ludewelle* c. 1130 OxonCh *et passim* with variant spellings *Ludewell', Ludewell* to 1300 Ipm, *Ludwell* 1316 FA
Lodewelle 1241 FF *et freq* with variant spelling *Lodewell* to 1320 Os, *Lodelewell* 1275 Ch (p)
Lydewell 1270 Ch
Ledewelle 1285 *Ass, Ledwell* 1608–9 *Survey, Ledwell Farm* 1797 Davis, 1822 O.S.

'Stream called *Hlȳde*,' cf. Ledwell 280.

MILFORD BRIDGE (6″) is *Meolcforda, Meolforda* 958 (12th) BCS 1042 *Milford Bridge* 1606–7 *Survey, Millforde* 1608–9 *Survey*. Ekwall (RN 129) suggests that the first of the charter forms is the better one, and that *Meolc-* may represent an earlier name of the river Dorn. The water of the stream has, he says, a somewhat milky colour. There is a *stream called Millke* in Clanfield (313) and a *Milkwell* in Newton Purcell (232).

STRATFORD BRIDGE is *Stratford'* c. 1200 (13th) S, *Stratford Bridge* 1606–7 *Survey*. The strǣt is Akeman Street.

WOODLEYS is *Widelie* 1086 DB, *Wideli* 1109 Eynsh, *Wytteleya* 1239 Eynsh, *WoodLays* 1797 Davis. 'Wide lē(a)h' or 'willow lē(a)h,' *v.* wiðig.

FARLEY LANE (6″). Cf. *Great and Little Farley* 1606–7 *Survey*. THE LANKET (6″) is *The Langet* c. 1840 *TA* (*v.* lanket). WOOTTONDOWN FM. Cf. *le Downe hedge, way* 1606–7 *Survey, Downs Fm* 1797 Davis, 1822 O.S. WOOTTON WOOD and KING'S WOOD (latter in Stonesfield). Cf. *bosco de Wutton'* 1236 Cl, *bosco Regis de Wutton'* 1237 Cl, *bosco de Wotton* 1238 Cl *et freq* with variant spellings *Wotton', Wottone* to 1298 Eynsh, *bosco Regis de Wotton'* 1252 Cl.

FIELD-NAMES[1]

(a) In c. 1840 (*TA*) Great and Little Ashtree Ground (cf. *Ashe close* 1606–7), Beechentree Ground, Behind Town, Chapel Lays (*v.* lē(a)h), Dean Hill (*v.* denu), Engine House Meadow, Honeysuckle Ground, The Paddock, The Pix (*v.* picked), Upper and Lower Rowsome Ground, Old Sainfoin Ground, Upper and Lower Slough Lane Ground, Slough Lane.

(b) In 1608–9 *Footeball close* (also 1606–7), *Gamfeld close* (possibly 'game field'), *Partingmeade* (also 1606–7, *v.* parting), *Queens Cushinges* (*Queen's cushion* is a dialect term for the mossy saxifrage, *Saxifraga hypnoides*), *Westislesellmeade* (*Westerselmeade* 1606–7, *v.* mǣd). In 1606–7 *Abrahams shard* (second word *sceard*, 'cleft, gap'), *Beame meade*, *Bitton Cliffe or Buttons Cliff*, *le Buttes* (*v.* butts), *Cansfield*, *Coestowe hille* (*v.* cot-stōw), *Copredlow or Copned low* (possibly 'peaked barrow,' with first element coppede, second hlāw: references to tumuli are common in this area), *le faire Mile* (the name appears on the modern map in Badgemore: it is a fairly common name for a good road), *le Goginge plat* (*v.* plat), *Hookes*, *Lampe acre* (*v.* church), *Marins furlong*, *Peece close*, *Pleasden*, *Pontasse or Poulasse magna and parva*, *Little Punlesse*, *Prattehaye*, *Rope acre* (*v.* church), *Rowes crofte*, *Water Close*, *la Were* (*v.* wer). In 1300 Wych *Benteleye* ('clearing full of bent grass,' OE *beonet-lē(a)h*; the compound is a common one in place-names), *Poddeleye* ('*Podda*'s wood or clearing,' *v.* lē(a)h). In 1257 (Os) *Aluyuedene* ('*Ælfgifu*'s valley,' *v.* denu), *Bikeweyesforlonge* (first two elements weg and the personal name *Bica*), *la Gore* (*v.* gāra), *Grenedichesforlonge* (*v.* grēne, dīc), *Hanghedelonde or Hangendelonde* (*v.* hangende), *Meyesheuedlonde* (possibly '*Mæg*'s headland'; the existence of the personal name is doubtful, however), *Smocacre* (*v.* smoke), *Wrighedelond*. In 958 (12th) BCS 1042 *eadweardes ge mære* ('*Ēadweard*'s boundary,' *v.* (ge)mǣre).

33. Worton

WORTON, NETHER AND OVER

Ortune 1050–2 (13th) KCD 950 (p) *et freq* with variant spellings *Orton'*, *Orton(a)* to 1246 Ch, *Ouerorton'* 1200 P *et freq* with variant spellings *Uuerorton'*, *Ou'orton'*, *Overorton'*, *Overortone*, *Over Orton* to 1337 Ipm, *Nitherortun'* 1220 Fees *et freq* with variant spellings *Netherorton'*, *Netherorton(a)*, *Nether Orton*, *Nether Orton'* to 1428 FA, *Nerer Orton*, *magn' Orton*, *Orton major* 1278–9 RH, *Little Orton* 1350 Ipm, *Orton* (=Over Worton) 1401–2 FA

Hortone 1086 DB, *Horton'* 1199 P, 1229 Ch, 1242–3 Fees, *Nothe(r)-horton'* 1240–1 Ass, *Netherhorton'*, *Overhorton'* 1242–3 Fees,

[1] Except where otherwise stated, the forms are from *Survey*.

Nitherhorton' 1246 Ch, *Netherhorton* 1272 FF (p), *Nether Horton* 1346 FA

Wurtton' 1194 P

Wrtton' 1220 Fees

Overton' 1236 (c. 1300) Fees, 1275–6 RH, *Overtone* 1285 *Ass*, *Overton* 1316 Fine, 1341 Cl

Oerton 1252 FF

Nutheroverton' 1273–4, 1275–6 RH, *Netheroverton'*, *Over Overton* 1284–5 FA, *Northouertone*, *Netherouertone* 1285 *Ass*, *Nether Overton'* 1314 Ipm, *Overe Overton* 1316 Ipm, *Overoverton* 1362 Ipm

Ouer Euertone, *Nethereuertone* 1285 *Ass*

Overwortone, *Netherwortone* 1526 LS

'tūn by a bank or slope,' *v.* ōra, ōfer.

BLACKPITS FM. Cf. *Blacke pitt* 1591 *Survey*. HAWK HILL is *Hawkshill* 1795 *EnclA*. HEATH FM. Cf. *Upper and Lower Heath, Heath Close* c. 1840 *TA*.

FIELD-NAMES

(a) In c. 1840 (*TA*) Long Ancot, Great Ancot Meadow, Great and Little Bald hill, Batten, Berry Leys, East and West Berry Fields (*Berry Field* 1685 (c. 1700) *BodlT*, *v.* burh), Churchill, North and South Hays (*v.* (ge)hæg), Heartwell, Hemp Slade (*v.* slæd), The Nursery, East and West Oat Hill, Parsonage House and Farm, Pleasure Ground, Upper and Lower Sands, The Slade (*v.* slæd), The Works (possibly dialect *wergs*, 'willows').

34. Yarnton

YARNTON

(æt) *Ærdintune* 1005 (late 12th) Eynsh

Harbintone, Hardintone 1086 DB

Aerdintona 1091, 1109, 1155–61, 1197–8 Eynsh, *Aerdinton'* 1192 P

Eardeton' c. 1185 CartAntiq

Herdintona 1186–96 Eynsh, *Herdinton'* 1194, 5 P, 1278–9 RH

Erdinton' 1206 P *et passim* with variant spellings *Erdintun'*, *Erdint(h)one, Erdynton'*, *Erdynton(e)*, *Erdinton* to 1390 Eynsh

Erdington' 1273–4 RH *et passim* with variant spellings *Erdyngton(e)*, *Erdingtone* to 1592 BM

Ersyngtone 1285 *Ass*

Eardyngton 1285 *Ass*

Yarnton 1529 Eynsh, *Yarneton* 1517 D Inc, *Yarneton al. Erdington*
1592 BM
Yardington alias Yarnton 1623 Cai
Yarrington 1660 Stapleton

'*Earda*'s farm,' *v.* ingtūn. Cf. Ardeley (PN Herts 151), which was
known as Yardley till the 19th century.

OXEY MEAD takes name from *Oxhay* 1774 Stapleton. Probably
'ox-enclosure,' *v.* (ge)hæg. The same name occurs in Cropredy 419.

FROGWELLDOWN GORSE AND LANE and PATERNOSTER FM (all 6″). Cf.
Fog hill Down and *Paternoster* c. 1840 *TA*. YARNTON OR WEST MEAD
(6″) is *Westmead* 1774 Stapleton, c. 1840 *TA*.

FIELD-NAMES

(*a*) In c. 1840 (*TA*) Bank Windmill field, Bark Orchard and Plantation,
Boddington, The Clay (*the Clay pieces* 1800 *Bodl*), Clover Marsh, Great and
Little Couch (the name *couch* is given to various creeping grasses), Deal
Ground and Plantation, Hay Day, The Lancot (*v.* lanket), Lot Meadows
(*v.* lot), The Marsh (cf. *Marshfield* 1800 *Bodl*), The Pound, Ramclose, Big
and Long Rutton, Rutton Lane, The Rutton (*Ruttons close* 1800 *Bodl*), Great
and Picked Sands, The Sand, Lee Sands (cf. *the Sandpieces* 1800 *Bodl*),
Seed Lake, Spring Piece, Stertfield (first element steort), The Strip, The
Tithalls or Tidals (cf. *tetherhal de bladene* c. 1300 (c. 1450) Godstow, under
Cassington: *v.* h(e)alh, there is a word *titter* recorded once in 1573, meaning
some kind of weed, which would be a possible first element; *bladene* is the
old name of the Evenlode, *v. supra* 7). In 1800 (*Bodl*) Oxhurst (*v.* hyrst).

(*b*) In 1285 (*Ass*) *Blakenhul* (*v.* blæc, hyll). In 1278–9 (RH) *Fretescroft*
(second element croft).

XI. BAMPTON HUNDRED

Bampton' 1219 Fees *et freq* with variant spellings *Bampton*(*e*)
Baunton' 1220 Fees

v. Bampton *infra* 304. The district originally contained two hundreds annexed to the royal manor of Bampton (*Bentone...Soca
duorum hundredorum pertinet huic Manerio* DB, *ii hundreda de Benton*'
1182 P). Only in the case of this and Bloxham have the royal manors
to which the jurisdiction over Oxfordshire hundreds was attached
given names to the modern hundreds.

1. Alvescot

ALVESCOT [ɔ·lzcot, ælvzcot or ælvezcot][1]

Elfegescote 1086 DB, 1185 P (p), Elfegescota 1186 P (p)
Alfegecoto 1185 RR
Ælfegescota 1187 P (p)
Alueseicuth' 1198 (c. 1300) Fees
Elfeiscote 1200 P et freq with variant spellings Elfeiscot, Elfeiscot'
   to 1250 FineR, Elveiscot 1249 Ipm
Alfincot' 1214 Cur
Elwescot' 1219 Fees
Alfescot' 1220 Fees, Alvescot' 1246–7 Ass et passim with variant
   spelling Alvescot(te), Alfiscot 1249 Ipm, Alfiscote 1268 Ass
Alfestcote 1241 Fees
Elfescot', Elvescot' 1242–3 Fees, Elfescote 1253 Cl
Delvescote 1250 (c. 1302) Fees
Elfycote 1268 Ass
Efeiscote 1268 Ass
Afiscote 1268 Ass
Alfayscote, Alfeyscote 1278–9 RH
Alwescote 1285 Ass
' Ælfhēah's cot(e).'

BROMSCOTT and PEMSCOTT (not on map). The first of these is
Bumerescote 1086 DB, Burmerscot 1250 Ipm, Bormerescote 1357 Cl,
Burmerscote 1360 Cl, Bromscot(t) 1797 EnclA, which means ' Beornmǣr's cottage(s).' The second is Pismunscote 1086 DB, Pithmundiscote
1250 Ipm, Pythmundescote 1357 Cl, Pemscott Close 1685 (c. 1700)
BodlT, Pemscott 1797 EnclA: second element cot(e), first an unrecorded personal name *Peohtmund. The Vicar, the Rev. B. Lloyd,
informs us that both names are still known, though not in frequent
use, and that at his suggestion some new council houses on the land
known as Pemscott fields are to be named Pemscott Villas.

KENN'S FM takes name from the family of John Kenn, who is mentioned
1797 EnclA.

BATES'S LAND FM. Cf. Baytesland 1654 Bodl. CALCROFT LANE (6")
is Colcroft Lane 1797 EnclA. ALVESCOT DOWN. Cf. the Downs 1797
EnclA. LANGHAT DITCH. Cf. the four Langetts 1797 EnclA, v.

[1] The late Professor H. C. Wyld, a resident of Alvescot, averred that the railway
porter pronounced the name as a monosyllable.

lanket. Ruxhill Fm (6″), Lower Rookshill Fm. Cf. *Great Ruxell, the Barn Ruxell* 1655–9 Burford, *Rookshill* 1797 Davis, *Ruxhill* 1797 *EnclA, Rookshill Farm* 1822 O.S. Shield Fm is so named 1797 *EnclA, Shill Farm* 1797 Davis: *Shield Ford and Hedge* and *Shield-hill* are also mentioned in the *EnclA*, and *Shield Foord* appears 1685 (c. 1700) *BodlT*. These names probably contain a corruption of the name of Shill Brook, which is itself probably a back-formation from Shilton 328–9: as the brook is called *Sheilds brooke* 1685 (c. 1700) *BodlT*, the corruption is evidently fairly old.

FIELD-NAMES[1]

(*a*) In 1797 (*EnclA*) Aslet (*Astlott* 1685), Barn Ground, Barrell (also 1685), Black pitts, Blagroves or Forty Acres, Boneham (*v.* hamm), the Burnt House, Churchill (the church is on a hill), Church Ley, Coppice Ground, Cow Moor, Drift Road and Way (*v.* drift), Dunsbrook (*Dun brooke meade* 1685), Elm Ground, Far Ground, the Furzen, Furzy Ground (cf. *Furzy common* 1739 *Bodl*, *furzen* is a dialect word for *furze*), Gassons (*v.* gærs-tūn), the Green or the Horse Common, Green Meads (*the green mead* 1739 *Bodl*), the Home Close (so named 1739 *Bodl*), Home Ground (*v.* home), Lanes piece (*Lanes pieces* 1739 *Bodl*), Long Lands, Louseham (*v.* Fan), the Marsh, Michaelmas Grounds (*v.* Lammas), Millan, the Mortar Pitts, Murrel(l) Green, New Leaze, Old Court, Pen Mead and Coppice, Pinn Mead (*Little Pen mead* 1739 *Bodl*), Pitlands (*Pittlands* 1685), port lane (probably a variant of the common Port Way, on which *v. supra* 2–3), Round Close, Round Hill (also 1685), Seabrook (*Sea brooke Furlonge* 1685), Sheephouse Close, Stoney, Touchings, the upper Field, Water Mead, Winsmores, Woolands (also 1685, *v.* wōh).

(*b*) In 1739 (*Bodl*) Thorne Furlong. In 1685 *Base Land, Borrough way meadow, the Brush furlonge, the Clay furlong, Middle Edge furlong Fullwell furlong, Gospell Bush furlonge* (*the Gospell bush* 1634, *v.* gospel), *Grip*(*e*) *Furlonge, Hanging land* (*v.* hangende), *high bush furlong, Margh Thornes* (*v.* mangthorn), *Mill end and way, the Mill Furzes, Peartree furlonge, picked halfe Close* (*v.* picked), *the Redland Furlonge* (*Redland* 1606–7 *Bodl*), *the southside, Swallow*(*e*)*s furlong, the Watry furlonge*.

2. Asthall

Asthall

(*æt*) *Eást Heolon* early 11th Ælfric Pentateuch (p)[2]
Esthale 1086 DB *et freq* with variant spellings *Esthal*(*l*)*a, Esthall*(*e*), *Esthalles* to 1354 Ipm

---

[1] Except where otherwise stated, the forms are from *BodlT*, and are (c. 1700).

[2] There is no proof of the identification, but no other place of the name is known, and Asthall is only some eight miles from Eynsham where Ælfric was writing.

Asteles c. 1185 OxonCh (p), *Astal* 1275–6 RH, 1797 Davis

Estlihall 1205 Cl

Estale 1220 Fees, *Estal* 1237 (c. 1300) Fees, *Estalle* 1242–3 Fees, *Estall'* 1278–9 RH

Hesthall 1219 FF (p), *Hesthalle* 1285 Ass

Asthall' 1246–7 Ass (p) *et freq* with variant spelling *Asthall* to 1428 FA, *Astehalle* 1526 LS

Easthalle 1278–9 RH

Aschall 1285 Ass

v. ēast, h(e)alh. Probably the original name was plural, *ēast-healas*, and the earliest form represents the dative, unless the *eo* goes back to an ablaut variant (with Germanic *e:a*). The sonant *l* grade is represented in *holh*.

The same name, also in the plural, occurs in KCD 1279 in the boundaries of land in Arncott in the east of the county, *v.* 162. Grundy identifies this with some hollows in a hillside.

ASTHALL LEIGH

Esthallingel' a. 1270 Queen, *Esthallynggelegh* 1325 Cl

Estallingeleye 1272 Ipm

Astallingeleye 1278–9 RH, *Astallingele* 1316 FA, *Astallyngley* 1597 Queen

Asthallingeleye 1270–90 Queen, *Asthallinglegh* 1290 FF, *Asthallynglye* 1406, 10, 47 Queen

Asthawyngleye 1406 Queen

Astally 1797 Davis

'Woodland of the people of Asthall,' *v.* ingas, lē(a)h.

FIELD ASSARTS is *Field Asarts* 1797 Davis. The name looks like 'assart(s) belonging to Leafield,' *v.* sart.

FORDWELLS. Cf. *Sewkeford', Sewkeden'* 1300 Wych, *Fordwell Bottome als. Duckpoole Bottome als. Sukedene, Fordwell Poole als. Duckpoole als. Sewkeford* 1641 Wych. The first names are '*Seofeca*'s ford' and '*Seofeca*'s valley,' *v.* denu. The others are self-explanatory. The personal name *Seofeca* is the first element of Seacourt Berks.

PINNEL SPRING (marked on first edition of 1″ O.S. but not on present maps) takes name from *Pinele* 1226 Cl. Perhaps '*Pinna's spring', OE *Pinnan* w(i)elle.

STANDRIDGE COPSE (6″) is (*wood called*) *Stourygge* (? *Stonrygge*) 1448 *Queen, Standridge* 1597 *Queen*. 'Stony ridge,' OE stān-hrycg.

STOCKLEY COPSE takes name from *Stochelie* 1086 DB, *Stocleye* 1278–9 RH (p), *Stockleye* 1300 Wych, *Stockelegh* 1320 Cl (p). Cf. *Upper and Nether Stockley* 1608–9 *Survey*. Either stocc-lē(a)h or stoc-lē(a)h; the former is perhaps more probable.

WORSHAM MILL, TURN (both 6″) take name from *Wolmaresham* 1278–9 RH. '*Wulfmǣr*'s hām or hamm.'

ASTHALL BARROW and DODD'S PLAIN (6″) are *Asthall Barrow* and *Dods Plain* 1814 *EnclA* and 1822 O.S. respectively. THE CLEEVE (6″). Cf. *the Cleeves Hill, Cleeves Wood and Meadow* 1814 *EnclA*: 'land on the river bank,' *v.* clif. HICK'S PLANTATION (6″). Cf. *Hyckesene* 1551–2 *Survey, Hickswell* 1630 *Bodl, Hickswell close* 1699 *Bodl, Hicks Hill Stile, Hix Hill* or *Hickshill Barn* c. 1840 *TA, Hick's Copse* 1857 *EnclA*: a *Jone Hykes* appears 1551–2 *Survey*. KITESBRIDGE FM AND POUND (6″) are so named 1814 *EnclA*. LEIGH HALE PLAIN (6″). Cf. *Leigh Hall Gate, Leigh Halegate, Leigh Hale* 1814 *EnclA*. For *plain* here and *supra, v.* 389. SHORTHAZEL BOTTOM (6″). Cf. *Short Hazle* 1814 *EnclA*. WISDOM'S BOTTOM AND COPSE (both 6″). Cf. *Wisdom* 1822 O.S.

FIELD-NAMES

(*a*) In 1814 (*EnclA*) Bangey Gate, Beggarsbush Hill (*v.* Fan), Bow Furlong, Briary Ham (*v.* hamm), Combrouse Field, Combecouse field, Costals or Costall's piece (*v.* cot-steall), Coxhead ham (*v.* hamm), Upper Dean Ground (*v.* denu), Dog Hill, Duckham Meadow, Duckhams (*v.* hamm), Field Search (this may be another version of the name of Field Assarts (300): *serch* occurs frequently in this area for sart), Heath furlong, the Heath Field, Old Hitching (*v.* hechinge), In(n)mead (*v.* in), the Land-dues (*le Landewe* no date *Queen, v.* landew), Maddox or Maddock's Close, High Meer Furlong, Newstage Field and Hill, Odney Ham (*v.* hamm), Osney or Odney Meadow (a *crofti Abbatis de Osneye* is mentioned 1300 Wych), Pebbly Furlong, Punt-house Ground (cf. *Puntus als. Pumbas Corner* 1641 Wych), Settle Green and Gate, Shepherds Close, Tile House Close, The Waste, Water Close, Water-gall field (this is a term which occurs frequently in the field-names of Nth describing spongy ground, *v.* PN Nth 263), Well Spring Hill.

(*b*) In 1608–9 (*Survey*) Weedell Waste. No date (*Queen*) Abenacre ('*Aba*'s acre'), *le Churchstie* ('church path,' *v.* stīg), *la Gorebrodefurlong* (*v.* gore-brode), *le Schornindel'* (there is a Warwickshire word *shorning*, 'sheep-shearing,' which is a possible first element; second element *dell*, 'hollow'), *la Stocke* (*v.* stocc).

3. Aston Bampton

ASTON

Eastun 987 (14th) *Hengwrt*
Esttun 1069 OSFacs, (æt) *Est tune* c. 1080 Ex, *Eston'* c. 1130–42
   Eynsh *et passim* with variant spellings *Eston(a)*, *Estun'*, *Estune*,
   Estonia to 15th Ex
Aston Pogeys 1328 Cl, *Aston* 1346 FA *et passim*, *Astone* 1360
   Eynsh, *Aston le Riche* c. 1384 Eynsh, *Aston Rytes* 1551–2 *Survey*

'East tūn.' A member of the *Pugeys* family is mentioned 1239 Ch
in connection with land here, *v.* Broughton Poggs 309–10. An earlier
reference to the place is found in (*on*) *east hæma* (*gemære*) 958 (c. 1250)
BCS 1036, *v.* hǣme. No reference has been found to a family
surnamed *le Riche*.

CHIMNEY

Ceommanyg 1069 OSFacs, (æt) *Ceommenige* c. 1080 Ex
Ciminia c. 1140 Ex
Chymene 1241 Ass (p), 15th Ex, *Chimeneye* 1285 Ass, *Chymeney*
   1316 FA, *Chymeneye*, *Chymoneye* 1345 Cl
Chemeneye 1278–9 RH, 1284, 1285 (bis) Ass, 1327 AD, *Chemene*
   1285 Ass
Chymneye c. 1360 Eynsh
Chimley 1797 Davis

'*Ceomma's island,' *v.* (ī)eg. The personal name is a hypocoristic
form of such names as *Cēolmǣr*, *Cēolmund*, with assimilation of -*l*-
to -*m*-: it is found also in the name of a brook at Chimney—*Ceomina
laca* 1005 (late 12th) Eynsh and *Ceoman lace* 1069 OSFacs—and in
Ceomman bricg KCD 652 and *Ceomman treow* BCS 820 in other
counties.
   The 1797 form is identical with a 19th-century form of the word
chimney.

COTE

la Cot(e) 1203 Cur (p), *Cote* 1278–9 RH *et freq*, *la Cote* 1278–9
   RH (p), *Coat* 1797 Davis
Cotes 1203 Cur *et freq* to 1285 Ass, *Cootes* 1517 D Inc

v. cot(e).

BULL INN and HAM LANE (both 6″) are so named 1855 *EnclA*. KINGSWAY'S FM (6″). Cf. *Kingeshull* 1218 FF, *Kingswayfield* 1732 *Bodl*.

FIELD-NAMES

(a) In c. 1840 (*TA*) Upper and Lower Bawgey (*berhtulfing yge* 1069 OSFacs, perhaps '*Beorhtwulf*'s island,' with connective -ing; but a personal name *Beorhtwulfing* is recorded once: v. (i)eg), Beanlands, Beanhill Slade (cf. *Northbenehellefurlong*, *Westbenhulfurlong* 1328 Cl, v. bēan, hyll, slæd), Short Beer Furlong (v. bere), Cross and Short Bittham (v. bytme), The Blacken, Bleach pit mead, Brandy ham (the first element is possibly the side-form of *branded*, applied in dialect to animals, and meaning 'brindled'; here the sense would be 'variegated': second element hamm), Broadcutt (v. cut), Bun furlong, Burn House, Bussenger corner (cf. *Bosengaye*, *Bosingaye* 1661 *Bodl*), Butts (v. butts), The Caveat, Long and Short Cindhurst, Clerkinway, Cock up hat (v. Des), Cricklade Ham (v. hamm), Crutch furlong, Dead Knowle, Dolehams (v. dole), Duck puddle (v. Des), Duxford Hays (v. (ge)hæg; Duxford is in Berks), Favrey furlong, Frost furlong, Galley shares (*Gall(e)y acres* 1661 *Bodl*: gally is recorded as a dialect form of yellow: there is a *Galley Hill* in the Tithe Award for the nearby parish of Curbridge), Ganderfield furlong, Garsons (v. gærs-tūn), Gather Hill (the word *gather* has several dialect meanings, for which v. EDD), Hatchway Furlong, Hog breach (v. breche), Holymans tithe, Holywell Field, Long Horny, Huckrell, Inmead, the Outmead (*In Medowe*, *Oute Medowe* 1551–2 *Survey*, *Inn mead* 1715 *Bodl*, v. in), Long Kendall, Ladys Close (v. Lady), Longlains (v. lain), Lameway furlong, Lapinland, Last Laying out (a Quack-mans Laying Out appears in the *EnclA* for Bampton), Lower Linton, Lock Ham (v. hamm), May furlong, Mallange, Merry Headland, Milking Pan (v. Des), No mans plot, Flat and Scrubbed Oatlands, Oatmoor, Short and Long pease lands, Peal furlong, Penny ham (v. penny), The Pikes (v. picked), Long Reedy, Rod Eyott (v. rod), Aston Russia, Great Russia, Home Russia (*Russia* in these names is a corrupt form of the name *Rushy* in Rushy Weir 304), Rye fuelong, Sheepmarsh, Sheepway hill, Showels Mead (cf. Showell 249, 291), Sickle Ground, Sinbury ham, Slip lands (v. slipe), Small Gains (v. Fan), Southbroad, Sparrowhawks Close, Short Starnham (Starnham Ground appears in the *TA* for Ducklington), Great and Little Steach (v. stiche), Swift Lake Hay (v. *supra* 15), Thisabed furlong, Eight Vernals, Wead furlong, Who furlong, Windmill Field (*Windmill feld* 1728 *Bodl*), Withy Eyot (v. wiðig, eyt), Woodway ford (so named 1705 *Bodl*), Wrenches hedge.

(b) In 1722–3 (*Bodl*) Golds. In 1681–2 (*Bodl*) Calmore. In 1218 (FF) *Brodelonde* (v. brād, land), *Chalchulle* ('chalk hill,' v. c(e)alc), *Warnforulong*.

4. Bampton

BAMPTON

Bemtun 1069 OSFacs, (*æt*) *Bemtune* c. 1080 Ex, *Bemtona* 1140, 3 OxonCh, *Bemtonia* c. 1175 Ex

Bentone 1086 DB, *Bentona* 1123–33 OxonCh, *Bentun'* 1156, 7 P, *Benton'* 1158 P *et freq* to 1203 P, *Bent'* 1203 Cur

Betton' 1160 P, *Beton'* 1162 P

Beanton' 1195 P

Baunton' 1199 FineR, 1235 FF *et passim* in late 13th, *Bauntun' comitis*, *Bauntun' de Oylli* 1220 Fees

Bannton' 1199 MemR, *Banton* 1200 Eynsh, *Banton'* 1207 P

Bamton' 1208 Pat, 1217 Cl, *Bamton* 1233 Ch, *Bamtone* 1247 FF

Bampton 1212 Cl *et passim* with variant spellings *Bamptun*, *Bamptun'*, *Bampton Doyly* 1349 Ipm, *Bampton Talbot* 1361 Ipm, *Bamptoune* 15th Ex, *Bampton Doyley* 1596 AD, *Bampton in the Bush* 1797 Davis, 1822 O.S.

Baynton 1457 Cl

OE *bēam-tūn*, either 'tūn made of beams' or 'tūn by a prominent tree.' The same name occurs in Cu and We. A family named *Talbot* is mentioned 1362 Ipm as holding the manor of Bampton, and the *Doyl(e)y* family have given their name to Ascot d'Oyley in this part of the county. For *-comitis* in 1220 cf. Fees i, 104, "Comes Bolonie habet manerium de Bamptun'." For the suffix *in the Bush* cf. F. G. Brabant, *Oxfordshire* (London 1906) 54, "This region was formerly common land called 'the bush' and up to 1750 there were no roads across it, so that travellers to and from Bampton had to make the best of their way across the scrub. It may be added that even now the roads are none too good."

BURROWAY BRIDGE (6″) AND BROOK take name from (*pratum de*) *Burweia* c. 1210 Os, *Borewe* c. 1240 Os, *Burwe* c. 1241 Os, *Burewey* 1284 Os. 'Path by or to a burh,' *v.* weg.

HAM COURT. Cf. *pastura q.v. Hamm* 1239 Ch. *v.* hamm, courte. The building incorporates the gatehouse of Bampton Castle, built by Aymer de Valence, Earl of Pembroke, in the early 14th century.

RUSHY WEIR takes name from *hrisyge* 1069 OSFacs, *Russeya* 1233–4 Os *et freq* with variant spelling *Russeye* to 1280 Os, *Russheya* c. 1280 Os, *Russhey* 1509–10 Os. 'Rush island,' *v.* rysc, (ī)eg.

WEALD

> *Walda* 1188 P, *Walde* 1224 FF, c. 1275 Os
> *Welde* 1216 Cl *et freq* to 1509–10 Os, *Westweld* 1246–7 *Ass* (p),
> 1361 Ipm, *Weld* 1280 Os, 1608 BM, *Westwelde* 1315 AD
> *Wealde* 1239 Eynsh
> *Waulde* c. 1275 Os
> *Westwold* 1316 FA

v. w(e)ald, and cf. Claywell Fm 317–18.

A place called *Wich'*, *Wicha* is mentioned in connection with Bampton 1156, 7, 8, 1162 P, and there is a *Neutone by Bamptone* mentioned 1285 *Ass* which has not been identified.

COWLEAZE CORNER. Cf. *Cow Leys* 1812 *EnclA*. ISLE OF WIGHT BRIDGE (6″) and TADPOLE BRIDGE are so named 1855 *EnclA*: cf. *Tadpoll House* 1761 Rocque in the adjacent parish of Buckland (Berks).

FIELD-NAMES

(*a*) In 1855 (EnclA)[1] Back Lane, Briar Furlong, Chimney Gate, Cross Bank Gate, Greenacres Close, Hatch Gate (*v.* hæcc-geat), Old Hays Close (*v.* (ge)hæg), Huckett Close, Kentsham (*v.* hamm), Lake (*v.* lacu), Little End Corner, The Mays, Mil(l)ford, Piece Meadow, Sheepbridge (*Shepesbrig'* c. 1241 Os, *v.* scē(a)p, brycg), Slippery, Squire's Lane, Truelands (*Trowelond* 1406 Eynsh, *Trulands furlong* 1675 *Bodl*), Westmoor. In c. 1840 (*TA*) Arch Ground, Bibury Ham (*Byberry Ham* 1685 (c. 1700) *BodlT*, *v.* burh, hamm), Cox's Farundel (*v.* fēorðan dǣl), Old Nans Weir, Queenborough (*Queneburgheye* 1238, 9 Ch, *Quenbereweye* 1267–84 Os, *Quenborueya* 1275 Os, *v.* (ī)eg; the first element is the woman's name *Cwēnburh*: in 1239 Ch it is said to be an island), Studdy Meadow. In 1812 (*EnclA*) Bowery Ground, Hapse Field, The Monks Field, The Paddock, First and Further Ringborough Fields, Little and Great Row Fields (cf. *Rughemede* 1238 Ch, *Rugheueld* 1239 Ch, 'rough field,' *v.* rūh, mǣd, feld).

(*b*) In 1433 (Os) *Goldborewys* (*Goldeberge* 1187 (c. 1200) Thame, *v.* be(o)rg, first element probably *golde*, 'marigold'). In 1275 (Os) *Lyndwere* (*Lindwere* 1233–4 Os, 'weir by the lime-tree(s)'), *Newewerewater* (cf. *Newerehamme* 1238 Ch, 'stream and hamm by the new weir,' *v.* wer, nīwe), *Northlongewater*, *Roweneye* (*Rughenhey* 1238 Ch, *Ruganhey* 1249 Ch, 'rough island,' *v.* rūh, (ī)eg: it is said in the 1239 reference to be an island). In 1239 (Ch) *Athestaneshamm* (possibly '*Æðelstān*'s hamm'), *Crohamm* (*v.* hamm; the first element might be *crōh*, 'saffron'), *Forthamm* (*v.* forð), *Prestenhamm* ('priests' hamm,' with weak genitive plural of prēost), *Rodfordhurst* (*v.* ford, hyrst), *Sworenehamm*, *Thatcheshamm* (*v.* þæc-hamm).

---

[1] Some of these fields may be in neighbouring parishes.

5. Black Bourton

BLACK BOURTON [bɔˑtən is commoner than bəˑtən]

Bortone 1086 DB

Bvrtone 1086 DB, *Burtona* 1122–33 OxonCh *et passim* with variant spellings *Burthona, Burton', Burthon(e), Burtun', Burton* to 1385 Cl

Burgton' 1268 *Ass*

Abbodesbourton 1323 Cl, *Bourton* 1360 Ipm, 1385 Cl, 1526 LS, *Bourtone* 1433 Os, *Boorton* 1526 LS

v. burhtūn. The Abbot is the Abbot of Osney: *v.* Os iv, 475 ff. for the possessions of Osney in this town. E. Carleton Williams, *Companion into Oxfordshire* (London 1935), p. 240, suggests that 'Black' was prefixed because "the land belonged to Osney Abbey, and the Austin Canons, in their black habits, worked the Manor Farm."

GARSON'S COPSE is so named c. 1840 *TA*. Cf. *Horsgarstone* 1230 Os. 'Horse paddock,' *v.* gærs-tūn.

ELMWOOD HOUSE is *Elmwood Farm House* c. 1840 *TA*.

FIELD-NAMES[1]

(a) In c. 1840 (*TA*) Workhouse Close.

(b) In 1498–9 (*PreQuen*) *le Grenesty* ('green path,' *v.* stīg). In 1267–84 *Derdesham* (second element hamm; the first might be a personal name, possibly *Dæggræd*), *Huntemede* ('*Hunta*'s meadow,' *v.* mǣd), *le Muleam* (*v.* myln, hamm), *Shodforde*. In c. 1275 *Cleyteforlonge* (first element *clǣgiht*, 'clayey'), *Mileburne* (*Mileberewe* c. 1240, possibly 'hill where millet is grown,' first element the obsolete word *mile*, second element be(o)rg), *Morforlonge* (Þ*emoforlunge* c. 1240, *v.* mōr), *Mulestieweye* ('mill path,' *v.* myln, stīg, to which weg has been added), *Pinkelesco*, *Rugge* (*v.* hrycg), *sclade* (*v.* slæd). In c. 1250 *Clodecroft* (*v.* croft; *clod* in the sense 'lump of earth' is not recorded till c. 1420), *Waterslede* (*v.* slæd), *Wodeford'* (*v.* wudu, ford). In c. 1240 *Berenhulle* (the first element could be byrgen, 'burial place,' in which case the name refers to the tumulus in the south of the parish, *v.* hyll), *Breich* (*v.* breche), *Burthemeleye* ('woodland of the people of Bourton,' *v.* hǣme, lē(a)h).

6. Brize Norton

BRIZE NORTON

Nortone 1086 DB *et passim* with variant spellings *Norton(a)*, *Nortune, Nortun', Norton', Northone* to 1300 Ipm, *Suthnorton*

[1] Except where otherwise stated, the forms are from Os.

1235 FF, *Northone Brun* 1264–8 Eynsh *et freq* with variant spellings *Northon(a) Brun, Norton' Brun, Norton Brun* to 1316 FA, *Northone Bruyn* 1320 Eynsh *et freq* with variant spelling *Norton Bruyn* to 1517 D Inc, *Brunesnorton* 1341 Ipm, 1365 Ch, *Norton le Bruyn* c. 1384 Eynsh, *Brimesnorton* 1388 Cl, *Norton Broyn* 1509–10 Os, *Bresenorton alias Norton Bruyn* 1517 D Inc, *Norton Bryne* 1526 LS, *Norton Broyne* 1539 Eynsh, *Breames Norton alias Norton Broyne* 1560 AD, *Brice Norton* early 18th ParColl

'North tūn belonging to *Brun*.' William le *Brun* is mentioned 1200 Cur in connection with land here. It is 'south' in relation to Chipping, Over and Hook Norton.

The prefix may have been altered to Brize by influence of the church dedication to St Brice, but K. E. Kirk (*Church Dedications of the Oxford Diocese*, Oxford 1946, pp. 62–3) suggests that there is no apparent reason why this church should have been dedicated to St Britius, bishop of Tours in the 5th century, and that it may have been because of the corruption of *Brunes Norton* to *Brice Norton* that the saint's name became attached to the church, whose original dedication is now lost.

ASTROP FM takes name from *Estrope* 1086 DB *et passim* with variant spellings *Estrop(a), Estrop', Estorp, Esthropp* to 1316 FA, *Eistrope* 1185 P, *Astrop* 1261 FF *et freq* with variant spellings *Asthorp, Ast(h)rop', Astropp', Astthrop* 1285 FF, *Estthrop* 1300 Ipm, *Asthorp Farm* 1797 Davis. 'East þrop.'

HADDON FM (6″), MARSH HADDON FM take name from *Haddon'* 1225–8 Eynsh (p) *et passim* with variant spellings *Haddon(e), Haddune, Eddone* c. 1235 Os (p), *Heddone* c. 1240 Os (p), *Mershaddon* 1278–9 RH. OE hǣp-dūn, 'uncultivated hill slope.' 'Marsh' has been prefixed to the 1278–9 form.

CHEQUERS INN, GRANGE FM, ROOKERY FM and TEN ACRE COPSE (all 6″). Cf. *the Chequer Garden and Orchard, the Grainge Homestead, The Rookeries* and *Ten Acres* 1777 EnclA. GROVE FM is so named 1822 O.S. Cf. *Norton Grove* t. Hy 8 AugmOff. STONELANDS. Cf. *Stone Lands* 1777 EnclA, *the Stonelands road* 1814 EnclA. VEN BRIDGE is so named 1822 O.S.

FIELD-NAMES

(a) In 1777 (*EnclA*) Barn Close, the Barn Stable and Yard, Great and Little Beany, Blind Lane, The Brackes[1], Broad Mead, Bull Ham (*v.* hamm), Chandry Close (possibly *Caneneye* c. 1300 Thame, '*Cana*'s island,' *v.* (i)eg), Cherry Hayes Close (*v.* (ge)hæg), the Cow Common, the Crofts, Cudmoor, Long Cut Coppice (*v.* cut), The Downs, Drift Way (*v.* drift), Farm Close, The Fens, Forty Acres Spiney, Gasson Paddock, Gassons, Little Gasson Coppice, Little Gastons (*Garstone* 1187 (c. 1200) Thame, *v.* gærs-tūn), Gate Stile Close, Grass Close, The Hades (*v.* hades), Great and Little Hagborough, The Ham Coppice (*v.* hamm), the Hays (*v.* (ge)hæg), the Heath, the Home Ground (*v.* home), Honey Ham (*v.* honey), Horse close, Island Coppice, the Ivy House, the Leys, Limborough (*Linberwe* c. 1280 Os, 'flax hill' or '*Lina*'s barrow,' *v.* līn, be(o)rg), The Mansion Homestead, Millway, Moor Furlong, Little Moor Way (*Lytlemor* c. 1280 Os, *v.* lȳtel, mōr), The Nursery, Nutting Close, Oak Piece, Old Orchard, Oxpen Ground, The Paddock, The Picked Ground (*v.* picked), Rick Yard Coppice, Robinhoods Close (*Robinhood* is used in dialect of several plants), Rushy Moor, Saint Foin Ground, Sandpit Furlong, Thames Meadows, the Vicar's Mead, Wash Bridge, Wetherstones Pleck (*v.* plek, first element the name of the owner), Woosam Gap.

(b) In 1551–2 (*Survey*) *Grene Rydge*. In c. 1300 (Thame) *terra Pomerey*. In c. 1280 (Os) *La Nouele Breche, La Uele Breche* ('new breche'). In 1231 (FF) *Alweyesham* (*Elwyesham* 1230 Bract, '*Ælfwīg*'s hamm'). In c. 1200 (Thame) *Netlewrde* (*Netle Widonis* 1187 (c. 1200) Thame). In 1187 (c. 1200) (Thame) *Benefurlong* (*v.* bēan), *Brokeneberge* (cf. the field-names of Garsington 175), *Depe Crundele* (*v.* dēop and cf. the field-names of Goring 55), *Haneberge* (*v.* be(o)rg; first element the personal name *Hana* or the identical noun meaning 'cock'), *Langeberge* (*v.* lang, be(o)rg), *Langefurlong* (*v.* lang), *Merslade* (*v.* mersc, slæd), *la Steorte* (*v.* steort), *Suðereslade* (*v.* slæd; first element *sūðerra*, 'southern').

7. Broadwell

BROADWELL

Bradewelle 1086 DB *et passim* with variant spellings *Bradewell'*, *Bradewell, Bradeuell'* to 1369 Ipm, *Bradwella* 1194 P
Bradeswell' 1190 P
Brodewell 1517 D Inc

'Broad stream,' *v.* brād, w(i)elle.

COTTESMORE (lost) is (*æt*) *Cottesmore* c. 980 (15th) ASWills, *Cotesmore* (ter) 1185 Templars, *Cottemor* (bis) 1244 RegAntiquiss. '**Cott*'s marsh,' *v.* mōr.

---

[1] Cf. the same name in Warborough 140.

BROADWELL GROVE, FIVE BELLS PUBLIC HOUSE (6″), MANOR FM and PUMPHOUSE PLANTATION (6″). Cf. *Grove Piece* and *The Grove Enclosures*, *The Five Bells*, *Manor Homestead* and *Pumphouse Barn* 1776 *EnclA*.

FIELD-NAMES

(*a*) In 1776 (*EnclA*) Burnt Barkside, Bark House Ground, Great and Little Barley Hill, Bull Close, Burden Hill, Bushey Ground, Calf Close, Cat Closes, Crooked Piece, Crooked Oak Piece, Cuckow Pen (*v.* cuckoo pen), Cutmoor Laines (*v.* lain), Dean Furlong (*deane furlonge* 1607–8 *Bodl*, *v.* denu), Little Down, Dye Close, Ferney Piece, Gallows Close, The G(l)assons, The Gores (*v.* gāra), The Ham (*v.* hamm), Hindmoor Furlong, The Horse Leys, Lower Horse Pools, Hothsted Farm, The Hurst, Kates Hay (*v.* (ge)hæg), Kings Lane, Lot Meadow (*v.* lot), Maggets or Maggots Lane, The Marsh, The Moors, The Morleys, Nettle Piece, The Nursery, The Paddock, Old Pits, Purbrick's Lands, The Quire (*v.* church), The Ridge, Old Saint Foin Ground, St John Leys (Broadwell St John[1] is given as an alternative name for the parish), Sheep House Piece, Summer Leaze or Leys, The Thirkett (evidently a corruption of *thicket*; it is said to be woodland), Lower Town Close, Townsend Furlong, Varney Mead, The Great Varrey.

(*b*) In 1607–8 (*Bodl*) *the hasse*, *Lynchewaye* (*v.* hlinc, weg), *Mydlynche* (*v.* hlinc), *Morrybushe* (the name *merry* is used in this part of the country for a kind of cherry; it is first recorded in 1595, and the NED considers it an altered form of *merise*: alternatively this name could contain *morel*, 'a morello cherry,' first recorded in 1611), *Newbrokelandes*, *Tuckwell*, *Woode Way*.

8. Broughton Poggs

BROUGHTON POGGS

Brotone 1086 DB

Broctona 1192 Eynsh *et freq* with variant spellings *Brocton'*, *Broctun'* to 1236 (c. 1300) Fees

Brochton' 1242–3 Fees, 1268 *Ass*

Braxston' 1246–7 *Ass*

Burthon' (bis) 1246–7 *Ass*

Brouctone 1254 Eynsh

Brouton' 1268 *Ass*, *Brouton* 1278–9 RH, *Brouthton* 1303 Ipm

Broghton 1316 FA, 1345 Ch, 1347 Cl

Broughton 1330 FA, *Broughton Maulditz* 1401–2 FA, *Broughton Pouges* 1526 LS

Brouztone Mauduyt 1347 Cl

'tūn by the brook.' Cf. Broughton 396–7. John *Maudut* holds the

---

[1] From the Hospitallers of Clanfield, who took over the Templars' property at Broadwell, on the suppression of that order.

manor 1285 *Ass* by the service of mewing a falcon and carrying it to court. Sir Robert *Pugeys* appears ib. in connection with land in the nearby village of Broadwell.

BROUGHTONDOWNS PLANTATION. Cf. *Downes* 1736 *BodlMap*. OX-LEAZE COMMON AND FM. Cf. *Ox Lees Piece* 1736 *BodlMap*, *Oxleys* 1797 Davis. SHIRE GATE is so named 1822 O.S.: it is on the County boundary.

FIELD-NAMES

(a) In c. 1840 (*TA*) Burril piece (*Birril Piece* 1736 *BodlMap*), Cats brain (*Catsbraine Farme* 1685 (c. 1700) *BodlT*, *v.* catsbrain), the Chaslins, Coneygre (*v.* conygree), Cow pen ground, Deep corner (so named 1736 *BodlMap*), Hand post ground (*v.* handing post), Long Hirons (*v.* the field-names of Stratton Audley 240), Old Hitching (so named 1685 (c. 1700) *BodlT*, *v.* hechinge), Hopcopse, Hop yard ground, Kingsway, Lamplands (so named 1736 *BodlMap*, *v.* church), Picked Ground (*v.* picked), Old Saint foin ground (*Old St. Foin Ground* 1736 *BodlMap*), The Several (so named 1736 *BodlMap*, *v.* several), Withy Bed (*v.* wiðig).

(b) In 1736 (*BodlMap*) *Ash Hill, Burton hill* (possibly identical with Burden Hill in Broadwell), *Green Hill, Hanging Lands* (*v.* hangende), *Hedge Piece, Mead Furlong, Three Shire Stone, Twentynine acre, White Quarry piece.* In 1685 (c. 1700) (*BodlT*) *Brooke furlong, Dip Cornhill, Hoarestone* (*v.* hār), *hurst furlonge* (*v.* hyrst), *East and west outlands* (*v.* in). In c. 1500 (Eynsh) *fyrbuskys, the myll ham* (*v.* myln, hamm), *Oteland* (*v.* āte), *Thortoneslond, Sondputtez* (*v.* sand, pytt), *West Lacy Myll*.

9. Burford

BURFORD

Bureford 1086 DB *et passim* with variant spellings *Bureford', Bureforde, Bureforda, Burefford* to 1380 Cl
Burghforde 1285 Ass
Bereford 1301 AD, 1349 Ipm
Boreford 1341 Ipm *et freq* to 1393 Cl
Burford 1316 FA *et passim* with variant spellings *Burforda, Burfford, Burford upon the Wold* 1449 Cl, *Burford in the Olde* 1502–3 Burford, *Burforde on the Wolde* 1510 Burford
Bourford 1322 Ch
Borford 1362 Cl
Berford 1327 Ipm

Many of the early forms suggest that this name is identical in origin with Burford Sa, in which the first element is OE **burh**, 'fortified place'. This place cannot be identified with the (*æt*) *Beorg feorda* of ASC 752 A, of which the first element is beorg 'hill.' For *Wold v.* w(e)ald.

NOTE. GUILDENFORD is *Gildenford lane* 1456 Burford, *Geldenford* 1551–2 *Survey*: 'guildsmen's ford' seems the most appropriate etymology, although names with this weak genitive plural as first element usually have the initial consonant [j], as in *Yelden bridge* in Benson (118–19). The first element may mean 'golden' with reference to flowers. HIGH ST is mentioned 1404 Burford. PRIORY LANE is so named 1594 Burford, when it was applied to only part of the present street: the name has since been extended to what was formerly *Synt Jones Street* 1392 Burford, *Seynt Johns stret* 1551–2 *Survey*, so called from the Priory of St John. SHEEP ST is *Shepstrete* 1551–2 *Survey*. TANNER'S LANE is so named 1795 *EnclA*: the *Bark Lane* mentioned in the same document may have the same meaning, the first element being a shortened form of ME *barkere*, 'tanner.' There is a lost Bark Hill in Banbury (412). WITNEY ST is *Wytteneystrete* 1396 Burford.

Lost street-names include *Bordemwetlane* 1493 Burford, *Batts Lane* 1552, 1607, 1706 Burford.

THE TOLSEY. Cf. Burford 187: "the first mention of the Tolsey by that name occurs in 1561." It is *the court house commonly called the Towlsey* 1581 Burford. The name represents a compound of OE *toll* and *seld*, 'seat,' or *sele*, 'hall,' and is the ancient name in some English and Irish towns for the guildhall, tolbooth or borough courthouse (NED *s.v. tolsel, tolzey*).

WHITE HILL is *Whit hyll* 1501 Burford, *Whyttehill* 1551–2 *Survey*.

FIELD-NAMES[1]

(*a*) In 1797 (*EnclA*) Abigal's Bush Quarter, Apple Pye Corner (*apple-pie* is used in dialect of various plants), Butt Furlong (*v.* butts), Church Land (cf. *the churche land* 1501), Down Ground and Bottom, Fern Furlong (*ferny furlong* 1576, *the Ferne Furlong* 1698), Garden Ground, Glebe Piece, Hallicroft Close (*Halcrafte ende* 1501), Holl Acre, Hull Bush Furlong (so named 1695), Lady Ham (*le ladys hame* 1549, *v.* Lady, hamm), Upper Leasow (*v.* lŋēs), Ludwall Meadow, Picked Close (so named 1515, *v.* picked), the Pikes (*v.* picked), Pump Ground, St John Ground, School Land[2], Whore's Quarter, Windsmoor Hedge Quarter (this may be connected with *Wilmore* 1435–6, *Wyldmore, Wyldemoremeade* 1551–2 *Survey*, probably 'wild marsh').

(*b*) In 1734 *High Mead* (this is mentioned frequently in the 16th; it is *le common lott meadow vocatur le High meade* in 1631). In 1706 *the Barley Closes, Bear Close* (*the Beere close* 1652, *v.* bere), *the Lanes* (*the Leynes* 1599 *et freq, v.* lain), *the Water Crooke*. In 1698 *Dyneacre Wey* (*Denacre* 1438, *Dean acre furlong* 1576, *Dean Acre, Deane Acre way* 1661, *v.* denu), *the High Cross, the Long Bushy Close* (so named 1607), *the Two Butts* (*v.* butts). In

---

[1] Except where otherwise stated, the forms are from Burford.
[2] Presumably an endowment of the Grammar School (VCH O I, 464–6).

1695 *the great Bush, the Greene banck, the Leaze Wall, the Oares* (so named 1661). In 1661 *the Conigree end* (v. congree), *Fulden Bottom* (*fuldene, fuldenslade, fuldenschull, fuldeane hill* 1576, v. fūl, denu, slæd), *Grove Way*. In 1655 *Berrie Orchard* (*Biriorchard* 1435–6, v. burh). In 1631 *le Church-greene* (*le Cherchegrene* 1456). In 1598 *the Culverclose* (cf. *Culverhay* 1492, the first element refers to a dove-cot). In 1588 (*Bodl*) *Ivie house* (*Iveyhouse* 1539). In 1576 *Bright hyll, Cheyney furlonge, Cley furlonge, Cleyt furlong, Elerstubfurlonge, the Gowrys* (v. gāra), *hyllyslade, our ladys lande* (v. Lady), *Longe cross, the owld hull, the townsende, Whitslade furlong, Whyteslade, the worthye* (*le Worthe* 1462, v. worþ). In 1567 *Jesus Acre* (v. Lady). In 1551–2 (*Survey*) *Forest Wall, le Hades* (v. hades), *Hammes* (v. hamm), *le More* (v. mōr), *Wornam* (*Wirmham* 1435–6), *Wyldernes*. In 1545 *Le Holme* (v. holme), *Piggehill*. In 1538 *farme callyd the Rye*. In 1501 *Angecrosse, Bellam Furlonge* (*beldame furlong* 1416, *Beldamys furlong* 1462, *beldam(e)* is first recorded c. 1440 in the sense 'grandmother'), *Brod(e)hedden furlonge, comfast furlong* (*comefast furlong* 1419), *coppyd crosse, copyslade, copeslade* (*Coppdeslade furlong* 1419, it is said in Burford (p. 175) that *Coppedslade* abuts on *Copped Cross*, the latter name referring to a ridged cross-roads, perhaps the point where the path to Bampton crosses the Shilton road on a rise of ground: v. coppede), *Downe furlong, Hedsondye furlonge, Henfurlonge, Esterhenfurlonge, Westerhen-furlong* ('eastern and western bird furlong,' cf. *Henacres furlong* 1385), *Hiot, moresty furlong, Offley furlong, Sawnfyfe furlonge, Shednills, Uphedfurlonge, Whitstone furlong* (*Whitston furlong* 1462, probably 'white stone'). In 1488 *the Newlond* (*le newelond* 1423). In 1486 *the laund of Burford* (*Burfordlaund* 1478, v. launde). In 1462 *Myllonde* (*Mullelond* 1416, 'mill land'). In 1438 *Bunslade* (v. slæd). In 1435–6 *Overham* (v. hamm), *Powkputte* ('goblin pit,' first element pūca: there are two other examples of this name in the county), *le Serte, le Stertequarrell* ('steort quarry'), *Whiteladiesquarrell, le Wortquarrie*.

10. Clanfield

CLANFIELD

Chenefelde 1086 DB

Clenefeld' 1196 P, *Clenefelde* 1222–5 Os (p), 1247 FF, 1320 Ch, *Clenefeld* 1241 FF

Clanefeld 1204 FF *et passim* with variant spellings *Clanefelde, Clanefeld', Clanefeud, Clanefeud', Clanefelt* to 1395 AD

Kanefeld 1227 FF, *Canefeld* 1285 Ass

Clenesfeld(e) 1275–6 RH

Clanfeld 1275–6 RH *et freq* with variant spellings *Clanfelde, Clanfyld, Clanyfeld* 1380 Cl

LITTLE CLANFIELD is so named 1797 Davis.

'Clean field,' v. clǣne, feld. For other occurrences of this name, which probably describes open land free from weeds, v. PN W 70.

CHESTLION FM (6″) takes name from the family of *Chastilun, de Chastilon* who had property here in 1278–9 (RH), and for part at least of the next century.

EDGERLY FM takes name from *Heggerdoseye, Eggerdeseye* c. 1235 (c. 1280) Os, *Egerdesheye* c. 1240 Os, *Egerdeseye* (bis) c. 1241 Os, *Eggardeseye* (bis) 1278–9 RH (p), *Egaridiseye* 1347 Ipm. '*Ecgheard*'s island,' *v.* (ī)eg.

GREEN BENNY (not on map). Cf. *Cornbenneye, Greneben* c. 1235 Os, *Benneye* c. 1241, 1267–84, 1280 Os, 1278–9 RH, 1285 *Ass*, *Benney* 1316 FA, *Benny* 16th Os, *Green Benny* c. 1840 *TA*. Probably '*Benna*'s island,' *v.* (ī)eg. The personal name is found in Benham Berks. The prefixes *Corn* and *Green* are self-explanatory.

IPENHAM (not on map) is *Ippenham* c. 1200, c. 1225, c. 1240 Os, *Irpenham* 1253 FF, *Magna and Parva Ippenham* 1267–84 Os, *Nipenham* c. 1840 *TA*. '**Ippa*'s hām or hamm.' The personal name is only recorded in place-names.

PUTTS (lost) is *Putte* 1242–3 Fees, *la Putte* c. 1254 (c. 1425) Frid, *Puttes* 1275–6 RH *et freq* to 1360 Cl, *Pytys* 1346 FA. *v.* pytt.

FRIAR'S COURT is *Frier Court* 1797 Davis, *Friar Court* c. 1840 *TA*: from the Hospitallers of Clanfield. LANGLEY LANE (6″) is so named c. 1840 *TA*. MARSH LANE and MILL LANE (both 6″). Cf. *Marsh close* and *Mill Field* c. 1840 *TA*.

FIELD-NAMES

(a) In c. 1840 (*TA*) Betham Hays (cf. *Belham heydiche* 1519–20 *PreQuen*; final element probably (ge)hæg, to which 'ditch' has been added in the early form), Boam Bridge, Burrow or Barrow Field, Bushey Close, Duck Marsh, Ten Farundels (cf. *Tria fordella* c. 1240 Os, Þ*referthendels* 14th or 15th Os, *v.* fēorðan dǣl), The Lay(s) (*v.* lē(a)h), Linton Field, Litney (possibly identical with *Litleneyt* 1230 Os, *Lutleneye* 1267–84 Os, in Black Bourton: '(at the) small island,' the second element is eyt in the first form and (ī)eg in the second), The Moor (*More* c. 1235 Os, *la More* 1267–84 Os, *le More* 1517–18 *PreQuen, v.* mōr), Pound Close, The Shaft, Tarney Field and Furlong (*Torneye* c. 1235 Os, *Torneya* c. 1240 Os, *Thorneye* 1247 FF, 'thorn-bush island,' *v.* þorn, (ī)eg), Withey Bed (*v.* wīðig), Wymonds (*Wymundesplace* 1380 Cl, *Wymans* 1498–9, 1517–18 *PreQuen*, first element the personal name *Wīgmund, place* may have the sense 'manor-house').

(b) In 1519–20 (*PreQuen*) Bedestone. In 1512–13 (*PreQuen*) Honymede (*v.* honey). In 1511–12 (*PreQuen*) stream called *Millke* or *le lode milne* (cf. 294, *lode* is (*ge*)*lād*, 'watercourse,' *v.* myln), *Sainct Leonards diche* (*Saint Leonards Chappell* is also mentioned). In 1498–9 (*PreQuen*) *le Formede* (*Formede* c. 1240 Os, *Foremede* c. 1250 Os, *Foremed* c. 1280–90 *Bodl*, *v.* mǣd, the prefix is *fore*, 'in front of'). In c. 1250 (Os) *Longeherst* (*v.* hyrst), *Wereforlong* (*v.* wer), *Wommane Wayssche* (this looks very much like 'women's washing place,' though the word *wash* is not recorded in this form). In c. 1241 (Os) *Netherbenlond* (*v.* bēan), *Cleyputh* (*Cleypute* c. 1235 Os, *v.* clǣg, pytt), *Fokeneye* ('*Focca's island,' *v.* (ī)eg, and cf. PN Wo 341), *Garstun*', *Garsthona* (*Garstone* c. 1235 Os, *v.* gærs-tūn), *Kungewrthe* (possibly a poor form for *Kadewrthe* 1240 Os under Black Bourton, which means '*Cada*'s worþ'), *Matrebeddesfurlong* (the first element might be *mæddre*, 'madder'; second element 'bed'), *Themuge*, *Puffurlong*, *Rixe* (also c. 1235 Os), *Sprungwelle* ('wellspring'). In c. 1240 (Os) *Buleham* ('bull or *Bula's hamm'), *Welodessetere*. In c. 1235 (Os) *Bidemelne* (this name occurs several times in W, *v.* PN W 4–5: the second element is myln, and the first is a stream-name identical with Boyd Gl, probably from OE *byd, 'hollow, depression': *v.* also PN Nth 222).

11. Crawley

CRAWLEY

> *Croule* 1214 FF, 1285 *Ass*
> *Craule*(*e*) 1214 FF, *Craule* 1227 Cl *et passim* to c. 1384 Eynsh, *Crawle* 1285 FF, *Crawele* 1387 Cl

'Crow wood,' *v.* crāwe, lē(a)h.

BLINDWELL WOOD (6″) is *Blindewell Coppice* 1608–9 *Survey*. 'Blind' probably means 'hidden by vegetation,' for other occurrences of the name, *v. supra* 13.

BREACH BARN. Cf. *the Breaches* 1608–9 *Survey*, *v.* breche. CHASE-WOOD FM. Cf. *Chace Green* c. 1840 *TA*, *Chase Wood* 1857 *EnclA*. THE LINSH (6″) is *the Lynch* 1608–9 *Survey*, *The Linch* 1857 *EnclA*: *v.* hlinc. MAGGOTS GROVE. Cf. *Magottes close* 1526–7 *CourtR*, *Maggots Grove*, *Maggot's Corner* c. 1840 *TA*. SHOWELLS SPRING (6″) is *Showel Spring* 1822 O.S., *v.* 291.

FIELD-NAMES

(*a*) In 1857 (*EnclA*) Henley Knapp ((*on*) *hean leage* 969 (12th) BCS 1230, *v.* hē(a)h, lē(a)h; the modern name appears again on the 1″ map in Spelsbury, about six miles north north east, *v.* 380–1), Spoonley Copse (cf. (*on*) *swon leage*, (*on*) *swon weg* 969 (12th) BCS 1230, (*to*) *swondæne*, (*innan*) *swonlege* 1044 (c. 1150) KCD 775, *Sponden*' 1300 Wych: Grundy's suggestion that the -*w*- of the charter forms is a mistake for -*p*- is proved correct by the appearance of the name with a -*p*- in Wych; the first element must be OE *spōn*, 'chip, shaving,' which Ekwall (DEPN) gives as the first element of Spondon Db, and there was evidently a wood, road and valley (*v.* lē(a)h, weg, denu) with this name). In c. 1840 (*TA*) Broken Hatch Hill, Cats Close, Crawley Ridings (*v.* ryding), Dry Ground, Hanksley, Hemmitt Hill, Lanket (*v.* lanket), Rack Piece, Little Rack Close (*v.* rack), Sideland Close and Hill (*v.* sideland), Great and Little Smalley, Smalley Piece and Green (*Litle and Great Smal(l)ey* 1608–9 *Survey*, 'narrow island or lē(a)h,' *v.* smæl, (ī)eg), Water Vine (*Water Vynes Coppice* 1608–9 *Survey*).

(*b*) In 1608–9 (*Survey*) Worsell. In 1300 (Wych) *Colneyshacch'* (possibly 'Cola's island,' *v.* (ī)eg, to which hæcc has been added). In 1044 (c. 1150) KCD 775 (*to ðære*) *haran apeldran* ('hoar or boundary apple tree,' *v.* hār), (*to ðam*) *heafdam* (*v.* hēafod), (*andlang*) *surode* ((*on*) *suga rode* 969 (12th) BCS 1230, second element 'clearing'; the first might be *sugga*, 'sparrow'). In 969 (12th) BCS 1230 (*on norðe weardum*) *cynges steorte* ('king's tongue of land,' *v.* steort), (*on*) *lungan leage weg* (*v.* lang, lē(a)h, weg), (*on þa*) *wiðig rewe* ('row of willow trees').

12. Curbridge

CURBRIDGE

(*æt*) *Crydan brigce* 956 (c. 1200) BCS 972
Crudebrigg' 1200 Ch, *Crudebrug(g)'* 1240–1 Ass, *Cruddebrigge* 1277 FF, *Crudebrug'* 1278–9 RH, *Crudbrugge* c. 1384 Eynsh
Credebrigge 1209 PWint, 1225 FF, *Credebrugg'* 1268 Ass
Cradebregge 1242–3 Fees
Crotebruge 1316 FA, *Crotebrugge* 1342, 84 Eynsh, *Crotebrugg* 1368 Cl
Curbrigge 1517 D Inc
'Creoda's bridge.' *v.* brycg.

BURWELL FM takes name from *Burewell* 1226 Cl, *Berwelle* 1401 Cl (p). 'Stream by a burh,' *v.* w(i)elle. Alternatively the first element may be be(o)rg.

CASWELL Ho etc. take name from *Cauereswell'* 1166 P, *Cressewell'* 1182 *et seq* P, *Kerswelle* 1223–8 Eynsh, *Charswell* 1278–9 RH, *Karsewell'* 1297 CornAcc *et freq* with variant spellings *Carsewell(e)*, *Karsewell* to 1517 D Inc, *Karswelle* 1342 Eynsh *et passim* with variant spellings *Carswell(e)* to 1387 Cl, *Craswelle* 1384 Eynsh. If the earliest form is to be trusted, the first element is the personal name, probably **Cāfhere*, found in Caversfield 204, and in Caversham Berks. All the other forms point clearly to the etymology 'cress-stream,' *v.* cærse, w(i)elle, which is a common stream-name in the county (*supra* 13), and might have been substituted for that reason.

APLEY BARN (6"). Cf. *Appley Piece and Meadow* c. 1840 *TA*. CONEYGAR POND (6"). Cf. *The Coneyger* c. 1840 *TA*, *v*. conygree. CORAL SPRING and PARSONAGE BARN (both 6") are so named 1822 O.S. and c. 1840 *TA* respectively. WITNEY PARK FM (6"). Cf. *Witney Park* 1797 Davis, *Witney Park House* c. 1840 *TA*.

FIELD-NAMES

(a) In c. 1840 (*TA*) Ash Bed Piece, Ashmore Well (cf. *Ashforlong* 1315 *PWint*, in Witney), Back Ham Bleaching (*v*. hamm), Butter Croft (*v*. butere), China Lands, The Dogs Close (there is a Cats Close in the neighbouring village of Crawley), Folly Piece (*v*. folly), Fulling Mill, Grist Mill, Hawk(e)sley (this is named from the tumulus just south of Crawley Bridge and Mill, which appears as (*of*) *hafoces hlewe* 969 (12th) BCS 1230, (*into*) *hafoces hlæwe* 1044 (c. 1150) KCD 775, *Hauekeslewe* 1315 *PWint*; 'Hafoc's tumulus,' *v*. hlǣw, under hlāw; *hafoc*, 'hawk,' is not on independent record as a personal name), Hills and Mountains, Lady Ham (*v*. Lady), Meer Furlong, Minster Pike (*v*. picked, the first element is from Minster Lovell), Long Miskin (this is a side-form, with metathesis, of *mixen*, 'dunghill'), Mowing Park, Packsford Piece, Pound Lane, The Race Course, Rotton Moor (*v*. mōr, *rotten* is used in dialect to mean 'boggy'), Short and Long Stanning, Sidegate Stream, Little Spring Close, The Spurge, Stokenford Paddock, Little and Great Thorney Leys, The Wilderness, Withey Bed (*v*. wiðig), The Worlds End.

(b) In 1044 (c. 1150) KCD 775[1] (*to*) *hlæwan slæde* (*v*. hlǣw, slæd; the valley is on the north boundary of Lew, the name of which parish represents hlǣw), (*on*) *horninga mære* (also 969 (12th) BCS 1230[2]), (*into*) *kytelaceras* (cf. (*on*) *cytel wylle* 969 (12th) BCS 1230; the first element is 'kettle,' probably describing a spring in which the water bubbles up: the name has been transferred from the spring to the 'acres' in the later name), (*into*) *Leofstanes bricge* ('Lēofstān's bridge'), (*innon ða*) *wudestret* (*v*. wudu, strǣt). In 969 (12th) BCS 1230 (*on þane*) *ealdan weg* (*v*. (e)ald, weg), (*on*) *lythlan eorþ beorg* (the bounds go on *of þære byrig*, which suggests that the word in the preceding phrase should be *eorþburh*, 'earthwork'; lȳtel has been prefixed), (*on þa*) *on heafda*, (*of þas*) *on heafdon* (*v*. hēafod; the exact sense of this term with *on* prefixed is uncertain), (*on ða*) *myþy*, (*of þas*) *gemyþon* (possibly 'crossroads'; 'junction of streams' does not suit the topography), (*on*) *tycan pyt* ('Tica's pit'), (*on*) *wæredan hlinc* (*v*. hlinc; the first word is obscure).

[1] For the interesting term *dufan doppe*, which occurs in this charter, *v*. 9.

[2] A *Rosa de Horningem'e* is mentioned 1278–9 RH in connection with land at Lew, and this is doubtless the same place-name. It means 'boundary of the *Horningas*', the latter term, which means 'dwellers in a tongue of land' being also the first element in the name of Hormer Hundred in Berks, about six miles away. In the Berks hundred-name the **horna* is the projecting corner of Berks surrounded by the Thames (*v*. Anderson 214). It is possible that the *Horningas* who evidently lived near Witney came from that part of Berks.

13. Ducklington

DUCKLINGTON

Duclingtun, (*to*) *Duclingtune*, (*to*) *Duclingdune* 958 (c. 1250) BCS
    1036, *Duklyngton* 1428 FA, *Ducklingtone* 1526 LS
Duceling dune 1044 (c. 1150) KCD 775
Dochelintone 1086 DB
Dukelind' 1122–33 OxonCh *et passim* with variant spellings *Duke-
    lintona, Dukelindune, Dukelintun', Dukelinton', Dukelindon',
    Duchelintona* to 1292 Ch
Duclindona 1151 Os, *Duklynton* 1311 Ipm, 1346 FA, 1364 Cl
Dokelind' 1176 P (p) *et freq* with variant spellings *Dokelinton',
    Dokelinton*(*a*), *Dokelindon', Dokelynton*(*e*) to 1285 *Ass*
Dukelesdona 1200–18 Eynsh
Duglintona 1210–18 Eynsh
Dugkelintona 1247–64 Eynsh
Dogelinthone c. 1270 Eynsh
Doclindon 1278–9 RH, *Doklindon* c. 1284 (c. 1320) Frid, *Doklynton*
    1311 Ipm
Dokelingtone 1309 Eynsh, *Dokelyngton* 1428 FA, 1509–10 Os
Doklington 1512 AD

Ekwall (DEPN) gives the etymology of this name as 'the hill (dūn)
of **Duc(c)el*'s people.' The forms do not suggest, however, that it
contains -inga-, and it might be better to take it as '**Ducel*'s farm'
(*v.* ingtūn), with very early confusion of tūn with dūn. Evidence for
a personal name *Duc(c)*, of which *Ducel* would be a derivative, is
given in PN Ca 92–3. Alexander's etymology, 'the hill of the duck-
lings,' is unsatisfactory, as neither *duckling* nor *gosling* is recorded
till the mid 15th century.

BARLEYPARK FM, WOOD take name from *Byrnan lea* 958 (c. 1250)
BCS 1036, *park of Barley alias Barlowe parke* 1586 *Bodl, Barley Park*
early 18th ParColl. '*Beorna*'s wood or clearing,' *v.* lē(a)h.

CLAYWELL FM takes name from *Welde* 1086 DB, 1320 Eynsh, 1429–30
Extent, Wealde 1170–90, 79, 94–5 Eynsh, *Estwald'* 1268 *Ass, Estwelde*
1278–9 RH, 1316 FA. The original name is OE w(e)ald, to which
'east' was added, perhaps for distinction from Weald in Bampton
which is *Westweld* in 1246–7. If the identification be correct, the
name has been completely transformed by the substitution of 'clay'

for 'east' and the confusion of the second element with 'well.' The modern name appears as *Claywell Field, Claywell Hill* c. 1840 *TA*.

COURSEHILL FM takes name from *Coredeshell'* c. 1200–11 Eynsh (p), *Curteshull(e)* 1328 Cl (p). Possibly '*Cūþrēd*'s hill.'

DUCKLINGTON MILL (6″). Cf. (*to ðam*) *mylewere* 1044 (c. 1150) KCD 775: 'mill weir.'

GILL MILL FM takes name from *molendino aureo* 1278–9 RH (p), *Guilden Mill* 1638, 96 *Bodl, Guild or Guilden Mill* 1639 *Bodl, Guild Mill* 1642, 52, 1704, 12 *Bodl, Gill Mill* 1797 Davis. *Guilden* is used as an attribute of places in the sense 'rich, productive, splendid,' *v.* PN Ca 61.

THE MOORS takes name from the family of Richard de *Mora*, who is given 25½ acres in Ducklington c. 1200–18 Eynsh.

DAVIS'S COPSE (6″) and MOULDEN'S WOOD are *Davis Copse* and *Mouldings Wood* 1822 O.S., *Davis' Coppice, Davis's Copse* and *Mouldens Wood* c. 1840 *TA*.

FIELD-NAMES

(*a*) In c. 1840 (*TA*) Beanhill field, Bean field, Brick Kiln ground, Chancery Ground, Court Close, Upper and Little Dodnell or Dodnells, Down Hays (*v*. (ge)hæg), Ferney Ley, Fish House Ham, Fox Hill, Gander Field, Gatsen ground, Goose Ham, Grubbed Ground (*v*. grubbed), The Ham (*v*. hamm), Hanging of the Hill Furlong (*v*. hangende), Heath Ground, The Isle, The Lanket, the Long Lankett (*v*. lanket), Oxfar Close, Picked Close (*v*. picked), Pitchless Hill, The Rod Ham (*v*. rod), Sandy Leyes Plantation, Rose Close, North and South Three Hill, Tongue Furlong, Wood field, Wormwood Close.

(*b*) In 1429–30 (*Extent*) Lordesmede, Newmede (*v*. nīwe, mǣd), Oldefelde (*Aldefeld* 1200–18 Eynsh, *Eldefelde* 1328 Cl, *v*. (e)ald, feld), Seleham (*Selhampmede* 1328 Cl: second elements hamm and mǣd). In 1328 (Cl) *Castelfurlong, Cleydonefurlong* (*v*. clǣg, dūn), *Donynglondfurlong, Emedham* (*v*. hamm), *Eys(h)furlong, Morfurlong* (*v*. mōr), *Morghlesefurlong, Overeham* (*v*. hamm), *Overnglondfurlong, Thachampende* (*v*. þæc-hamm), *Thornefurlong, Godesthornefurlong* (*v*. þorn, *God(d)* is a personal name), *Wedemhofurlong, Worthfurlong* (*v*. worþ), *Wynna*. In 1327 (Ipm) *Oxelese* ('ox pasture'). In c. 1280 (Os) *Hecynges, Inhechinges* (there is mention in 13th-century sources of the practice of making an *inhoc*, i.e. enclosing for cultivation a part of the arable fallow which would in the normal course of tillage have lain uncultivated: *Inhoke* occurs as a field-name in Great Tew, the Ducklington term being evidently an alternative one, for the second element of which, frequent

by itself as a field-name with this meaning, *v.* hechinge). In 1200–18 (Eynsh)
Medhal (*v.* mǣd, h(e)alh). In 1044 (c. 1150) KCD 775[1] (*into*) *hocslew* ((*on
occan slæw*, '*Occa*'s slǣp'[2]), (*on ðone*) *mædham ðe hyrnð* (read *hyreð*) *into
Scylftune* (as pointed out by Grundy, this survives as a detached portion of
the parish of Shilton, which is about six miles from Ducklington; *v.* mǣd,
hamm), (*on ða*) *niwan dic* (*v.* nīwe, dīc, and cf. (*on þa*) *ealdan dic* in BCS 1230,
v. (e)ald), (*ofær ðone*) *wegean mor* (a poor form for *Wittan mor*, for which
v. 333). In 969 (12th) BCS 1230[3] (*on*) *fugel sled* ((*on*) *fugelslæd*, 'bird valley'),
(*on þa*) *stan bricge* (possibly connected with (*on*) *stanford*; 'stone ford and
bridge'). In 958 (c. 1250) BCS 1036 (*to þære*) *apoldre* ('apple tree'), (*on*)
blace þyrnan ('blackthorn'), (*on þone*) *byge* ('bend'), (*on*) *burh dic* (*v.* burh,
dīc), (*on þa*) *ealdan dic* ('old ditch'), (*on þone*) *ealdan ford* ('old ford'), (*on þa*)
ealdan Rode (probably 'old clearing,' *v.* rod), (*to þan*) *ellere*, (*to þan*) *oþern
ellene* ('elder tree' and 'other elder tree'), (*on*) *folgor hyrste* (*v.* hyrst, the first
element is obscure), (*on*) *gate þyrnan* (perhaps 'goat thorn'), (*to þan*) *heafdan*
(*v.* hēafod), (*æt*) *loppede þorne* (this is an early example of the name which
occurs as Lopthorne, Lapthorne PN D 169, 281, 323, meaning 'lopped or
pollarded thorn tree'), (*on*) *scottes healh* ('*Scot*'s h(e)alh'), (*on*) *swyllan healas*
(second element the plural of h(e)alh; the first is uncertain), (*on þa*) *wurtwalan*, (*to*) *uurt walan* (*v.* the field-names of Arncott 162), (*on*) *uuenburge
byrgge* (second element brycg; the personal name *Wenburh* is not recorded
elsewhere, and the first element might be a poor form for the woman's name
Cwēnburh, which appears in the field-names of the nearby Bampton).

14. Little Faringdon

LITTLE FARINGDON

Ferendone 1086 DB[4], *Parua Ferend'*, *Parua Ferenduna* 1156 P,
  Ferendona c. 1185 CartAntiq, (*Parua*) *Ferendon'* 1191, 3 P
Parva Farendon' 1220 Fees, *Parua Farenduna* 1233 Bract, *Farendon*
  1252 Cl, *Faryndone* 1285 *Ass*, *Parva Farindon* 1316 FA, *Farendon'*
  1337 Cl, *Little Farendon'* 1359 Ch
Farndon 1278–9 RH
Faryngtone 1526 LS

'Fern hill,' OE fearn-dūn. 'Little' by contrast to Faringdon in
Berks.

[1] The earlier forms in the brackets are from BCS 1230, date 969 (12th).
[2] The -*w* should probably be -*þ*, as in other forms from these charters (*v. supra*
314).
[3] The earlier forms in the brackets are from BCS 1036, the date of which is 958
(c. 1250).
[4] This includes Great Faringdon, Berks, and Little Faringdon, O.

15. Filkins

FILKINS

Filching 1173–4, 1194 Eynsh

Filkinges 1180 Os (p), *Filking* 1185 Templars *et freq* with variant spellings *Filking'*, *Filkyng*, *Fylkynge* to 1390 Eynsh, *Nether Fylkings* 1333 BM, *Netherfilkynge* 1347, 69 Ipm, 1347 Cl, *Netherfylkynges* 1360 Ipm, *Netherfilkyng* 1360 Cl, *Filkynges* 1383 Cl

Filkinch 1185 Templars, *Fylkynche* 1316, 36 Ipm

Filiking 1218 FF (p), *Filyking'* 1268 *Ass* (p)

Fulking 1229 Cl

Filechinge 1269, c. 1270 Eynsh, *Fileking* (ter) 1278–9 RH, *File-kyngges* 1285 *Ass*, *Fylekinge* 1316 FA

Over Filkins, Nether Filkins 1797 Davis

Possibly 'the people of *Filica,' but the forms are too late for any degree of certainty.

COCKEDHAT COPSE (6"): *v.* Fan.

THE PILLS. In *Archæologia* 37 (1857), p. 145, there is a reference to a spring in this neighbourhood called *Ewelme Pill*. *Ewelme* (for which there is an early form 1254 Cl, "abbas de Bruera...heremitagii sui del le Euuelme in Whiccheuuode") is from OE æw(i)elm, 'river-spring' (cf. the parish name Ewelme 126–7) and *Pill* is from OE pyll, used in place-names of a small stream.

16. Grafton and Radcot

GRAFTON

Graptone 1086 DB

Graftona 1130 P *et passim* with variant spellings *Graftun'*, *Grafton'*, *Grafton, Graffton'* 1244 RegAntiquiss

'tūn by or in a grove,' *v.* grāf(a).

RADCOT

Ratrotam c. 1150 (17th) GestS

Raðcota 1163 P

Redcote 1176 P *et freq* with variant spellings *Redcot'*, *Redcot* to 1272 Ch, *Redicote* 1268 *Ass*

Recot' 1219 Cl, *Reccot* 1236 (c. 1300) Fees

Rotcote 1220 FF, 1285 *Ass*, 1296 (1339) Ipm, *Rotcot* 1257 Ipm, 1428 FA, *Rotecote* 1369 Cl, *Rottecote* 1380 Cl

Radcote 1220 FF, 1235–6 *Fees*, *Radecote* 1285 *Ass*, *Radcott* 1761
  Rocque
Rutcot 1220 *Fees*
Retkot 1235–6 *Fees*, *Rettcot* 1257 Ipm, *Retcote* 1278–9 RH, 1316
  FA, *Rettecote* 1315 Ipm
Rethcot' 1242–3 *Fees*
Rockote 1285 *Ass*, *Roccote* 1296 Ipm

Probably 'reed cottage,' i.e. with a roof thatched with reeds,
v. hrēod, cot(e); but the early appearance of forms with *Rat-*, *Rad-*
indicates confusion with rēad, 'red,' and this may have been the
original first element. *Rocote* 1086 DB may refer to this place.

Ashton Pill Br. Cf. *Asshenbridge* 1511–12 *PreQuen*, *Ashton Peal
Bridge* 1869[1], *v.* pyll. Cradle Br. (6″) is so named c. 1840 *TA*.
Grafton Green Fm (6″). Cf. *Grafton Green* c. 1840 *TA*.

FIELD-NAMES

(*a*) In c. 1840 (*TA*) Cowleaze Common, Duck Puddle (*v.* Des), The
Duntles, Flat Mead, Little and Great Frogmore, The Garrison, The Ham,
The Common Hams (*v.* hamm), Hen Flat, The Highway, Little and Great
Honey Ham (*v.* honey), The Housey Ground, Leys Common, The Muddle,
Pound close, Prist Meadow, Quiddams (*Quedham* 1278–9 RH, *Whedam*
1519–20 *PreQuen*: second element hamm, the first may be OE *cwēad*,
'dirt'), Rye Mead.

(*b*) In 1285 (*Ass*) *Juresherde*.

17. Hailey

Hailey

Haylegh' 1240–1 *Ass*, *Hayle* 1278–9 RH, 1285 *Ass*, 1387 Cl,
  Hayles 1285 *Ass*, *Haylle* 1316 FA, *Haille* 1368 Cl, *Hayley* 1517
  D Inc
Hagele 1246–7 *Ass*, *Hagley* 1372 AD
Halylegh 1268 *Ass*
Hyle 1278–9 RH
Heyley 1797 Davis

'Hay clearing,' *v.* hēg, lē(a)h.

Delly Pool (6″), End take name from *Denle* 1278–9 RH (p), 1387
Cl, *Denleghe* 1316 FA, *Denlegh* 1368 Cl. Cf. *Dallys Close* 1529–30

---

[1] J. M. Davenport, *Oxfordshire Bridges*.

CourtR, Delly Brache close, Dellynge, Dally Sarte 1608–9 *Survey, Dellypool End* 1822 O.S. 'Valley clearing,' *v.* denu, lē(a)h. For *Brache* and *Sarte v.* breche and sart.

POFFLEY END takes name from *Pouwele* 1278–9 RH (p). Probably '*Pohha*'s stream,' *v.* w(i)elle. Poughill Co, which has the same etymology, is pronounced [pɔfil]. The same name in the form *Pochwele* occurs 1300 Wych, on the west boundary of Wychwood, about four miles away: it is not possible to identify the two.

SHAKENOAK FM takes name from *le Forsakenho(c), le Forsakenhok'* 1300 Wych, *Saken house* 1551–2 *Survey, Forsaken Hooke, Forsakenho(s)e* 1608–9 *Survey, Shekenhowe, Shakenhoofe* 17th *Survey*. The original meaning was 'the deserted oak,' referring perhaps to an oak tree in a clearing. The name had evidently ceased to convey this by the 16th century, and the later forms are due to popular etymology. Also, by the time of the earliest reference, the name had come to be that of an extensive wood. It occurs three times in the surveys of different parts of Wychwood Forest given in Wych; in the first reference it is near the north boundary of Stonesfield, in the second it is on the south-west boundary of Wychwood, and in the third it is near the modern farm.

BLACKBIRD ASSARTS LANE (6″). Cf. *Blackbird Sarts* c. 1840 *TA*. There is also a *Blackepitt Sarte* 1608–9 *Survey, Great and Little Blackpit Assarts* c. 1840 *TA*, and it is possible that the former name is a corruption of the latter. As they both appear in the *TA*, however, they may refer to different places, *v.* sart. BREACH FM, LANE (6″). Cf. *Lea Breache, Old(e) Breache* 1608 *Survey*: the farm is so named 1822 O.S. *v.* breche. BURY CROFT and CHARITY BARN (6″) are so named c. 1840 *TA*. COMMON LEYS BARN (6″). Cf. *Cummyns leaze* 1608–9 *Survey, Common Leys* c. 1840 *TA*. DOWNHILL FM (6″) is so named 1822 O.S. FOXBURROW BARN AND LANE (both 6″), THE HAYES, LEES BARN (6″), JOB'S COPSE, STARVEALL FM (6″) and WATER LANE (6″). Cf. *Foxborough Barn, Hayes Barn, The Leys, Jobs Coppice and Paddock, Starvehall House* and *Watery Lane* c. 1840 *TA*. GIGLEY FM, MERRYFIELD FM, PRIEST HILL (6″), SPICER'S LANE (6″), SWANHILL FM AND LANE (both 6″), TURLEIGH FM AND LANE (both 6″). Cf. *Gigley Sartes, Meryfeild, Meryfieldes, Priest close, Spicers Hurne, Swanhill Rudge, Turleigh Sarte* 1608–9 *Survey*. HATFIELD PITS LANE (6″). Cf. *Hatfield Corner, Hatforde* 1608–9 *Survey, Hatfield*

Pits Ground c. 1840 *TA*: the first element might be hǣþ. MIDDLE-
FIELD FM is so named 1822 O.S. Cf. *Middlefields* 1797 Davis.
SINGE WOOD and WITHERIDGE CROSS (6″) are *Singeat Coppice* (perhaps from *sænget, cf. Signet 331) and *Witheridge crosse* 1608–9
Survey. WHITEOAK GREEN is *Whitty Green* 1723 *Bodl*, *Witty Green*
1797 Davis, *Witty or Whiteoak Green* 1822 O.S., *Whitty Green*
c. 1840 *TA*.

FIELD-NAMES

(*a*) In c. 1840 (*TA*) Queen Anne's Bounty (this is the name applied to a
perpetual fund of first-fruits and tenths granted by a charter of Queen Anne
for the augmentation of the livings of the poorer Anglican clergy), Arbors
Close, Assarts Close (*v*. sart), Blackmore Breach, Box Piece, Boycroft,
Charneys (so named 1608–9 *Survey*), Chastill, Chastill Ditch Piece (*Casteldych'* 1315 *PWint*), Closen Piece, The Cockloft Ground (a *cock-loft* is a
garret), College Close, Copythorn (*v*. coppede), Great and Little Corkhill
Ground, Corkhill Coppice (*Caulkhill Coppice* 1608–9 *Survey*, this might just
possibly be CALCUTT's WOOD (6″)), Little and Great Costell (*v*. cot-steall),
Football Ground, The Handkerchief Ground (*v*. Fan), Hartshorn Close,
Hemplands, Hen furlong, Hickrall (*Hickrilles* 1608–9 *Survey*), Hill(e)y ley
breach (*v*. breche), The Lanket(t) (*v*. lanket), Upper and Lower Mob Hayes
(*Mobb Haies* 1608–9 *Survey*, second element the plural of (ge)hæg, 'en-
closure'), Navelands, Paddock, Paradise, Parrocks Ditch (*v*. pearroc), Paunch
Hill, Pebby Piece, Ploughed Stump Copse, Poors Allotment, Rainbow Piece
(*v*. Des), Rod Ham (*v*. rod), Sparrow hawk, Spring Closes, Streight lane
Close, Summerleys Ground, Swann Close, Tee Ground, Venneyend Close,
Vennyend Ground (*v*. fenn), The Warren, Willock.

(*b*) In 1608–9 (*Survey*) *Butt Close* (*v*. butts), *Cockes Wood Sarte* (*v*. sart),
Hyde Crofte (*v*. hīd), *Leazing grove* (*Losyng Grove* 1545–6 *PossColl*, *v*. lūs),
the Lopes, *Stony Rudge* ('stony ridge'), *Winchcroftes* (*v*. 64). In 1044
(c. 1150) KCD 775[1] (*innan*) *æcenes feld*, (*into*) *æceres felda* ((*on*) *yccenes feld*,
v. feld; probably the earlier charter has the more accurate form for the first
word, but it is uncertain what it is), (*innan*) *huntenan weg* ((*on*) *huntena weg*,
'huntsmen's way'), (*on*) *kicgestan* ((*on*) *cycgan stan*, 'Cycga's stone,' the
personal name is not recorded elsewhere but is presumably related to *Cyga*
in BCS 316), (*on*) *mætseg*, (*andlang*) *metseg* ((*on*) *met sinc*; the term is obscure),
(*on*) *sceapa weg* ('sheep path'), (*into*) *wicham* (also 969, *v*. wīchām), (*be ðare
wyrtruman* ((*be*) *wyrt wale*; the terms are synonymous, *v*. the field-names of
Arncott 162). In 969 (12th) BCS 1230 (*on*) *ealdan weg* (*v*. (e)ald, weg), (*on*)
ecgerdes hel ('*Ecgheard*'s hill'), (*on þane*) *grenan weg* (*v*. grēne, wēg), (*on ða*)
hege rewe ('hedge row'), (*on*) *ofling æcer* (second word 'acre'; the first might
be a personal name with connective particle *-ing*).

[1] The earlier forms in brackets are from the 969 charter dealt with below.

18. Hardwick with Yelford

HARDWICK

Herdewic' 1199 FF *et passim* with variant spellings *Herdewike, Herdewyke, Herdewick, Herdewyk'* to 1285 *Ass*, *Herddewyk* 1293 Ipm
Herdwich' 1200 Cur *et passim* with variant spellings *Herdwic', Herdwik', Herdwick(e), Herdwik* to 1295 Ipm
Herewyke 1275–6 RH, *Herewyk* 1285 *Ass*
Hurdewyke 1285 *Ass*

v. heordewīc, perhaps 'sheep farm.'

YELFORD

Aieleforde 1086 DB
Eleford 1200 Eynsh *et freq* with variant spellings *Eleforde, Elefor(d)'* to 1428 FA, *Elleford'* 1246–7 *Ass*, *Elevorde* 1328 Ipm
Elesford' 1220 Fees
Aleford 1235–6 Fees, 1333 Ipm
Eilesford 1245 Ch, *Eylesford* 1246 FF, 1304 Cl
Elford 1364 Cl (p), *Elford Walwyn* 1555 BM

'*Ægel*'s ford': the personal name is not on independent record, but occurs frequently in place-names, *v.* PN Bk 145. The same man is referred to in the name (*to*) *Æglesuullan broce* 958 (13th) BCS 1038 (on the portion of the Ducklington boundary adjacent to Yelford).

COKETHORPE PARK [koukθɔ·p]

Soctrop 1226 Cl (p)
Cocthorp (p), *Cocthrop* 1278–9 RH, *Cokthrope* 1293 Ipm, 1428 FA, *Cokthrop* 1406 Eynsh
Coketrope 1285 *Ass*

Possibly '*Cocca's þrop'; or the first element may be the farm bird, OE *cocc.*

Boy's Wood probably takes name from the family of Ernald de *Bosco*, whose wife inherits land in Standlake 1245–6 Ipm, and John du *Boys*, mentioned 1278–9 RH.

BERRYHAM PLANTATION (6″) takes name from *Berryeham* 1551–2 Survey, *Berry Ham* c. 1840 TA, *v.* burh, hamm. BREACH FM and MANOR FM (6″, in Yelford: there is another in Hardwick) are so named 1822 O.S. and c. 1840 TA respectively: *v.* breche. RICKLESS

HILL and SHERALD'S COPSE (both 6″) are *Rickby Hill* and *Sherrils Coppice* c. 1840 *TA*.

FIELD-NAMES

(*a*) In c. 1840 (*TA*) Codd Meadow, Ewster Ham (*v.* hamm, the first word might be from *ēowestre*, 'sheepfold'), The Heyes (*v.* (ge)hæg), Mear Common, Moor Lease, The Park, Little Sheep Lease, Wags Ham (*v.* hamm).

(*b*) In 1551–2 (*Survey*) *Redley, Shyppam, Wrappepitt*.

19. Holwell

HOLWELL

Holewella 1189 (1372) Ch, *Holewell* 1335 Cl, 1675 Ogilby, *Holewelle* 1366 Ch

Haliwell' 1222 Cl, *Halywell* 1278–9 RH, *Haliwell* 1278–9 RH, 1354 Eynsh

Halewille 1285 *Ass*, *Halewell* 1316 Ipm, FA, 1340 Cl, 1354 Ipm

Holwell 1675 Ogilby

'Holy spring or stream,' *v.* hālig, w(i)elle. The same name appears in Oxford in the form Holywell (21).

GLISSARD'S WOOD and OLD PITS PLANTATION (both 6″). Cf. *Glissards Coppice and Ground* and *Old Pits Field* c. 1840 *TA*. GODFREY'S BARN (6″) is so named c. 1840 *TA*. HOLWELLDOWNS FM is *Holwell Down Farm* c. 1840 *TA*.

FIELD-NAMES

(*a*) In c. 1840 (*TA*) Ashholt Field, Black Bushes, Butherop, Little and Great Clay Furlong, Coleway Ground, Ewe Pen Close, Fern Slade Field (*v.* slæd), Hill Sides, Long Lands, The lays field (*v.* lē(a)h), The Pens, Pumphill, Rectory Close, The Thirts Field, Little and Great Tumblers Ground, Two Bush Ground, Walnut Tree Close, Warren House Field.

20. Kelmscot

KELMSCOT [kemzkɔt or kelmzkɔt]

Kelmescote 1234 FF *et passim* to 1340 Cl

Kylmescote, Kelmecote 1285 *Ass*

Kemscot 1675 Ogilby

Kelmscott 1761 Rocque

'*Cǣnhelm*'s cottage(s),' *v.* cot(e).

FIELD-NAMES

(a) In 1799 (*EnclA*) Bullham (*v.* hamm), Bull Mead, Little Cockerills Close (*Cokerelles* 1421 (c. 1450) Godstow, owned by Thomas *Cokerell'*), the Cow Common, Drift Way (*v.* drift), Fernham Lands (*v.* hamm), the Green, Ham Croft (*v.* hamm), Henfield, Kingsham (*v.* hamm), Old Latch Corner (*v.* lache), Leyworth hades (*v.* hades), lingcroft, Reefham (*v.* refham), Upcroft, Water-hay, Waterhay Close (*v.* (ge)hæg), Westham (*v.* hamm).

(b) In 1302 (*Queen*) *Lacforlong'* (*v.* lacu). In 1268 (*Ass*) *Benheumemore* (*v.* mōr).

21. Kencott

KENCOTT

Chenetone 1086 DB, *Chenicota* c. 1130 OxonCh, *Chenigcote* 1163 Poole

Kenicot c. 1150–60 Frid (p) *et passim* with variant spellings *Kenicot'*, *Kenicot(h)e*, *Kenycote* to 1361 Ipm, *Kenigcot'* 1227–8 WellsR, *Kenecot'* 1229 Cl, *Kenecote* 1268, 85 *Ass*, 1278–9 RH, 1349 Ipm

Kencot c. 1190–1200 (c. 1425) Frid (p), *Kencote* 1428 FA

Kenningcote c. 1195 *AddCh*

Canicot' 1220 Fees

'*Cǣna's* cottage,' *v.* ing, cot(e). The personal name could be a diminutive of that contained in the nearby Kelmscot.

FIELD-NAMES[1]

(b) In 1767 (*EnclA*) the *Great and Little Down* (*the Downs* 1634), *Droveway* (also 1634, *v.* drove), *Glebe Land*, the *old Hitching* (*the old Hitchin* 1685, *v.* hechinge), *Kencott Common or the Cow Common*, *Kencott Green*, the *Parsonage Lane*, *Parsonage Close*, *Rick Yard*, *the Rough Mead*, *Style Mead*. In 1685 *blechmore hill*, *Brimsmore furlong*, *the Coppice end furlong*, *deadmans-shrubs* (*Deadmans scrubbes* 1634), *the Dean bottome* (*v.* denu), *the greensward*, *Hankes his Ham*, *the Lease hedge*, *Picks* (*the pickes* 1634, *v.* picked), *Scary furlong* (*scary* is mentioned by Plot, p. 247, as a term meaning 'bare of grass': there is a Scary Hill on the 1" map south of Kingston Lisle in Berks), *the Thames Meadow*, *Woodway*. In 1634 *Barrow way*, *the Hagge pitts* (*v.* 69), *Hamme Curwell* (*v.* hamm), *the home peece and close* (*v.* home), *Lock Furlong*.

[1] Except where otherwise stated, the forms are from *BodlT*, and are (c. 1700).

22. Langford

LANGFORD

Langefort 1086 DB, *Langeford'* 1155–8 RegAntiquiss *et passim* with
variant spelling *Langeford(ia)* to 1393 Cl, *Little Langeford*
1384 Cl

Lanfordia 1233 Bract

Langford 1316, 1428 FA

LANGFORD DOWNS FM is so named 1822 O.S.: cf. *Langford Downes*
1685 (c. 1700) *BodlT*.

'Long ford,' a fairly common place-name.

23. Lew

LEW

(*æt*) *Hlæwe* 984 (14th) *Hengwrt*

Lewa 1086 DB, *Lewe* 1185, 6 P (p), 1201 FF, 1316 FA, 1328 Ipm

Lewes 1195 Os *et passim* to 1338–9 (1346) FA, *Lewes Margerie*
1220 Fees, *Lehwes* 1225–8 Eynsh

Leawe 1331 (c. 1444) BC

Leuwe 1341 Ipm

Lawe 1384 Eynsh

'(At the) tumulus,' *v.* hlǽw (under hlāw).

24. Shifford

SHIFFORD

Scipford, (*to*) *Scypforda* 1005 (late 12th) Eynsh, *Scipford* 1086 DB,
1109, 1254 Eynsh, *Scipfort* 1091 Eynsh, *Scipford'* 1151–73
Eynsh

Schiford' 1159–62 Eynsh *et freq* with variant spellings *Schyfford*.
Schifford(e) to 1426 Eynsh

Sipford 1197–8 Eynsh *et freq* with variant spellings *Sipforde*,
Sypford(e) to 1278–9 RH, *Sippford* 1285 Ass

Shipford 1199 FF

Schipford 1240–1 Ass, *Schipford'* 1246–7 Ass (p)

Sibford' 1242–3 Fees

Scheford' 1268 Ass

Shifford' 1268 Ass, *Shyfforde* c. 1360 Eynsh

Sifford 1285 Ass

'Sheep ford,' *v.* scē(a)p, ford.

KNIGHTS BRIDGE (lost) is *Cnithebrugge* 1268–81 Eynsh, *Knytenebrugge* c. 1360 Eynsh, *Knights Bridge* c. 1840 *TA*. 'Bridge of the young men,' *v.* cniht. The same name occurs also in the parish of Shirburn 92.

COLD HARBOUR COTTAGES (6″): *v.* Fan.

FIELD-NAMES

(*a*) In c. 1840 (*TA*) Beggar Ground, Little and Great Claxes (cf. *Clax-hurste* c. 1360 Eynsh; *v.* hyrst, the first element might be the personal name *Clac*, which occurs again in combination with hyrst in Eynsham, about five miles away), Broad Fleet (*v.* flēot), Ham, Black Ham (*v.* hamm), Lancot (*v.* lanket), Pound, Red Lands (*le Redelond* c. 1360 Eynsh, first element hrēod or rēad), Black Rod Ham (*v.* rod), Sixpenny Ham (*v.* penny, hamm), Stoney Furlong (*Stonyfurlong* c. 1360 Eynsh), Turney Meadow, Well Furlong (*Wellefurlong* c. 1360 Eynsh, *v.* w(i)elle), Wood Way.

(*b*) In 1485–6 (*CourtR*) *Yeafurlong* (the first element might be ēa, 'river'). In 1484–5 (*CourtR*) *Cowbelleslane* (the term *cow-bell*, for a bell hung round a cow's neck, is not recorded till the 19th), *Medford yate* (*v.* geat), *le Whyte-cross*. In 1483–4 (*CourtR*) *Churchebrygge* ('church bridge'). In 1483 (*CourtR*) *le Rougheham* (*v.* rūh, hamm). In 1482–3 (*CourtR*) *le Dyche acre* (*v.* dīc), *Enefurlonges*, *lez hades* (*v.* hades). In c. 1360 (Eynsh) *Addehurst* (possibly '*Eadda*'s hyrst'), *Blethemanfurlong* (the first element might be the obsolete verb *blithe*, 'to make glad,' in which case the reference would be to a productive piece of land), *le Brech* (*v.* breche), *Clayfurlong*, *Clayhurste-furlonge* (*v.* clæg, hyrst), *Cowelesowe* ('cow meadow'), *Droueacres* (*v.* drove), *Euerlongwey* (*v.* weg), *Fysshefurlong* (cf. *Fysselondes* 1250 PN Ca 336, and the suggestion there that it might have been manured with fish), *Hastelege-furlong* (the first two elements might be ēast and lē(a)h), *Hollefurlong* (*v.* holh), *Horestone* (*v.* hār, stān), *Laundewes* (*v.* landew), *Mulnehulle* (*v.* myln, hyll), *Russhehammes* (*v.* rysc, hamm), *Shyppelonde*, *Shiplond* (*Sypland* 1241–64 Eynsh, 'sheep land,' cf. the parish name), *Walewyngacres*, *Weylond* (the first element could be weg), *Wyly* (possibly welig, 'willow'). In 1005 (late 12th) Eynsh (*on*) *Cynlafes stan* ('*Cynelāf*'s stone'), (*on*) *Kenewines treow* ('*Cynewine*'s tree').

25. Shilton

SHILTON

(*into*) *Scylftune* 1044 (c. 1150) KCD 775
Siltone a. 1180 Os (p)
Schelton' 1201 P
Selfton' 1204 Cl
Sulfeton', *Sulveton'* 1205 Norman
Selton' 1220 Fees
Shulfton' 1241 *Ass* (quater), 1242–3 Fees

Shilftun' 1242–3 Fees
Shulton' 1284 *Ass*, 1316 FA, *Shulton* 1347 Cl, 1348, 59 Ch
Shyltone 1428 FA
Sulton 1428 FA

'tūn on a bank or ledge,' *v*. scylf. The name occurs in a number of other counties as Shilton or Shelton.

HEN AND CHICKENS PLANTATION (6"): *Hen and chickens* is a dialect term for some plant, *v*. 150. STURT FM is so named 1795 *EnclA*: *v*. steort.

26. Standlake

STANDLAKE

Stanlache c. 1150–64 Eynsh *et passim* with variant spellings
  Stanlac(h), *Stanlak'*, *Stanlak(e)*, *Stanlayke* to 1636 *FF*, *Stanlega*
  1195 P
Standlac c. 1200 (c. 1225) Abingdon, *Standlake* 1302 Eynsh, 1544
  Bodl
Stanelake c. 1360 Eynsh

'Stony stream,' *v*. stān, lacu. There is a heartfelt piece of popular etymology early 18th ParColl, where the place is said to be "situate upon a damn'd standing Puddle, long Deep and Dirty."

GAUNT HO is so named 1645 Stapleton: cf. *Gauntes* 1544 *Bodl*. A tablet in the church dated 1465 in memory of John Gaunt and his wife Joan is mentioned early 18th ParColl, with the comment "this John Gaunt and Joan his wife did first of all as I conceive build Gaunt House in this parish." GAUNTHOUSE MILL (6") is so named c. 1840 *TA*.

BRIGHTHAMPTON

Byrhtelmingtum 984 (14th) *Hengwrt*
Bristelmestone 1086 DB, *Bristhelmeston* 1245 Ch, 1304 Cl
Brihtelmeston' 1161 P *et freq* with variant spellings *Bric(h)tel-*
  meston', *Bricthtelmeston'* to 1202 P
Brith' Helmton' 1226 Cl
Britholmeston', *Brithelingges* 1242 P
Bridhelmeston 1246 FF
Brichelminton' 1246–7 *Ass*, *Brithelminton* 1268–81 Eynsh, *Brithel-*
  minton', *Brithelme'ton'* 1278–9 RH

Brychampton 1284 *Ass, Brythamptone* c. 1360 Eynsh
Bristelmentone 1285 *Ass*
Brighthampton 1316 FA, 1364 Cl, *Brighthamton'* 1316–17 AD
Bryztyngton 1433 AD
Brittington 1675 *Bodl, Brittendon* 1696, 1728 *Bodl*

'*Beorhthelm*'s tūn.' Most of the forms are identical with the most frequent early spellings of Brighton Sx (PN Sx 291). Some, however, point to a compound of the personal name with ingtūn, perhaps alternating with the other form, or early superseded by it. The ultimate confusion with hāmtūn appears early also.

BLACK HORSE and GOLDEN BALL PUBLIC HOUSES (both 6″) are *The Black Horse Inn* and *Golden Ball Inn* c. 1840 *TA*. HORN'S WAY (6″) is so named c. 1840 *TA*. LANGLEY'S LANE AND WEIR (6″). Cf. *Langleys, Langleys Weir* c. 1840 *TA*. RACK END is *Rach End* c. 1840 *TA*, cf. *Rackend street* 1683 *Bodl*. The first element is probably dialect *rack*, 'a narrow passage,' which occurs also in the street-names of Oxford (42). SANSOM'S FORD (6″). Cf. *Orchard late Sansomes* c. 1840 *TA*. UNDERDOWN MILL (6″) is so named 1822 O.S., c. 1840 *TA*: cf. *Underdown Bottom and Ham, Underdown Way furlong* c. 1840 *TA*.

FIELD-NAMES

(*a*) In c. 1840 (*TA*) Albury furlong, Alders Hedge, Aldsworth or Addsworth, Bail furlong, Berry Butts, Bettham (*v*. bytme, this might be identical with the Bittham which occurs under Aston Bampton), Brake West field pieces, Burford close and Homestead, The Butts (*v*. butts), Cat's brain furlong (*v*. catsbrain), Chaddocks Ham (*Chettuchesham* a. 1192, 1194 Eynsh, *Cattokesham* c. 1360 Eynsh, *Shatokesham* 1388 Cl, *Chattokesham* 1481–2 *CourtR*, second element hamm: the first looks like a personal name, possibly a diminutive in *-uc* from *Ceatta*; the latter name is not well recorded, but almost certainly appears in a place-name in KCD 636), Clay Hill (*Cleyhill* 1551–2 *Survey*), Constable Way furlong, Costars, Costall bush furlong, Costhall (*v*. cot-stōw), Cross furlong, Crow Cross Butts, Middle Dole (*v*. dole), Dollop and piece, Outer Hams Dollop (*dollop* is used in dialect of 'a patch of ground among growing corn where the plough has missed; rank tufts of growing corn where heaps of manure have lain'), Ealong furlong (*v*. ēa), Lower and Upper Earnest, Greys Court, Hackington or Hatchington furlong, Middle and Outer Hams (*v*. hamm), Harbourmere, Kings hedge lane folly (cf. *Foley* 1551–2 *Survey, v*. folly), Limehouse Close, Moors close, Oatlands, Pease lands, Pen Close, Poors Close, Rawpit, Red Lands, Short Richland Trees, Rickland Field and furlong (*Richland field* 1685 Gray), Sanfoin piece, Sheepstead, Slough, Smith Mead furlong, Stone ham hook, Sydenham Meads, Upper and Lower Sydenham (*Sydnam* 1551–2 *Survey*, probably identical with the parish name Sydenham 114–15), Weaving lane, Wheaten Pipe, Bush piece wheaten ripe, Whettington furlong, Whit Ox furlong.

(b) In 1469 (AD) *Deperwite*. In 1368 (Cl) *Brodecroft* (v. brād, croft). In c. 1360 (Eynsh) *Langenhurst* (*Langehurst* c. 1150–64 Eynsh, *Langenhurst* a. 1192, 1194 Eynsh, '(at the) long hyrst'). In 1302 (Eynsh) *la Landmede* (v. mǣd). In 1194 (Eynsh) *Sumerforde* ((on) *Sumerford* 1005 (late 12th) Eynsh, *Sumerforde* c. 1150–64, a. 1192 Eynsh, 'ford used in summer,' cf. the same name 253), *Wdefordhurst* (also a. 1192 Eynsh, v. wudu, ford, hyrst).

27. Upton and Signet

UPTON

Upeton' 1200 Cur (p)
Hupton' 1200 Fine (p), *Huptone* 1214 FF
Upton' 1203 NRS v (p) *et passim* with variant spellings *Upton(e)*
Opton 1295 Ipm

'Higher tūn,' first element upp-.

SIGNET

Senech 1285 *Ass*
Seynat, Saynet 1299 Ipm
Seynet 1307 Ipm
Seynate 1316 FA
Synett, Seignett 1551–2 *Survey*

The original form of this name may have been **sænget*, 'place cleared by burning.' Cf. *bærnet*, whence Barnet in Herts and Mx (PN Herts 70). **sænget* also occurs in Sencley (or St Chloe) in Minchinhampton (PN Gl 136).

BATTLE EDGE (6″) is *Bateling* 1435–6 Burford, *Batelenche* 1551–2 *Survey*, *Battledge Field* 1706 Burford, *Batledge* 1795 *EnclA*. This is considered locally to be the site of the battle of *Beorg feorda*, which was considered to have been fought at Burford (v. 310–11): it is accordingly marked "Site of Battle A.D. 752" on the 1919 edition of the O.S. 1″ map. From the above forms, however, it appears that the modern form has been evolved by recent popular etymology from an original name in which hlinc was compounded with an uncertain first element.

BURY BARNS is *Burybarnes, Ber(e)ybarre* 1551–2 *Survey*. Possibly 'barns by, or belonging to, the burh,' i.e. the town of Burford.
FERNHILL COPSE (6″). Cf. *Fernehill* 1435–6 Burford, *Veron Hill*,

Vyrynhille, Vernellmedow 1551–2 *Survey*: the modern form shows the correct etymology. STURT COPSE (6″) AND FM may take name from *the Stert* 1501 Burford, *le Sturte* 1551–2 *Survey*: 'tongue of land,' *v.* steort. There is another STURT FM, however, rather more than a mile east in Burford, and these forms may refer to that.

FIELD-NAMES

(*a*) In 1773 (*EnclA*) the Bird in Hand Road (an inn with this name is mentioned in the *EnclA* for Burford), the Downs, the fifteens (presumably part of the Burford property known as the Fifteen Lands, first mentioned in 1382, which was held in trust for the purpose of relieving the burden upon the town when a tax of tenths or fifteenths was levied, *v.* Burford), the Hand and Post (*v.* handing post), the Home Close (*v.* home), the Mill Way, Tythe Ham (*v.* hamm).

(*b*) In 1551–2 (*Survey*) *Seignet Downe*.

28. Westwell

WESTWELL [westəl]

Westwelle 1086 DB *et passim* with variant spellings *Westwell'*, *Westuell'*, *Westewell* 1428 FA

WESTWELL COPSE. Cf. *Westwell great and little Coppice* 1770 *EnclA*.

'West spring or stream,' *v.* west, w(i)elle.

FIELD-NAMES

(*a*) In 1770 (*EnclA*) Long and Little Coppice Close, the Cuckow pen (*v.* cuckoo pen), the Demesnes, Fairford Gate, the Farm Close, Holliday Hill (*Hollyday hill* 1601 (c. 1700) *BodlT*, the same name occurs in Marston 182), the Home Close (*v.* home), the Hop Yard, Mill Way, the Parsons Long Ground, Little and Great Picked Ground (*v.* picked), Pricketts Gap, Great and Little Pump Pen, Lower and Upper Rails Ground, Rough Ground, Stow Gate, the Waste or Wash-way, Wast or Wash way (*v.* wash-way), Upper and Lower William Smith.

(*b*) In 1601 (c. 1700) (*BodlT*) *Crowe bush*, *Dean-bottom* (*v.* denu), *Horne-stone*, *Longston waye*, *penny furlonge* (*v.* penny), *platt squarre* (*v.* plat), *Southhill*, *Thornehill*, *three shongs furlong*. In 1513–14 (*PreQuen*) *Dricote* or *Draycote* (*Drycote* 1498–9 *PreQuen*), *le Kingesdown* (also 1498–9 *PreQuen*, *v.* dūn). In 1498–9 (*PreQuen*) *Borowy*, *Dolmede* (*v.* dole), *Elizabeth ham* (*v.* hamm), *Heyweyes ende* (*v.* hēg, weg, ende), *Ridindoll* (*v.* ryding and dole), *Stertes* (*v.* steort).

29. Witney

WITNEY

(*æt*) *Wyttanige* 969 (12th) BCS 1230, (*to*) *Wittannige* 1044 (c. 1150) KCD 775

Witenie 1086 DB *et freq* with variant spellings *Witen(e)ia, Witenega, Witene, Wyten', Witeneie, Witeneye, Wytenay, Wyteneye* to 1285 *Ass, Witten'* 1151–73 Eynsh *et passim* with variant spellings *Witteneia, Wittenega, Wittenay, Wittene, Witteneie, Witteneya, Witteney(e), Wytteney(e), Wyttene(i)* to 1471 Eynsh

Witheneia 1163 P, *Wittheneye, Wytheneya* 1268–81 Eynsh

Whyteneye 1285 *Ass*

Wytney 1316 FA, *Long Wytney* c. 1530 Frid

'*Witta*'s island,' *v.* (ī)eg. The Windrush divides into numerous branches here, and there are several pieces of land surrounded by streams. *Wittan mor* ('*Witta*'s marsh') is mentioned in the boundaries of Witney in BCS 1230.

NOTE. CROWN LANE. Cf. *The Crown Hotel and Close* c. 1840 *TA*. DARK LANE is so named c. 1840 *TA*. HIGH ST is *the high streete* 1637 *Bodl*. PUCK LANE is so named 1829 *Bodl*. THE BUTTER CROSS (erected in 1683) is so named c. 1840 *TA*: the term denotes a market cross near which butter is sold.

COGGES [kɔgz]

Coges 1086 DB *et passim, Kogis* 1195 FF, *Cogges* 1201–3 Eynsh *et passim, Koges* 1253 FF, *Kogges* 1285 *Ass, Coggis* 1428 FA, *Coggys* 1517 D Inc

Cogas c. 1160, 1172–90 Eynsh, 1166 (c. 1425) Frid

Cokes 1200 Cur

Coghes 1216 Cl, 1246 FF

Gogges 1285 *Ass* (p)

Coggs 1526 LS

Ekwall (DEPN) suggests that the name is the plural of an OE **cogg*, identical with ME and Modern *cog*, 'cog of a wheel,' and meaning 'hill.'

CASTLE (6"). Cf. "on the south side of Cogges Church is ground called by the name of the Castle Yard, where frequently large and thick foundations have been dugg up. The vulgar people, that live here, think that in old time here was a Castle but I have not read of any such thing" early 18th ParColl.

LANGEL COMMON (6″) is *Langdale Common* 1822 O.S. Cf. the odd statement "a mead… (as the inhabitants report) called Langdell Mead valued at £30 per annum where any stranger of what condition soever, living in any part of the kingdom may putt his Horse therein" early 18th ParColl.

CHURCH GREEN (6″) is so named c. 1840 *TA*. CLEMENTSFIELD FM (6″) and NEWLAND are so named 1797 Davis.

FIELD-NAMES

(*a*) In c. 1840 (*TA*) Bacon House, Bear Close (*v.* bere), Brewery Close, Highworth Piece, Maddox Close, Market Standings, The Moor, Pleasure Ground and Garden, Slip by the River, Whiting Yard Close. In 1761 (*Bodl*) Bogcroft, Rudges.

(*b*) In 1680 (*Bodl*) *the Hayes* (*v.* (ge)hæg). In 1598 (*Bodl*) *Goldefinch close.* In 1315 (*PWint*) *Borewell* (cf. *Borehull* 1242 Cl; *v.* w(i)elle, hyll; the first element could be *bār*, 'boar,' or the element found in Boreham (PN Ess 238), which Ekwall (DEPN) takes to be a word meaning hill), *Calvecroft* ('calf croft'), *Chenest' apud Wodefordesmulle* (*v.* wudu, ford, myln; the first name is obscure), *Crandelhulle* (*v.* hyll), *Goldclyf* (*v.* clif; first element possibly *golde*, 'marigold'), *Hankyndelonde*, *H'modeshey'* (perhaps '*Heremōd*'s enclosure,' *v.* (ge)hæg), *Holdechurcheheye* ('old church enclosure'), *Inlond* (*v.* in), *Lonegoreshamme* (*v.* gāra, hamm), *le Slydyngclyf* (*v.* clif; the first element is the present participle of the verb *slide*, used to mean 'slippery' or 'steeply sloping': there are only three occurrences of its use in this sense recorded in NED, one from c. 1325 and the others from 1605 and 1616[1]), *Swenheye* (*v.* (ge)hæg), *Swonham* (*v.* hamm), *Waleismulle* (*v.* myln). In 1300 (Wych) *Grimeshevedesden'*, *Grimesmede*[2] (the first element is the personal name *Grīm*; the others are hēafod, denu and mǣd). In 1278–9 (RH) *Bissopeswode* (*v.* wudu: the Bishops of Winchester owned the manor from before the Conquest). In 1242 (Ch) *Langefurlong* (*v.* lang), *Mesherg* (if the *-r-* is in the wrong place, the elements are mersc and (ge)hæg). In 1195 (FF) *Ripesfeld* ('*Rippe*'s field'). In c. 1172–90 (Eynsh) *Hengestesei* ((*æt*) *hengestes ige* 969 (12th) BCS 1230, '*Hengest*'s island,' or 'island of the stallion,' *v.* (ī)eg; identical with Hinksey, Berks), *þegmed* (*v.* mǣd). In 969 (12th) BCS 1230 (*on*) *fulan yge* ('muddy island,' *v.* fūl, (ī)eg), (*on*) *tidreding ford* ('*Tīdrēd*'s ford'; -ing is connective).

XII. CHADLINGTON HUNDRED

Chedelinton' 1168–9 P *et freq* with variant spellings *Chedelinton(e)* to 1278–9 RH
Chedelington' 1192 P

---

[1] The word occurs in this sense in *le Slydinge dell* PN Herts 271.
[2] The latter name was still in use in the late 19th, *v.* Wych.

Chadelinton' 1195 P *et freq* with variant spellings *Chadelinton(a)*, *Chadelintun, Chadelynton* to 1344 Ipm
Chaderington' 1242 Cl
Chadelington' 1275–6 RH, *Chadelyngtone* 1285 *Ass*
Chadlington 1314 Ipm *et freq* with variant spelling *Chadlyngton*

v. Chadlington *infra* 338–9.

According to DB, the soke of three hundreds belonged to the royal manor of Shipton under Wychwood. Two of these are mentioned in the 12th century as the two hundreds of Chadlington. The third is mentioned by name as *Cheneward'berge* 1156 P, *Kenesward'* 1162 P, *Kenewardes* 1163 P, *Kanewardesberga* 1192 P, *Kineswardesburg* 1195 P, *Kinewardesburc* 1197 P, *Kinewardesberg* 1199 P. This is the old name of Shipton Barrow, which is called *Kenners Barrow* by Plot in 1676, and which was evidently the meeting place of the hundred. The name means '*Cyneweard*'s barrow,' *v.* be(o)rg.

There is a *Hundredum de Linham* (*v.* Lyneham 362) mentioned late 13th Os, which Salter says is one of the hundreds of Chadlington. If so, the meeting place may have been the 'speech hill' (*Spelberwe, Spelberwesfurlong*) mentioned late 12th *Dodsworth*, in Fifield.

1. Ascot under Wychwood

ASCOT UNDER WYCHWOOD

Estcot' 1220 Fees
Estone 1220–8 (13th) Sar[1]
Ascote 1291 FF

ASCOT D'OYLEY

Esthcote 1086 DB
Escota c. 1124–30 (c. 1425), c. 1130–40 (c. 1425) Frid, *Escot(e)* c. 1150–60 (c. 1425) Frid *et passim*, *Eskote* 1202–3 FA
Estcota, Estcote c. 1124–30 (c. 1425) Frid *et passim* with variant spellings *Estcot, Estkote* to 1302–3 FA, *Estkote Doyliuorum sub Wicchewode* c. 1280 Os, *Estcote Doyliuorum* 1389 Os
Astcote 1258 FF

[1] In spite of the form it seems more probable that this is Ascott under Wychwood than Aston Bampton. The context is "Marcam...quam reddit capella de Swin-broch ecclesie de Schiptone...Marcam quam soluit capella de Estone...ecclesie de Schiptone." *Schiptone* is Shipton under Wychwood, which is contiguous with Swinbrook and with Ascott under Wychwood. Aston Bampton is over eight miles distant.

Ascote Doyly 1346 FA, 1349 Ipm, *Ascote Toly* 1362 Ipm, *Ascote* 1384 Cl, *Ascott* 1428 FA, *Ascot Doiley* 1797 Davis

ASCOT EARL

   Estcote 1086 DB
   Astcote comitis 1316 FA
   Ascote Earl 1362 Ipm, *Ascote Earls* 1362 Cl, *Ascote* 1376 Fine

'East cot(e).' *d'Oyley* from the family of Wido *de Oileio*, who held *Escota* c. 1100 RegAntiquiss. Ascot Earl takes its suffix from the le Despensers, earls of Winchester: cf. the *Calendar of Fine Rolls* for 1326—"the manor of Ascote, co. Oxford, late of Hugh le Despenser, earl of Winchester."

BOYNAL COPSE is (*bosco q.v.*) *Boynale* 1278–9 RH, *Boynhal(l)e* 1298 Eynsh, *Boynhale* early 15th *Rental*, *Boynoll Coppes*, *Great and Little Bonnelle* 1591 *Rental*. '*Boia*'s nook or corner,' *v.* h(e)alh.

PRIEST GROVE is *Prestegraua* 1163 P, 1276 Cl, *Prestegrave* 1278 Cl, *Prestesgrove-end*, *Prestegrove* 1298 Eynsh, *Prestesgrovesende*, *Prestes-grove* 1300 Wych. 'Priest's grove.'

COLD WELL (6") is so named 1822 O.S. WOEFIELD GREEN (6") is *Woofeild Greene* 1641 Wych. Cf. *By Woful Road, Above Woful Road* c. 1840 *TA*.

FIELD-NAMES

(*a*) In c. 1840 (*TA*) Ascot Hangings (*v.* hangende), Balls Acre (*Bales acre* 1591 *Survey*, *Balls Acre* 1641 Wych), Great Balls Close (*Balles close* 1551–2 *Survey*, *v.* balle), Bonny Hay, Broad Ground (cf. *le Brodestrete, le Brode-furlong* early 15th *Rental*). In Coombe (cf. *le Coumbe* early 15th *Rental*, *Come hed* 1591 *Survey*, *v.* cumb, for the modern name *v.* in), College Orchard, Cuts Close (*v.* cut), Days Ground, Above Hemp Plot, Holly Bush Hill, Hutchings ground (*v.* hechinge), above Meadlands (cf. *le Medlond* early 15th *Rental*, *v.* mǣd), Ruttam Crook and Meadow (cf. *Rattan headge* 1591 *Survey*), Town Meadow (cf. *Mecheltounstede, Lyttletownstede* early 15th *Rental*, *v.* mycel, lȳtel, stede), Waterloo (*v.* Fan), Wilmer Hays (*v.* (ge)hæg), Wyars ground.

(*b*) In 1591 (*Survey*) *Little Beassell in Woodfield, Black hedge furlong, Haye hedge* (*v.* (ge)hæg), *Holliewell Head, Longe Kemplands, Kingeswood, Longe land side, Leaze hedge* (*v.* lǣs), *Skirettes, Sow mead, Wilgostham, Withihill* (probably identical with *Whythel* early 15th *Rental*, 'willow hill,' *v.* wiðig, hyll). In 1551–2 (*Survey*) *Corfes* (Ekwall (DEPN) derives Corfe Do from an unrecorded OE *corf*, 'pass'), *Waterfeld, Woodfeld*. In early 15th (*Rental*)

Banefurlong, le Lyttlebenefurlong ('bean furlong,' *v.* bēan), *le Longebedefurlong, le Blakelond, Bermersdene* (from this form the etymology could be ' *Beornmǣr*'s valley,' *v.* denu), *Borfortheweye, Shorteboteforlong* (*v.* butts), *Bycroftfurlong, Bycrofte* (*Bicroft* 1278–9 RH), *Cotmanecroft* (*v.* cotman), *Esthalfthethornes, le Garebrod* (*v.* gorebrode), *Grashey* (*v.* gærs, (ge)hæg), *Holham* (*v.* holh, hamm), *Honydole* (*v.* honey, dole), *le Newebrech* (*v.* nīwe, breche), *Penyham* (*v.* penny), *Reedham* (*v.* hrēod, hamm), *Shorham, Slonham, Smokacre* (*v.* smoke), *le Spore, Techham, Thagham* (*v.* þæc-hamm), *le Walforlong* (first element possibly **wælle** (*v.* under w(i)elle), *le Lytlewatfurlong* ('little wheat furlong,' *v.* hwǣte), *Lytleswynham, Mecheleswynham* ('little and great swine hamm').

2. Bruern

BRUERN

Bruaria 1159, 62 P

Bruir' 1162 P

Brueria 1172 Os *et passim* with variant spellings *Bruera, Bruere, Bruer'* to 1447 Cl, (*abbas et fratres de*) *Brueria' Tretoniæ* late 12th Madox, *Bruiera* 1208 Cur, 1230 P

Bruern c. 1200 OsReg, *Bruerne* 1241 FF, 1526 LS

Bruwere 1217 Cl, *Brewere* c. 1220–30 (c. 1425) Frid, *Briwer* 1221 Bract, *Briwer', Bruwer'* 1246 Cl, *Breware* 1384 Cl

Boruerne c. 1242–3 AD

Brewerne 1395 Cl, 1526 LS

Bruarne t. Hy 8 *Valor*

Probably the name is OFr *bruiere,* 'heath,' as in Temple Bruer (L), which suits the topography and accords with the earliest forms. The modern name and the later forms support Ekwall's etymology (DEPN), 'brewery' from OE *brēowærn*.

TANGLEY HALL, WOODS take name from *Tengle* 1189 (1372) Ch, *Teinglea* c. 1190 *AOMB, Tengeley* 1205 Ch, *Tengle* 1212 (c. 1300) Fees, *Tengel'* 1278–9 RH, *Tengele* 1366 Ch, *Teyngley* 1517 D Inc. 'lē(a)h by the River Teign,' *v.* Taynton 385.

TRETON (lost) is *Treton'* c. 1130 OxonCh, *Treiton'* 1176 P, *Trettin* 1178 P, *Treinton'* 1180 P, *Treutona* 1186 Os, *Treithoniam* 1189 (1372) Ch, *Treiton'* 1194, 5 P, *Tretona* 1259 Os *et freq* with variant spellings *Treton*(*e*) to 1526 LS. 'tūn by the tree(s),' *v.* trēo(w).

COCKSMOOR COPSE (6″) is *Coxmore Coppies* 1551–2 *Survey;* cf. *Cokysmore mede* t. Hy 8 *Valor.* This may be the same tract of land as that referred to as *Cox Moor* in the Kingham *TA*, and the meaning is probably 'marsh frequented by wild birds.' It is very near Henmarsh (341), with the same meaning. GRANGE FM. Cf. *the Graynge Grene* t. Hy 8 *Valor, the Grange hill* 1608–9 *Survey*.

FIELD-NAMES[1]

(*a*) Modern names (supplied by Mr W. Mason) Ashleighs, Bares Leaze, Furzy Broads, Hay Broads (cf. *the Overbrode, the Netherbrode*), Cabbage Ground, Big and Little Cycles, Dimansdale, Dry Ground, Hell Patch (so named c. 1840 *TA*), Highwood, Hill Leaze, Hop Garden, Ingreen (*v.* in), Little Mead, Long Meadow (*Longe mede*), Oak Ground, Oxleaze (*Oxelese*), The Park, The Patches, Picked ground (*v.* picked), Quarry Piece, Sandpits, Sawpit Close, Square Close, Thomas's Ground (cf. *Dan Thomas grove* 1551–2 *Survey, Dan* is an obsolete title of respect, used especially for members of the religious orders), Two Bush, Vestry Light (*v.* church), Watermarsh, Watermeadows.

(*b*) In 1551–2 (*Survey*) *Asheholde* (*Ashold wody, Asshe close*, the second element might be *holt*, 'wood'), *Barnefeld, Bayerdes leyes* ('horse pasture'), *the Calfes lease, Chappelle close, Chappell Coppies, Coweleys, the Fursey pasture, Hachewell leyes* (*Hachewelle lease*), *Nether and Upper Hey Coppies, Horseheys* (*v.* (ge)hæg), *Horseley close* (*the Horselease*), *le Infelde* (*v.* in), *le Launde* (*the Lande, v.* launde), *Milbourne Coppies* (*v.* myln, burna), *le Newe leyes, Nether pole* (*the Powles*), *Shepherdes leys, le Sheres, Trey meade* (*v.* trēo(w)). In t. Hy 8 (*Valor*) *the Barowe fyld* (*v.* be(o)rg), *Candesdene* (*v.* denu), *Course mede, Gyttyng, Nether Getyng*[2], *Hynchelwyke, the mede close, the Newfyld, the New close, Sewell Graynge, The Shalkes, Thornlese, Town Close*.

3. Chadlington

CHADLINGTON

> *Cedelintone* 1086 DB
>
> *Chedelint'* c. 1130 *Bodl* (p) *et passim* with variant spellings *Chede-linton(a), Chedelintone, Chedelinton'* to 1208 Fine (p)
>
> *Chadelinton'* c. 1180–90 (c. 1425) Eynsh (p) *et passim* with variant spellings *Chadelintun, Chadelint(h)one, Chadelinton(a), Chadelynton* to 1346 Ipm, *Chadelintun' Simonis, Chadelintun' Belet, Chadelintun' Willelmi* 1220 Fees, *Chadelinton Wahull* 1278–9 RH, 1302–3 FA, *Chadelynton Shuppenhull* 1358 Ipm
>
> *Chadelington'* 1196 P (p) *et freq* with variant spellings *Chadeling-tone, Chadelyngton(e)* to 1316 Ipm, *Chadyllyngton* 1517 D Inc

---

[1] Except where otherwise stated, the forms are from a *Valor* of t. Hy 8.

[2] Guiting Power and Temple Guiting in Gl seem to be named from an old name of the upper Windrush, a derivative of OE *gyte*, 'flood' (DEPN). The west boundary of Bruern is just over two miles from the Windrush, however, so this may be the same stream-name applied to another stream.

Chaderinton' 1196 P (p)

Chedlington' 1196 FF (p)

Chellinton' 1199 Cur (p), *Chelinton'* 1206 Cur (p)

Chatelinton 1216 Cl

Cadelinton' 1235–6 Fees, *Cadelyntone* 1268 Eynsh

Chadelygton' c. 1250 AD

Chaldelinton' 1262 Ipm

Cedredon' 1268 *Ass*

Chadlington 1304 Ch, *Chadlingtone* 1320 Eynsh, 1526 LS, *Chadlington Shipponhull* 1331 (c. 1444) BC, *Chadlington Wahull* 1361, 1362 (c. 1444) BC, *Chadlyngton Schepenhull* 1361 (c. 1444) BC, *Chadlington Shippenhull* 1364 (c. 1444) BC, *Chadlyngton* 1517 D Inc

Chaderyngton 1316 Ipm

Chadlinton Wahull 1346 FA, *Chadlynton* 1361 Cl

'*Ceadela's farm,' *v.* ingtūn. Identical with Chillington PN D 332. *Simon de Wahull* is mentioned 1216 Cl in connection with land here, and John *Belet* 1242–3 Fees in connection with land in the nearby parish of Swinbrook.

Shippenhull, the name of a manor in Chadlington, has scipen, 'cattle-shed,' as first element, and hyll as second. It appears as (manor of) *Shuppenhull* 1346 Ipm, (manor of Chadlington called) *Shippenhull* 1362 (c. 1444) BC, *Sharpenhull* 1358 (c. 1444) BC.

CATSHAM LANE AND BRIDGE (both 6″) are *Caytisham Lane* 1551–2 *Survey*, *Catsham Bridge* 1822 O.S. The same name occurs as that of a lost place in Tackley—*C(h)attesham* 1241–64 Eynsh, *Cattesham* 1278–9 RH, *Catte(s)ham* 1328 Eynsh, *Catesham* 1539 Eynsh, cf. *Catesham brigge* 1442–4 Eynsh, *Catsham* or *Catsome Leys* c. 1840 *TA*—and there is a *Catsham Way* 1679 Blo in Middleton Stoney, probably leading to the place in Tackley. There is also a *Cattesham meadow* 1551–2 *Survey*, in Shipton under Wychwood. 'River meadow frequented by cats,' *v.* hamm.

BARLEY HILL, BROOKEND, GREENEND and MILLEND are so named 1825 *EnclA*. BLAYTHORNE HO, OLD DOWNS FM and GREENHILL COPSE (6″). Cf. *Bleythorn, The Down, Down Fm and Quarter* and *The Green Hill* 1825 *EnclA*. CHADLINGTON DOWNS FM (6″) is *Chadlington down Farm* 1822 O.S. UPPER AND LOWER COURT FMS (latter 6″). Cf. *Overcourt Ground and Coppice, Lower Court Homestead* 1825 *EnclA* (*v.* courte). CROSS'S LANE (6″) is *Crosses Lane* 1825

EnclA: *Cross's Homestead and Barn* are also mentioned. EASTEND and WESTEND (latter 6″). Cf. *in campo del Est et...in campo del West* 1264–8 Eynsh. The former is *Estend* 1316 FA. KNOLLBURY CAMP, a rectangular earthwork (VCH O II, 317–18), probably contains OE *cnoll*, 'knoll,' and burh, 'fort.'

FIELD-NAMES

(*a*) In 1825 (*EnclA*) The Angle or Turn, Ashcroft Road and Furlong, Ashmore Side, Great Bandlands (*v.* bēan: *Bandlands* for earlier *Banlond*' occurs in Cassington), Banks Quarter, Berry Hills or Berryhill, Betweenways Furlong, Blackman Brakes Quarter, Blackthorn, Bowldown Smith's, The Bratch (*v.* breche), Bridge Meadow Furlong, Broadham Meadow, Broadham Nap Furlong (*v.* hamm), Broadslade Quarter (*v.* slæd), Buds Close (*bud* is a dialect term for a yearling calf), Burman Hill Furlong, Burnt Ground, Burrow Ash Furlong, Butt Furlong (*v.* butts), Cannons Breach (so named 1701–2 *Bodl*, *v.* breche), Cannon Grave Furlong, Castle Furlong, Chantry Piece, The Chauntry (*v.* church), Upper and Lower Churchway Furlong, Cockcroft Stone Quarter, Coll(e)y Coppice, Common Close, Cordwell, Cordwell Bottom (this is probably connected with the name Cordialwellhead which appears in the field-names of the adjoining parish of Churchill), Costive Piece and Banks, Costiff, The Cow Pasture, Crab-tree Hill, The Crofts, Crooked Oak Furlong, Diamond Acre, Ditched Piece, Dog Furlong, Easy Furlong, Fawdry Piece, Fernymoor, Fish Pool Slade Furlong (*v.* slæd), Fletchery Headge, Ford Meadow, Forest Pond, Gardens Quarter, Gilton Piece, Gorfen Furlong (this might be a cognate of OE *gyrwefenn*, *v.* 242), Grassey Close, Green Benches Quarter (*v.* bench), Green Furlong, Green Hedge Meer, Great Greenslade (*v.* slæd), Greenway Furlong, Gulliver's Quarry Furlong, Holborn Lane, South Horn Slade, Hornwood, Horse Bridge and Close, Hovel Ground, Kingswell Close(s), Lady Croft Meadow, Lady Mead (*v.* Lady), Lamas Close (*v.* Lammas), Lice-hill, Limekiln Lane, Litch Furlong, Lockland Quarter, Loneland Hill and Piece, Long-lands, Maycroft, Mill Ham and Hill (*v.* hamm), Newfoundland Furlong and Piece (*v.* Fan), New Meadow, Nine Lays (*v.* lē(a)h), Nockway Butt, (*v.* butts), Oldhorse Hitching Furlong (*v.* hechinge), Oxhay Meadow (*v.* (ge)hæg), The Paddock, Park Furlong, Pear Tree Piece, Peas Furlong, Pebley Furlong, The Common Pen, Picked Piece (*v.* picked), Play-close Lane, Pool Ground, Prior's Side, Ratley Meadow, The Saltham, Several Close (*v.* several), Shepherd's Hill, Short Hedge, Shots-down Furlong, Shots Down Quarter, The Sidelands (*v.* sideland), The Slade (*v.* slæd), Slat Pit Furlong, Hough or Slough Pool Road, Small Gains Furlong (*v.* Fan), Smallwell Hill, Sour Furlong (*v.* sūr), Southorne Slade Furlong (*v.* slæd), The Springs, Squires Brush, Standal(l)'s Pit Furlong (the first word might be stān-gedelf), Stone Stile, Swiftwater Furlong, Thorn Close, Tower Furlong, Town Furlong, Turbridge Leys, The Valley, Wakeston Furlong, Walnut Tree Piece, Water Furrows, Well Close, Upper and Lower Wheat Close, White-wall, White Hill Furlong, Long Woren Furlongs.

(b) In 1551–2 (*Survey*) (*close called*) *Seynt Jones at cross*. In 1264–8 (Eynsh) *Lintone* (v. lin, tūn), *Wlgaresham* (also c. 1180–97 Eynsh, '*Wulfgār*'s hamm').

4. Chastleton

CHASTLETON

Ceastelton '777' (12th) BCS 222

Cestitone 1086 DB

Chestelton' c. 1100 (late 12th) EHR xlviii, *Chestylton* 1397 Os, *Chestelton* 1509–10 Os

Cestretona 1129–33 OxonCh *et passim* with variant spellings *Cestreton*', *Cestreton(e)* to 1320 Os, *Cestretona in Hennemers* 1276 Os, *Cestreton in Hennemersh* 1320 Ch

Cestrenet' 1143 OxonCh, *Cestrent*' 1143–7 OxonCh

Chestertone c. 1180 (c. 1280) Os, 1321 Eynsh, *Cestertona Bardulfi* 1206–21 Os, *Cestertone in Hennemerhs* c. 1208 Os, *Cestertona* c. 1245 AD (p), *Cesterton*' 1246–7 *Ass*

Ceteltun' 1220 Fees

Chastelton 1286 FF, 1349 Ipm, 1355 Ch, 1428 FA, *Chastellone Bardulf* 1329 Eynsh, *Chastilton* 1509–10 Os, *Chastleton* 1589 AD

Chestertona 1315 Os, *Chestertone* 1328 Eynsh, *Chesterton* 1389 Os, 1428 FA

Chastertone 1341 Cl (p)

Casterton 1346 FA

Chestlington 1568 AD

'tūn by the prehistoric camp.' The first element is OE *ceastel*, for which v. Holthausen. There is a prehistoric camp in the vicinity[1], and the forms show a considerable amount of confusion with ceaster. *Bardulf* from *Bardulfus f. Rogeri* (probably a second cousin of the first Henry d'Oilli), who held Chastleton 1160–91, and his descendants, two of whom had the same name. Henmarsh (Gl) means 'marsh frequented by wild birds.'

BROOKEND HO etc. take name from *Brokende* 1316 FA *et freq* to 1406 Eynsh. v. brōc, ende.

HARCOMB FM (not on map) is called *Wyton*'s 18th DickinsC. Miss Dickins says there is still a field called Wyton's Harcomb (*Wyton Harcombs* c. 1840 *TA*) on the farm. For the modern name, cf. *Harckum, Harckum Gate* 1597 DickinsC, *Harkum* 1608 DickinsC. HARCOMB WOOD (6″) is in Gl. Second element probably cumb. The

[1] See Hawkes, pp. 75–6.

forms are too late for definite etymology of the first element, but 'boundary valley' is likely, *v.* hār. The Wood is on the county boundary. hara, 'hare,' is formally possible.

DURHAM'S FM (6″) takes name from the family of Nathan *Durham*, who occupied a house called *Simmond's* in 1789 (DickinsC). Miss Dickins says there is still a Symonds Meadow on Durham's Fm and it is mentioned c. 1840 *TA*. HOGG'S BARN (6″) takes name from the family of William and Henry *Hogges* 1363 Eynsh.

CHASTLETON BARROW and COWLEY'S COPSE (6″). Cf. *Barrow ground* and *Cowleys grounds* c. 1840 *TA*. FOUR SHIRE STONE is *Fourshire stone* c. 1840 *TA*: the shires are O, Gl, Wa and Wo: *v.* PN Wa 303 for an earlier form. GROVE FM is so named c. 1840 *TA*. HILL FM, CHASTLETON HILL. Cf. Johannes de la *Hulle* 1363 Eynsh: Chastleton Hill is so named 1596 DickinsC. KITEBROOK HO. Cf. *Kyghteboroughe leyes* 1596 DickinsC: *Kiteborough* and *Kitebrook* are both mentioned c. 1840 *TA*. STUPHILL COVERT (6″). Cf. *Stupple* 1596 DickinsC, *Stuphill coppice* c. 1840 *TA*.

FIELD-NAMES[1]

(*a*) In c. 1840 (*TA*) Burnt Hill, Catsram close (cf. *Cats Close* c. 1798), Coney gree coppice (cf. *Great Conygree* 1597, *v.* conygree), Ducksnest meadow (so named 1596), Fatting ground, Green sands (cf. *the Sands* 1596, c. 1789), Broad Hades (*v.* hades), Hale Meadow, Overhale (*v.* h(e)alh), Hand Brake, The Holt ('wood'), Hounsells (*Hundeshulle* c. 1180 (c. 1280) Os, '*Hund*'s hill'), The Knowle (*the Knowl* 18th), Lady's ground (*v.* Lady), Lay ground (*v.* lē(a)h), Langate (*v.* lanket), Motley hays (*Motley Hades* c. 1798, *v.* hades), The Moors (cf. *Blakemor* c. 1180 (c. 1280) Os, 'black marsh,' *v.* mōr), Pickett ground (*v.* picked), Plock at Church, Rug piece (*v.* 376), Sally bed ('willow plantation'), The Slad (cf. *Heremoneslede* c. 1200 Os, *Bowslade, Hillslade, Longslade* 1596, *v.* slæd; the c. 1200 name has the personal name *Hereman* as first element), Home and Hillocky splats, Near and far splatts (*the Splatts* 1596, 1667, *the Home Splatts, Hillocky Splatts, Splatts lane* 18th, *splat* is a dialect term for 'a piece of ground'), Sweet Piece (*v.* sūr), Long and Furzy white hill (*Whitehill* 1596), Green and Ploughed Winshills (*Wynshill leyes* 1596, *Winshill* 1667, probably identical with Winshill St, which means '*Wine*'s hill').

(*b*) In 1596 *Allmescote meadow, the Coombes* (*v.* cumb), *Rysum* (probably the dative plural of *hrīs*, 'brushwood'), *Woolland* (*v.* wōh). In c. 1240 (Os) *Smaleweye* ('narrow way,' *v.* smæl, weg). In c. 1200 (Os) *la Siede*. In c. 1180 (c. 1280) (Os) *Rugge* (*v.* hrycg).

---

[1] Except where otherwise stated, the forms are from DickinsC.

5. Churchill

CHURCHILL

Cercelle 1086 DB *et passim* with variant spellings *Cercell(a)*, *Cercell'*, *Cerchil*, *Cerchull(a)* to c. 1220–30 (c. 1425) Frid, *Cerzhulla* 1168 P, *Cerceill'* 1220 Cl, *Cershull'* 1235–6 Fees, *Sercellis* 1246–7 *Ass*, *Cerccell* 1346 FA

Langechurchehull' 1140–1 (c. 1425) Frid, *Churchehull'* c. 1170–80 (c. 1425) Frid *et freq* with variant spellings *Churchehull, Churche-hill(e)* to 1480 Frid, *Churchull* c. 1195 (c. 1425) Frid *et freq* with variant *Churchulle* to 1385 Cl, *Churechehulle* 1284 FF, *Churchill* 1537 Frid

Lankechirchilla 1140–1 (c. 1320) Frid, *Chirchehull'* c. 1170–80 (c. 1425) Frid *et freq* with variant spellings *Chirchehull(e)*, *Chirchehill(e)* to 1375 Frid, *Chirchell'* c. 1195 (c. 1425) Frid *et freq* with variant spellings *Chirchella, Chirchull(e), Chirchille* to 1378 Cl

Chirhull (bis) c. 1195 (c. 1425) Frid

Cherchell' 1199 Ch *et freq* with variant spellings *Cherchull'*, *Cherchull(e)* to 1298 Ipm, *Chercelle* 1199 (c. 1320) Frid, *Cherche-hulle* 1247 FF *et freq* with variant spellings *Cherchehelle, Cherche-hill, Cherchehull* to 1387 Cl, *Chershull'* 1268 *Ass*, *Cherchenhulle* 1285 *Ass*

Churhull 1241 (c. 1425) Frid, *Churehull* 1366 Ch, *Churhell* (bis) 1372 (c. 1425) Frid

Certell 1278–9 RH, *Certelle* (bis), *Certel(e)* 1285 *Ass*

Chirkenhulle 1307 Winchcombe (p)

CHURCHILL MILL (6″) is *Melle of Churchehull* 1336 Cl (p), *Churchill Mill* 1788 *EnclA*.

v. PN Wo 106–9. In this village the old church was not on the hill, but there is a round barrow which is practically on top of it. 'Hill with a tumulus,' from British *crouco- and OE hyll, would be a suitable etymology, but can only be accepted on the assumption that there is very early confusion of the first element with OE cirice, 'church.' *Lange-, Lanke-* means 'long.'

STANDBOW BRIDGE (6″) is so named 1778 *EnclA*. Cf. *Stanboge* 1210 Cur, *Standbawham* t. Hy 8 *Valor*, *Stande Bawham* 1551–2 *Survey*. This is OE *stān-boga*, 'stone arch,' which occurs in *Beowulf*, ll. 2545 and 2718, and survives as Stonebow, the name of one of the gates of Lincoln. hamm has been added to two of the forms.

BESBURY LANE (6″), CONDUIT FM (6″) and CHURCHILL HEATH FM AND WOOD. Cf. *Bes(s)barrow Way Furlong, The Conduit* and *Heath Way Common* late 18th HistChurch, and *Churchill Heath* 1788 *EnclA*. THE GRANGE (6″) and RYNEHILL FM. Cf. *Grange Grounds* and *Rynehill* 1788 *EnclA*. THE MOUNT is so named late 18th HistChurch. SARSGROVE FM AND WOOD (latter mostly in Sarsden) are so named 1788 *EnclA*. SWAILSFORD BRIDGE (6″) is *Swailesford Bridge* 1788 *EnclA*.

FIELD-NAMES

(a) In 1934 (HistChurch) Dovehouse close (so named 1788 *EnclA*), Lamp-acre (*v.* church), Ox-leaze, Saintfoin ground. In c. 1840 (*TA*) Fitchet Moor, Fiddixmoor, Fidexmoor (*Fiddicks Moor or Fiddixmoor Quarter* late 18th HistChurch). In 1788 (*EnclA*) Ash Close, Great and Little Backslade (*v.* slæd), Beggars Lane, Broad Mead and Close, Brookleys, Burhill Meadow, Chapel Close (*the Chappell close* t. Hy 8 *Valor, Chaple close* 1608–9 *Survey*), Churchstreet, North Claypits Furlong, Constables Ley, Cordialwellhead, Cotfield, Flood Leys, Ham Close and Bridge, The Hams (*v.* hamm), The Hays, Hay Bridge, Wither Hays (*v.* (ge)hæg), Hencroft Field, Hockley Close, Home Street, The Lawn or Home Ground, London Road, Little London (*v.* Fan), Madplots Close (*v.* mæd), Nethill Grounds, Newbridge Furlong, New Farm, New Ground, Furzey and Rushey Norhill, Bruern or Nothill Lane, The Park, The Pasture, Pickshill (*The Pick Hill* late 18th HistChurch, *v.* picked), Poolwalks (possibly identical with *le Pollakk, la Pollak* 1253–4 (c. 1425) Frid, *v.* lacu, first element 'pool'), Quarhill Field (*v.* quar), Raghay, Ramwell Field, The Roundabout (*v.* Des), Ryfen Piece (possibly identical with *Refham* c. 1210, c. 1217 (both c. 1425) Frid, *v.* refham), Shills, Shillsfield, Upper Shurborn, Lower Sherbourn, Shuttenham Gate and Meadow and Bridge (*Shyttenham* 1299 Cl, '*Scytta*'s hamm'; the personal name is only found in place-names), Stork Bridge, The Sturts (*v.* steort), Town Furlong and Butts (*v.* butts), William Meadow, Woodside Field, Woodside Hill Field. In 1782 (HistChurch) *Dogkennel ground.* In late 18th (HistChurch, from various sources) Apple-Pye Butts (*apple-pie* is used in dialect for various plants), Ashen Thorns, Ash Slade (*v.* slæd), Beanhill, Little and Great Bedminster, Besdown Slade (*v.* slæd), Bickwell, Briar Slade (*v.* slæd), Broad Corner, Brook Furlong, Budd's Hedge, Bull Plot, Burnhill Wood, Butt Furlong (*v.* butts), Casenham Pool Furlong, Catsbraine (*v.* catsbrain), Challenge Moor (*Challenge* is used of land of which the ownership has been disputed), Chirls Furlong, Clay Ground, The Cleves (*v.* clif), Clump Ground, Coney Furlong, Cot Mead, Cowpen, Croakham Way, Crookhorn Way or Swan's Nest, Crooked Elbow, Dirty Headlands, Dirtymeere, Small Doles (*v.* dole), The Down, Five Bushes Furlong, Lower and Upper Football, Fullwell, Glebe Piece, Goose Acre, Grass Furlong, Grey Goose Leys, Grove

Way, Great Gutter Furlong, Hensdon(e) Quarter, High Thorn, Holland's Moore Furlong, Hollowback Furlong, Lower and Upper Hoping Hill (*v.* Hopping Close in Mapledurham 61–2), Jone's Stone Bushes, Kernal Pit Furlong, Hither and Further Kidmoorhill, Leadwell Hill, Leazow Hedge (*v.* lǣs), Lock Furlong, Long Ends, Long Lands Furlong, Lords Corner, May-thorn Breaks, Meer Piece, Milham (*Milnhamme* 1298 Fine, *Mulleham* 1299 Cl, *v.* myln, hamm), Money Furlong, Mortar Pit Hill, Mousepit Ground, Osemoor Furlong, Second and Third Picked Furlongs (*v.* picked), Qualmstone Pieces, Redford Piece, Round Hill, Sheep Common Pasture, Shooting Piece, Shooting to Sarsbrook, Sloe Bushes, Great Sloe Marsh, Square Hide, Steersmoor, Swire Furlong and Leys (*v.* swēora), Thornhill, Varndels, Varndell Bottom, Water Furrows, Small Wergs, Highspring Wergs (the NED gives a quotation from 1707 "A Willow-Tree was Anciently call'd *Willig*; whence the Modern *Werg* (a Willow) us'd in Berkshire and some other Countreys, seems corrupted"), Wheel Leys, Whitehill, Whore's Slade (*v.* slæd), Whorewell Lake Furlong, Long and Short Woolham, Woundhill.

(*b*) In 1299 (Cl) *Bynuthe Merethornes* (first word 'beneath'; the second could mean either 'thorn trees by the pool' or 'boundary thorn trees'), (house called) *Hachus*, *Mullecroftes* (*v.* myln, croft), *Smythemers* ('smooth marsh,' *v.* smēðe). In c. 1230–40 (*Bodl*) *Huruardesberewe* ('*Heoruweard*'s hill or tumulus,' *v.* be(o)rg). In c. 1230 (*AddCh*) *Hordelpoleshulle* (*v.* hyll: the second element is 'pool' and the first looks like 'hurdle'). In c. 1220 (Frid) *Sitham* (also c. 1210 (c. 1425) Frid). In c. 1217 (c. 1425) (Frid) *Micheleslade* (*v.* mycel, slæd).

Mrs Rose (HistChurch 54) says that the village had four Lot Meads, which were divided yearly by the drawing of lots. They were evidently sub-divided into sets (the word *set* is not recorded in this sense), and each set sub-divided into ten hides. Names of sets include: *Acres set*, *Long Bezzle*, *Broken set* (this contained two lots known as *Duck* and *Drake*), *Bull Mead set*, *Double set*, *Inn Mead set* (*v.* in), *Single set*, *Way Acres set*, *Whole set*, *Over Yard Mead set*. Names of hides include: *Axtree hide*, *Blank hide*, *Dungpike hide*, *Four Notches hide*, *Ladle hide*, *Knott hide*, *R hide*. These hide names were apparently (to judge from the wording of the terrier quoted HistChurch 54) used for the sets in all the Lot Meads. Mrs Rose suggests that the names may have some relation to the actual lots that were drawn.

6. Cornbury Park

CORNBURY PARK

Corneberie 1086 DB *et passim* with variant spellings *Corneberia*, *Cornebiria*, *Corneberg'*, *Cornebyri*, *Cornebir(y)*, *Cornebiri*, *Cornebur(e)*, *Cornebery*, *Cornebyry*, *Cornebury* to 1310 Ipm

Acornebir' 1223, 38, 40 Cl, *Acorebir'* 1238 Cl

Cornbury 1301 Cl, *Cornbiri* 1307 Cl, *Cornbir(y)* 1311 Cl, *Cornbury Park* 1337 Cl

'Fort frequented by herons,' v. corn, burh, and cf. PN Wo 54 and Cornbrough PN NRY 32. There is an earthwork here. ME *parke* means 'an enclosed tract of land for keeping beasts of the chase.'

TOWER LIGHT and WITNEY LIGHT in this parish, and HAZEL LIGHT and SHAMSPIRES LIGHT on the 6″ map in Wychwood and Spelsbury, contain *light* EDD sb 6, 'a long footpath by the side of a wood.' TOWERLIGHT GATE and VISTA GATE (both 6″) are so named 1857 EnclA.

FIELD-NAMES

(a) In c. 1840 (*TA*) The Streights als. Bondmans Mead (v. Des).

(b) In 1337 (Cl) (*house called*) *Logge* (this is the ME form of *lodge*, generally at this date used of a temporary shelter). In 1300 (Wych) *Nunnechirche* ('nuns' church'), *le Puntfold de Cornbury* ('pinfold').

7. Cornwell

CORNWELL

Cornewelle 1086 DB *et passim* with variant spellings *Cornewell(a)*,
    Cornewell' to 1428 FA, *Corneuelle Punsolt* 1239 Eynsh
Cornwelle 1148–61 Eynsh *et passim* with variant spellings *Corn-
    well(a)*, *Cornwell'*
Corwelle 1151–73, 1193–1200 Eynsh, 1201 Cur
Corenwelle 1285 *Ass*
Crumwelle 1285 *Ass*

'Stream frequented by herons,' v. corn, w(i)elle. A *Craneswell furlong* appears in the Tithe Award for the neighbouring parish of Kingham. Stephen de *Pontsold* and his wife granted the church to Eynsham 1151–73 Eynsh. Cf. Cornbury, *supra*.

FIELD-NAMES[1]

(b) In 1635 *the Combe, the Combe head, Combe Brooke* (*Cumba* c. 1210 Os, *Combe brooke* 1614, 'valley,' v. cumb), *Corn(e)well Hill, the Cunnytree hedge* (*the Conygree* 1614, v. conygree), *Henhills* (*Heanhulle* c. 1210 Os, *Hen Hill* 1614, '(at the) high hill,' v. hē(a)h), *Kingham way* (*via de Kangham* c. 1210 Os, Kingham is an adjoining parish), *Meare Mead, Quarr furlonge* ('quarry furlong'), *Sharp Stone furlong* (*Sharpston* 1614), *uper Thetcham* (*over Thetcham* 1614, v. þæc-hamm), *Woodstock way*. In 1614 *Bushey furlonge, the Grove Close, the Mill Banck, the revell Mead, Stow way* (Stow is in Wo). In c. 1210 (Os) *Sunderham* ('separate hamm,' first element OE *sundor*).

---

[1] Except where otherwise stated, the forms are from *BodlT*, and are (c. 1700).

8. Enstone

ENSTONE

Henestan 1086 DB, *Hennestona* 1175 (13th) Winchcombe, *Hennestan*
1309 Winchcombe

Ennestane 1185 (13th) Winchcombe *et passim* with variant spellings
Ennestan(a), *Enestan'*, *Eneston*, *Enneston(e)*, *Ennestann'*, *Enestan'*
to 1349 Winchcombe

Anestan c. 1260 Os

Ennstan' c. 1265 RegAntiquiss (p), *Enstan* 1285 *Ass*, 1428 FA,
Enston 1381 Cl, 1428 FA

Ennaston 1284–5 FA

Eynstone 1463, 75 Dean

CHURCH ENSTONE

Churchenstane 1415 Dean, *Church Enston* 1587 AD

'*Enna*'s stone,' v. stān.

BOX WOOD (6″) is *Boxwode* 1298 Eynsh, *le Boxe* 1300 Wych, *Box(e)*
1356, 1425 Dean (p), *Boxewood* 1672 *Bodl.* v. box, wudu.

BROADSTONE PLANTATION (6″), BROADSTONEHILL

Bradestan 1194–1221 Winchcombe (p) *et freq* with variant spellings
Bradestane, *Bradeston* to 1331 Dean

Bradenestan(e) c. 1215 Winchcombe (p) *et freq* with variant
spellings *Bradeneston(e)* to 1280 Winchcombe (p), *Bradenistan*
c. 1260 Os (p), *Brademeston* 1316 FA

Bradenstan c. 1220 (13th), c. 1240 (13th) Winchcombe (both p),
Bradynstane c. 1270 Winchcombe

Second element stān. There is a monolith about half a mile away.
The first element could be either the personal name *Brada* or the
adjective brād, 'broad': the former is perhaps more probable. There
are references to a place called *Bradenhull* c. 1235 Winchcombe,
muchele Braden-hulle c. 1240 (13th) Winchcombe, and it looks as if
this name, which could mean either '*Brada*'s hill' or '(at the) broad
hill,' has coalesced with *Bradenestan(e)* to give the name of BROAD-
STONEHILL, which is found as *Broadstone-Hill* early 18th ParColl.
The names Lidstone and Enstone are composed of a personal name
and the element stān.

CHALFORD

Celford 1086 DB

Chalkford c. 1200 Dean (p) *et passim* with variant spellings *Chalcford'*, *Chalcford*, *Chalkeford*, *Chalkforde*, *Parva Chalkeford* 1285 *Ass*

Chauford' 1242–5 Fees

Chalford' 1242–3 Fees, *Overchalford*, *Netherchalford* 1400, 1450 Dean, *Lower Chalford* 1409 Dean, *Overchalford* 1412 Dean, *Nether and Overchalleford* 1415 Dean

Chalkesford 1266 FF

Chacf(f)ord c. 1300 Dean, *Chakford* 1315, 38 Dean

Calford 1450 Dean

Overschalford, *Netherschalford* 1511, 36 Dean, *Overschalkford*, *Netherschalkford* 1536 Dean

Chaford early 18th ParColl

CHALFORD OAKS (6") is *Charlford Oaks* c. 1840 *TA*.

'Chalk ford,' cf. Chalford in Aston Rowant (102). There are frequent 14th- and early 15th-century references in Dean to Lower and Upper, Nether and Over *Chalcford* and *Chalkford*.

CLEVELEY

Clivelai (ter) 1194–1221 Winchcombe *et passim* with variant spellings *Clivele(h)*, *Clivel(e)ia*, *Cliveley(a)*, *Clyveleye*, *Clivel'*, *Clivele(ye)*, *Clyvele(ya)* to 1341 Cl

Clevele 1319 Winchcombe

Clieveley 1587 AD, *Clievely* 1797 Davis

'Wood or clearing on a clif,' *v.* lē(a)h. In this name clif may mean 'river bank' or 'hill slope.'

GAGINGWELL

Gadelingwelle c. 1173 (13th) Winchcombe *et freq* with variant spelling *Gadelingwell* to c. 1280 Winchcombe, *Gadelingewelle* 1193 (13th) Winchcombe

Gudelingwell' 1207 Cur

Gedelingwell (bis) 1221–32 Winchcombe

Galdingewell 1316 FA

Gageinwell early 18th ParColl

Gogingwell 1797 Davis

Second element w(i)elle. Ekwall (DEPN) takes the first to be OE *gædeling*, 'kinsman, relative.' This word is recorded in ME, however, as a term of reproach, and later, in the 16th century, with the meaning 'wanderer, vagabond.' If it is used in one of these latter senses here, the name is similar to that of Sugarswell in Shenington (403 and PN Wa 285) and Hook Norton (354).

HOAR STONE is *le horestone* 1331 Dean, *Hoare Stone* c. 1840 *TA*. *v.* hār, stān.

LIDSTONE

> *Lidenestan* 1235 FF *et passim* with variant spellings *Lideneston*,
>   *Lydenestane, Lidenestane* to 1331 Dean
> *Lidunstan* 1285 *Ass*
> *Ledeneston* 1316 FA
> *Lydenstan* 1316 Winchcombe
> *Lidelestane* (bis), *Ledelestane* 1318 Dean
> *Lidestane* 1338, 57 Dean, *Lydestane* 1368, 75 Dean
> *Ledestane* 1357, 68, 79 Dean
> *Lidston* 1797 Davis

'*Lēodwine*'s stone.' Ekwall (DEPN) considers that this name contains the parish name Enstone with a distinguishing prefix. But there is a monolith at Lidstone, as well as one at Enstone, and another quite near to Broadstonehill. It seems reasonable, therefore, to interpret the three names separately as having only the element stān in common.

NEAT ENSTONE is *Net Enestan* 1300 Wych, *Netenestane* 1379 Dean, *Netenstane* 1413 Dean. Second element 'Enstone.' The first may be nēat, 'cattle.'

RADFORD

> *Radeford* 1086 DB *et passim* with variant spelling *Radeforde* to
>   1324 Dean
> *Rodeford* 1316 FA

The absence of *-e-* and the solitary form with *-o-* suggest that the first element is OE rād, 'riding,' rather than rēad, 'red,' as in most occurrences of the name. The meaning here may be 'ford which can be crossed on horseback.'

BAGNEEDLE BARN (6"), LEYS FM and OATHILL FM. Cf. *Bagnell house, The Leys piece* and *Oat hill* c. 1840 *TA*. CUCKOLD'S HOLT.

Cf. *Cuckoo Close, Cuckholt* c. 1840 *TA*. SHREWSBURY ARMS (6″). Miss R. M. Marshall, *Oxfordshire By-Ways* 58, speaks of this inn as the Talbot Arms. Under either name it commemorates, as she points out, the Talbots, the Catholic earls of Shrewsbury, who owned the manor of Heythrop in the 18th century.

FIELD-NAMES[1]

(a) In c. 1840 (*TA*) Abbey Close and Ground, Apple pie piece and corner (*apple-pie* is used in dialect of various plants), Batch Close (cf. *Bacheden* 1247–82, v. denu, first element *bæc*, 'stream'; Hollow Bach occurs as a modern field-name in Spelsbury), Bricknell Meadow, Brooksed, Burn Barn ground (*Burn Barn piece* 1743 MapsOx), Cane Close, Cats Brain (*Cattesbrayn* 1315 Dean, v. catsbrain), Cling Clang Lane ("so called because a gate once swung here, cling-clang on rusty hinges"[2]), Copped Lands (v. coppede), Corcrup Common, Cracknell Close, Dames ground, Dirty hock ground, Lower and Upper Dislings (*Lower and Upper Distins* 1743 MapsOx), Drift acre (v. drift), Dry Ground, Fenny Close, The Folly House and Piece (v. folly), Fulwell Corner (cf. *Foulwellingemere* c. 1278, 'boundary of the people of Fulwell,' v. -inga-, (ge)mære; Fulwell is in Spelsbury), Goody Lands, Gramham(s) hill, Greensward Moors, Hangings (cf. *Hongindelonde* c. 1280, v. hangende), Harrow Hill, Hind Jones piece and meadow, Hugh Oak (*Great and Little Ews Oaks* 1743 MapsOx), Ironmonger way piece, The Little Jew Road, Kitchen piece (v. kitchen), Knock Oak piece, Leasow Ground (v. læs), Nore Meadow, Prigborough Ground, Quakers piece (so named 1743 MapsOx), Rods Close (v. rod), Rug Piece (*The Rugg Piece* 1743 MapsOx, v. 376), Saintfoil ground (presumably a corruption of *sainfoin* or *cinquefoil*), Scaresbrook Close, Shear pen Close, Shop acre piece, Side land ground (v. sideland), Shew Barn and ground, The Slip (v. slipe), Snipe Moor, Town piece (cf. *Tunfurlong* c. 1280, *The Towne Piece* 1743 MapsOx, v. tūn), Wash Pool Hill (*Wash Poole Hill* 1743 MapsOx, v. supra 15), Water gate ground, Water lands (cf. *Waterseclede* c. 1233, v. slæd), Whinchcomb Assarts (*Winchcombe Sartes* 1608–9 *Survey*, the reference is to the monastery of Winchcomb in Gl, which had property here: v. sart), Woodford Close and Meadow (*Wodefordmede* c. 1270, *Wodeford* c. 1278, c. 1280, *Wodeford(d)eswey* c. 1300 Dean, v. wudu, ford, mæd, weg).

(b) In 1743 (MapsOx) *The Chappel Hill and Heath, Sally Bed* ('willow plantation'). In 1324 (Dean) *Northbrok* (*Norsbrocfurlong* c. 1300 Dean, *Northebroke* 1315 Dean, v. norþ, brōc). In 1315 (Dean) *Blakemixerne* ('black dunghill,' v. mixen), *Westcumbe, Cumbemede* (v. cumb, mæd), *Cutegrene* (cf. *Cutestonfurlund* c. 1300 Dean), *Drove* (v. drove), *Ederslade* (v. slæd; there is a rare word *eder*, 'ivy,' but the first element is more likely to be a poor spelling for 'elder': there is an *Alslade* mentioned in the same source, the first element of which could be a poor spelling for 'alder' or 'elder,' and an

---

[1] Except where otherwise stated, the forms are from Winchcombe.
[2] R. M. Marshall, *Oxfordshire By-Ways*, Oxford 1935, p. 66.

Ellerneden c. 1235 Winchcombe, which contains OE *ellern*, 'elder' and denu, 'valley'), *Hicheforde* (*v.* ford, the first element might be identical with that of Wychwood 386), *Merslade* (*Merstlade* c. 1300 Dean, *v.* mersc, slæd), *Newebreche fardel* (cf. *Breche* c. 1280, *v.* nīwe, breche and fēorðan dǣl). In c. 1300 (Dean) *Mannesdene* ('*Mann*'s valley,' *v.* denu). In c. 1280 *Baldeþurne* (cf. *Baldeburne* c. 1250–60, '*Bealda*'s thorn-tree and/or stream,' *v.* þyrne, burna), *Fureberewe, Oveberewe* ('in front of' and 'over the hill,' *v.* be(o)rg), *Buteresden* (*Botereden* c. 1278; second element denu, cf. Butterhill in Hook Norton 354), *Cateslade* ('cat valley,' *v.* slæd), *Estrot, Godingeslonde* (*Godesland* c. 1233; God and Goding are both recorded as personal names, second element land), *Gosemershulle* (*v.* gōs, mersc, hyll), *Grenewey* (*v.* grēne, weg), *Hardelonde* ('hard land'), *Tipperston* (cf. *Stipperstane* c. 1233, *Stepestonefurlong* c. 1278, *v.* stān), *Wodewey* (*v.* wudu, weg). In c. 1278 *Blakeputte* (cf. *Nigreputte* c. 1250–60, *v.* pytt; the earlier form has Latin *niger* for OE blæc), *Hauekhulle* (cf. *Hauekwelle* c. 1240 (13th), *v.* hyll, w(i)elle, first element 'hawk'), *Helde* ('hill slope,' *v.* h(i)elde), *Lottreden* (*Lottresden* c. 1233; the first element might be OE *loddere*, 'beggar', second element denu). In c. 1270 *le Galbare.* In 1247–82 *Bertheden* (*v.* denu), *Honebumwe.* In c. 1240 (13th) *Aswedene* (*v.* denu), *Garleford* (*v.* ford), *le grene diche* (*v.* grēne, dīc). In c. 1235 *Havedlonde* ('headland'), *Stanberewehavede* (*v.* stān, be(o)rg; final element 'head'), *Suthhwetewrþe* ('south wheat enclosure,' *v.* sūþ, hwǣte, worþ), *Þikkeþornefurlong* (*v.* þorn, first element 'thick'). In c. 1233 *Lepegeite* (*leapgate*, 'a low gate in a fence that can be leaped by deer, while keeping sheep from straying,' is found also in Lypiatt Gl and Lypiate So).

9. Fifield

FIFIELD

Fifhide 1086 DB *et passim* with variant spellings *Fifhid*(*a*), *Fifhid'*, *Fifhyd'*, *Fyfhide*, *Fyfyde*, *Fifhyde* to 1400 Cl, *Fyfhid Mirymouth* 1401–2 FA

Fifide 1241 FF *et freq* with variant spellings *Fifyde*, *Fyfyde* to 1399 Cl, *Fiffide* 1285 *Ass*

Vifhid 1282 Dean (p)

Fixhyde (bis) 1285 *Ass*

Fifede 1346 FA

Fyffehide 1428 FA

Fyfield merrymonte 1676 Plot, *Fifield Merrymouth* early 18th ParColl, *Fyfield* 1797 Davis

'Five hides,' *v.* hīd. Groups of five, of ten, and other multiples of ten hides were common, and have given rise to the various Fyfields and Fiveheads, and to such names as Tinhead W and Piddle Trenthide Do. *Merrymouth* etc. from the family which has given its name to the Merrimouth Inn.

ROUGHBOROUGH COPSE (6"). Cf. *Rowborough* c. 1840 *TA*. It is not safe to base an etymology on modern forms, but the topography gives full support to the obvious derivation, 'rough hill': *v*. rūh, be(o)rg.

MERRIMOUTH INN takes name from John *Muremonth* 1316 FA, John *Murimont* 1346 FA, John *Murimouth* 1361 Ipm. Cf. *Fifield nuper Johannis Mormount* 1428 FA.

HERBERT'S HEATH is *Herberts Heaths* c. 1840 *TA*. STARVEALL WOOD (6"). Cf. *The Ham Stamveall* c. 1840 *TA*. The last word is obviously an error for *Starveall* (*v*. Fan): the first is hamm. WARREN FM. Cf. *Fyfield Warren* 1797 Davis.

FIELD-NAMES

(*a*) In c. 1840 (*TA*) Barren Ground, Blandy Lake, Bogs Close, Crying Corner, Foxholes (*v*. fox-hole), Full Bush ground, Hanging furlong (*v*. hangende), Hen Plott (cf. *Henmede* 1538–9 *Valor*, second element mǣd, first 'wild bird'), Larksparrow Ground, The Melholds, Old Seed, Parsonage Close, Picked Ground (*v*. picked), Pikes Corner (*v*. picked), Ploughed Heines Ground, Rugged piece, Sentsfield Ground, Sidelong ground, Snow Hill, Summer Eating ground, Trooping ground, Turnpike Road piece, Twopool ground, Welcome Meadow.

(*b*) In late 12th (*Dodsworth*) *Brerforlong* (first element brǣr, 'thorn-bush, briar'), *Chalcumba* (*v*. c(e)alc, cumb), *Fifberwe* ('five hills or barrows,' *v*. be(o)rg), *Tuamberewe* (*Tuambeordhe* 1160–80 Eynsh, 'two hills or barrows,' OE (æt) twǣm be(o)rgum), *Utlongelonde* (first element ūt, 'out'), *Wichull* (*v*. wīc, hyll). In 1189 (1372) (Ch) *le Steort* (bis) (*v*. steort).

10. Fulbrook

FULBROOK

Fvlebroc 1086 DB, *Fulebroc* 1156–66 Os *et passim* with variant spellings *Fulebroch, Fulebrok(e), Fulebrok'* to 1316 FA, *Fullebroc* 1168 P *et freq* with variant spellings *Fullebroke, Fullebrok'* to 1275–6 RH

Fulbroc 1167 P, *Fulbrok* 1326 Fine *et passim*

Folebrok' 1246–7 Ass *et freq* with variant spelling *Folebrok(e)* to 1302–3 FA, *Follebrok* 1346 FA

Folbrok' 1297 CornAcc

Foulbrock 1311 AD, *Foulbrok* 1322–3 AD

Felebrok 1327–8 *Extent*

'Foul brook,' *v*. fūl, brōc.

Cobbler's Bottom (6″) takes name from (*on*) *cobban hyll* and (*on*) *cobban broc* 1059 (11th) *St Denis*. '*Cobba*'s hill and stream'; the personal name is only found in place-names.

Smalloaks Copse (6″) is *Smelnoc* 1230 P, *Smalnoke* 1271–2 *For*, *Smaleock* 1538–9 *Valor*. Probably 'at the slender oak,' v. smæl, āc.

Westhall Hill (6″) is *Westhal'* 1268 *Ass*, *Westhalle* 1300 Ch *et passim*, *West Hill* 1797 Davis. 'West h(e)alh.'

FIELD-NAMES

(*a*) In c. 1840 (*TA*) Westgrove Coppice (*West grove* 1538–9 *Valor*).

(*b*) In 1551–2 (*Survey*) le Fullbroke Hache (v. hæcc). In 1538–9 (*Valor*) *Bradley, Fardelles* (v. fēorðan dǣl), *Holvey stret, Lowsing Grove* (v. lūs), *le Ouerende, Tyldhouse* (presumably 'tiled house').

11. Hook Norton

Hook Norton

    (*æt*) *Hocneratune* c. 925 (s.a. 917) ASC A

    (*æt*) *Hocenertune* c. 1000 (s.a. 913) ASC B, c. 1070 (s.a. 913) ASC C, *Hokenertona* 1140–2 (c. 1197), 1153–4 (13th) Os, *Hokenertun'* c. 1195 *Bodl*, *Hokenertone* 1199 FF, 1203–6 (13th), 1206 Os, *Hokenertune* 1320 Ch

    (*æt*) *Hocceneretune* c. 1075 (s.a. 913) ASC D

    Hochenartone 1086 DB

    Hokenarton' c. 1100 (late 12th) EHR xlviii (p) *et passim* with variant spellings *Hokenart', Hokenartona, Hokenartune, Hokenartuna, Hokenarton(e), Hokenarthon'* to 1292 Ipm

    Hokenortona c. 1130–50, 1219–23 Os, *Hokenortone* (freq) 1285 *Ass*, 1509–10 Os, *Hokenorton* 1302–3 FA, 1509–10 Os, early 18th ParColl, *Hoke Norton* 1568 ParColl

    Hochenert' 1143, 1143–7 OxonCh, *Hochenertune* 1233–4 WellsR

    Hoc(h)anertona 1164–6 OxonCh

    Okenartona 1186–91 Os, *Okenarton'* 1246–7 *Ass*, 1263 Fine, *Okenardton* 1263 Ipm

    Hocnert' late 12th *AOMB* (p), *Hocnertone* a. 1196 Os

    Hoconortun' 1220 Fees

    Hogenartone c. 1228 Os, *Hogenerton* 1231 Cl, *Hogenarton* 1242–3 Fees, *Hogenorthon* 1251 Cl *et passim* with variant spellings *Hogenorton(e), Hoggenorton(e)* to 1476 AD, *Hogemorton'* 1275–6

RH, *Hegenortone* 1285 *Ass, Hognorton* 1305 Cl *et freq* to 1435
Ch, *Hogesnorton* 1381 Cl, *Hognotton* 1428 FA
Poke Norton 1285 *Ass*
Hook Norton early 18th ParColl
HOOK NORTON LODGE (6″) is so named 1795 *EnclA*.

Cf. Ekwall (DEPN): "The first element is clearly the genitive of
a folk-name. It may be suggested that the original name was *Hoccan
ōra,* '*Hocca*'s hill slope,' from which was formed *Hoccanēre,* 'the
people at *Hoccanōra.*' Hook Norton would then mean 'the tūn of
the people at *Hoccanōra.*'" In the appendix he mentions the name
Hokernesse, which appears c. 1260, c. 1270 Os. This is evidently the
eminence in question, the second element being *næss,* 'headland.'

The humorous corruption to Hogs Norton, recently employed by
Mr Gillie Potter, goes back at least to the 16th century, when the
village had become proverbial for rusticity and boorishness, and the
form from 1381 Cl suggests that it is a good deal earlier. E. H.
Sugden (*A Topographical Dictionary to the works of Shakespeare and
his fellow dramatists,* Manchester 1925) quotes a number of literary
examples of the joke. There was evidently a jingle about "Hogs
Norton, where pigs play on the organ."

UPPER AND LOWER BERRYFIELDS FMS (6″). Cf. *Westbury Felde* 1534
Bodl, Estbury feldes, Westbury feldes 1551–2 *Survey.* v. burh, be(o)rg:
it is impossible to say which *Berry-* represents.

BUTTER HILL is *Buterhul* 1154–63 Os, c. 1160 OxonCh, *Buterhull'*
1183–5 Os, *Buterhil* 1320 Ch. The name probably refers to the
richness of the pasture. v. butere, hyll.

HAYWAY LANE (6″). Cf. *Heiweies furlung* c. 1220–30 *Bodl.* v. hēg,
weg.

OATLEYHILL FM. Cf. *Othull'* a. 1185 (late 12th) Os, *Athelle* c. 1200–5
Os, *Otehulle* c. 1230 Os, *Othulle* c. 1270 Os. First element āte, 'oats.'
Second element hyll, which has been corrupted to *-ley,* the modern
word 'hill' being added afterwards.

SOUTHROP (6″) is *Suthrop* 1316 FA, *Southropp* 1705 *Bodl.* 'South
þrop.'

SUGARSWELL FM (6″). Cf. *Shokerewellemore* c. 1260 Os, *Schokeres
Welle* c. 1270 Os, *Sugerswell or Sugarswell Quarter* 1709 Dickins, and

Theroberewes Lake c. 1230 *Bodl*. The same name occurs about five miles north in Shenington (*v.* PN Wa 285). It means 'robbers' spring or stream,' *v.* w(i)elle, the first element being OE sceācere, which appears also in the minor names of Banbury and Watlington. mōr has been added to the first form. The name which occurs c.1230 *Bodl* is evidently an alternative one, with lacu as second element, and the word *robber*, adopted from French, as the first.

COUNCIL HILL may be connected with William *Counser*, who is mentioned 1521 Os.

ARCHELL FM and HIGHWOOD FM (both 6″). Cf. *Lower and Upper Archill* and *Highwood Copse* 1774 *EnclA*. COLEMAN'S ELM BARN (6″). Cf. *Coleman's Elme* 1683 Dickins. COWPASTURE and LEYS FM. Cf. *Cowpasture Lane* and *The Ley(e)s* 1709 Dickins. CRADLE HOUSE is *Cradle Farm* 1797 Davis: cf. *Cradle Hedge* 1685 (c. 1700) *BodlT*, *v.* 410. EAST END (6″). Cf. *Easte ende* and *westende* 1590 *Bodl*. FANT HILL and ROUND HILL (both 6″) are so named 1718 Dickins. The name Fant Hill occurs again about five miles away in Brailes (PN Wa 278) with a form from 1608. Cf. also *Fantwell* and *Fant close*, 1551–2 in Shipton under Wychwood, and possibly Fant Ho, Upper Fant PN K 141, with a form from 1782. Fanville Head Fm, less than a mile from the O Fant Hill, may earlier have been Fantwell Head Fm. It is Fanbullhead Fm on the 6″ map. No etymology can be suggested. GIBRALTAR FM (6″): *v.* Fan. MANOR FM is *Lampits Farm* 1797 Davis, cf. *Lampets Hedge* 1795 *EnclA*, 'loam pits.' THE MOORS (6″) are so named 1709 Dickins. NILL FM. Cf. *Nill* 1706, 18 Dickins. The farm appears from the O.S. map to be on a hill, and the name may be OE **cnyll*, 'hill': *v.* PN Sx 169, or from ME *atten hille*, 'at the hill.'

FIELD-NAMES

(*a*) In 1928 (Dickins) Bakehouse Hill, Bells Tewer (this is said in Dickins to be a passage by the Bell Inn; the word *tewer*, 'a narrow passage,' is given in EDD as used in Wa, O and Gl), Betty Croft, Braile way (*viam de Brayles* c. 1190 (c. 1280) S, *Braylesweye* c. 1270 Os, named from Brailes in Wa), Brown Meadow (*Browne mead* 1672–3 *Bodl*), Clay Bank, Cownham (*Cuham* 1219–23 Os, *Cownum* 1685 (c. 1700) *BodlT*, 'cows' hamm'), Cross Bank, The Dovehouse Close, Garrett Lane (*Gurrett Lane* 1774 *EnclA*, it is said in Dickins to be named from a 16th-century house known as 'the Garrett'), Flexhill (*Flexhulle* c. 1260 Os, *v.* fleax, hyll), The Marsh Farm (*Mershe* c. 1260 Os, *The Marsh* 1739 Dickins, *v.* mersc), Maydenberrow (*Maydene-*

berewe c. 1270 Os: *v.* PN Cu 255–6; the name probably refers to the pre-
historic camp in the north-east corner of the parish, but the second element
is apparently be(o)rg: the more usual name is 'maidens' burh' or 'fortress'),
Mobbs Lane (cf. *Mobbs Close* 1765 Dickins), Nitting, Priest Top (cf.
Prestefeld 1153–4 (13th) Os, *Prestesfeld* 1182–5 OxonCh, 1320 Ch, *Prestless,
Prestlese, Prestfeld(e)* 1509–10 Os, *Pitfield or Preistfield* 1672–3 Bodl, *v.*
prēost; second elements feld and lǣs), Ramthorne, Great and Little Rydon
(*Ruydone* c. 1260 Os, *v.* ryge, dūn), Sheering Close (*Shearing or Sheering Close*
1774 *EnclA*), Staplehill (*Stapehulle* c. 1260 Os, *Stapenhulle* c. 1270 Os,
Stapele late 13th Os, *Stapen Hill* 1774 *EnclA*, '(at the) steep hill,' *v.* stēap,
hyll[1]), Tite Lane (*v.* tite), Townesend, Watery Lane. In 1808 (Dickins)
Longdon (*Langedene* c. 1260 Os, *Langdon* 1706 Dickins, *v.* lang, denu). In
1797 (Dickins) Ledwell Hill (*Ludewelle* c. 1230 Os, *Leadwell Hill* 1709
Dickins, for the stream-name *v.* 280). In 1774 (*EnclA*) Barnard Ground,
Blackmoor, Brimsbury Ground, The Butts (*v.* butts), Cats Ash Close,
Cliftons Way, Colings Piece (*Coleings peice* 1709 Dickins: cf. *Cowlaing Spring*
1795 *EnclA*, in Wigginton), Cottage Cow Common, Farm Land, Flaxland
Meadow (*Flexlond* c. 1240 Os, *Flex land* 1728 Bennett, *v.* fleax, land), Ground
Sheep Commons, Horsepools, Hovell Croft, Lamp Acre (*v.* church), Leasow
Gate (*v.* lǣs), Limekiln Gate, Linch (*v.* hlinc), Lodge Pool, North Penwell
Meadow, Redwell Hill (cf. Radwell Leys and Close in the adjoining parish
of Little Tew), Round Close, Rylands (so named 1700 *Bodl*), The Spiney.

(*b*) In 1739 (Dickins) *Meadow furlong* (also 1709 Dickins), *The Sands*
(also 1709 Dickins). In 1709 (Dickins) *Arnewell Slad* (*v.* slæd), *Chisley Leys,
Chrishill, The Greensword Ground, Keepers Close, longcutt furlong* (*v.* cut),
the Lott ground (*v.* lot), *Mill Way, The Shoules* (*v.* 179), *Wadbridge furlong*
(*Watbrech* a. 1185 (late 12th) Os, *Wadbrech* c. 1230 Os, *Watbrech, Wadbreche*
c. 1260 Os, 'breche where woad is grown'), *Whitehill, White quaris ffurlong.*
In 1692 (*Bodl*) *Overbury fields.* In 1683 (Dickins) *Grasse Ground.* In 1672–3
(*Bodl*) *Hey or Little mead.* In 1551–2 (*Survey*) *Courte place* (*v.* courte), *Ferne
Combes* (*v.* fearn, cumb), *le Orcherde close.* No date (Os) *Merewelle furlunge*
(*v.* w(i)elle; first element (ge)mǣre), *Rowenhullesdiche* (*Rivenhulle* c. 1180
(c. 1280) S: if these two spellings are to be trusted, the first element is
identical with that of Rivenhall Ess, *v.* PN Ess 295; second element hyll;
dīc has been added to one form), *Swchewirthebede* (the last part of the name
is probably a poor spelling of the common term *withy-bed*, 'willow plantation'; the first element is obscure). In late 13th (Os) *Rolhememere* ('boundary
of the people of Rollright,' *v.* hǣme, (ge)mǣre). In c. 1270 (Os) *Bottedediche*
(*Bottededich* c. 1260 Os, *v.* dīc; the first element might be a derivative in -*ede*
from the personal name *Botta*), *Forthshetere* (*v.* forthshetere), *Oldegore*
(*v.* (e)ald, gāra), *Heme Mede* (*Hememed* a. 1185 (late 12th) Os, *v.* heme),
Hertelston (*v.* stān), *Kingestroustrete* (*Kingestreu* c. 1230 Os, 'King's tree,'
to which strǣt has been added), *Lambecotestrete* ('cot(e) where lambs are
kept,' to which strǣt has been added), *Milborewes Slade* (*Mildburges slade*
c. 1260 Os, *v.* slæd; the first element is the woman's name *Mildburh*),
Rokeshulle ('rooks' hill'), *Northlongeslade* (*v.* slæd), *Smalestrete* (also c. 1260

---

[1] Cf. the same name in Goring 53.

Os, *v.* smæl, stræt), *Smethedole* (*Smededel* c. 1185 (late 12th) Os, *v.* dole;
the first element is *smēðe*, 'smooth'), *Thremthorne* ('(at the) three thorn
trees'), *Wodeweye* (*v.* wudu, weg), *Wowelonde* (*v.* wōh, land), *Wychemestrete*
('stræt of the people of Whichford,' *v.* hǣme; Whichford is about 2½ miles
west in Wa). In 1267 (Os) *Asterlongehelle* ('long hill,' to which ēasterra,
'eastern,' has been prefixed). In c. 1260 (Os) *Alueshammesfurlong* (*Aluedesham*
c. 1230 Os, possibly '*Ælfweard*'s hamm'), *Cattesbreyn* (*v.* catsbrain), *Cot-
mannesforlong* (*v.* cotman), *Doune* (*v.* dūn), *Fifburghe* ('five hills,' *v.* be(o)rg[1]),
Icheford (*v.* ford), *Sewynes dich* ('*Sǣwine*'s ditch,' *v.* dīc), *Witefelde* (*v.* hwīt,
feld), *Longe Wodefordesweye* (*v.* wudu, ford, weg), *Wolstane crofta* ('*Wulfstān*'s
croft'). In c. 1250 (Os) *Holecumbe* (*v.* holh, cumb), *Wyggelcuam* ('*Wicga*'s
barrow,' *v.* hlǣw (under hlāw)). In c. 1230 (Os) *le Scheld* (the same name
occurs in the field-names of Kidlington; this could be OE *sceld* in the sense
'shelter,' which Ekwall (DEPN) suggests for the first element of Sheldwich
K), *Siffacra*, *Stamwellehulle* (*v.* stān, w(i)elle, hyll). In 1229–32 (Os) *Parroc*
(*v.* pearroc).

12. Idbury

IDBURY

> *Ideberie* 1086 DB *et passim* with variant spellings *Idebyre, Idebire,
> Idebur', Idebury, Ydebery, Ydebury* to 1428 FA, *Iddebir* 1241
> *Ass* (p) *et freq* with variant spellings *Iddebir', Iddebur(y),
> Yddebury* to 1428 FA
>
> *Edebur'* 1268 *Ass*
>
> *Edbury* 1675 Ogilby
>
> '*Ida*'s burh.'

BOULD [bould]

> *Bolda* t. Hy 3 AD (p), *la Bold* 1278–9 RH (p), *la Bolde* c. 1300
> Winchcombe, *Labolde* 1302–3 FA (p), *Bold* early 18th ParColl
> *Folda* 1316 FA
>
> BOULD WOOD is *Bold Wood* 1797 Davis.
>
> OE (Anglian) bold, 'building.'

FOSCOT

> *Foxcote* 1086 DB *et freq* with variant spelling *Foxcot'* to early
> 18th ParColl, *Focscothe* c. 1181 Gor

Cf. PN Wo xxxix. It is most probable that such names as Foxcote,
Foxcott, Forscote, Foscott, Foscote contain OE fox-cot(e) used in
the sense 'foxes' earth.'

[1] Cf. the same name in Fifield 352.

FIELD-NAMES

(*a*) In 1932 (supplied by the Local History Committee of the Oxford Rural Community Council, from a map) America's Head or Hill, Barn Ground, Black Thorn, Little Blackwell, Bratch Ground (*v.* breche), Brick Kiln, Broad Green, The Butts (*v.* butts), Camp Ground, Church Piece, Church Sidlings (*v.* sideling), Big and Little Cow Ground, Cow Fen, Crooked Bushes, Cuckoo Pen (*v.* cuckoo pen), Cuckoo Ground, Curtiss Haig, All Cut, Far All Cut, River Cut (*v.* cut), Dean or Bean Bottom, Duck Pits, Five Ash Bank, Lower Five Ash, Garsons (*v.* gærs-tūn), Green Ground, Green Seed, Grinsid Caudle, Big Heath, Little Heath Ground, Hill Close, House Ground, Leasow (*v.* lǣs), Long Ground, Low Field, First and Middle and Far Marsh, Monkums, Oat Furlong, Large and Little Pan (*pan* is used in dialect of 'a depression in a field; a hollow in hills'), Pen Lane, Pied Piece, The Plain, Ploughed Allborough, Ripslade, Old Sainfoin Ground, Sandfoin Ground, Sharp Marsh Hill, Spruce Field, Strut Field, Swinesty, Twenty Lands, Turkey, Warboro' Bank, Lower Warboro' (this could be a name for Idbury Camp, from weard and burh, *v.* 138), Wet Foot, Whitey Corner, Yellands.

13. Kiddington with Asterleigh

KIDDINGTON

> *Chidintone* 1086 DB
> *Kidigtun* 11th Heming
> *Cudintone* 1148–61 Eynsh (p) *et passim* with variant spellings *Cudinton*(*a*), *Cudintun*', *Cudinton*', *Kudintona*, *Kudintone*, *Cudynton*, *Kudynton* to 1360 Ipm, *Nethercudinton*' 1242–3 Fees, *Norhcudinton* 1284–5 FA
> *Cudigton*', *Codinton*' 1230 P
> *Cudington*' 1230 P (p) *et freq* with variant spellings *Cudington*(*e*), *Kudington*, *Kudyngton*, *Cudyngton*(*e*) to 1428 FA, *Niþere Cudington* 1278–9 RH, *Nether Cudyngton* 1327 Cl
> *Crudynton* 1287 Ipm
> *Kedyngton* 1517 D Inc

OVER KIDDINGTON

> *Chidintone* 1086 DB
> *Soukudintona* 1231 Bract, *superiori Cudintone* 1241 FF, *Kudinton*' *superior* 1242–3 Fees, *Overe Cudynton*' 1300 Wych, *Overe Cudinton* 1302–3 FA, *Over Cudinton* 1316, 46 FA, *Over Cudynton* 1428 FA
> *Ouerkudingtona* 1232 Bract, *Uuer Cudincton* 1232 FF
> *Oueretudyntone* 1327–8 Extent

'*Cydda*'s tūn,' *v.* ingtūn.

ASTERLEIGH

Exle 1185 Templars

Esterleg' 1220 Fees *et passim* with variant spellings *Esterleia, Esterley(e), Esterl', Esterle(e), Esterlegh(e)* to 1428 FA, *Esterele* 1285 *Ass*

Asterle 1300 Wych *et freq* with variant spellings *Asterleye, Asterlegh(e), Astreleyge* 1346 FA, *Arstally Fm* 1797 Davis, *Asterley Fm* 1822 O.S.

OE ēasterra lē(a)h, 'eastern wood or clearing.'

WOOD FM. Cf. *Wodewell'* 1268 *Ass*. There is a spring marked on the 6″ map very close to the farm. *v.* wudu, w(i)elle.

ASSARTS COTTAGE (6″). Cf. *Kiddington Sartes* 1608–9 *Survey, Great Assarts, the Further Assarts* c. 1840 *TA, v.* sart: WOOD FM (6″) is called *Kiddington Assarts Farm* 1822 O.S. BALLHALL BOTTOM, BROOKLANDS COPSE, BURCHIESS COPSE, NEWMAN'S COPSE and THE ROUNDABOUT (all 6″). Cf. *Ball Hall* (a wood), *Near Brook Lands, Burchies Brake and Coppice, Newmans Coppice and Meadow* and *The Roundabout Meadow* c. 1840 *TA*: BURCHIESS COPSE is *Burgess Copse* 1822 O.S. HILL WOOD and OUT WOOD are *Hillwood* and *Outwood* 1608–9 *Survey*; for the latter name *v.* in. KINGSWOOD BRAKE (6″) is so named c. 1840 *TA*. MAISEY COPSE (6″) is *Mazey's Copse* 1822 O.S., *Maisey's Coppice* c. 1840 *TA*. WHITEHOUSE FM is so named 1822 O.S. Cf. *The White House* c. 1840 *TA*.

FIELD-NAMES

(a) In c. 1840 (*TA*) Black Bottom Wood, Bridle Downs, The One Bush Ground, The Two Bush Ground, Coppied Hill (Copped lands occurs in the neighbouring Enstone: *v.* coppede), Near and Further Dandridge, Dog Bank, First and Second Fiddle Piece (*fiddle* is used in dialect of several plants), Lower and Upper Follys Ground (*v.* folly), Freeboard (several) (*v.* freeboard), Hell Piece, Hellditch Brake, Hell Hills, The Langcott, Langcott Brake (*v.* lanket), The Lezzer, Lezzer Coppice (*v.* læs), The Lots, The Lots Coppice (*v.* lot), Moor Lake Coppice and Meadow, The Little and Great Picks, the Picked Ground, The Picked Cone Ground (*v.* picked), The Rides, The Sidelands, Sidelands Brake, The Sidelings (*v.* sideland), Stone Quarry Ground, Towns End Piece, Turnpike Roads, The Warren, The Warren Hill, Westerbury Ground, White Way Bottom, The Wilderness, Wood End, Great Oxford Yatt, Clap Yatt Piece (*v.* geat).

(b) In 1271–2 (*For*) *wood of Esterle called Pedersle* (*v.* lē(a)h, the first element might be the word *pedder*, 'pedlar,' obsolete except in dialect).

14. Kingham

KINGHAM

Caningeham 1086 DB, *Canyngesham* 1285 Eynsh
Keingaham 11th Heming, *Keingham, Keyngham* 1235–6 Fees *et passim* to 1397 Cl, *Keynkham* 1526 LS
Kaingham c. 1160 (13th) *Harl et freq* to 1251 Cl, *Caingeham* c. 1160 (13th) *Harl*, 1163 P, *Kaingeham* 1220, 1242–3 Fees
Kangham c. 1210 Os
Kengham 1254 FF *et freq* to 1377 Cl
Kehingham 1268 *Ass*
Kyngham 1285 *Ass et freq* to 1428 FA
Keygham 1346 FA

'Homestead of *Cǣga* and his people.' Identical with Keyingham PN ERY 32. *v.* -inga-, hām.

SLADE FM. Cf. *Slade Furlong* c. 1840 *TA*, *v.* slæd. WHITEQUARRY HILL is so named c. 1840 *TA*: *Red Quarry Hill* is also mentioned.

FIELD-NAMES

(a) In c. 1840 (*TA*) Apple Dumpling Butts (*v.* butts, *apple-dumplings* is a name given to the great hairy willow herb), Babden furlong, Babdens Pieces, Baborn Greensward, Balden furlong, Upper and Lower Batstead Piece, Bibury Gap furlong, Upper Birdsmore furlong, Blakeworth furlong, Breakworth, Blakeworthy, Bond furlong piece, Broadgate furlong, Broadmoor Piece, Burn Close and Butts, Bury Pen Close, Great Butt (*v.* butts), Castle Crook furlong, Lower Catsbrain furlong (*v.* catsbrain), Cheesecake Butts (*v.* butts and cf. the field-names of Shipton under Wychwood 376), Cock Crow Piece and Furlong, College Lane, Coney Grey (*v.* conygree), Court field (*v.* courte), The covered Piece, Cousen Lane, Cuckoo corner furlong, Culverpit furlong (first element 'wood pigeon'), dindry or Dendry or dinday furlong, The Dinge Bank, Dinge or Brookside Quarter, dinges (probably OE *dyncge*, 'manured land'), Disslings piece, distings (the same name occurs in Enstone 350), Dogdole Meadow, Dognell furlong (*Dognel Meadow* 1778 *EnclA*), Downs thorns furlong, Dynesham Close, Effhill furlong, Embleditch furlong, Every Years Land (*Every yeares Feild* 1679 *Bodl*; Gray (92) quotes from a book published in 1781 "extensive common fields...cropped, year after year, during a century, or perhaps centuries; without one intervening whole year's fallow. Hence they are called 'Every Year's Land'"), Fernhill Lake furlong, The Folley (*v.* folly), fordens or Ford on hill, Fox Cover, Broad Gores piece, Hailesmere furlong, Hanging piece (*v.* hangende), Hatchet furlong, Hatchets ditch (*v.* hæcc-geat), The Hay(s) (*v.* (ge)hæg), Hens Nest, Upper henslade furlong, The Hooks, Hossicks Moor and Close, Hadsicks Moor, (H)assix Moor (first element probably the plural of *hassock*, 'tuft of coarse grass'), Howell Park, How lane furlong, Huckstone furlong, Haxstone furlong, Knolesham or Knowle Hams Gate furlong, The Knowle, Lady Acre (*v.* **Lady**), Langmead or Langmeadow, Langmere Piece, Lawless Acre, lot Meadow (*v.* **lot**), Madams Close, The March, Monking Hays Piece (*Monkynges heyres* t. Hy 8 *Valor, Monkyng Leys* 1551–2 *Survey, Monking Laris* 1608–9 *Survey, Monking Hayes* 1609 *Survey*), Mount Pleasant furlong, The east odd Swarths (*v.* **swath**), Owel Piece, Parting close Piece (*v.* **parting**), Ragnell Piece, Rough hade(s) furlong (*v.* **hades**), The Running Yard Mead, Ryeworth Piece, Sharpway Furlong, Shear Butts, Great Stone furlong, Sugar Acres, Throthedge Greensward, Upper toby's Hedge furlong, Lower Tooty's Hedge furlong, Townhill Piece, Trigmire Lane (*Trikmor* c. 1217 (c. 1425) Frid, *Trigmoor Lane* 1778 *EnclA*), Uppersets (for *sets v.* the field-names of Churchill 345), Wellham or Whellam furlong, Whetstone or Wetsone furlong (*v.* 394), Withcombe Piece and Quarter, Yanthill Meadow (*The Yantals, Yantal Meadow* 1778 *EnclA*).

15. Leafield

LEAFIELD

la Feld', la Felde 1213 Cur *et freq* with variant spelling *la Feld* to 1298 Eynsh, *the Feld* 1517 D Inc, *le Feild* 1641 Wych
Aldefelde 1220–8 (13th) Sar
Felde 1220–8 (13th) Sar *et passim* with variant spellings *Feld(a)* to 1366 Ch

'The field,' *v.* **feld**: probably an open space in Wychwood Forest. The first element of the modern name is the French definite article. One of the forms from Sar apparently has (e)ald, 'old,' prefixed.

LOUGHBOROUGH (6″), LOWBARROW HO etc. take name from *Lunebur'*, *Lunebir'* 1232 Cl, *Luburg'* (ter) 1246–7 *Ass* (p), *Lovebyri* 1270 Ch, *Loveburyhurn'* 1300 Wych, *Louberes* 1551–2 *Survey, Lowbery* 1608–9 Wych, *Lowborow alias Loueburie Corner, Lowborow alias Loueburie coppice* 1641 Wych. '*Lufa*'s fort.' The *-n-* in the earliest forms should doubtless be *-u-*. The burh is the camp near Lowbarrow Ho. *-hurn'* in the 1300 form is **hyrne**, 'corner': cf. LOWBARROW CORNER (6″). Loughborough Lei appears to contain the personal name *Luhhede* and **burh** (DEPN).

STUDLEY ALLOTMENTS, COPSE (6″) take name from *Stodleye* 1300 Wych, *Studlye alias Stodlye* 1641 Wych. Cf. *Studley Copies, Stodley Serte* (*v.* **sart**) 1551–2 *Survey, Studley Coppes, gate* 1608–9 *Survey*. OE stōd-lē(a)h, 'pasture for horses.' Cf. the same name 179.

BLACK'S LANE, LEAFIELD BARROW and WITNEY ROAD (all 6"). Cf. *Blacks Close, The Barrow* and *Witney Lane* c. 1840 *TA*. THE GREEN and ROYAL OAK PUBLIC HOUSE (both 6") are so named c. 1840 *TA*; the former is *le Feild Greene* 1641 Wych. GREENWICH LANE (6") is probably *Green(a)ways Lane* c. 1840 *TA*. HATCHING LANE (6"). Cf. *Hatching Lane Gate* 1641 Wych. THE RIDING (6") is *Road called Low Barrow Riding from Hicks Hill Stile* (cf. Hick's Plantation in Asthall) *to the Green* c. 1840 *TA*, *v*. ryding. SIDE FM is so named 1822 O.S. THUMPER'S ELM (6") is so named 1857 *EnclA*.

FIELD-NAMES[1]

(a) In c. 1840 (*TA*) Ashmead (*Ashemede* 1551–2), Broad and Long Assarts (*Broade Sarte* 1608–9, *Broade and Long serte* 1678 *Bodl*, *v*. sart), Bitley Lane (*Bytley* 1551–2), Blind Lane, Burying Ground, Bushy Close Grove (*the Bushy close* 1678 *Bodl*), Chase Ground, Cinquefoil Ground, Clay Assarts (*Cleysart Corner and Hedge* 1641 Wych, *v*. sart), Colley Ground (*Colley* 1551–2), Gadley Coppice (*Gateley coppice* 1608–9, *Gadley* 1641 Wych), Gill Rose (*Childe rosens* 1551–2), Hollond Lane (*Holland Lane* 1641 Wych), Hollow Oak (*Hollow Oke* 1608–9, *Hollow Oake Close* 1641 Wych), Honeybones, Honey Lane (*v*. honey), Field of Industry (so named 1822 O.S.), Lancott (*v*. lanket), Manor Pound, Paddock, Purrance or Purrence (*Purveaunce* 1300 Wych, *Barrons, Perryans, Purrens, Porryans serte* 1551–2, *Astall Sartes als. Purrens* 1608–9, *Porrians* 1678 *Bodl*, *Purance Field* 1814 *EnclA* (*Map*), evidently the word *purveyance*[2]), The Running Close, Sandy Piece, The Scrubbs, The Slipe (*v*. slipe), Lower and Upper Sperrings, Lower and Upper Warren (*Warrens* 1551–2), Watcham Assarts (*Little Wacheham Serche* 1551–2, *Watcham Sarte* 1641 Wych, *v*. sart).

(b) In 1678 (*Bodl*) Deepewell acre. In 1608–9 Churchill (*Churchehille* 1551–2). In 1551–2 Brecheland (*v*. breche), *Brodesall, Cleyacre, Cowham* (*v*. hamm), *Pelsse padocke, le Towere felde*.

16. Lyneham

LYNEHAM

Lineham 1086 DB, 1216 Cl, *Lyneham* 1244 Cl
Linham 1137–9 Farrer, *Early Yorkshire Charters, et passim* with variant spelling *Lynham, Leynham* 1285 *Ass*

'hām or hamm where flax is grown,' *v*. lin.

---

[1] Except where otherwise stated, the forms are from *Survey*.

[2] The word is recorded in 1439 to mean the compulsory purchase of provisions for the royal household, which could be made at much less than the market price. In W. E. Tate's book *The Parish Chest* (181) there is a reference of 1625 to a piece of land which was evidently an ancient endowment to discharge parishioners of liability for such expenses: possibly this field-name means something of the kind.

MERRISCOURT FM is *Merry Court* 1797 Davis, *Merriscourt Fm* 1822 O.S. It is probably named from the family called *le Mire* 1244 Cl, 1302–3 FA, *le Myre* 1278–9 RH, 1316 FA, *le Mirye* 1310–11 (1336) FA, *le Mirie* 1346 FA, *Murie* 1361 Ipm, *Murye* 1361 Cl, *Merie* 1376 AD, *Myry* 1401–2 FA, *Mury* 1428 FA, who held land in Lyneham.

FIELD-NAMES

(*b*) no date (AD) *Poeresham* (*v.* hamm: possibly an early version of the common later names such as Poor's Allotment, for land devoted to the upkeep of the poor people of the parish, but the first element might be a surname).

17. Milton under Wychwood

MILTON UNDER WYCHWOOD

Mideltone 1086 DB *et passim* with variant spellings *Midelton(a)*,
  Mid(d)elton', *Middelton(e)*, *Middelthona*, *Middilton'*, *Midleton* to
  1393 Cl
Mitdeltona (ter) late 12th Madox
Midelinton' 1219 Fees
Milton 1390–1 AD, *Miltone* 1414–31 Eynsh

'Middle tūn.'

BUTCHERS' ARMS PUBLIC HOUSE (6″) is *Butchers Arms Inn* c. 1840 *TA.* CROW'S CASTLE HILL, LITTLE HILL, RECREATION GROUND and THE SANDS (all 6″) are so named c. 1840 *TA.* FROG LANE (6″) is *Frogglane, Frogelane* 1551–2 *Survey, Froglane* c. 1840 *TA.* HABBER GALLOWS HILL. Cf. *Upper Abber Gallows furlong, Lower Abbey Gallows furlong, Abber Gallows Butts* c. 1840 *TA.* HEATH FM. Cf. *The Heath* 1849 *EnclA.* MILTON FIELD (6″) is so named 1797 Davis. OLD QUARRIES PLANTATION (6″). Cf. *Old Quarries* c. 1840 *TA.*

FIELD-NAMES

(*a*) In 1849 (*EnclA*) Bear Stile and Furlong, Beer Furlong (*v.* bere), Black Pit Furlong, Callace Close, Common Close, Grange Stile and Gate, The Green, Hedduth Gate, Hifield Furlong, Lammas Closes (*v.* Lammas), Great Landcroft Furlong (*Landcroft* 1160–80 Eynsh, *v.* land, croft), Oats Land Furlong, Ray Meadow (*Reymedowe, Reymede* 1551–2 *Survey,* the first element might be identical with the river-name Ray, *v. supra* 9–10), Vesta Gate (possibly a poor form for Vestry Light, *v.* the field-names of Bruern: Vista Gate (346) is several miles away), Water Shore, Whitfield (*Whytfeld, Whitefeld* 1551–2 *Survey, v.* hwīt, feld). In c. 1840 (*TA*) Black Bush furlong, Bog furlong, Bow furlong, Brushy furlong, Breeches Lot (*v.* breche and lot),

Bright furlong, Bulls tail, Burnet Close, The Burnets, Barnets (*Burnetes close* 1608–9 *Survey*, possibly from OE *bærnet(t)*, 'place cleared by burning': Signet, just over two miles away, has a name with this meaning, *v.* 331), Catstail furlong and Lots (*v.* lot), Coggleston Hill, Crabtree furlong and Slad (*v.* slæd), Crane Headland, Cleaver furlong (*cleavers* is used in dialect of goose-grass, *Galium Aparine*, and of tufts of coarse grass or rushes turned up by the plough on recent grasslands), Flag Ditch Slad, Floodgate Acre, Foxhole piece furlong (*v.* fox-hole), Gilton Acre Headland, Gilton Ford (*v.* gylden), Gog furlong (*v.* gog), The Hams (*v.* hamm), Hollow Patch, Hollow Slad, Key furlong, Labouring Poors Allotment, Lays (*v.* lē(a)h), The Leas, Great and Little Ledwell Brakes, Next Well Mead Patch, Peble furlong, Pencham furlong, Pies Nest furlong ('magpie's nest'), The Pound, Sand pit Allotment, Starvington Downs furlong, Stomacher patch (cf. EDD "Stomacher-piece, an irregular, awkward shaped piece of land": *Stomacher* appears in the *TA* for Stokenchurch Bk), Thanky furlong (*v.* Fan).

(*b*) In 1551–2 (*Survey*) *Abuttes hey*, *Cankeclose* (for the place-name element *cank*, meaning apparently 'hill,' *v.* PN Wa 292–3), *Cleylandes*, *Colens lesowe* (*v.* lǣs), *le Gores* (*v.* gāra), *le Penne*, *Wellheys* (*v.* (ge)hæg). In late 12th (Madox) *Grundeles* (*v.* lǣs: the first element must be OE *grund*, 'bottom, foundation,' in some sense which is not clear), *Thegla*. In 1160–80 (Eynsh) *Athulle* ('oat hill'), *Beorcfurlonga* (*v.* be(o)rg), *Cleitlanda* ('clayey land,' first element OE *clǣgiht*), *Eordnuteslede* (first element OE *eorðnutu*, 'pig-nut,' second element *slæd*), *Fifþornesfurlunche* ('five thorn-trees furlong'), *Gerstuna* (*v.* gærs-tūn), *Pesternehulla* (*v.* hyll; the first element might be the weak genitive plural of *prēost*, which is sometimes found in place-names, in this spelling with the -*r*- in the wrong place), *Utlangafurlunga* ('long furlong,' to which *ūt*, 'out,' has been added).

18. Minster Lovell

Minster Lovell

> *Minstre* 1086 DB, 1297 Cl, 1390 Eynsh, *Minstra* 1173, 4 P, *Mynstre Magna* 1316 FA, *Magna Minstre* 1346, 1428 FA, *Minstre Lovel* 1347 Ipm, *Mynstre Lovel* 1348 Cl, 1362 Ipm, *Mynstre* 1428 FA, *Mynster Lovell* 1517 D Inc
>
> *Ministre* 1109 Eynsh *et freq* to 1371 Cl, *Ministr' Lovel* 1278–9 RH, *Mynistre* 1287 Ipm, *Ministre Lovel* 1325 Fine
>
> *Menistra* 1163 P *et freq* with variant spellings *Menistr'*, *Menistre* to 1224 FF, *Menistres* 1215 Cur
>
> *Menstra* 1197 (c. 1200) Thame, *Menstre Lovel* 1310 Ipm
>
> *Meunistre* 1216 Cl
>
> *Munstr'* 1278–9 RH (p), *Munstre* 1285 Ass, 1314 Ipm (bis), 1384 Cl, *Mangna Munstre* 1302–3 FA, *Munstre Lovel* 1341 Cl, *Munstre Lovell* 1392–3 AD, *Munstreloval* 1442 Ch
>
> *Munistre* 1285 Ass

LITTLE MINSTER

> *Minstre* 1086 DB, *Mynstre Parva* 1316 FA, *Mynstre Laundell* 1429 FA
>
> *Parva Munstre* 1242–3 Fees, 1302–3 FA, 1349 Ipm, 1429 FA, *Lutlemunstre* 1325 Cl, *Little Munstre* 1333 Ipm, *Munstre Parva* 1346 FA
>
> *Parva Menistre* 1242–3 Fees, *Menistr'* 1246–7 Ass
>
> *parva Ministr'* 1268 Ass, 1278–9 RH, *Little Ministre* 1327 Ipm
>
> *Munestr'* 1370 Eynsh
>
> *Lettlemenstre* 1324 Ipm, *Lutlemenstre* 1324–5 Ipm
>
> MINSTER WOOD is *Mynsterwood* 1551–2 *Survey*.

OE **mynster**, 'monastery.' Lovell from the family of William *Luvel* or *Lupellus*, who appears in this connection 1206 Cur. The same family name is found in Lillingstone Lovell Bk. Little Minster is called *Laundell* from the family of John *Laundell*, who appears 1429 FA. The priory of Minster Lovell was founded 1200–6 by Maud, widow of William Luvel, and was attached to the abbey of Ivry in Normandy, but there must have been a monastery, to which no reference has been found, before 1086, or at any rate a church of some importance.

BANGRY BOTTOM and TUB HOLE (both 6″). Cf. *Great and Little Bangory Hills* and *Tub Mead* c. 1840 *TA*. CHARTERVILLE ALLOTMENTS are named from the Chartist movement in the 19th century. Cf. F. G. Brabant, *Oxfordshire*, London 1906, p. 191: "In 1847 the 'National Land Company' started by the Chartist leader, Feargus O'Connor, bought here a farm of 300 acres, divided it into allotments with cottages, and set eighty-one North country mechanics to live on them. The scheme was unsuccessful." COT FM and LADYWELL POND (6″) are so named 1822 O.S. and c. 1840 *TA* respectively. MINSTER RIDING (6″). Cf. *Minster Ridings* 1822 O.S., *The Ridings* c. 1840 *TA*, *v.* **ryding**. POSTERN BOTTOM (6″) takes name from *Postern* 1822 O.S., c. 1840 *TA*. RINGWOOD FM. Cf. *Ringwood Oak* 1822 O.S.

FIELD-NAMES

(*a*) In c. 1840 (*TA*) Back Pike (*v.* **picked**), Back Ditch, Broad Mead, Burn Ground, The Causeway, Cockshoot Hill (*v.* **cockshoot**), Double Ditch Plantation, Minster Freeboard (*v.* **freeboard**), The Ham, Broad and Long Ham (*v.* **hamm**), Harbor Hill, Hedge Acre Plantation, Hunger Hill (*v.* **Fan**), Lower and Upper Land Ewes (*v.* **landew**), The Long Lankett, The Lanket,

The Lankett Plantation (*v.* lanket), Lifeless Close, The Lynch (*v.* hlinc), Monk Ham, Musele Pond, The Nap Plantation, The Paddock, Parsons Piece and Meadow, The Patch, Pig Rooting Plantation, Pike Lane (*v.* picked), Plat Field (*v.* plat), Pool Field, Pound Ground, Quarry Ground formerly Colmels Hill (the second name appears later as Colonel's Hill), The Ruins, School Room, Sheer Ash and Groves, Shyless Field, Sidegates, Great and Little Sideland (*v.* sideland), Squitch Field (*squitch* is used in this part of the country for couch-grass, *Triticum repens*), Stonepit, Sunday Close, Town Field, Long Turnwall, Warren Hill, Level and Middle and Home Warren, Wash Mead, Water Pool Lane, Water Close, Weir Mead, Great and Little Woodcock Pieces.

(*b*) In 1551–2 (*Survey*) *le Moore land, Notley medow* (cf. (*on*) *hnut clyf* 969 (12th) BCS 1230, *Nutcliua* 1197 (c. 1200) Thame, 'nut slope,' *v.* clif), *Thornbury, Whyte hege.*

19. Northmoor

NORTHMOOR

> (*to þam*) *more* 1059 (11th) *St Denis, la More* 1200 Cur *et freq* to
> 1361 Cl, *la Mora* 1203 Cur, *Mora* 1203 Cur *et freq* to 1285 *Ass*,
> *Mor'* 1242–3 Fees, *More* 1285 FF, 1301, 1347 Cl, 1416 AD,
> 1428 FA, *la Moore* 1316 FA, *La More Sancti Dijonisii* 1343
> St John
>
> *Northmore* 1367 Cl

'North marsh,' originally simply 'marsh,' *v.* mōr. *Sancti Dijonisii* from St Denis of Paris (land here is included in the grant made by Edward the Confessor to that Abbey in 1059), or from the church dedication which is to St Denis.

BABLOCK HYTHE takes name from *Babbelack* 1277 Ipm, *Babbelak* 1278–9 RH, 1361 Cl, *Babelake* 1280 Os, *Babbelake* 1291, 1368 Cl, *Bablick Hithe* 1797 Davis. '*Babba*'s stream,' *v.* lacu. Hythe seems to be a late addition of the word *hithe* derived from OE hȳþ, 'landing place,' which remained in use till the late 19th century. The ferry is referred to as *passagium de Eatona* 1212 FF (from Eaton in Berks) and as a *ferry in More* 1476 AD.

MOORTON

> *Merton'* 1207 Cur
> *Morton'* 1208 Cur, *Mortone* 1211 FF, 1285 *Ass* (p), *Moretune*,
> *Mortona* 1239 Eynsh

'tūn in swampy ground,' *v.* mōr.

RAMSEY FM takes name from *Rames'* 1203 Cur (p), *Rumesia* 1206 Cur, *Rameseia* 1206, 12 FF, 1223, 6 Bract (p), *Rameseye* 1239 Eynsh, *Ramesey* 1246–7 *Ass* (p), *Romesy* 1280 Os (p). Probably 'garlic island,' OE hramsa-(i)eg. Cf. PN Wo xl and PN Ess 346.

THE ARK WEIR (6″). Cf. *Ark Ground and Close* c. 1840 *TA*. LITTLE BLENHEIM FM (6″). Cf. *Blenheim Homestead* c. 1840 *TA*. NEW-BRIDGE MILL (6″) and NEW BRIDGE are so named 1822 O.S. and c. 1840 *TA*. PENCOTS. Cf. *Pincots* 1822 O.S., which seems, however, to be the name of Watkins Fm, while the present Pencots is called *Old Farm*. RADGNOLL FM is *Radnell Farm* 1822 O.S., *Ragnel Homestead* c. 1840 *TA*.

FIELD-NAMES

(*a*) In c. 1840 (*TA*) Achim Mead, Ashen Copse, Bull Bridge Ground, First and Lower Burnbake (*v.* bake), Charcroft mead (cf. *Chagrate or Chalcroft* 1699–1700 *Bodl*), Damasks Piece (the word *damask* appears also in the field-names of Finstock 423), Fair Ground, Frog Ham (*v.* hamm), Gainge Meadow or Gaingey Mead, Ham(s) (*v.* hamm), Handing Post Common (*v.* handing post), Hockhill, Lancot (*v.* lanket), Lot Mead (so named 1699–1700 *Bodl*, *v.* lot), Meadow Platt (*v.* plat), No mans patch, Oaken Copse, Paddocks, Parting Close (*v.* parting), Pin Hay, poors Ground, Pull Close, Rhyme Acre, Rod Eyot, Rod Ham (*v.* rod), Allotment Rollspiece, Rushney, Sainfoin Ground, Sheepbridge Ground, Spensavence, Staff (this appears as 'Staff by the Brook' in the *TA* for the neighbouring parish of Standlake), Stonebridge Ground, Walnut Tree Ground, Water Mead, Weer Ham ('hamm by the weir').

(*b*) In 1699–1700 (*Bodl*) Six Swathes (*v.* swath), *Wyre furlong* (first element probably wer). In 1689 (*Bodl*) *Cowleaze* (so named 1638 *Bodl*), *Dedwick alias Derrick* (*the Upper Common alias Dedwicke alias Derricke* 1638 *Bodl*), *Pryery close*. In 1674 (*Bodl*) *the June common*. In 1661–2 (*Bodl*) *dryhedge close, the hades* (*v.* hades). In 1367 (Cl) *Kathyngeye* (*Kadengeye* 1247 FF, final element probably (i)eg). In 1361 (Cl) *Northurst* (*v.* hyrst). In 1334 (AD) *la fenne* (*v.* fenn), *More Hill* (*v.* mōr), *Opfelde* ('higher field'), *Pykethorne* ('spiky thorn,' identical with the place-name Pickthorne in Sa, the first element being OE pīc, 'point'). In 1247 (FF) *Widewere* ('wide weir'). In 1059 (11th) (*St Denis*) (*on*) *beafolces ears* (second word 'arse,' used in place-names of a rounded hill; the first word, which might be an animal name, is not recorded anywhere else), (*on*) *ryðeraford* ('cattle ford'), (*a*) *wilstede*, (*on*) *wireneges þorn* (the first elements of both the last names are uncertain, the second elements are 'thorn' and stede, 'place').

20. Chipping Norton

CHIPPING NORTON

Nortone 1086 DB *et freq* with variant spellings *Nortunie, Nort(h)on',
Nortun', Norton(a)* to 1285 *Ass, Chepingnorthona* 1224 Bract
et passim with variant spellings *Chepingnort(h)on, Chepingnortone,
Cheping Nort(h)one, Cheping Norton, Chepingnorthton, Chepinge-
northon, Chepyng Norton, Chupyngnorton* 1302 Ipm, *Norton
Mercatoria* 1246 Ch, *Chip Norton'* 1268 *Ass, Chebyngnorton* 1297
Ipm

'North tūn with a market,' *v.* cīeping[1].

NOTE. CONYGREE TERRACE. Cf. *the Con(e)ygrees* 1770 *EnclA*, *v.* conygree.
HIGH STREET and NEW STREET are so named 1695 *Bodl* and 1770 *EnclA*
respectively. THE LEYS may be *Leys Lane* 1770 *EnclA*. WEST STREET.
Cf. *the West End* 1770 *EnclA*.

THE CLEEVES (6″). Cf. *Clyve* 1387–8 AD, *la Clyue* t. Hy 6 *Valor,
the Cleves* 1770 *EnclA*. This is a strip of land on the bank of a small
stream, and the name is another example of the word clif used of
land by the side of a river.

PRIMSDOWN FM (6″) takes name from *Prenesdone* a. 1217 (c. t. Ric 2)
AD, 1302 Ipm, t. Hy 6 *Valor, Prunesdoune* 1331–2 *Valor*. 'Prǣn's
hill,' OE *Prǣnes* dūn. *Prǣn* is found as a nickname, *v.* PN Wa 142.

CASTLE (6″). Cf. *molendino sub castello de Norton* 1268 *Ass, Castle
Ground* 1770 *EnclA*. THE COMMON. Cf. *the Great Common* 1849
EnclA. THE FOLLY (6″): *v.* folly. OLDNER HO. Cf. *the Oldner*
1701–2 *Bodl*. PRIORY FM is so named 1770 *EnclA*: it is on the site
of St John's Priory.

FIELD-NAMES

(*a*) Modern names (from Chipping Norton Secondary Modern School)
Pickett's Andy, Butcher's Andy (this name appears as The Handy, Picket
Handy Ground in a list of modern names in Spelsbury), The Deer Pens,
The Plotter's Field, The Pole Ground, Whettle (*Whittall Stile* late 18th
HistChurch). In 1770 (*EnclA*) Berry piece, Burgesses Gate, Clay Lane,
Glebe Land, The Ham (*v.* hamm), Heath Ditch, The Hide (*v.* hīd), the pest
House (*v.* pest-house), the Poors Allotment, Ragnail Close, Serpents Well,
Simmon's Homestall, Tite End (*the Tytend* 1659 *Bodl, Tyte end street* 1686
Bodl, v. tite), Watery Lane, The Wool Way.

---

[1] See F. E. Harmer, 'Chipping and Market: A Lexicographical Investigation',
in *The Early Cultures of North-West Europe*, Cambridge 1950, pp. 335–60.

(b) In 1701–2 (*Bodl*) *Drove way* (*v.* drove), *Hade acre* (*v.* hades), *Heathfield Quarter*, *Smallridge furlong*, *Whippfeild*, *Whitington bottome*. In t. Hy 6 (*Valor*) *Boysbrubbe* (*Boysrolle* 1302 Ipm, *Bosroppe* 1387–8 AD), *Dependencroft* (*Depeden* c. 1280 Winchcombe, *Depyngdene* 1387–8 AD, 'deep valley,' *v.* dēop, denu), *la Groue* (*the Grove* 1302 Ipm, *v.* grāf(a)). In 1387–8 (AD) *Sederysmille*. In 1302 (Ipm), *Hememede* (*v.* heme).

21. Over Norton

OVER NORTON

Parva Norton' 1213 Cur, *Spitulnorton'* a. 1217 (c. 1400) AD, *Norton'* 1188 P *et freq* with variant spellings *Norton*, *Northan*, *Northun*, *Northon'* to 1278–9 RH, *Caldenorton'* c. 1217–18 Ipm *et freq* with variant spellings *Colde Norton'*, *Caldenorthon'*, *Calde Norton'*, *Kaldenorton*, *Coldenort(h)on'*, *Cold(e)norton*, *Cold Norton* to t. Hy 8 *Rental*, *Ou' Norton*, *Wolde Norton'* 1268 *Ass*, *Overenorton* 1302 Ipm, *Over Norton* 1316 FA, *Overnorton* 1376 AD

Coldevuerton 1233 Cl

Kaldemorton 1237 (c. 1300) Fees

'Over north tūn,' earlier 'cold north tūn.' The various prefixes distinguish it, of course, from Chipping Norton. *Spitul-* is 'hospital.' The priory of Cold Norton was founded in the days of Robert, Bishop of Lincoln, by Avelina, the daughter of Ernulf de Hesding, lord of the manor of Norton in 1086. Bishop Robert de Chesney says that at the presentation of Avelina he has "canonically instituted the priory of the church of St John the Evangelist, the hospital house of Cold Norton, and the Church there built." The date must have been between 1148 and 1158 (VCH ii, 96). This is the only hospital in Oxfordshire mentioned in the list drawn up about 1200 by Gervase of Canterbury (*Opera*, Rolls Series, ii, 434).

CHAPEL HO and SOUTHCOOMBE are *Chaple House* and *Southcomb* 1770 *EnclA*. KITENEY COPSE (6″). Cf. *Ketney* 1616 *Bodl*. PRIORY MILL is so named 1797 Davis.

FIELD-NAMES

(a) In 1770 (*EnclA*) the Winyards (*Wynyerd* t. Hy 6 *Valor*, the term *wineyard* was replaced by *vineyard*).

22. Ramsden

RAMSDEN

Rammesden' 1246-7 *Ass*, 1278-9 RH, *Rammisden'*, *Ramesden'* 1268
Ass, *Ramesden* 1307 Ipm, 1341 Cl, *Rammesden* 1316 FA,
Ramesdem 1449 Eynsh
RAMSDEN HEATH is so named 1641 Wych.

'Wild garlic valley,' OE *hramsa*-denu. Cf. Ramsey 367.

HULWERK (only on 1″ map) is *Hulwerk'* 1300 Wych, *Ramsden Heath
als. Hulwerk* 1641 Wych. There was also a family surnamed *de la
Helworck, de Helwer'* 1250 Cl, *del Hulwerk* 1278-9 RH, which evidently
took its name from here. The name means 'earthwork on a hill,' and
its occurrence on the O.S. map is due not to the survival of the name
but to Mr O. G. S. Crawford's investigations of the earthworks
in this region, which he described in *Antiquity*, September 1930,
pp. 303-15. For another occurrence of the term, cf. "a place of
land called le Hulwerk" t. Ed I Ipm in Stoke Bruern (Nth).

BRIZE'S LODGE and RIDGE POOL (both 6″) are so named c. 1840 *TA*
and 1822 O.S. respectively. EASEWELL COPSE (6″). Cf. *woods called
Easewelle* 1608-9 *Survey*, *Easewell* 1822 O.S., *Easewell Coppice* c. 1840
TA. MOUNT SKIPPITT is *Mount Skippert* c. 1840 *TA*. Cf. Mount
Scipett Fm on the 1″ map in the parish of Bray Berks, and Mount
Skeppet on the 1″ map in Bk, about 11 miles south of Penn.

FIELD-NAMES

(*a*) In c. 1840 (*TA*) Bean Headland and Hill, The Butts (*v.* butts), Cherry
Orchard, Codling Corner (a *codling* is a kind of apple), Cold Wells, Crabtree
furlong, Upper and Lower Crack Hill Sarts (*v.* sart), Cross Acre, Fernhill
furlong, Harrow Sarts (*Harrowe serte* 1551-2 *Survey*, *v.* sart, the first element
is the agricultural implement), Horse Itchen or Itchin Furlong (*v.* hechinge),
Kilsby Garden, Lamber Leaze or Leys ('lambs' pasture'; the OE plural of
lamb was *lambru*), Public Pond, Pool Close, The Pound, Robrush Coppice
(*Rowghbarowes* 1551-2 *Survey*, *Rowbarrowes* 1608-9 *Survey*, *Robrush* 1822
O.S.; the forms are late, but the etymology is most probably 'rough barrows,'
v. rūh, be(o)rg), Saintfoin field, Saintfoin Wall furlong, New Sart (*newe serte*
1551-2 *Survey*, *v.* sart), Swillpot Field, Winter Close.

(*b*) In 1608-9 (*Survey*) *Shutley* (also 1551-2 *Survey*), *Swimpie*. In 1551-2
(*Survey*) *Cropewelle sarte* (*v.* sart), *Downe Hales* (*v.* dūn, h(e)alh), *Esthames*
(*v.* hamm), *Godefeld*, *Herwelle serte*, *Horwelle serte*, *Horolle sert* (*v.* sart),
Lucerte, *Shot(t)elake* or *Shutlake*, *Swyne pytte feld*, *Tholdefeld* (probably 'the
old field').

23. Rollright

ROLLRIGHT, GREAT AND LITTLE

Rollendri, Parva Rollandri, Rollandri maiore 1086 DB, *Parva Rolendre* (bis) 1285 *Ass*

Rollendricht 1091 (late 12th) Eynsh *et passim* with variant spellings[1] *Rollendrit(h), Rol(l)endricht, Rolendrict', Rollendrict(h), Rollendriht, Rollendritt, Rollendright, Rol(l)endrich, Rollendrid, Rolendri(s)t, Rol(l)endryght, Rollendrida, Rollendricthe, Rollendret, Rollendrythe, Rollendrizt* to 1363 Eynsh

Rolindricd' c. 1160 RegAntiquiss, *Rollindricth* 1196 P, *Rollindrith* 1213–28 Eynsh, *Rollindrithe* 1222–3 WellsR, *Magna Rollindricht* 1233–4 WellsR, *Rolindrich* 1236 (c. 1300) Fees, *Little Rollyndryght* 1341 Cl, *Rollindrith* 1358, 60 Ipm, *Rollyndrith* 1359 Ipm, *Little Rollyndrygth* 1380 Cl

Rollenrith 1197 P, *Rollenriht* 1198, 1200 P

Rollinrith 1197 P, *Rollinriht* 1197, 8, 9, 1200 P

Kollendrit 1199 Ch, *Magna Bollendr', Parva Collendrih't* 1278–9 RH, *Boulondrych Magna* 1401–2 FA

Magna Rolaunderit' 1220 Fees

Parva Rolandr' 1242–3 Fees, *magna Rollandrich* 1268 *Ass, Rollandrithe Parva* 1286 Eynsh, *Rolandrith* 1297 Cl *et freq* with variant spellings *Rolandrit, Rollandrith, Rolandriche, Rollandrithe* to 1390 Eynsh, *Parva Rolandright* 1316 FA, *Great Rolandrith* 1317 Cl, *Great Rollandryght* 1380 Jeffery, *Rollondryght* 1424–5 Jeffery

Roulandrith' (p), *Magna Roulandrith'* 1246–7 *Ass, Roulandrith* 1247 *Ass, Magna Roulandrithe* 1286 Eynsh, *Roulandriht* 1346 Ipm, *Roulandright* 1346 Cl

Rolledrich 1268 *Ass*

magna Rollebyre, Rollebure 1285 *Ass*

Great Rodlandrich 1307 Ch

Great Rollywright 1346 Ipm

Rollyngdright 1401–2 FA, *Parva Rollyngrygthe* 1414–31 Eynsh, *Rollyngrith* 1425 Jeffery

Rollundryght magna 1419 Jeffery, *1428* FA, *Rollundryht magna* 1428 FA

Roulryght 1529 Eynsh, *Greate Rowlright* 1662 Jeffery, *Rowlright* 1682 Jeffery, *Rowlright magna* 1735–6 Jeffery

---

[1] These forms are frequently prefixed or followed by *Magna* and *Parva*.

Rollwrighte 1577 AD, *Litil Rolleryght, magna Rolryght* 1517 D Inc,
　　Rolwright 1765 Jeffery, *Great, Little Rolwright* 1797 Davis
Rolle erthe t. Hy 8 *Rental*
Rowelwrighte magna alias greater Rowelwryte 1586 *Bodl*

Cf. Ekwall (DEPN): "The numerous spellings with -*a*- suggest
that the middle element is *land*. The name may contain OE *landriht*
'privileges belonging to the owner of land' (Beowulf etc.), here
synonymous with *landār* 'property.' If so, the first element is no
doubt a pers. n., e.g. *Hrolla, a short form of *Hrōþlāf* or the like.
Rollandun (*Wrollendun*) 944 BCS 795 might possibly contain this
name."

DANES BOTTOM (6″). Cf. *Debedene* c. 1180 Jeffery, *Deanhulle* c. 1300
Jeffery, *Dean quarr'* 1630 Jeffery, *Deans quarry, Deans Bottom* 1713
Jeffery. The original name is 'deep valley,' *v.* dēop, denu. Only the
second element has survived.

TYTE END (6″). Cf. *Tite close* 1662 Jeffery, and the same name in
Chipping Norton (368). *Tite* is an obsolete Gl and O word meaning
'a fountain of water; a small rivulet or rill dammed across to collect
water for family use.'

COOMBE FM. Cf. *Rolwright Coombs* 1797 Davis, *The Coombs* c. 1840
TA. ROLLRIGHT HEATH FM. Cf. *le Hethe* 1363 Eynsh, *the Heath*
1662 Jeffery, *v.* hǣþ.

FIELD-NAMES[1]

(*a*) In 1927 Crooked Hades (mentioned fairly frequently in 17th, also
known as Hall's Hades from the family owning it in 1927, *v.* hades), The
Forbury (*le forthebiri* c. 1310, *forbury* 1716, cf. PN Ess 596; this is the word
forbury recorded in EDD as used of an open space near a town wall: *forth*
sometimes appears in OE and ME words as a substitute for *fore*, 'in front
of'), Frog Lane (*Frogglane* 1662, the name occurs several times in the county),
Herd's Drift (*the Heards, Heards drift* 1662, *v.* drift), Keckshill (so named
1662), Robin Close (*Robin peese furlong, Robin peast, Robin pease* early 18th),
Shelswell (*Chelswell* 1662), the Slade (*Churchslad* 1662, *v.* slæd). In c. 1840
(*TA*) Barrow ground, Cockbills (cf. PN Wa 145: there are three examples
of Cockbill in that county, one of which has been traced back as far as 998,
and it is suggested there that the term was applied to sharp-pointed boundary
projections), Fatting Field, Five knights (this refers to the remains of a
cromlech, consisting of five stones called the Whispering Knights[2]; it is about

---

[1] Except where otherwise stated, the forms are from Jeffery.
[2] Hawkes, pp. 173–5. The stone circle is *Rolle-rich stones* 1607 Camden's
Britannia.

a quarter of a mile from the famous stone circle), The Hamm (*v.* hamm), Summer Leazons (*v.* lǣs), The Leys, Picked piece (*v.* picked), Pool Close, Great and Little Quarr piece (*v.* quar(r)), Sheep Ground, Shepherds Knowl, Spring field, The Warren, Well ground.

(*b*) In 1794 *Wain furlong and Ground* (*Waine forlonge, Longwaineborough* 1662). In 1747 *Hareslade* (*Areslade* 1170–85, *Hareslat* c. 1180, *v.* slæd; the first element is probably *hara*, 'hare'). In 1662 *Aishway, Beaneleyes, Beans hill, Droveway* (*v.* drove), *Great Hole, Grey flegg path, Greyflegge, the homer furlonge* (*v.* 453), *Lotte meadow ground* (*v.* lot), *Luckslad* (*v.* slæd), *Meadow hades furlong* (*v.* hades), *the Mith furlong, Oxfordway, picked stint furlong* (*v.* picked), *the Plower acre, priory peece, Middle Sands, Sweetmowe*. In 1363 (Eynsh) *Brodestrete, le Brodewey* (*v.* brād, strǣt, weg), *Byxemor* (*v.* byxe, mōr), *Dedelond* ('dead land'), *Flexlete* (*v.* fleax, lete), *le Hegge* (*v.* hecg), *Holeweye, Holeweyestretes* (*v.* holh, weg, strǣt), *le Hoste, le Knorre, Knorre-furlonge, Knorrespece* (this looks very much like the word *knor(re)* or *knur(re)*, first recorded c. 1400 and of uncertain origin, which means 'a hard excrescence, swelling or concretion in the flesh': here it is presumably used of a hill or tumulus), *Leyecroft* (*v.* lē(a)h, croft), *la Mereston, Merestonpeece* (*v.* stān, first element probably (ge)mǣre), *la Merse* (*v.* mersc), *le More* (*v.* mōr), *le Re(e)de* (Ekwall (DEPN) suggests that Rede in Sf represents either a collective use of *hrēod*, 'reed,' or an unrecorded *rēod*, 'clearing'), *Reemeade* (*v.* ēa, mǣd), *Saltegras(s)* (apparently 'salt grass,' though the sense of the compound is not obvious), *Shrooedole* (*v.* dole), *Luttelsladepece* (*v.* lȳtel, slæd), *Wythyhullebuttes, le Wythyhull* (*v.* wiðig, hyll, butts). In 1240 *Smokacre* (*v.* smoke). In c. 1230 (Os) *Wiþecombe* (*Withecombe* c. 1190, *v.* wiðig, cumb). In c. 1225 *Hudenhill* ('Hūda's hill'), *Pushil* ('pease hill,' cf. the parish name Pishill 84). In c. 1200 *Wintercombe* (*v.* cumb, the first element is probably 'winter'). In c. 1190–1200 (c. 1425) (Frid) *Eggemede* (*v.* mǣd; the first element is probably the personal name *Ecga*). In c. 1190 *Trembergh* ('three barrows,' *v.* be(o)rg). In 1170–85 *Berenhulle* (*v.* hyll), *Fenikfurlong* (the first element might be a shortened form of ME *fenecel*, a side-form of the word *fennell*), *Hegmeda* (*v.* mǣd), *Heilricamore* (probably 'Æþelrīc's marsh,' *v.* mōr), *Lodesled* (*v.* (ge)lād, slæd), *Patrikesfearn* ('Patrick's fern'), *Stodfold* ('horse enclosure'), *Stonstret* (*v.* stān, strǣt).

24. Salford

Salford

Saltford '777' (12th) BCS 222 *et passim* with variant spellings *Saltfor, Saltford', Saltforde* from 1220 Fees to 1428 FA

Salword, Salford 1086 DB, *Salford* c. 1100 (late 12th) EHR xlviii, 1302–3 FA, *Salford'* 1243 Cl, 1246–7 *Ass* (p), 1363 Eynsh, *Salforde* 1376 AD

Scandeford' 1208 Cur

Sanford' 1213 Cur

Samford', Sauford 1242–3 Fees
Shalteford 1285 *Ass*
Saleford 1284 FF

'Salt ford,' *v.* s(e)alt. *v.* PN Wo 7, where it is suggested that this village was on a Saltway which led from the Four Shire Stone to Chipping Norton. The nearby Rollright had salt-rights in Droitwich in 1086.

CROSS HANDS INN is *the Cross Hand* 1770 *EnclA*.

FIELD-NAMES

(a) In 1770 (*EnclA*) Fernhill (*Fernhulle, Farnhulle* 1241 FF, *v.* f(e)arn, hyll), Grass Land Ground, the Hollow Ground, Langley Hill furlong, Law Close. (From an undated map of the Rectory in the Bodleian Library) Barn Ground, Bell Piece (*v.* church), Cowpasture, Hemestal (*v.* hāmst(e)all), Home Leys (*v.* home), low Field, Mill Ground, Oxleys, Paddock, Quar Ground (*v.* quar(r)), Townsends, Turnpike Ground.

25. Sarsden

SARSDEN

Secendene 1086 DB
Sercend' c. 1130 *Bodl* (p)
Serchedene c. 1170 Madox, 1414–31 Eynsh
Cercheden c. 1173 (13th) Winchcombe (p), *Cercheden'* 1232 Cl,
  Cerchedene 1251, 4 Eynsh, 1368 Cl
Cerchesdena c. 1180 Eynsh, *Cerchesdene* 1181–97 Eynsh, 1332 Ipm,
  Cerchesden 1375 (c. 1425) Frid
Cercendone 1180–1200 (early 13th) Thame (p) *et passim* with
  variant spellings *Cercenden(n)e, Cercenden'* to 1239 Eynsh
Cerceden' (bis) 1200 Cur *et passim* with variant spellings *Cerceden(e),*
  Cercedon to 1428 FA
Carceden' 1204 Cur
Certeden' 1205 Fine (p), late 13th AD, *Certedon'* 1246–7 *Ass*,
  Certeden (bis) 1278–9 RH, *Certedone* 1285 *Ass*
Cerdene ?1236 Fees
Certesden' 1246–7 *Ass*, *Certesdene* 1285 *Ass*
Certendone 1285 *Ass*
Circ(h)esden 1375 (c. 1425) Frid
Serchesden 1375 (c. 1425) Frid, *Serchesdene* 1397 Cl
Schercheden 1398 (c. 1425) Frid

Serseden 1428 FA
Cersden 1476 AD
Saresden 1539 Eynsh
SARSDEN LODGE. Cf. *Sarsden Lodge Farm* 1788 *EnclA*.

Ekwall (DEPN) suggests that the name means 'church valley,' OE *circan denu*, and that it has been strongly modified owing to Norman influence. The forms in -*s*- he regards as due to a late change.

NO MAN'S LAND (6″). This is a common term for land on a boundary. For other occurrences in the county *v.* 460.

26. Shipton under Wychwood

SHIPTON UNDER WYCHWOOD

Sciptone 1086 DB, 1220–8 (13th) Sar, *Scipton*' 1185 RR
Sipton 1144 (c. 1215–30) RSO *et freq* with variant spellings *Siptona*, *Sipton*', *Siptone*, *Siptun*', *Sypton*(*e*) to 1235 Cl
Scipestuna 1146 (15th) Holtzmann
Septon' 1194 Cur (p), 1216 Cl
Schipton' 1195 P *et passim* with variant spellings *Schipton*(*e*), *Schypton*' to 1346 FA
Shipton 1210 (c. 1425) Frid *et passim* with variant spellings *Shipton*', *Shypton*, *Shiptone* to 1362 Cl, *Shipton under Whicchewood* 1322 Fine, *Shipton Undreweichewode* 1362 Cl
Shuptune c. 1220 (13th) Sar, *Shupton under Wichewode* 1362 Ipm, *Shupton* 1366 Ch, *Shupton under Wycchewode* 1391 AD
Scupton 1226 RSO
Skipton 1252 Cl (p)
Shepton underhuchewode 1398 Cl

'Sheep farm,' identical with Shipton on Cherwell 280. For Wychwood *v.* 386.

LANGLEY

Langeleiam 1199 (early transcript) Frid *et passim* with variant spellings *Langel*', *Langele*(*e*), *Langeleg*(*h*)', *Langeleya*, *Langelegh*(*a*), *Langeley*(*e*), *Langeleie* to 1390 Eynsh
Langlhe 1213 Cur (p)
Lankeleg' 1219 Fees
Laungel' 1246–7 *Ass*, 1278–9 RH (bis) (p)

Langleya 1268–81 Eynsh (p)
LITTLE LANGLEY (6"). Cf. *Litle Langley, Litle Langley house* 1608–9
Survey, Little Langley Gate 1641 Wych.
LANGLEY MILL (6") is *Langley Milne* 1551–2 *Survey*.

'Long wood or clearing,' *v.* lang, lē(a)h. This is a common place-
name.

NOR GROVE (6") is *Norgrove* 1551-2 *Survey, Norgrove Coppice* 1608–9
Survey. Probably 'north grove': it is north of Langley.

UFFCOT (lost) is *Hoffecote* (bis) 1197 Thame (p), *Uffecot* 1220–8
(13th) Sar. Probably '*Uffa*'s cot(e).'

DOG KENNEL LANE (6"). Cf. *Kennelle or Kennyl Hoke* 1551–2 *Survey,
Kennel Slade, Dog Kennel Slade* c. 1840 *TA. v.* hōc, slæd. RUG
SPINNEY (6"). Cf. *Rug Furlong* c. 1840 *TA. Rug Piece* occurs in
Chastleton (342) and Enstone (350). Mrs Rose (HistChurch) men-
tions the term *rug* as applied in this region to large stones[1]. SHIPTON
DOWN and DOWN'S FM (both 6"). Cf. *The Downs* c. 1840 *TA.*
SHIPTON FIELD (6") is so named 1797 Davis. WESTHEDGE SPINNEY
(6"). Cf. *West Hedge Furlong* c. 1840 *TA.*

FIELD-NAMES[2]

(*a*) In c. 1840 (*TA*) Ashbed (cf. *Asshehall* 1551–2), Upper and Lower
Barn Close (*Barnecloses* 1551–2, *Barne close* 1608–9), Black Thorn Furlong,
Bowerham, Bowerham Meadow and Oaks (*Boreham, Bo(w)ram, Bouram*
1551–2), The Braid (*Bredemore* t. Hy 8 *AugmOff, le Bredes* 1551–2, 'broad
strip of land' to which mōr has been added in one form), The Breeches (cf.
Brecheland t. Hy 8 *AugmOff, v.* breche), Brizeham (*v.* hamm), Caper Meadow
(*Capronemede* 1391 AD, *Capedmede, Cappersmede, Capermede* 1551–2, *Cop-
mede* 1608–9, *Capermede* 1609, *Copermead* 1609–10, second element mǣd:
if the earliest form is to be trusted, the first element may be an early example
of the word *capron*, recorded once in 1693 as the name of a kind of straw-
berry), Cheesecake Furlong (*cheesecake* is used of the fruit of the common
mallow, *Malva sylvestris*, and the bird's foot trefoil, *Lotus corniculatus*), Cross
Lands and Furlong, Dean Bottom Furlong (*v.* denu), Dickars or Dickens
Pit (cf. *Dykerslane* t. Hy 8 *AugmOff, Dykerlane* 1551–2, probably identical
with Dicks Lane, which appears 1849 *EnclA* in Milton under Wychwood:
there is a ME word *dyker*, 'ten,' which is apparently the source of Dicker
PN Sx 439–40, of which this may be another example, though it is not

---

[1] It is perhaps a variant of *rag*, in the sense 'large stone,' for which *v.* W. J.
Arkell, *Oxoniensia* vii, 14. Dr Arkell quotes from the Bursar's Accounts of Merton
College for 1278—"Pro magnis lapidibus qui vocantur ragghes."
[2] Except where otherwise stated, the forms are from *Survey*.

possible to suggest a meaning for the term here), Dippings, Dippys, Dip Acre (probably referring to the dipping of sheep in a liquid preparation to destroy parasites), Dogmidge, Dowell and Dowell Pend Furlong (cf. *Daywell* t. Hy 8 *AugmOff*), the Farthings (*le Fardynge* 1551–2, *the Farthinges* 1608–9 *v.* fēorðing), Fernhill Ground (*Fearnehill* 1608–9), Foredrift (*v.* drift), The Ham (*v.* hamm), Hanging Lands Furlong (*v.* hangende), Hayes Meadow (first element the plural of (ge)hæg), Lower and Upper Hen or Hon Furlong, Hidworth (*Hedworthe or Edworthe* 1551–2, second element worþ), Hoarstone Furlong (*meer-stone called Hoorestone* 1591, *Horestone* 1641 Wych, 'boundary stone,' *v.* hār), Horn Furlong, Horsebrake Furlong, Howberry Hill Furlong, Juggs Grave Hollow and Jugg's Bottom, Hither and Further Kernocks, The License, Mayseys Close (*Meyses close* 1551–2, *Mayes close* 1608–9), Farther Morton, Newland Furlong, Newpool or Nowpool Furlong, Parlour Ground, Parrots Close, Peat Pit, Picked Close and Ground, Pikes (*v.* picked), Pollard Furlong (*Pollard Hill Coppice*, *Pollardes* 1608–9, *Pollard* 1617 *Prince Charles*, a *pollard* is a tree cut back so as to produce a rounded mass of young branches; the word is first recorded in 1611), Poors Close, Queens Piece (cf. *Quyne Copies* 1551–2, *the Queen's lands* 1591 (under Ascott under Wychwood), *Queenhill* 1608–9), Rice Furlong, Scab Hill, Shepherds Bench (*v.* bench), Stock Acre and Stock Cross Furlong, Homeward Stony Gaston (last word probably gærs-tūn), Suby Moor (*Shrubbymoor* 1745 *Bodl*), Thorn Close (*Thorney close* 1551–2), Tutton Furlong, Tyses Close (*Tysez close* 1551–2), Tythesmans Plot, Watery Ground, Well Head (*Well hed(d)es* 1551–2), Widford Meadow (*Wydforde meade* 1551–2, evidently named from the nearby Widford).

(*b*) In 1551–2 *Aldebury and Aldebury fee*, *Fant close*, *Fantwell* (*v.* 355), *le Feldowne* (*v.* feld, dūn), *Hammynge Hoke* (*v.* hōc), *Kellam Hoke* (*v.* hōc), *Lamburleye* ('lambs' pasture,' *v.* lē(a)h; first element *lambru*, plural of *lamb*), *le Langell*, *Lokinges*, *Nonnes close*, *Oldeheys or Oldehay* (*v.* (ge)hæg), *Penyheye* (*v.* penny), *Petwayes*, *Quyrnalles* (*Quernhale* 1300 Wych; the elements are *cweorn*, 'mill,' and h(e)alh), *Sawsam*, *Brode Serte* (*v.* sart), *Stody Serte* (*v.* sart), *Stokeryke*, *Stowberyker*, *Sturbrigges*, *le Wyrsen*. In t. Hy 8 (*AugmOff*) *Bushamore* (*v.* mōr), *le Buttes* (*v.* butts), *Cademore* (*v.* mōr), *Coppidmore* (*v.* coppede), *Depdene* (*Dupedene* 1160–80 Eynsh, 'deep valley,' *v.* denu), *le Hay*, *Oxles* (*v.* lǣs), *Redwardmore* (*v.* mōr), *Slademore* (*v.* slæd, mōr), *Taddesworthe* (second element worþ), *Tatham*, *Wodeswardesmore* ('marsh of the wood-keeper'). In 1235 (Cl) *Oldefrith* ('old wood,' *v.* fyrhþ(e)).

27. Shorthampton or Chilson

SHORTHAMPTON

> *Scorhamton* 1227 FF
> *Sorthampton* 1232 Cl, *Sortham(p)ton'* 1242–3 Fees
> *Schormanton* 1246–7 *Ass*
> *Scorthamptone* 1262 FF, *Scorthampton'* 1268 *Ass* (p), *Scorthampton* 1278–9 RH

Shorthamtone 1291 Eynsh, *Shorthampton* 1301 Cl *et passim*
Schorthamton 1293 Ch *et freq* with variant spelling *Schorthamtone*
   to 1320 Eynsh

'Short hāmtūn.'

CHILSON

Cildestuna c. 1200 Abingdon
Childestune early 13th (13th) Miss *et passim* with variant spellings
   Childestona, Childestuna, Childeston(e), Childeston' to 1390
   Eynsh, *Childiston'* 1235–6 Fees
Chiltestune 1234–49 (13th) Miss, *Chiltesdon'* 1235–6 Fees
Chiligtone (by Cherleburghe) 1285 *Ass*
Childston 1401–2 FA

'tūn of the young nobleman,' *v.* **cild**. Chilston K has the same
origin as this name, and the common name Chilton usually represents
OE *cilda tūn*, with the genitive plural of *cild* as first element.

PUDLICOTE HO [pʌdlikʌt]

Pudelicote 1176 P (p) *et passim* with variant spellings *Pudelicota,*
   Pudelicot', Pudilikote, Pudilicote, Pudelecote to 1428 FA
Pudlicot c. 1173 (13th) Winchcombe (p), *Pudlicote* 1390 Eynsh,
   1428 FA
Pudricot' 1241 Cl
Pudelekirke 1254 Eynsh
Podelicothe 1264–8 Eynsh *et freq* with variant spellings *Podelicot(e),*
   Podelycote, Podelecote to 1346 FA
Putelicote 1278–9 RH
Podlicote 1320 Eynsh, 1368 Cl
Podelcote 1397 Cl

Probably '**Pudel*'s cot(e),' with connective **ing**. **Pudel* would be
a diminutive of *Puda*.

THORNGREEN COPSE (6"). Cf. *Thurn* 1210 (c. 1425) Frid (p), *le Turn*
1218 (c. 1425) Frid (p), *la Thurne* c. 1220–30 Frid (p), 1232 Cl (p),
la Thirne, Thirna, Thurna 1230 P (p), *Thierne* 1231 Cl, *la Thirn*
1233 Cl, *la Thurn'* 1235 Cl (p), *la Thirne* 1241–2 P. 'Thorn-bush,'
v. þyrne.

KNIGHTON'S COPSE (6") is *Knighten* 1608–9 *Survey, Knighten Coppice,*
Knighton Coppice 1641 Wych. WATERMAN'S LODGE (6") is so named
1822 O.S.

FIELD-NAMES

(a) In c. 1840 (*TA*) Lower and Upper Arbour (this could be OE eorþ-burh, 'earthwork': there is a prehistoric camp in the vicinity), Cuckoo Pen (*v.* cuckoo pen), Dovehouse Close (cf. *Dufcote close* 1551–2 *Survey*), Hither and Further Elm Hatchet (cf. *Hellmone Hatchett* 1608–9 *Survey*, the first word is obscure, for the second *v.* hæcc-geat), Glim Hill (*Glime Hill* 1825 *EnclA*, the River Glyme is several miles north), King's Meadow (*Kinges meadow* 1608–9 *Survey*), Parish Pound, Spinnage (*Spinidge* 1608–9 *Survey*), Woodstock Green (*Woodstocke grene* 1551–2 *Survey*). In 1822 (O.S.) Sweedentree Plain (a *sweeting tree* is a kind of apple-tree).

28. Spelsbury

SPELSBURY

(*æt*) *Speoles byrig* early 11th BCS 1320

Spelesberie 1086 DB *et passim* with variant spellings *Spel(l)esbury*, *Spelesberi*, *Spel(l)esbir'*, *Spel(l)esbur'*, *Spelesbure*, *Spelesbyre*, *Spellesbery* to 1428 FA, *Spelusbury* 1375 Dean, *Spellisbury* 1487 AD

Speleberi 1220 Fees, *Spelebure* 1285 *Ass*

Spelsberi 1230 Eynsh

Spillebire 1285 *Ass*

Spillesbury 1343 Ch, *Spillesbure* 1358 Cl, *Spillisburye* 1478 Dean

'*Spēol's burh.' Cf. PN Wo 61.

DEAN

Dene 1086 DB *et passim* with variant spellings *Dena*, *Den'*

Deyne 1473 (early 18th) ParColl (p)

DEAN GROVE is *Deyne Grove* 1542 Dean.

'Valley,' *v.* denu. Cf. Dean 2: "at one time the greater part of it must have been down at the bottom of the hill on which it now stands," and "fields called Town's End Hill lying well to the south of the village suggest that in the late Middle Ages Dean was still a village in a valley" (ib. 10).

DITCHLEY

Dicheleye 1208 FineR *et freq* with variant spellings *Dichelega*, *Dichele*, *Dycheleye*, *Dicheley(a)*, *Dychele(gh)* to 1551–2 *Survey*

Dichle 1251 Eynsh (p), *Dichlee* 1268–81 Eynsh (p)

Decheleye c. 1260 Os (p)
Ditchl(e)y, *Ditchlie* 1608–9 *Survey*

'lē(a)h by the ditch': the latter is obviously Grim's Ditch. *v.* dīc.

FELLEY (lost) is so named 1142–8 (bis), 1142–50 Eynsh, *Pheleleie* 1142–8 Eynsh, *Feleleye* 1271–2 *For.* Cf. *Felleyehegge* 1298 Eynsh, *Felleyeshegg'* 1300 Wych, which is near Grim's Ditch in Spelsbury. The meaning may be 'wood where fellies are cut,' from OE *felg* and lē(a)h. Cf. PN Sr 115.

FULWELL

Fulewell c. 1250–60 Winchcombe
Folewell 1278–9 RH (p), 1316 FA

'Dirty stream,' *v.* fūl, w(i)elle.

SHILCOTT WOOD is *Chilcott Wood* 1608–9 *Survey. v.* cot(e). The first element may be OE ceole, 'throat,' which seems to be used in place-names with the sense 'gully.' There is a ditch here.

TASTON

Thorstan 1278–9 RH, *Thorstane* 1316 FA
Torstone 1492 Dean
Taston 1608–9 *Survey*

Apparently '*Þor*'s stone,' *v.* stān; but it may be suspected that the first element was originally *Þunres-*, with reference to the god *Þunor*, as in *Þunresdæg*, now Thursday. The earliest example of *Thors-* as the first element of the day of the week given in NED is from Robert of Gloucester, 1297. Cf. R. M. Marshall, *Oxfordshire By-Ways*, Oxford 1935, pp. 57–8, "giant monoliths—the Hoar Stone at Enstone, near the cross-roads; the Hawk at Dean; and Thor's Stone at Taston in the south of the valley." The stone is marked on the 6″ map, but no name is given, and the corruption of the village name has obscured the connection between the two. Cf. Tusmore (216).

CHALFORD GREEN is so named 1779 *EnclA*. DEADMAN'S RIDING (6″) is *Deadman Ryding*, *Deadman Riding* 1608–9 *Survey*, *v.* ryding. DEVIL'S POOL and NEWBARN FM (both 6″) are so named 1822 O.S. DOGKENNEL WOOD. Cf. *The Dog Kennell* 1779 *EnclA*. HAWK STONE is so named 1743 MapsOx. HENLEY KNAPP is so named 1803

EnclA[1]. Inott's Clump and Laurel Wood (both 6″). Cf. *Inotts Lane* and *Laurel Hill* 1803 *EnclA*. Sheers Copse is *Shire Wood* 1822 O.S. Spelsburydown Fm. Cf. *Spilesbury Downs* 1797 Davis, *Spilsbury down Farm* 1822 O.S.

<h2 style="text-align:center">FIELD-NAMES</h2>

(a) Modern names (supplied by Miss E. Corbett) Middle and Lower Ainutt, Blaythorn, Blylands Corner, Long Brake, Briar Furlong (so named 1803 *EnclA*), Broad Mead, Bushey Close, Caterhill, Cherry Orchard, Church Furlong (*Church Furlongs* 1803 *EnclA*), Claylands (so named 1743 MapsOx), Conagee (*v.* conygree), Court Close (cf. *le Towne house and le Courte house, Courte close* 1551–2 *Survey, v.* courte), Cow Close and Pastures, Cracklands, Dam Ham, Small Darnells (*Darnwell Spayne* 1551–2 *Survey, Darnille* 1608–9 *Survey, Darnwell* might be a compound of d(i)erne, 'hidden,' and w(i)elle), Little and Top Downs (*Little Downs, Down Hill Fields and Close* 1803 *EnclA*), Elm Tree Ground, Far Piece and Side, Fern Close (*Fe(a)rn Close* 1803 *EnclA*), Furze Green and Piece, Great Ground, Greystones, The Ham (so named 1779 *EnclA, v.* hamm), Hell Ground, Hollow Ground, Hop Ground, Horsley (*Horseleys* 1803 *EnclA*), Hovel Ground, Judge Piece, The Kennels, Lame Close (possibly identical with *Lammas close* 1608–9 *Survey, v.* Lammas), Landlords Ground, Lindsay, Meadlands Close, Medlands (*Meadlands* 1779 *EnclA*), Mill Ham (*Mylne ham* 1564 *Bodl*), The Moors (cf. *Great and Little Moore* 1743 MapsOx), Mortar-pit Hill (*Mortar Pit* 1803 *EnclA*), Oak Tree Ground, Oat Hill (*Out Hill Furlong* 1803 *EnclA*), The Paddock, Paddy Land, Pedlars Close, Picked Ground, Picket Piece (cf. *The Pikes* 1803 *EnclA, v.* picked), The Pits, The Pumps Ground, Quarry Furlong, Claridge Sands, The Sands (*Little Sands, Great Sand Piece* 1743 MapsOx), Sanfoin Close (*Saintfoin Long Down Furlong* 1803 *EnclA*), Seed Ground, The Seven Acres, Shortway Furlong, Sidelands, Sid(e)lings (*Sidelong Mead* 1743 MapsOx, *Sideland Meadow* 1779 *EnclA, v.* sideland), Six Men's Mead (*Six Mans Mead* 1743 MapsOx), Six Penny Mead (*v.* penny), Lower Slade (*v.* slæd), Snappy Field, Sour Acres (*v.* sūr), The Squire's Piece, Stitchings (*v.* stiche), Stone Ground, Upper Sun Close, Tennants Ground, Townend Piece (*Town's End Furlong* 1803 *EnclA*), Wheat Close (so named 1743 MapsOx), Whitlass Close, Will Close, Wigwell (*Wigwell Closes, Field Wigwell* 1803 *EnclA*), Winter Beer (*Winter Beer Furlong* 1803 *EnclA, v.* bere; *wynter bere* is first recorded 1398 (NED) with reference to barley which stands through the winter), Wit Close, Big and Little Woodlands.

[1] This is presumably the place referred to in the doggerel verse on a wall in Ditchley House under a pair of antlers from a red deer killed by James I when the king hunted at Ditchley—
"In Henley Knap to hunt me, King James, Prince Henry found me.
Cornbury Park River to end their hunting drowned me."
v. E. Carleton Williams, *Companion into Oxfordshire* (London 1935), 52. The name Henley Knapp occurs also in Crawley (314).

(b) In 1803 (*EnclA*) *East Binn Broad Mead*, *The Common* (also 1743 MapsOx), *Costar Hill Furlong* (*v.* cot-stōw), *Culver Mead* (first element 'wood-pigeon'), *Elder Bush Furlong*, *Foxholes Wood* (*Great and Lytle Foxwelle* appear 1551–2 *Survey* in a list of coppices and *Fox Holes* appears 1743 MapsOx; in 1822 O.S. *Foxhole Wood* is the name of New Park), *Hurdle Furlong*, *Langford Orchard*, *Limekiln Lane*, *Noaks Hill*, *Pit Furlong*, *Pockett Close*, *Pool Close* (*Poole Close* 1743 MapsOx), *Redlands Furlong*, *Norton Ridings* (*v.* ryding), *Shagg Hill*, *Slat Pits*, *Town Furlong*, *Tythe Yard*, *Small Varnels or Varnils Furlong*, *Well Close*, *Whitehill Gap*, *Whittle Hedge and Gap Furlong*, *Wollands Furlong* (*v.* wōh), *Yards Way*. In 1779 (*EnclA*)[1] *Constables Plot and Piece*, *Cow Ditch Lane*, *Dean Downs*, *Manor Farm*, *Ray Meadow* (*Ray Mead* 1743 MapsOx, first element probably identical with the river-name Ray, *v. supra* 9–10, and ēa), *Upper End Close*, *Westbury Piece and Lane*. In 1743 (MapsOx) *The Benches* (*v.* bench), *Glebe*, *Greendall pitt*, *Green Thorn furlong*, *Green Way furlong*, *The plain*, *Pole Bush furlong*, *Ruarr Hill* (*Rore hill Lane*, *Rorehill* 1608–9 *Survey*), *Winter Thorn*. In 1610 (*SP*) *Sharcelles Coppice als. Sharcells wood* (for the family name *Sharshill v.* Steeple Barton 248–9). In 1608–9 (*Survey*) *Ashe Coppes*, *Bottom close sarte* (*v.* sart), *Boxden Lake* (*Boxden* 1300 Wych, 'box tree valley,' *v.* denu), *Boxwood*, *Cunditt Close* (first element 'conduit'), *Netten Wood*, *Broade Sartes*, *Sarte closes*, *Common Sartes* (*v.* sart), *The Snosson*, *Spannryding Wood*, *Spanriding Lane* (*v.* ryding: for OE *spann*, 'hand's breadth,' in place-names *v.* PN Wa 168), *Spelesbury Woodes als. Saintley*, *Wardley Wood* (cf. *Rydynge Wordeley* 1551–2 *Survey*, *v.* ryding). In 1566–7 (ChurchAcc) *Sydenowle* (*Sydnall* 1524 ChurchAcc, *Sydnoll* 1556–7 ChurchAcc). In 1551–2 (*Survey*) *Great and Little Handgrove*, *lytle Hary House*, *Pitleyton*, *Serteland* (*v.* sart).

29. Swerford

SWERFORD

Svrford 1086 DB

Suereford 1122–33 OxonCh, c. 1166 Madox, 1359 Cl, *Suer(r)eford'* 1199 Cur, *Suerefordia* 1216–17 Os

Swereford' 1194 Cur *et passim* with variant spellings *Swereford(e)* to 1428 FA

Sueresforde 1227–8 WellsR

Swerford' 1230 P (p), *Swerforde* 1290 Eynsh, *Swerford* 1328 Cl, 1349 Ipm

Swureford 1275–6 RH

Swirford (bis) 1337 Ch, 1359, 78 Cl, *Swyrford* 1337 Cl

Swyreford 1337, 46 Cl

Swarford 1494, 1587 AD, *Swarwood* 1667 St John

Swaford 1504 AD

[1] This award is for the hamlet of Dean.

Swareford 1587 AD

SWERFORD PARK is *Swerford parke* 1685 *Bodl*, *Swerford Park* 1774 *Loveday*.

'Ford by a col,' *v.* swēora.

DIGGER'S WELL (6″) is *Digeneswella* c. 1160–70 Eynsh (p). Apparently identical with Digswell PN Herts 124. '*Dicen's spring,' *v.* w(i)elle.

POMFRET CASTLE. Cf. *Pomfret Farm* 1794, 1803 *EnclA*, *Pumphery Castle* 1797 Davis. SWERFORD HEATH is *The Heath* 1803 *EnclA*.

FIELD-NAMES

(a) Modern Names (from Chipping Norton Secondary Modern School) Topper's Paradise, The Yes Field. In 1803 (*EnclA*) Ash Hill, Barbridge Furlong (cf. Carbridge Lane 1795 *EnclA* in South Newington), Beef Bush Furlong, Berrydale or Berridale, Briar Furlong, Bryce Furlong, Buck Leap Furlong (*v.* 387), Cliff Close, Coppice Ground, The Droves (*v.* drove), Frog Lake, Hawking Balk, Grunt Hole Furlong (*groundehole* ? c. 1240 (c. 1450) Godstow), Haywoods, Highway Cross, Ireland Piece, Lamas Moor (*v.* Lammas), Lays under the Heath (*v.* lē(a)h), Lyons Spinney (*v.* lain), Master Lays Ditch, Mead Furlong, Moon Slade (*v.* slæd), Out Furlong (*Owteforlong* 1506–7 *Valor*, *v.* in), Park acre and Slade, Plank Meadow (*v.* plank), Rye Furlong, Sheephouse Piece, Slate Pit Furlong, Town Meadow, Town Well, Town Furlong, Town Street, Walnut Tree Close, Close Withey (*v.* wīðig), Woodway Ford and Lays (*Wodeweye* 1268 Os, 1329 (c. 1450) Godstow, *v.* wudu, weg), Yern Hill Quarter.

30. Swinbrook and Widford

SWINBROOK

Svinbroc 1086 DB, *Suinbroc'* 1216 Cl, *Suinbroc* 1235 FF
Swinbroc 1196 FF *et passim* with variant spellings *Swinbroch*,
    Swynbroc, *Swinbrok(e)*, *Swynbrok'*, *Swynbrok(e)*, *Swynbrook*
Sunbroc 1146 (15th) Holtzmann, *Swnbroc* 1196 FF
Simbroc 1220 Fees
Swenbroc 1268 *Ass*
Swynesbroke 1273 FF, *Swynesbroc* 1278–9 RH
Swenebroc 1278–9 RH, *Swenebroke* 1285 *Ass*, *Swenebrock* 1311 AD
Swynebrok' 1278–9 RH *et freq* with variant spellings *Swynebrok(e)*,
    Swinebrok to 1351 Ipm
Swunebrok 1322–3 AD

'Pig brook,' *v.* swīn, brōc.

WIDFORD

> *Widiforde* 1086 DB
> *Wythiford'* 1232 Cl
> *Wydeford* 1279–80 AD

'Ford by the willow tree,' OE **wīðig-ford**. Cf. Widley Copse *infra*.

FAWS GROVE (6″) is (*on*) *fæste graf* 1059 (11th) *St Denis, Fasshe grove* 1551–2 *Survey, Fosgrove Coppice* 1608–9 *Survey, v.* grāf(a). The first element is OE *fæst*, 'firm, stiff, dense,' possibly used to describe a thick wood, though it is not recorded in precisely that sense.

WIDLEY COPSE is (*on*) *wiðilea* 1059 (11th) *St Denis*: OE **wīðig-lē(a)h**, 'willow wood.'

BOCKETT'S CORNER and SALTER'S CORNER (both 6″) are so named 1857 *EnclA*: for the latter *v. supra* 3. CAPP'S LODGE (6″) is *Caps Lodge* 1797 Davis. HANDLEY PLAIN, NUTOAKS COPSE (6″) and FURZEY LEAZE. Cf. *Hanley Plain, Nottox Copse* (*v.* nattock) and *Furzey Leys Copse* 1857 *EnclA*. HEN'S GROVE is *Hemegrove* 1300 Wych, *Hengrove* 1608–9 *Survey, Hengrove als. Hemegrove* 1641 Wych, *Hensgrove Copse* 1814 *EnclA*(*Map*): 'border grove,' *v.* heme, grāf(a); it is on the parish boundary. LADIHAME CORNER is *Ladyham, Ladyham Corner in Hengrove* 1641 Wych, *v.* Lady, hamm. NINETY CUT HILL (6″) is so named 1813 *EnclA*. PAIN'S FM is so named 1797 Davis. TUDHILL BUSHES (6″). Cf. *Tudevin* 1300 Wych, (*crucem vocatur*) *Tudvin als. Tudhill Crosse* 1641 Wych.

FIELD-NAMES

(*a*) In 1813 (*EnclA*) Ash Close, Black Bush Quarter, Bridge-Ham, Broad-Ham (*v.* hamm), Cowpath Road, Culvert Closes, Dicky Berrys, Eight o'clock Gate, Fawdrus Green, Flat Quarter, Forest Road, Fox Grove Wood, Grove Meadow, The Grove, The Ham (*v.* hamm), The Heath, Joseph's Close, Meadow Between The Waters, Mill Ham (*v.* hamm), Morter Pit Hill, Pageants, Woody Pageants, Paradise (*v.* Fan), Park Lane, Pasture Hill Quarter, Plumbtree Brake Quarter, Rightham Meadow (*v.* hamm), Sand Quarter, Standbridge Hill Field, Standridge Coppice, The Sturt (*v.* steort), Summer Hays (*v.* (ge)hæg), Sweet Well Piece, Town Quarter, Walnut Walk, Water Close.

31. Taynton

TAYNTON

(*æt*) *Tengetune* c. 1055 (11th) *St Denis*

Teintuna 1059 (11th) *St Denis et passim* with variant spellings *Teinton(e)*, *Teynton(e)*, *Teinton'*, *Teynton'* to 1676 Plot, *Teinton' Sancti Dionisii* 1163 P, *Teintona Sancti Dionisii* 1167 P

Tængtune 1059 (11th) *St Denis*

Tentone 1086 DB

Teigtone 1086 DB

Taynton 1675 Ogilby

The first element is probably a river-name identical with that of the Teign in Devonshire, presumably an older name of Hazelford Brook. Teign is related to W *taen*, 'a sprinkling,' and seems to mean simply 'stream.' Cf. Tangley 337. Second element tūn. -*Sancti Dionisii* from the Abbey of St Denis in Paris, to which Edward the Confessor granted land here in 1059.

HAZELFORD BRIDGE (6″) is (*on*) *hæselford* 1059 (11th) *St Denis*, *v.* hæsel, ford, and cf. the same name in Broughton 397.

BLACKHEATH CLUMP. Cf. *Blackheath Quarter* 1811 *BodlT*. MILL. Cf. *Milneham* 1551–2 *Survey*, second element hamm. TAYNTON DOWN (6″). Cf. *the down close* 1650–1 *Bodl*, *v.* dūn. TAYNTON QUARRIES (6″). Cf. *quarraria de Tegton'* 1163 P[1].

FIELD-NAMES[2]

(b) In 1650–1 *Burham* (also 1559), *the Coniger* (*the Coneygree or Warren* 1605, *v.* conygree), *the hades* (*v.* hades), *Odenham* (*Odneyham* 1605, *v.* hamm), *the poole hay* (*Pooleheys* 1551–2 *Survey*), *Segeham* (*Sedgeham* 1559, *v.* hamm). In 1641–2 *the leaze*. In 1559 *Berry Grenes* (*v.* burh), *Chaffordes waye, Hearringes meade, Hyll meade*. In 1059 (11th) (*St Denis*)[3] (*on*) *ælfredes denn* ('Alfred's pasture'), (*on*) *drygepytt* ('dry pit'),(*on þone*) *haran stan* (*v.* hār), (*on*) *magnhilde beorh* (*v.* be(o)rg: the first element is apparently an unrecorded woman's name *Mægenhild*), (*of þam*) *readan clife* ('red slope,' referring probably to land by the Windrush, *v.* clif), (*on þa*) *rugaðyrna* (*v.* rūh, þyrne), (*on þone*) *stapel* ('post').

[1] The best building-stone in the Oxford district comes from Taynton, where there was a quarry at the time of Domesday.

[2] Except where otherwise stated, the forms are from *Bodl*.

[3] For *cobban hyll* and *cobbanbroc*, which occur in this charter, *v.* Cobbler's Bottom in Fulbrook: the stream-names have been dealt with among the river-names *supra* 18.

32. Wychwood or Whichwood

WYCHWOOD

Huiccewudu[1] 840 (early 11th) BCS 432, *Hwichewod* 1230 P,
  Hwicchewod' 1237 Cl

Hucheuuode 1086 DB, *Huchewode* (bis) 1316 Cl

Wichewude 1185 P *et passim* with variant spellings *Wic(c)hewod*,
  Wic(c)hewude, *Wichewud'*, *Wychewud(e)*, *Wichewod'*, *Wyche-
  wod(e)*, *Wichewud*, *Wycchewud*, *Wyc(c)hewode*, *Wichewode* to
  1362 Cl, *Wichchewode* 1217 Cl

Whichwde 1205 Cl

Wichlewude 1218 Cl

Wigewde 1219 Fees

Wuchewud 1230, 2, 3 Cl

Wychwod 1231 Cl, *Wichwud* 1247 Cl, *Wychwode* 1266 Ch

Whichewud 1231 Cl *et passim* with variant spellings *Whicheuud'*,
  Whycchewod', *Whichewud'*, *Whichewod(e)*, *Whicchewod(e)*,
  Whiccheuuode, *Whyc(c)hewode* to 1449 Eynsh

Quichelwud 1236 Cl

Whycchwod' 1247 Cl

Whischewod' 1260 Fine

Whicheswod 1275 Cl

Whucchewode 1280 Cl, 1284 Ch, *Whucchewod* 1329 Cl

Whytewode, Wytewude 1285 *Ass*

Chicchewode 1298 Cl

Whecchewode 1302 Cl

'Forest of the *Hwicce*,' *v.* **wudu**. "This name is the only surviving
memorial of the people known as the *Hwicce*, who in the seventh
century occupied the territory now represented by Gloucestershire,
Worcestershire, and the western half of Warwickshire" (F. M.
Stenton, *Anglo-Saxon England*, 43). For the tribal name *v.* PN Wo xv.

BRASSWELL CORNER, GATE (both 6″) take name from (*cornerium de*)
Brestaneshalle, Brestenhalle 1298 Eynsh, *Brestanhale* 1300 Wych,
Brosteshale early 15th *Rental.* Cf. *Brasholl hedge* 1591 *Survey*,

---

[1] This is the name of a district ("ubi ruricoli nominantur Huiccewudu"), not
a village. Cf. VCH 1, 377: "The Bishop of Worcester's 10-hide manor of Spelsbury, included anomalously in the (Domesday) survey of Warwickshire, had been
granted to his church by Berhtwulf king of the Mercians between 838 and 845
(KCD 775). It can safely be identified with the 10 hides in Wychwood Forest
which Berhtwulf gave to Bishop Heahberht of Worcester by a charter dated on
Christmas Day 841, that is, 840 by modern reckoning."

Braswell als. Brastenhall Pointe, Corner and Gate 1641 Wych, '*Beorhtstān*'s nook,' *v.* h(e)alh.

BUCKLEAP COPSE (6″) is *Bocklepe* 1551–2 *Survey, Bucke Leape, Buckleape* 1608–9 *Survey*. This name and SORE LEAP (6″) are analogous to Hindlip (PN Wo 139) and to Lypiatt (Gl), Lypiate (So) or Leapgate, from OE *hlīepgeat*. These names denote a gate or a low place in a fence or hedge where deer may leap over. *sore* is an obsolete term for a buck in its fourth year, *v.* NED sb².

COCKSHOOTHILL COPSE (6″) takes name from *Cockeshotehulle* 1298 Eynsh, *Cokschuteshull'* 1300 Wych, *Cokeshottes Hill* 1551–2 *Survey, Cockshutt hill, Cockshethill* 1608–9 *Survey*. *v.* cockshoot.

CRANEHILL COPSE (6″) takes name from *Cranehill, Cranwell* 1608–9 *Survey*. The first element is probably OE cran (*v.* corn), 'crane' or 'heron.'

DOGSLADE BOTTOM (6″). Cf. *Dockeslade* 1300 Wych. 'Sorrel valley,' OE docce, slæd.

EVENDEN COPSE (6″) is *Eveden, Evenden als. Eveden* 1608–9 *Survey, Eueden* 1617 *Prince Charles*. 'Level valley,' first element *efen*, 'even', second element denu. The copse is on the side of a level valley.

FARFIELD CORNER is *Furfield Corner* 1641 Wych, *Farfield Corner* 1857 *EnclA*. Cf. *Furtherfilde close* 1551–2 *Survey*. The original name was perhaps 'further field.'

FIVEOAK COPSE (6″) is *Wyfhokes* 1298 Eynsh, *Wysok'* 1300 Wych, *Fyve Oakes Coppice, Five Oaks* 1608–9 *Survey, Five Oake alias Wyseoke* 1641 Wych. 'Five oaks,' *v.* āc. No stress should be laid on forms with initial *W-* and medial *-s-*, which are probably due to misreading of *Vyf-*, with the voicing of initial *f-* to *v-*.

KINGSTANDING FM: cf. *King's Standing* 1857 *EnclA*. This name has been noted in Sx, Wa, Nth and Nt, and there are other examples in Ewelme (127) and on the 1″ map about a mile west of Moulsford in Berks. The second element is *standing* NED vbl. sb. 4c, 'a hunter's station or stand from which to shoot game': cf. the first quotation (c. 1400) "Þenne shulde þe maister of þe game...meete þe kynge and brynge hym to his stondynge and telle hym what game is withinne þe sette." The reference to royal hunting is, of course, particularly appropriate near Wychwood Forest. *v.* Introduction xxvii.

25-2

LANKRIDGE COPSE (6″). Cf. *Langrygyate* 1298 Eynsh, *Longeruggeyate* 1300 Wych, *Lankeriche* 1551–2 *Survey*, *Lankridge*, *Great and Little Lankidge* 1608–9 *Survey*, *Lankeredge* 17th *Survey*. 'Long ridge,' *v.* lang, hrycg. geat, 'gate, gap,' has been added to the first two forms.

NOTTERIDGE COPSE (6″) takes name from *Naterigge* (bis) 1231 Ch, *Naterigg* 1231 Cl, *Notteriche* 1551–2 *Survey*, *Nuttridge* 17th *Survey*, *Notte ridge* 1822 O.S. Ekwall (DEPN) assumes an OE **næt*, 'wet,' corresponding to OHG *naz*, OLG *nat*, for the first element of Nateley and Netley Marsh Ha and Notgrove Gl, and this word would be a possible first element here. Second element hrycg, 'ridge.' *v.* liii.

ROUSTAGE is *Roustyge Copies* 1551–2 *Survey*, *Rowstage* 1608–9 *Survey*, *Rowstede* 17th *Survey*, *Rowstedge* 1822 O.S. Cf. *Rowstidge Corner and Way* 1641 Wych. Second element probably ecg, 'edge.' The EDD gives a Berkshire word *rouset(t)*, 'rank, dry grass not eaten by cattle,' which would be a possible first element.

SLATEPITS COPSE takes name from *Slattpiche* 1551–2 *Survey*, *Slatpitt*, *Slattpitts* 1608–9 *Survey*, *Slatpittes* 1617 *Prince Charles*. The thinnest in bed of the Forest Marbles (flatstones) were used as slates (Arkell, p. 88).

SMALLSTONES FM (6″). Cf. *Smalestonesweye* 1298 Eynsh, *Smalstoneswey* 1300 Wych, *Smallestones* 1551–2 *Survey*, *Smalestones* 1608–9 *Survey*. The name evidently means what it says.

SOUTH LAWN. Cf. *la Launde* 1300 Wych, *the Laund, South laund waste* 1608–9 *Survey*. 'Glade,' *v.* launde.

WALCOT QUARTER (6″). Cf. *Little Wades Gate alias Walcott Gate*, *Wallcott Feild, Walcott Feild Hedge* 1641 Wych. The modern name is from Walcot in Charlbury (416). The earlier name of the gate appears as *Lutleswadesyate* 1300 Wych: the meaning is obscure.

WASTIDGE SPINNEY (6″). Cf. *Wastidge Hill waste, Wastage* 1608–9 *Survey*, *Wastedge* 1617 *Prince Charles*, and possibly (*wood of*) *La Wayse* 1281 Cl. *wastage* is recorded in the 19th century meaning 'waste ground, desolate place,' and if the 1281 form is disregarded this name looks like a similar use of the word.

WHITLEY HILL (6″) may take name from *Whitele* 1300 Wych: *v.* hwīt, lē(a)h.

BROADQUARTER ALLOTMENTS (6″). Cf. *Brode Quarter* 1551–2 *Survey*, *Broad Quarter, Broade quarr* 1608–9 *Survey*, *Broadquarters* 1822 O.S. FAIR SPEAR (6″) is *Fair Speir* 1822 O.S. FRIAR'S BOTTOM (6″) and

RANGER'S LAWN are so named 1758 *EnclA*. GADDING WELL (6″) and
LAYCROFT BARN (6″). Cf. *Gadding Gate* and *Laycroft* 1857 *EnclA*:
the first name is *Gaddinge Gate als. Gatesdene hend* 1641 Wych:
Gadding might be a corruption of *Gatesdene*, for which *v.* 390.
GOSPEL OAK: *v.* gospel. HAZELWOOD COPSE (6″) is *Haselle woode*
1551–2 *Survey*, *Hasel(l)wood* 1608–9 *Survey*. HAWKSNEST COPSE.
Cf. *Hawkes coppice* 1608–9 *Survey*, *Hawkes* 1617 *Prince Charles*.
JUMPBERRY CORNER and SHOCK'S COPSE (both 6″) are *Tumpberry
Corner* and *Shocks Coppice* 1857 *EnclA*: *Jumpberry* might represent
Juniper berry. KINGSWOOD CLUMP (6″) is *Kingeswood* 1608–9 *Survey*,
1617 *Prince Charles*. NEWHILL PLAIN is *Newwell Plain* 1822 O.S.:
cf. also STAG'S PLAIN in this parish, and DODD'S PLAIN, LEIGH HALE
PLAIN (301) in Asthall, HANDLEY PLAIN (384) in Swinbrook. These
places are patches of ground beside woodland: cf. *Archæological
Journal* lxxviii, 36, where O. G. S. Crawford gives quotations from a
15th-century book on hunting in which *plain* is evidently used as a
hunting term for open country, unobstructed by trees, as opposed to
woodland. POTTER'S HILL. Cf. *Potters Hill, Potters quarre* 1608–9
Survey (*v.* quarr), *Potter Hill Lodge* early 18th ParColl.

FIELD-NAMES

(a) In 1857 (*EnclA*) Barley Green, Biggerstone or Biggarsden (*Bykeresden'*
1300 Wych, *Biggersden Corner and Gate* 1641 Wych, *Biggastone Close* c. 1840
TA: *v.* denu; the first element looks like OE *bēocere*, 'bee-keeper,' which
Ekwall (DEPN) takes to be the first element of Bickershaw and Bickerstaffe
in La, and of Bickerston Nf and Bickerton Ch), Boseley Riding (*v.* ryding),
Bunstock (so named 1641 Wych), Burnthouse Close (*Burndehouse close*
1551–2 *Survey*), Chetfield, Crackle Assarts (*v.* sart), Cock and Hen Woods,
Dampost, Dampool or Chadlington Gate (*New Crosse Gate als. Dampoole
Gate* 1641 Wych), Upper and Lower Deans, Dean Copse (*v.* denu), Duck
Pools (*Duckpoole* 1641 Wych), Little or Farthing Green, Farthing Stile
(*v.* fēorðing), Fretheless Stone ((*of*) *friðeles stane* 1059 (11th) *St Denis,
Fretheleston'* 1300 Wych, *Frethelstone* 1641 Wych, *v.* stān, first element the
personal name *Friðugils*), Grassless Field, Greenfield Gate, Gunsgrove Hill,
Gungrove Copse (*Gunnildegrove* 1251 Cl, 1300 Wych, *Gondilgrave, Gunnilde-
grave* 1278–9 RH, *Gurnell grove* 1606–7 *Survey*, 'Gunnhild's grove'[1]), Hayes
Close (*v.* (ge)hæg), Hazel Hill and Stile (*Hasill Stile* 1641 Wych), Langley
Scrubbs, Lilly's Cross (*Lillies Crosse* 1608–9 *Survey*, 1641 Wych), Lovegrove
Hill, The March, Pay Lane, Pebley Lane, Picket Piece (*v.* picked), Pigstye

---

[1] A *Gonnilda* de Bosseby is a tenant in South Newington 1278–9 RH, and there
was another landholder with a Scandinavian name in Barford 393–4. The early
references to this place show that part, at least, of the wood was nearer Wootton,
but it was perhaps extensive. cf. Shakenoak Fm (322).

Lane, Purlieu Waste (a *purlieu* is a piece of land on the border of a forest), Old Ridings (*v.* ryding), Southeram Lane, Summer Hayes (*v.* (ge)hæg), Swivle Close, Threepenny Copse (*v.* penny), Tile-House Ground, Townshend Meadow, Waddon Field and Riding (*Waddon*' 1300 Wych, *Waddon Green* 1641 Wych, 'woad hill,' *v.* dūn), Wall-acre, The Warren, Watervine Copse, Westgrove Copse (*Westgraue* 1230 P, 1271–2 *For*, *Westgrove* 1300, 1641 Wych, *v.* grāf(a); an *Estgraue* also appears in the 1271–2 reference), Whittal or White Stile (*Wittall Stile* 1641 Wych, *Wittle Stile* c. 1840 *TA*), Wood-gate, Woodmark Field.

(*b*) In 1641 (Wych) *Bene Hedge als. Bennetts Hedge, Cutchatch Gate* (*Cutteshacch*' 1300 Wych, *Cuttchatch* 1608–9 *Survey*, second element hæcc), *Elderne Stumpe* (*le Ellerverstobbe* 1300 Wych, 'elder stump'; the 1641 form is a later version of the original name, *eldern* (earlier *ellerne*) being first recorded in 1608; -*stobbe* is OE *stubb*), *P'adise Coppice and Hedge* (*Paradice* 1608–9 *Survey*), *Rode Gate, Little Sarte, Kinges Sarte* (*v.* sart), *Shippengate* (probably 'Shipton gate'; it was evidently near Shipton under Wychwood). In 17th (*Survey*) *Hasley, Ruffich*. In 1617 (*Prince Charles*) *Lefferedg* (*Levericke Copies* 1551–2 *Survey*, *Layfridge, Leyfridge* 1608–9 *Survey*). In 1608–9 (*Survey*) *Lowzie Grove* (*Losengraue* 1271–2 *For*, *Losnegrave, Losnegrove* 1300 Wych, *v.* lūs). In 1605 (*Bodl*) *Farrington* (*Farendone* 1271–2 *For*, *v.* f(e)arn, dūn, the name is identical with Little Faringdon 319). In 1551–2 (*Survey*) *Ereswelle, Ivyden Copies, Satley, Walsted*. In 1300 (Wych) *Asperleyehurn*' ('corner by the aspen wood,' *v.* lē(a)h, hyrne), *le Croswey* ('cross way'), *Ewardesfeld*' (*v.* feld), *le Newefrith* (*v.* fyr(h)þe), *Gatesdene Heved*' ('goats' valley,' *v.* denu, to which 'head' has been added), *Hawe* (*haga*, 'enclosure'), *Hevedweye* ('head way'), *Hodleye* (*v.* lē(a)h, the first element is probably the personal name *Hūda*), *Poreshull*' (*v.* hyll; the first element might be OE *porr*, 'leek'), *Rouwereshull*' (*v.* hyll), *Longeruggeyate* (*v.* lang, hrycg, geat), *Schet'esho* (*Shiterisho* no date Frid; this looks like another version of the Kentish and Northamptonshire name Shooter's Hill, with hōh as second element and ME *schetere*, 'archer,' as first: *v.* PN Nth 177, and cf. the field-names of Steeple Aston 248). In 1271–2 (*For*) *Bradeleye* (*v.* brād, lē(a)h), *Ewstane* (second element stān), *le Fricheshaleweye* (*v.* h(e)alh, weg; the first element might be the personal name *Friþ*, with -*c*- in error for -*t*-), *Grendone* (*v.* grēne, dūn), *Meredene* (*v.* denu, first element (ge)mǣre or mere), *Smaleweyes Ende* ('narrow way's end').

XIII. BLOXHAM HUNDRED

Blockisham, Blokesha' 1174–5 P *et passim* with variant spellings
   Blo(c)kesham, Blochesham to 1275–6 RH
Bloxham 1275–6 RH *et passim* with variant spellings *Bloxsham, Bloxam*

v. Bloxham *infra* 394. In 1086 this district contained two hundreds annexed to the royal manor of Bloxham and Adderbury.

1. Adderbury, East and West

ADDERBURY

(*æt*) *Ead[b]urggebyrig* ? c. 950 ASWills, (*æt*) *Eadburgebyrig* 1015
ASWills

Edbvrgberie 1086 DB, *Edburgebir'* 1192 P, *Edburgeber'* 1214 Cl,
Edburgebir' 1218 Cl

Ædburgebir' 1193 P, *Adburgebir'* 1199 FF, *Adburgbury* 1238 Cl

Hedberberia 1204 Cur

Edburberia 1204 Cur *et passim* with variant spellings *Edburbir'*,
Edburberi, *Edberbury*, *Edburber'*, *Edburburi(a)*, *Edburbur'*, *Edbur-
bury*, *Edberbur'*, *Edburbyri* to 1320 Ch

Edburgesbir' 1205 Cur

Auberbur' 1217 Cl

Ebblebir' 1224 Cl

Eaburebir' 1229 Cl, *Eabberbury* 1379 AR

Eburbir' 1230 Cl, *Ebberbury* 1288 Os

Adberbur', *Adbburbury* 1235–6 Fees, *Adburbir'* 1246–7 Ass (p)
et freq with variant spellings *Adburburia*, *Adburbyry*, *Adburbur'*
to 1294 Cl, *Adberbyry* 1280 Os

Edburubir' 1236 (1302) Fees

Atborebur' 1237 (1302) Fees, *Atburnbury* 1285 Ipm

Eadburbiry 1239 Eynsh, *Eadbirbir'* 1274 AD, *Eadburbury* 1387 AR

Abberebyr' 1240–1 Ass, *Abberbyr'* 1268 Ass *et freq* with variant
spellings *Abberbur'*, *Abberburi*, *Abberbury* to 1373 Cl, *Abbirbiry*
1270–1 Os, *Abbreby* 1285 Ass, *Abbreburi* 1290 Ipm, *Aberbury*
1297 Cl, *Abbresbury* 1307 Ipm (p), *Abburbury* 1346 FA *et freq* to
1397 Os

Alberbury 1273–4 RH, *Albrebyr'*, *Albrebyry* 1275–6 RH, *Alberbiry*
1288 Os

Elbrebyr' 1275–6 RH

Addenbure, *Addenbire* 1285 Ass

Ap(p)erbury 1307 Ipm (p)

Adderbury 1366 Cl, *Adirbury* 1372 AD, *Ad(d)erbury* 1378 Cl,
Addurbury 1428 FA

'*Ēadburh*'s burh.' *Ēadburh* is a woman's name.

TWYFORD BRIDGE (6"), LANE (6"), WHARF take name from *Twyford*
1246 Cl *et freq*. 'Double ford,' first element OE *twī-*: a common name,
for other occurrences of which *v*. DEPN.

Bushy Furze Barn (6") and Greenhill Fm. Cf. *Bushy Furze* and *Greenhill* 1774 Sale Catalogue. Cotefield House. Cf. *Coat Field* 1768 *EnclA*, *v.* cot(e). The Folly (6"): *v.* folly. Nell Bridge is so named 1768 *EnclA*.

FIELD-NAMES

(*a*) In 1774 (Sale Catalogue[1]) Acre Plot, Ass Pits, Barn Close, Upper and Lower Berry, Boggy Ground, Brick Kiln Ground, Cherry Orchard, Church Low Close, Claybank Spiney, Colly Pits (*colly* is used in dialect as a term of endearment for a cow), Cow Holm Meadow (*v.* holme), Cuttle Pit Hill and Pasture (*Cattle Pit Leys* 1768 *EnclA*), The Dog Kennel and Yard, Doe Cover Ground, Experiment Field, Fell Meadow, Hither and Further Fern Hill, Foxhole Bank (*v.* fox-hole), the Guide Post, Highwood, Hog-Lane, Home Ground and Close (*v.* home), Knight's Grave Hedge, Lane Way, Low Hedge Close, Ludacre Hill, Mickleham (*cf. Mic(k)ledge Meadow, Micklow Furlong* 1768 *EnclA*), Miller's House and Holm, Myse Meadow (*Mize Meadow* 1768 *EnclA*), New Pasture Lands, Nursery Ground, Ox Close, Penny Close (*v.* penny), The Pightle (*v.* pightel), The Pix (*v.* picked), the Pleasure Ground, Pudding Bush Close (*Pudding Bush Furlong* 1768 *EnclA*), Little and Great Rifeham (*Reeveham* 1768 *EnclA*, *v.* refham), Seven Mowers, The Shrubs or Upper Cow Common, Stone Pit Ground, Sydenham Plain and Meadow (cf. Sydenham 114–15), Three Cornered Close, Town Furlong, Vicarage Piece, Wantcatcher's Hook (a *want-catcher* is a mole-catcher), Weymoors, Windmillhill Ground. In 1768 (*EnclA*[2]) Billham Meadow, Bleach Moor Furlong, Byfarn Meadow, the Church Land (*le Chirchelonde* 1381 AR), the Cowpasture, Dove House Close, Hensington Land (Hensington is about 11 miles south), Hills End Meadow and Butts, Honyham, Honeyhams (*v.* honey), Kingstone Pieces and Furlong, Mare Meadow and Hades (*v.* hades), Long Moors, Moor Close, Nast Hill (*nast* is used in dialect of dirt, and of weeds in fallow land), the Northcroft, Oatlands, Pil Leys (*v.* pyll), Round Close, Stoney Pool Bank, Sturtones. In 1722 (Gray) Berryll quarter, the Flags quarter, Langland, Poinfurlong.

(*b*) In 1551–2 (*Survey*) *Fyfeldes* ('five fields'), *Ryssham, le Westende* (*v.* ende).

2. Alkerton

Alkerton [ɔˑlkətən]

Alcrintone 1086 DB *et freq* with variant spellings *Alcrintun', Alcrinton, Alcrinton', Alcrynton(e)* to 1472 BM, *Alkrinton* 1242–3 Fees, *Alkrinton'* 1246–7 Ass, *Alkrynton* 1472 BM
Alcretona 1087 (15th) EHR xl, *Alcretone* 1220 Fees
Ailcrinton' 1163, 1206 P

---

[1] Lent by Dr Loveday.
[2] Some of these might be in Bodicote. The list is not complete, as some sheets of the Award were being repaired.

Acrinton' 1187, 94 P (p), 1268 *Ass* (bis), *Acrenthon* 1236 (1302) Fees

Alcerinton' 1196 P (p), *Alkerynton* 1284–5 AD

Aucrinton 1200 Cur, 1231 Cl, *Aucrinton'* 1204 P (p), *Aucrintona* 1235–6 Bract

Aclinton' 1200 Cur

Argent' 1200 Cur

Aukelinton' 1240–1 *Ass*, *Auklinton* 1241–2 P

Alerinton 1284–5 FA

Alkynton 1472 BM

Alkertone 1526 LS

'*Ealhhere*'s farm,' *v*. ingtūn. The same name occurs in Gl.

FIELD-NAMES

(*a*) In 1777 (*EnclA*) Hadlands Cap, The Rick Yard, Tanner's Lane, Town Green.

3. Barford St John and St Michael

BARFORD ST JOHN

Bereford 1086 DB, 1282 Fine, *Bereford'* 1212 Fees, *Bereford' Plaice* 1220 Fees, *Northbereford* 1240–1 *Ass*, *Parua Bereford* 1240–1 *Ass*, 1346 AD, 1349 Ipm, *Bereford' Parua*, *Parva Bereford'* 1242–3 Fees, *Bereford Sancti Johannis* 1299 Cl, *Little Bereford* 1364 Cl, *Bereforde Little* 1377 Ipm
Parva Berford 1428 FA

BARFORD ST MICHAEL

Bereford 1086 DB *et freq* with variant spellings *Bereford'*, *Berefordia* to 1278–9 RH, *Bereford Olaui* 1194, 9 P, *Bereford' Olaf* 1220 Fees, *Bereford Chayney* 1242–3 Fees, *Bereford Olof* 1242–3 Fees, 1278–9 RH, 1305 Cl, 1346 FA, *Bereford Sancti Michaelis* c. 1250 AD *et freq* to 1346 FA, *Beryford* 1278–9 RH, *Bereford Olef* 1284–5 FA, *Bereforde sancti Michaelis* 1311 Os, *Bereforde Seynt Michael* 1327 Ipm, *Bereforde Oleffe* 1428 FA
Bureford Olaui 1199 MemR
Berford Olof 1359 Cl

'Barley ford,' OE bere-ford. The present suffixes are from the church dedications. Barford St John is called *Bereford' Plaice* from the antecedents of Hugh de *Plesy*, who is mentioned in connection with it 1364 Cl. Garin de *Plaiz* is found c. 1170 AD in connection with Barford St Michael. The latter place is called *Bereford Chayney* from the family of Dionisia de *Cheineto*, who appears ib. The suffix *Olaf* etc. in the forms for Barford St Michael probably preserves the name of an 11th-century tenant of Scandinavian origin. The dedication to St Olave of the church of Fritwell (211) six miles away is a curious coincidence, but probably nothing more.

BLACKINGROVE FM takes name from *Blackingrove* 1808 *EnclA*. BLOXHAM BRIDGE is so named 1794 *EnclA*. BUTTERMILK FM. Cf. *Butter Milk Hall* 1797 Davis: the same name occurs in Prescote 424. COOMBE HILL is *Comb Hill* 1794 *EnclA*. IRON DOWN and IRONDOWN SPINNEY (latter 6″ in Sandford St Martin) are *Yron down* 1506–7 *Valor* and *Irondown Spinney* c. 1840 *TA*: cf. Ilbury Fm (257).

FIELD-NAMES

(a) In 1794 (*EnclA*) Blood end furlong, Briar Furlong, The Butts (*v.* butts), Catsbrain (*v.* catsbrain), Clay furlong and Close, Dadford Meadow, Dadwell Meadow, Dangeway furlong, The Doles (*v.* dole), Elder Stump, Eldor Stump Furlong, Ham (*v.* hamm), Hilton Grounds, Knipple furlong, Knipple Waste Land, Knipplewell Close, The Leys, Meer furlong, Sawlop furlong, Weaveldon, Long and Short Whetstone (this field-name occurs also in Crowmarsh and Kingham, cf. PN Mx 100–1; it probably refers to the presence of a stone used for sharpening tools), Upper and Middle Withy bed (*v.* wiðig).

4. Bloxham

BLOXHAM

> *Blochesham* 1086 DB *et freq* to 1183 P, *Blocchesham* 1142–8 Eynsh
> *Blokesham* 1170 P *et passim* to 1319 Cl, *Blockesham* 1175 P *et passim* to 1287 Cl, *Blockisham* 1179 P, *Block'* 1241–2 P, *Blocesham* 1278–9 RH
> *Bloxham* 1227 Cl *et freq*, *Bloxsham* 1285 Ipm, *Bloxam* 1307 Winchcombe (p), 1401–2 FA
> *Blexham* 1284–5 FA
> *Blaxham* 1290 Cl
> *Brokesham* 1290 Cl

'**Blocc*'s hām.' For the personal name, which is only recorded in place-names, *v.* PN Wo 98.

Lower (6″) and Upper Grove Mill are probably named from Osbert de la *Grave*, who is mentioned 1238 Cl as the owner of a mill in Bloxham. Cf. *Grove Mill* 1768 *EnclA*.

Cumberford, Hog End and Nayland Fm. Cf. *Cumberfoot Slade and Road, Hog Lane* and *Nayland* 1802 *EnclA*. Hobb Hill is *Hobhill* 1802 *EnclA*.

FIELD-NAMES

(a) In 1802 (*EnclA*) Astwell or Asthill Quarter (*Astwell quarter* 1746 *Bodl*), Blackmoor (*Blakemore* 1506–7 *Valor*), Blegginton, Bog Lane, Bond Lands (there is a Bond Leys in the adjoining parish of Milcombe, the first element is probably 'bean,' *v*. 340), Bow Furlong, Broadwell Hill, Brook Mead Quarter, Butt Ley(s) Close, Clay Butts (*v*. butts), Chadwell Meadow (*v. supra* 13), Lower Chalk Meadow, The Coggs (cf. Cogges in Witney 333), College Close, Collis Leys, The Conduit, Cowhill Quarter (so named 1711 *Bodl*), Crabtree Corner (so named 1738 *Bodl*), Dairy Ground, Deep Moor, Fox Holes Furlong (*v*. fox-hole), The Green, Gutter Furlong, Hillocks, The Holm (*v*. holme), Bloxham Hook, House Ground, Hovel Ground, Lawrence or Lawrance Leys (Milcombe Church is dedicated to St Lawrence), Great Leys (so named 1739 *Bodl*), Loadhill Quarter, Lockway Furlong, Mann Meadow (*la Manne mede* 1240 Ch, *v*. mǣd, the first element might be the personal name *Manna*), Mill Way, Miller's Holm (*le Mylne holme* t. Hy 8 *AugmOff, v*. myln, holme), Morter Pitts, Muddings Leys, Northside Fields (so named 1746 *Bodl*), Ovenhill Quarters (*Olden Hill quarter* 1739 *Bodl*), Pike Hall, The Pikes (*v*. picked), Pope Furlong (*pope* is a dialect term used in this part of the country for the common red poppy, *Papaver Rhoeas*), Pound Close, Priestlands, Sallow Beds ('willow plantations'), Shackle Butt Hill, Snap Dragon Spring (*snap-dragon* is used of yellow toadflax, *Linaria vulgaris*), Southway Furlong (*Southway* 1739 *Bodl*), Stone Hill Furlong, Tadmarton Meer (*v*. (ge)mǣre), Tenants Meadow, Tippenny Meadow (*v*. penny), Townsend Road and Green, Townshend Piece, Wickell Leys.

(b) In 1784 (*Bodl*) *Dortway baulk, The Well Head*. In 1745 (*Bodl*) *Batts Gutter, Greensward, Whitehill*. In 1739 (*Bodl*) *Pile path*. In 1738 (*Bodl*) *Upper Staff furlong, Trowshooter*. In 1694 (*Bodl*) *Harris Hooke* (*v*. hōc). In 1328 (Cl) *The Churcheheye* (*v*. (ge)hæg). In 1240 (Ch) *Lukenden* ('*Luca's* valley,' *v*. denu).

5. Bodicote

Bodicote [bɔdikʌt]

Bodicote 1086 DB *et passim* with variant spellings *Bodicota, Bodicot', Bodikot', Bodycote* 1247, 1285 *Ass*
Budicote 1180, 1190 P (p)
Boidecot 1220 Fees

Bidicote 1239 Eynsh
Bedecote 1285 *Ass*
BODICOTE MILL is *Bodicot Mill* 1797 Davis.

'*Boda*'s cot(e),' with connective -ing.

WEEPING CROSS (6") is *Weeping-Cross* "a noted Place, where 4 Ways meet" 1675 Ogilby. There is a full discussion of this name (of which the O.S. maps show five examples in various counties) in the NED. The earliest occurrence of the phrase given there is *Crucem Lacrymantem* a. 1500, referring to a cross near Bury St Edmunds: but *v.* PN Sx 563 for a *Wepyngcros* mentioned in 1462. The NED mentions Beesley's *History of Banbury* 1841 as stating that the remains of an actual cross were removed from the Oxfordshire site in 1803. Various conjectures have been made as to the significance of the name—that acts of devotion at these crosses were enjoined on penitents, that the cross marked the place where bodies carried to interment were set down for the bearers to rest—but there is no evidence to support them. All the places seem to be at cross-roads. There is also a proverbial phrase *To come home by Weeping Cross*, 'to suffer grievous disappointment or failure,' for which cf. *Pennyless Bench* 22.

FIELD-NAMES

(*b*) In 1768 (*EnclA*) *Odkey Meadow* (*Nadkey* 1685 (c. 1700) *BodlT*), *Swetneys* (*the Swetneyes* 1685 (c. 1700) *BodlT*). In 1685 (c. 1700) (*BodlT*) *Brier furlonge, Congway, Ditch Well Hill, Greenway, Keck furlonge, the parsons Hamm* (*Parsonesham* 1381 AR, *Personesham* 1397 AR, *v.* hamm), *path way furlonge, Shulsand Hill and way, Shulsan Way, starlins, the Towne furlonge.*

6. Broughton

BROUGHTON

Brohtone 1086 DB, 1285 *Ass* (p)
Broctun c. 1166 Madox (p) *et freq* with variant spellings *Brocton'*, *Broctun'* to 1268 *Ass*
Brochton' 1242–3 Fees, 1251 Cl
Broucton' 1242–3 Fees
Broghton' 1246–7 *Ass* (p), *Broghton* 1301 Ch, 1316 FA, 1322 Ipm, 1382 Cl, *Brogton* 1316 Ipm[1]
Brouton' 1268 *Ass*, *Browton'* 1286 Cl (p)
Brocgton' 1268 *Ass*

[1] "Brogton uel Brougthon."

Brumton' 1268 *Ass, Brumpton* 1285 *Ass* (p)
Bromton' 1268 *Ass*
Brougthon 1316 Ipm[1], *Broughtone* 1324 AD, *Broughton* 1336 Frid
Wroughton (sic) 1333 Frid

'tūn by the brook,' *v.* brōc.

HAZELFORD MILL (6") is so named c. 1840 *TA*. It takes name from
(*on*) *hæsl ford* 956 (c. 1200) BCS 964; *v.* hæsel. The charter also
mentions (*on*) *hesl burh*, (*of*) *hæselbyrg*, evidently the name of the camp
marked on the 6" map less than half a mile west, *v.* burh. Cf. 385.

PIKE FM (6"). Cf. *the little and Great Pike, The Pike Barn* 1803
EnclA, *v.* picked.

7. Drayton

DRAYTON

Draitone 1086 DB *et freq* with variant spellings *Draiton'*, *Draitun'*,
   Draiton to 1328 Ch, *Drayton* 1228 Cl *et passim* with variant
   spellings *Draytona, Drayton'*
Dracton' 1204 OblR
Dreiton' 1268 *Ass, Dreyton* 1286 FF, *Dreyton'* 1316 FA
Haytone 1285 *Ass*

The first element is dræg, which is sometimes used of a portage
as in Drax WRY. *v.* DEPN under Drayton. It is difficult to see in
what sense it can be used in this particular name. Second element
tūn.

WITHYCOMBE FM is *Withecomb Farm* 1797 Davis; probably 'willow
valley,' *v.* wiðig, cumb.

FIELD-NAMES

(*a*) In 1926 (from a Redemption of Corn Rents in the County Record
Office with the Enclosure Award) [2]The Ashholes, [2]Calves Meadow, Clumps
Ground (*Clump Ground* 1802 *EnclA*), [2]Dairy Ground, [2]The Eyott (*v.* eyt),
[2]Grimes Hill, [2]High Ground, [2]Hill Ground, Home Ground (*v.* home), Hot
Hill (*Hob Hill* 1802 *EnclA*), [2]Little and Great Luke's Ground, Little and
Long Meadow, [2]Parsonage Meadow, Pond Ground, [2]Rough Meadow,
[2]Shirley's Little and Lower Ground, [2]Torketts Ground, [2]The Turnpike
Ground. In 1802 (*EnclA*) Ash Pits, Barkham, Beggars Piece, the Church
road, Clay furlong, the Cow pasture, Dustcomb(e), Fish Ponds, Gospel
furlong (*v.* gospel), Guild Close, Gill Close, Common and Lower Hades

---

[1] "Brogton uel Brougthon."
[2] These are all so named 1802 *EnclA*.

furlong (*v.* hades), the Handpost (*v.* handing post), Lane furlong, Lower Leys furlong, the Mill Ham(s) (*v.* hamm), Mistresses Grounds, Nineteen lands piece, the Pound close, the Town Green, Townsend close. In 1717, (*Bodl*) Little Bayford, Furzey close. In early 18th (ParColl) Little London.

8. Hanwell

HANWELL

Hanewege 1086 DB, *Hanewen'* 1154 Eynsh, *Haneweie* 1220 Fees,
    Haneweya 1233–4 WellsR, *Hanewey(e)* 1242–3 Fees
Haneuell' 1235–6 Fees, *Hanewell'* 1240–1 *Ass et passim* with
    variant spellings *Hanewell(e)* to 1476 Cl, *Hanywelle* 1346 FA
Enewell 1218 FF
Henewell c. 1242, c. 1245 AD
Hanwell 1428 FA
Haunewell 1428 FA

'*Hana*'s road.' w(i)elle has been substituted for the original **weg** of the second element.

MOOR MILL (6″) is so named 1783 Estate Act.

FIELD-NAMES[1]

(*a*) Modern names (supplied by Mrs Berkeley) Blackmoorland (cf. the field-names of Bourton 415), Bull's England, Camp Ground, Clayper Clays, Coach Road, Upper and Lower Deckburn or Dickburn, Nicklin Corner (*Nickling Corner* 1802 *EnclA*), Noble Patch (so named 1783 Estate Act), Big and Little Pinfold (*the pinfold* 1680 (c. 1700)), Pingle's Field (*v.* pightel), Springfontain.

(*b*) In 1680 (c. 1700) *the Bretch* (*the breach* 1601 (c. 1700), *v.* breche), *Catsbraine* (so named 1601 (c. 1700), *v.* catsbrain), *Chatswell way* (perhaps a poor form for *Shotswell way* 1601 (c. 1700); Shotteswell is in Wa), *Chesterland, over downe, over* and *nether Endland(e)s, Lotrum Quarter, Lothrum Hill* (*Lotsam* (bis) 1601 (c. 1700)), *the Mead yeards* (*the mead yeard* 1601 (c. 1700)), *Mill Way* (so named 1601 (c. 1700)), *the New Close, peasely slade, Pitt Acre Quarter* (*pitt acre* 1601 (c. 1700)), *Radway Hill* (*Rode way hill* 1601 (c. 1700)), *Ramwell leas* (*Rinnwell hades* and *Leas* 1601 (c. 1700)), *Roomor* (possibly 'rough marsh,' *v.* rūh, mōr), *over Smith Mead, Stonyford, Stonyland* (*Stoney Land* 1601 (c. 1700)), *the Thorne, the towne furlonge, well head, West Feild Quarter, wilslade way* (*Wool Slade, Wool Slade way* 1601 (c. 1700)). In 1601 (c. 1700) *Church way, the Dole Meadow* (*v.* dole), *nether hanging* (*v.* hangende), *Myll pond, prengewell slade, Small way.*

[1] Except where otherwise stated, the forms are from *BodlT*.

9. Horley

HORLEY

Hornelie 1086 DB *et freq* with variant spellings *Hornele(ia)*, *Hornel'*
 to 1344 Cl
Hornlege 1222 FF *et passim* with variant spellings *Hornle(e)*,
 Hornley(e), *Hornlegh* to 1428 FA
Hornilegh' 1239 (14th) RegAntiquiss
Hemele, Horuele, Houele 1285 *Ass*

Probably as suggested by Ekwall (DEPN) 'clearing in a tongue of
land,' with first element **horna* (*v.* DEPN under *horn*) and second
lē(a)h. Horley is between two streams.

10. Hornton

HORNTON

Hornigeton' 1194 Cur (p), *Hornigton'* 1240–1 *Ass*, *Hornygtone* (ter)
 1285 *Ass*
Horningtun' c. 1195 *Harl et passim* with variant spellings *Horning-
 ton'*, *Hornington(e)*, *Hornyngton* to 1385 Cl
Hornintun' 1212 Cur *et freq* with variant spellings *Hornint(t)on*,
 Horninton', *Hornynton* to 1346 FA, *Hornintun' Jurdan'* 1220
 Fees
Hormintun 1213 Fine, *Horminton* 1229 Cl
Horniton' 1236 Cl
Horlington 1275–6 RH, *Horlyngton* 1285 *Ass*
Horygtone, Horingtone 1285 *Ass*, *Horynton* 1327, 8 Ch
Horndon 1302 Cl, *Hornton* 1317 Ipm *et freq*

'tūn of the *Horningas*,' the latter being no doubt the dwellers in
the *horna* or tongue of land between the two streams on either side
of the village, which is the first element in the name of the neighbouring parish of Horley. For another occurrence of the term
horningas v. 316. Hornington (WRY) has the same etymology as
Hornton.

HORLEY AND HORNTON FIELD-NAMES

(*a*) Modern names (supplied by Mr A. Stockton) Angre Moor Hill, The
Butts (*v.* butts), Enter Common (the term *entercommon* is recorded in EDD
for Durham, meaning 'common to everybody'), The Common, Furze Hill,
Gallows Hill (cf. *Gallows Stile* 1766 EnclA), Picket Piece (*v.* picked), Vine
Yard, The Woods. In 1766 (EnclA) Berril or Berrell Gap, Callcotts Lane,
Croft Close, Driftway (*v.* drift), Gore Lane (*v.* gāra), Grindon Furlong,

Hellway Hedge, Holway, Lockway, the Poors Close, Townsend Close, Yellow well Close.

(b) In 1674 (*Bodl*) *Fearne furlong*. In 1615 (*Bodl*) *Quarry Hill*. In 1611 (*Bodl*) *Noe mans pleacke* (*v.* plek). In 1607 (*Bodl*) *Cozen Close*.

11. Milcombe

MILCOMBE

Midelcvmbe 1086 DB, *Midelcumba* 1159–62 Eynsh, c. 1160 RegAntiquiss, *Middelcumbe* 1209–35 RH, *Midelcumb'*, *Middelcumbe* 1268 *Ass*, *Middelcombe*, *Midelecombe* 1285 *Ass*

Mildecumba 1109 Eynsh *et passim* with variant spellings *Mildecumb'*, *Mildec(o)umbe*, *Myldecumb*, *Myldecombe*, *Mildecombe* to 1399 Cl, *Mildcombe* 1316 FA (p)

Melecumbe (bis) 1206 Cur (p)

Milecumbe 1206 Cur, 1268 *Ass*, *Mylcombe* 1530 Eynsh, *Millcome* 1586 AD

Midecumbe 1206 Cur

Meldecombe 1379 Cl (p)

'Middle valley,' *v.* cumb.

DODERS MILL (lost) is *molendino Dotardi* c. 1270 Eynsh, *molendino Dotard* 1390 Eynsh, *Dotard Mylle* 1414–31 Eynsh, *Dodar Myllys* c. 1513 Eynsh, *Dodersmyll* 1539 Eynsh. This is clearly the word *dotard*, 'simpleton,' used as a nickname, presumably for the miller. The word is not recorded till c. 1386, when it occurs in Chaucer in the Wife of Bath's Prologue. For another mill which takes its name from an uncomplimentary nickname of the miller, *v.* 181.

FERN HILL and RYE HILL are so named 1794 *EnclA*. LESSOR FM. Cf. *The Leazows, Further Leasow* 1794 *EnclA*, *v.* læs.

FIELD-NAMES

(a) In 1794 (*EnclA*) Bacon Furlong (*Bacunforlonge* c. 1235 (c. 1450) Godstow), Bond Leys, Marsh Bond Leys, Breakenhill Furlong, Brier Furlong Quarter, Brook Furlong Quarter, Butt Furlong (*v.* butts), Castle Leys, Chesnutt Tree, Church Close, Coney Tree Hill (this might be an error for conygree), The Coombs (*v.* cumb), Coppice Closes, Dovehouse Close, Furlong shooting to the Windmill, The Furt, Gallow Furze Leys, Hanging Furlong (*v.* hangende), Hawthorn Tree Lane, Short Heath, Hideway Furlong (*hydewey* c. 1235 (c. 1450) Godstow, *v.* hīd, weg; Hyde Fm is in the neighbouring parish of South Newington 277), Horse Croft Leys Pits, Horsehill Leys, Low and High Leys, Maltuns Close, Maltun Leys, Marsh Part, Mill

Holms (*v.* holme), Nettlebed Furlong (cf. Nettlebed parish 131), Northill, Marsh North Hill, Paradise Lane and Orchard, The Pike (*v.* picked), Pool Close Lane, Quarry Banks, Sheep House, The Simples, Tithes Furlong, Torve Furlong, Town Furlong, The Below Town, Low Town Grove Hill, Windmill Furlong, Wrestling close.

(*b*) In c. 1235 (c. 1450) (Godstow) *longebreche* (*v.* breche), *dichehurne* (*v.* dic, hyrne), *north(e)dun* (*v.* dūn), *morewelleforlonge* (*v.* mōr, w(i)elle), *Shotforlonge*, *shouelbrode* (*v.* shovelbrode), *theneldeford'* ('at the old ford,' *v.* the field-names of Tadmarton 407), *vtforlonge* (first element *ūt*, 'out,' *v.* in), *wayteburgeforlonge* (*v.* burh).

12. Milton

MILTON

Middelton' 1199 FF, 1268 *Ass*, *Middelton*, *Middilton* 1284–5 FA, *Middeltone* 1285 *Ass*, *Middelton* 1316 FA, *Middletone* 1367–8 FA
Medilton 1379 Cl
Milton 1386 Cl

'Middle tūn.'

13. Mollington

The name of this parish is dealt with in PN Wa 271. The whole parish was transferred to Oxfordshire in 1895: part of it was always in Oxfordshire. The name means '*Mol(l)*'s farm.'

FIELD-NAMES

(*a*) Modern names (supplied by Mr R. H. A. Holbech) Acre Ditch, Long Bar, Barley Piece, Beachmore, Beggar's Bush Ground, Upper Bilsbrook, Bludwell, Bridge Meadows, Chalk Pits, Church Close, Dassett Ham (*v.* hamm), Elder Clump, Elm Tree Close, Farm Sides, Fernhill, Hand Post Field (*v.* handing post), Old Hay (*v.* (ge)hæg), The Holdern, Home Close, Lark Furlong, Liquors Hirons (*v.* 240), Longyards Ground, Long and Great Marsh, Mill Close, Oat Hill, Oxbush, Oxslade (*v.* slæd), Pool Close, Prescombe Lake, Red Sag Meadow (*sag* is used in dialect of various species of rushes, reeds and sedges), Round Hill, School Ground, Little Seed Ground, Seed Field, Sheep Hill, Spearton, Spinney Side, Stonepit, Three Cornered Spinney, Three Trees Closes, Town Ground, Wheat Piece, Whitemoor.

14. North Newington

NORTH NEWINGTON [nu·tən]

Neweton' 1200, 1 Cur, *Northneweton'* 1268 *Ass*
Newinton' 1200 Cur, 1235–6 Fees, *Neuinton'* 1203 Cur, *Northnewynton* 1324 AD

Newenton' 1204 Fine *et freq* with variant spellings *Newentun'*,
Newentone to 1428 FA, *North Newenton'* 1299 Ch, 1381 Cl,
Northnewenton' 1340 AD, 1377, 1385 Cl, 1402 Ch, *Newnton'*
1428 FA
Niewenton' 1204 P
Neuton' 1204, 5 Cur, 1240–1 *Ass* (p), *Neutone* 1220 FF, *Neuton*
1401–2 FA, *North Newton* 1675 Ogilby

'The new tūn,' OE (*æt þām*) nīwan tūne. North to distinguish it
from South Newington (277).

CASTLE BANK (6″). Cf. *Castle Balks furlong, the Castle yard* 1803
EnclA. CLAYDON HILL is so named 1803 *EnclA*. KEEPER'S LODGE
AND COVERT and PADSDON SPRINGS AND BOTTOM (all 6″). Cf. *the
Keepers Meadow* and *Padgedon Bank* 1803 *EnclA*. THE KNOWLE (6″).
Cf. *Upper Knowler's furlong, Upper Knowles, Lower Knowes* 1803
EnclA.

FIELD-NAMES

(a) In 1803 (*EnclA*) Acre Hade, Acre Slade, Athen Hedge furlong, Brandy
Bridge Ground, Upper and Lower Breach (*v.* breche), Brewell Hill and Leys,
Brook Furlong, Bull Leys, the Bush Park, the Butt Furlong, Butt Leys
(*v.* butts), Calcots Ground and Hill, Upper and Lower Clover Ground, the
Constables Bank and Ley, Upper and Lower Corn piece, Crow Quarters,
the Dairy Ground, Football Ground, Fuzzey Ground, Great Meadow and
Ground, the Green, Green Hill, the Greensword hades Balk, Greensward
Ground, the Lower Ham (*v.* hamm), Hay Lands, High Ground, the Hill
Ground, Holyhead Furlong, Holly Head Ground, the Home Ground (*v.*
home), Limekiln Ground, the Lower and Upper Lowance, Hither and
further Marsh Furlong, Marsh, the Mill Barn and Ham (*v.* hamm), Moat
Close, New Broken grounds, New Close, the orchard, the Park, Pen Ground,
the Poor Plot, the Rick Yard, Round Hill, Sheep Pen Ground, The Shoulder
of Mutton (*v.* Des), The Slade, Deep Slade (*v.* slæd), the Slinket (*v.* slinket),
Spring Ground and Close, Stone Stile Furlong, Tomlow Furlong, Towers
end Ground, the Town Green, the Town Street Green, the Upper Ground,
Warren Hill (so named 1594 *Bodl*), the Warren, Washbridge, Weymore
Slade, Wrack Close (*v.* rack), Yelford Wood (Yelford is over 20 miles south).

15. Shenington

SHENINGTON

Senendone 1086 DB
Shenedon' c. 1180 (c. 1280) S (p)
Scheni'gton' 1246–7 *Ass* (p)
Shanynton 1283 Fine (p)

Schenyndon 1305 Eynsh, 1309 Ipm, 1393 Cl
Shenyngton 1388 Cl, *Shennington* 1797 Davis

'Beautiful hill,' OE (*æt þām*) sc(ī)enan dūne. Alternatively it is possible that the first element is a personal name **Scīena*, a weak form of **Scīene* (for which *v.* PN Ca 65), and that Shenlow Hill (*infra*) means '**Scīena*'s burial mound.'

ROUGH HILL (6″). Cf. *Rougftons hill, Lower and Upper Rufhills furlong* c. 1741 Bennett. Probably the name should be interpreted literally, *v.* rūh. The first form is obviously a bad one, and it is not possible to tell whether there was a tūn as well as a hill.

SHENLOW HILL is *Shenlowe* c. 1741 *Bennett*. Apparently identical in meaning with the parish name. *v.* sc(ī)ene, hlāw.

SUGARSWELL FM. *v.* PN Wa 285, and cf. the same name 354–5.

CHRISTMAS CORNER is so named 1780 *EnclA*. LODGE FM and STOCKING BARN. Cf. *Lodge Leys* and *Lower Stocking* (*v.* stocking) 1780 *EnclA*. SHENINGTON HIRONS COVERT. Cf. *Shenington Iron(s), Iron Close(s)* 1780 *EnclA*, *v.* 240.

FIELD-NAMES

(*a*) Modern (supplied by Dr T. Loveday) Duffus or Duffers (Dr Loveday informs us that this is a corruption of *dove-house*), Gally Hill (*Gallow Hill* 1780 *EnclA*), Golden end, Jacob's ladder (the term is used in dialect of various plants), Oxley, Tigers Hill, Tinckley Meadow, Tiverton, Turpits. In 1823 (*Bennett*) the Cuhard, Hell Pitts, the Leys, the Orchard.

(*b*) In 1780 (*EnclA*) Bancroft (*v.* bēan), *Barnscomb Common, Bowling Leys, Catsbrain* (*Catts Braine* c. 1741 *Bennett*, *v.* catsbrain), *Cotman Leys, Cotmans Well* (*the Cottman yard land* c. 1741 *Bennett*, *v.* cotman), *Dawshill Slade* (*v.* slæd), *Doe Bank, Drinkwater Mead, Elm Close and Garden, Foxholes Water Furrows* (*v.* fox-hole), *Broad Gores* (*v.* gāra), *Short Hedge Hadeway* (*v.* hades), *Hollow Hill Close, Hollow Well Head, The Holt, Home Leys, King Acres* (*Ring* (? *King*) *acres* c. 1741 *Bennett*), *Kinwell Leys and Spring, Mare Leys, Mariorn or Mariarn Furlong* (*Maryon* c. 1741 *Bennett*), *Meer Hill* (*Mearhill* c. 1741 *Bennett*), *Mugnells, Long Nettle Cliff, Parshill, Pertland Close, Peartland Stile, Pool Close, Pound Furlong, Rattlecomb* (*v.* 136), *Rynhill, Shootershill* (*v.* 247, 390), *Shortland Furlong, Small Thorns, Smiths Knobs* (*Smithes Nobbs* c. 1741 *Bennett*), *Sweet Furlongs* (*v.* sūr), *Tee Close, Wickham Slade* (*v.* slæd), *Winchcomb, The Yards at Broad Gores* (*v.* gāra), *Long Yeards*. In c. 1745 (*Bennett*) the Shrubb acre. In c. 1741 (*Bennett*) Scholars Close, *Vernycombe* ('ferny valley,' *v.* cumb).

16. Sibford Ferris

SIBFORD FERRIS

Scipforde 1086 DB

Sibbeford' c. 1153 (1280) S *et freq* with variant spellings *Sibbe-fordia, Sibbeford, Sybbeford', Sybbeford* to 1309 Ipm, *Sibeforde* 1185 Templars, *Parva Sibeford'* 1242–3 Fees, *Sibbeford* 1316 Ipm

Sibford c. 1200 *AOMB* (p)[1], *Sibford Temple* 1316 FA, *Temple Sibford'* 1327 S

Sippeford, altera Sippeford 1268 *Ass*

Sifford Temple 1285 *Ass*

Subbeford (bis)[1], *Subbeford Templanorum* 1285 *Ass*

Sabbeford 1285 *Ass*

Sibberts 1675 Ogilby[1]

Sibbard Ferreys early 18th ParColl

'*Sibba*'s ford.' Ferris from the family of Robert de *Ferrers*, second earl of Derby, who is mentioned in the charter (368 in S) by which William Fitz Roger of Sibford grants 9 hides of land, which he holds *de comite de Ferers*, to the Knights Templars. It is from these last tenants that the place is called *Temple* etc., *v.* Templars cxxi–cxxii.

THE FOLLY (6″): *v.* **folly**. MILLHILL BARN (6″) takes name from *Milhul* c. 1190 (c. 1280) S, *Mulnehulle* c. 1240 Os, *v.* **myln, hyll**. WOODWAY FM (6″) takes name from *Wudeweia* c. 1185 *AOMB*, *v.* **wudu, weg**.

FIELD-NAMES

(a) In 1790 (Gray) Blackland Furlong, Boyer Furlong, Bush Furlong, Church Furlong, Gore Furlong (*v.* **gāra**), Long Stone Hill, Pitch Furlong, Seven Acres Furlong, Shroudhill Furlong, Stonewall Furlong, Townsend Furlong, Wagborough, White Butt Furlong (*v.* **butts**).

17. Sibford Gower

SIBFORD GOWER

Scipford 1086 DB

Sibeford 1086 DB *et passim* with variant spellings *Sib(b)eford', Sibbeford(e), Sybeford(e), Sibbefordia, Sybbeford, Sybeford'* to 1254 Os, *Sibbeford' Goyer* 1220 Fees, *Sybeford Goher* 1251 FF, *Sibbeford Gower* 1281 FF, 1294 Os, 1314 Cl, *Sibeford Gouhey,*

---

[1] It is not clear whether these forms refer to Sibford Ferris or to Sibford Gower.

Sibeford Gouwer, Magna Sibeford 1285 *Ass, Sibbeford Gowers, Sybbeford Gouwers* 1346 FA

Sibesford(e) c. 1225 Os

Sibleford 1231 Ch

Silbeford 1275–6 RH

Sabeforde 1285 *Ass*

Shibbeford Gower 1285 *Ass*

Sibford 1285 *Ass, Sibford Gower* 1316 FA, *Sybforde Gower* 1346 FA, *Sybford* 1401–2 FA, *Sibford Gowers* 1428 FA, *Sybforde Gouer, Sybforde Goure* 1519 AD

Sibbard Gower early 18th ParColl

For etymology *v.* Sibford Ferris 404. The family of *Go(h)er, Coher, Gu(h)er* appears frequently from 1222 Bract to 1242–3 Fees.

BURDROP is *Burithorp* 1314 Ipm, Cl (p), *Burdropp* 1727, 8 *Bennett*. 'Hamlet near the burh,' *v.* þrop.

DITCHEDGE LANE (6″) takes name from *ditch hedge* 1728 *Bennett*. TEMPLE MILL (6″) is so named 1774 *EnclA*. Named from the Knights Templars, *v.* Sibford Ferris *supra* 404.

FIELD-NAMES

(*a*) In 1728 (*Bennett*) Assland Burch, Barch (*Burchwell* 1715 *Bennett*), Barnehills (*Barnills* 1714 *Bennett*), *Blakeland* ('black land'), Bones End, Bryerton, Butts hedge (*v.* butts), Hither combe leys (*the hithermost Combes Leyes* 1714 *Bennett, v.* cumb), Cottagers lotts (*v.* lot), Dock Furlong (*Docfurlong* c. 1240 Os, first element probably *docce*, 'sorrel'), Eatens way (*Ettons way* 1708, 1714 *Bennett*), Farbeardwell (*Bardenhulle* c. 1240 Os, *the furbendall* 1708, 1714 *Bennett*; 'Bearda's hill,' to which 'far' has been prefixed: the personal name is only found in place-names), Foderas, Great and Little Gate, the hadeland (*v.* hades), Little Heath, holy Furzes, honny pitts (*Hunny pitts hedge* 1714 *Bennett, v.* honey), Kimwell craft (second word 'croft'), Kishymore (*v.* mōr), Millbush, Hither old Land (*Aldelaunde* c. 1190 (c. 1280) S, *Oldlonde* c. 1240 Os, *fur olde land* 1714 *Bennett*, 'hither and far old land'), Pale Quarter, Paleway end (*the Palle* 1714 *Bennett*), plain Leyes, Soden Trees (John *Soden* is the tenant), Towne Land and Ground, Other Veare Ground (this might contain a form of the dialect word *fare*, from OE *fearh*, 'a young pig'), waterfurrows, Whitemore (*Wittemore* c. 1240 Os; *v.* mōr, the first element is uncertain), Long Wythey Combes, Wythy Combes (*Widicumbe* c. 1240 Os, 'willow valley,' *v.* wiðig, cumb and cf. 397, 408). In 1715 (*Bennett*) Messenger's Ditch. In 1714 (*Bennett*) Crosway Combes (*v.* cumb), Stratfords way, the Towneside, Whitelands.

(*b*) In 1671 (*Bodl*) *The Capell or Capon ground*. In c. 1270 (Os) *Beredis* (so named c. 1240 Os), *Brerdene* ('briar valley'). In 1251 (FF) *Nordfeld* ('north field'), *Whetehill* ('wheat hill'). In 1242 (c. 1280) (S) *Holdefeld* ('old field'), *Littlebromes*. In c. 1240 (Os) *Alwinescrofte* (' *Ælfwine*'s croft'), *Benchfurlung* (*v.* bench), *Brodeweye* ('broad way'), *Chirchweye* ('church way'), *Croftes ende*, *Edwinesweye* ('Edwin's way'), *Estlongebreche* (*v.* breche), *Fenniforde* ('muddy ford'), *Frendhulle* (*v.* hyll; there is a Frendly Hill in Tetsworth, but this is probably only a coincidence), *Horestone* (*v.* hār, stān), *Quanthulle* (*Quantehull'* c. 1190 (c. 1280) S, *v.* hyll), *Sefledethorne* (*v.* þorn; first element the woman's name *Sæflæd*), *Tunfurlung* (*v.* tūn), *Wimmanefurlong* (*Wimanefurlong'* c. 1180 (c. 1280) S, 'woman's furlong'). In c. 1220 (c. 1280) (S) *Stelesclive* (*v.* clif; the first element might be the word discussed in DEPN under Steel, apparently meaning 'steep place'), *Subina*. In 1209–13 (c. 1280) (S) *Cokeslaunde*, *Netheresmedemedwe* ('meadow called Nether Mead'). In c. 1180 (c. 1280) (S) *Sclofurlong'* (*v.* slōh).

18. Tadmarton

TADMARTON

Tademær tun, (*æt*) *Tademærtune* 956 (contemporary) BCS 965, *Tad(e)mærton* 956 (18th) BCS 967

Tademertun 956 (c. 1200) BCS 964, *Tademertone* 1086 DB *et passim* with variant spellings *Tademertuna*, *Tademerton'*, *Tademerton(a)* to 1285 *Ass*

Tadmertun, (*to*) *Tadmertune* 956 (18th) BCS 966, *Tadmertuna* 1103–4 (c. 1225) Abingdon

Thademertona 1146 (c. 1225) Abingdon, *Thadem'ton'* 1200 Cur (p), 1268 *Ass*, *Thademerton'* c. 1230 AD, 1241 *Ass* (p)

Tademarton' c. 1180–90 (c. 1425) Frid, *Tademartune* c. 1180 Thame (p), *Tademarton'* 1241 *Ass* (p), *Tademarton* 1284–5 FA, 1285 FF, 1316 FA

Thademarton' c. 1180–90 (c. 1320) Frid

Tadmereton' 1209–13 (c. 1280) S (p)

Tidemerton' 1242–3 Fees

Tedem'ton' (bis) 1268 *Ass*, *Tedemartone* 1285 *Ass*

Tamertone 1285 *Ass*

Eadmertone 1285 *Ass* (p)

Tadmarton 1428 FA

Tadmortone 1526 LS

Ekwall (DEPN) suggests 'tūn by a frog pool,' OE *tādemere-tūn*. This is not wholly convincing, but no alternative etymology can be offered. The -mær- of the earliest forms suggests (ge)mǣre 'boundary' rather than mere 'pool.'

HOLY WELL is *Halywelle* 1346 FA (p). *v.* hālig, w(i)elle.

FULLING MILL (6″). Cf. *Fulling Mill Quarter* 1676 (c. 1700) *BodlT*. TADMARTON HEATH is *Tad-Marton Heath* early 18th ParColl. There is also a reference to an intrenchment called *Tad-Marton Castle*, doubtless the camp on Tadmarton Heath.

FIELD-NAMES[1]

(a) In 1892 (Sale Catalogue[2]) Banky Ground, The Bank (cf. *longe bank* 1676), Barn Ground and Meadow, Blane Hill, Bush Ground, Calves Meadow, Church Ground, Dairy Ground, Far Meadow, The Flat, Hen Moor, High Meadow, Home Close (*v.* home), Home and Far Junts, Mickleton (*Mickleton hill* 1676), Moor Butts (*v.* butts), Park Furlong, Picket Ground (*v.* picked), Red Hill (so named 1676, cf. *Red Slade* 1676, *v.* slæd), Side Furlong, Smine Hill.

(b) In 1676 *Barly peece corner, Blackland Quarter and hedge, blackwell Slade* (*v.* slæd), *Brodshow furlonge, the Chase, Come hill, Comon hill, Cover wall furlonge, the Dean* (*v.* denu), *Dumbelong, Dumberlonge, long hale furlong* (*v.* h(e)alh), *the hanging lands* (*v.* hangende), *hixen way and Gate, the lea way, Lea brouck Quarter, marsh way, olden hedge, picked land* (*v.* picked), *pillmaster* (*v.* pyll), *Ratt Mill Quarter, short hedge, Stantile furlongs, Swakley feild, Swakly hedge* (these contain forms of the name of the neighbouring parish of Swalcliffe), *well leyes, White Butt* (*v.* butts), *the little yeards*. In 956 (contemporary) (BCS 965) (*of*) *eadwardes mylne* ('Edward's mill'), (*on ða*) *ealdan dic* (also in BCS 964, *v.* (e)ald, dīc), (*on ðane*) *ealdan garan* (*v.* (e)ald, gāra), (*on ða*) *ealdan styge* ('old path'), (*on þa ecge* ('edge'), (*be*) *heafdan* (*v.* hēafod), (*on ðone*) *mær pyt, (on*) *mær stan* ('boundary pit and stone,' the latter appears also in BCS 966), (*on þ′*) *riscbed, (of ðam*) *riscbedde* ('rush bed'), (*on*) *wilbaldes ecge* ('*Wilbeald*'s edge'). In 956 (c. 1200) BCS 964[3] (*on þone*) *ealdan ford* (*v.* (e)ald, ford; this might be identical with *theneldeford'*, mentioned c. 1235 (c. 1450) Godstow, under Milcombe, but it is more likely to be on the east boundary of Tadmarton than in Milcombe), (*on ðone*) *heafod æcer* ('head acre'), (*on*) *hun burhge leage* ('*Hūnburh*'s lē(a)h'; the woman's name *Hūnburh* is only found in place-names), (*on þone*) *læg æcer* ('fallow acre,' first element OE *læge*, only found in place-names), (*on*) *lang dices brigce* (the variant reading (*on*) *landgares bricge* is quoted by Birch in a foot-note, and the name appears in this form also in BCS 966; *v.* brycg), (*on*) *scearpannesse* ('sharp headland'), (*on ðone*) *steort* (*v.* steort). In 956 (18th) BCS 966 (*on*) *halhford* (*v.* h(e)alh, ford; but this may be, as Grundy suggests, an error for the (*e*)*ald ford* of BCS 964), (*on ða*) *heafod stoccas* (*v.* hēafod, stocc), *sandford* ('sandy ford').

---

[1] Except where otherwise stated, the forms are from *BodlT*, and these are (c. 1700).

[2] There is a copy of this in the Bodleian Library.

[3] For *hesl burh* and *hæsl ford*, which occur in this charter, *v.* Hazelford Mill in Broughton 397. The stream-names in the charter have been dealt with among the unidentified streams *supra*, and the 'ridge way' among the road-names *supra*.

19. Wigginton

WIGGINTON

Wigentone 1086 DB *et freq* with variant spellings *Wigent', Wigentona, Wygenton(a), Wigenton'* to 1364 Cl

Wigintun' 1220 Fees *et passim* with variant spellings *Wyginton(a), Wiginton(e), Wygintone, Wiginton', Wygynton(e)* to 1389 Cl

Wigingtone 1225–6 WellsR, *Wygyngtone* 1320 Os

Winginton 1242–3 Fees

Wydyngtone 1285 *Ass*

Wykyngton 1344 Os, 1370 AD

WIGGINTON HEATH is so named 1794 *EnclA*.

'*Wicga*'s tūn.' A '*Wicga*'s tumulus' appears c. 1250 in the field-names of the adjacent parish of Hook Norton, and could be named from the same man.

WITHYCOOMBE FM (6″) takes name from *Widecumbe* 1182–5 OxonCh, *the Withycombs* 1795 *EnclA*. 'Willow valley,' *v.* wīðig, cumb. The name occurs five times in the county.

HOLYWELL FM may take name from *Hollowell* 1685 (c. 1700) *BodlT*.

FIELD-NAMES[1]

(a) In 1806 (*BodlT*) Dash-Lake Furlong (*Dashlake* 1685), Hang-dog Leys (also 1795 *EnclA*, *hang-dog* is used in dialect to mean 'bad'), Milcomb Quarter (*Milcombe quarter* 1685), Plex Leys (*the Plext* 1685, *Plex Lane and Leys* 1795 *EnclA*, *v.* plek), long Slough (*short slow* 1685, *Long Slough Furlong* 1795 *EnclA*), Sweet Leys (*Sweet Leyes* 1685, *v.* sūr). In 1795 (*EnclA*) Abbots Brake, the Bowery (a dialect term for a bower or arbour), Broad Bridge Furlong, Brook Furlong, Broom, Chapel Close (*Chapple Close* 1685), the Cowpasture Road, Cross Leys, Dovehouse Close, Dunny Crofts Leys, Flag Meadow, Fuel Moor, Fuel Moor Bank, Hemplands, Hempland Butts, Hitching Leys (*Itchins Furlonge* 1685, *v.* hechinge), the Hollow Way, the Hooks, Long Midnell (*Midnill Quarter* 1685), the Mill Side Gate, the Moors, Nether Meadow (so named 1685), Oxhay, Pease Furlong, Pit a Bush Quarter (*Petye Bush quarter* 1685), Pit Furlong (so named 1685), Prior Wood Furlong, Ram Acres (*Romeaker* 1685), Rasberry Brake, Red Way (so named 1685), Shambles Close, Squire Hedge Furlong, Standwell Pits (*Standale* 1685, *v.* stān-(ge)delf), the Trough, Wadeley Leys, Wallowhill Furlong, Whirl Piece.

(b) In 1685 Castle Dich, Catsbraind furlonge (*v.* catsbrain), *course close, Dry hill, Elderne Stumpe furlonge, Foxhill furlonge, fox hill, Grass Ground, Marsh Willowes, The Millers hedge, Morral leyes, Oate furlonge, Rynoll, Rynell, Wosell furlonge* (perhaps *ousel*, 'blackbird').

[1] Except where otherwise stated, the forms are from *BodlT*, and are (c. 1700).

20. Wroxton

WROXTON [rɔkstən, occasionally ra·kstən]

Werochestan 1086 DB

Rochestane c. 1200 Abingdon

Wrokeston' 1203 Cur *et freq* with variant spellings *Wrokestan(e)*, *Wrokestone* to 1238 Cl, *Wrockestan* 1241 Eynsh, *Wrockeston'* 1242–3 Fees

Wrucestan 1204 Cur

Wroxtan 1204 Cur *et freq* with variant spellings *Wroxton'*, *Wroxton(e)*, *Wroxstan* 1205 Cur *et freq* with variant spellings *Wroxston(e)*, *Wroxstan'* to 1428 FA

Werkestan 1205 P (p)

Wrexstan 1214 Cur

Wrogstan 1226–7 WellsR

Wrokstan 1231–2 WellsR, *Wrocstan* 1275–6 RH, *Wrocston* 1310 Cl

Urocstan 1235–6 Fees

Rokesdon 1242 Fees

Wroskestan' 1242–3 Fees

Wractan 1275–6 RH

Wraxton 1285 *Ass*, *Raxston* 1675 Ogilby

Wrochstan 1285 *Ass*

Froxton (bis), *Froxstone* 1285 *Ass*

'Buzzards' or buzzard's stone,' OE **wrocca* stān or **wrocces* stān. *v.* PN Wa 229–30.

BALSCOTT

Berescote 1086 DB

Belescot(e) c. 1190 (c. 1200) Thame *et passim* with variant spelling *Belescot'* to 1241 FF

Balescot' 1219 FineR *et freq* with variant spellings *Bal(l)escote*, *Baleskote* to t. Hy 8 AugmOff, *Baliscot'* 1242–3 Fees

Belecot' 1233 Cl

Balscote 1242 P, 1285 *Ass*

BALSCOTT MILL is *mill in Ballescote* t. Hy 8 *AugmOff*.

'*Bæll*'s cot(e)'; for the personal name, which is only recorded in place-names, cf. PN Wa 54.

DOWNS BARN. Cf. *the Downes* 1538–9 *Valor*. GUIDE POST is probably *The Hand Post* 1805 *EnclA*, *v.* handing post. HEATH FM. Cf. *Heath*

Furlong 1768 MapsOx, *The Heath* 1805 *EnclA.* LUNSDON ROAD. Cf. *Lungedon Furlong and Well Head* 1805 *EnclA.* NEW INN is so named 1805 *EnclA.* RAGNELL BOTTOM. Cf. *Raynell Park* 1768 MapsOx, *Ragnall's or Ragnell's Path Furlong* 1805 *EnclA.*

FIELD-NAMES

(*a*) Modern names (supplied by Mr A. Stockton) Beggar Hill (*Begger Hill* 1768 MapsOx), Broken Back (*Breakback furlong* 1768 MapsOx, *Broken Back* 1805 *EnclA, v.* Fan), Butts Furlong (*Butt Furlong* 1805 *EnclA, v.* butts), Cobham Furlong, Cradle Ground (*cradle-land(s)* is given in EDD as a term for 'property passing to the youngest son'), Cuckoo's Close (*Cuckow Close* 1768 MapsOx, *Cuckolds Close* 1805 *EnclA*), Depcombe (*Deeplo(o)me* 1601 (c. 1700) *BodlT, Deptcomb* 1680 (c. 1700) *BodlT, Debtcomb bottom* 1768 MapsOx, *Depcomb Hill, Slade, Well Head and Spring* 1805 *EnclA, v.* dēop, cumb), Friar Hill (*Friars Hill* 1805 *EnclA*), Long and Short Friday (so named 1768 MapsOx, cf. *Long Thursday Furlong, Short Friday Furlong, Long Friday* 1805 *EnclA; Long Thursday* also appears 1768 MapsOx), Hounswell, Leys (*la Lea* 1180–1200 (early 13th) Thame (p), *v.* lē(a)h), Moor Meadow, Quick Close (*quick* is a dialect term for 'a young thorn plant for making hedges'), Raydon Hill (*Ruedenehulle* c. 1242–3 AD, *Reydown Hill* 1768 MapsOx, *v.* ryge, denu, hyll), Redhill (*Red Hills, Red Hill Furlong* 1805 *EnclA*), Rolow (*Roughlow quarter* 1768 MapsOx, *Rowlow Furlong and Quarter* 1805 *EnclA*), Salt Furlong (also 1768 MapsOx, 1805 *EnclA*), Sharlow Furlong (*Sharley Furlong* 1768 MapsOx, *Sharlow Furlong* 1805 *EnclA*), Shouls (*Long and Short Shoal's Furlong* 1805 *EnclA, v.* 179), Slatt Pitts (*Slatt Pit* 1805 *EnclA*), Townleys (also 1805 *EnclA*), Wyarmitter, Wych Ground (cf. *Whitchill Furlong* 1768 MapsOx, *Wych Pool* 1805 *EnclA*, the first element is probably 'wych elm'), Wydlow Furlong (cf. *Hydelow Hill, Hydlow Furlong* 1805 *EnclA*). In 1805 (*EnclA*) Ash Close, Bare Furlong (*Lower and Upper Bear Furlong* 1768 MapsOx, *v.* bere), Beggar's Bush Furlong, Beggar's Slade, Black Furlong, Boars Close, The Boggs, The Bower, Bridge Ground, Caldicot Water Mead, Catsbrain Furlong (*v.* catsbrain), Cherry Hedges Furlong (*Cherryhedge* 1768 MapsOx), Church Furlong (also 1768 MapsOx), Coarse or Course Furlong (*Course Furlong* 1768 MapsOx), College Land, Cox Hill Furlong, Craft Lands, Cross Furlong (cf. *the Cross pasture* 1538–9 *Valor, Cross Lands* 1768 MapsOx), Desmesne or Abbey Lands[1] (there are a number of *Abbey Lands* 1768 MapsOx), Dovehouse Furlong, Driftway Road (*The Drove or Drift Way* 1768 MapsOx, *v.* drift), Gallows Corner, Golden Ground, Hanging Cliff Furlong (*v.* hangende), Short Hoo Furlong (*v.* hōh), Horse Pasture, House Ham (*v.* hamm), Inn Lands (cf. *the Inniland, the Inne mede* 1538–9 *Valor, v.* in), Lamp Lands (*v.* church), Lang Furlong (so named 1768 MapsOx, *v.* lang), Langway, Baker's Leazow (*v.* lǣs), Long Lands, The Meadow (*The Mead* 1768 MapsOx), Pass Furlong (so named 1768 MapsOx), Path Furlong, Pen Ground, Penny Furlong (so named 1768

---

[1] The house called "Wroxton Abbey" preserves slight remains of the Austin Priory.

MapsOx, *v.* **penny**), Pond Furlong, Reynolds Den (*Reynolds den Bottom* 1768 MapsOx, *v.* **denu**), Rommell Hills (*Romerhill* 1768 MapsOx), Round Leys, Row Cross, Lower and Upper Rye Grass, Sketchall Piece (*Seatchel-piece* 1768 MapsOx), Balscot Slade Road (*v.* **slæd**), Sleak Slade Furlong (*v.* **slæd**), Stretthall or Streethall Piece, Swines Hook, Swingewick Corner, Town Street and Furlong, Wallbank, Water Mead Furlong (so named 1768 MapsOx), Whit(e)worth or Whitforth Hill, Withy Meadow (*v.* **wiðig**), Workhouse Leys and Garden, Yard Furlong (*Ȝerdefurlonge* c. 1242–3 AD, *Yeard Furlong* 1768 MapsOx, first element g(e)ard, 'enclosure').

(*b*) In 1768 (MapsOx) *Blackenhill Abbey Lands, Block Furlong, Butts, Abbey Butts* (*v.* **butts**), *Hanging Croft* (*v.* **hangende**), *Idler piece, Kite Furlong, the Lands ends, Lower Lasting, Upper Lasting Furlong, Madden Hill, Ousehill, Long Ouse, Pent Furlong, Picks* (*v.* **picked**), *Roughland, Shoulder of Mutton* (*v.* Des). In 1538–9 (*Valor*) *Lendge Close, the Oxelese* (*v.* **læs**), *Shepehouse close, Townefyld.* In c. 1242–3 (AD) *Ludeswellehulle* (*v.* 280 for the stream-name, to which hyll has been added).

XIV. BANBURY HUNDRED

Banneb'r 1193 P *et passim* with variant spellings *Bannebur*(*y*),
    Bannebir(*y*), *Bannebyr* to 1346 FA
Banbury 1428 FA

v. Banbury *infra.* The hundred, which consists of three different portions, belonged to the Bishop of Lincoln and was annexed to his manor of Banbury. The Bishop of Lincoln's three hundreds (the others are Dorchester and Thame) all have detached portions, cf. Dorchester Hundred 149.

1. Banbury

BANBURY

Banesberie 1086 DB

Banabereie c. 1100 EHR ix

Banneberia 1109 Eynsh *et passim* with variant spellings *Banne-beri*(*e*), *Banneber', Bannebiri*(*a*), *Banneburia, Bannebir', Banne-byri, Bannebire, Bannebur', Bannebyry, Bannebiry, Bannebery, Bannebyr', Bannebyre, Bannebere, Bannebyris, Bannebure, Banne-bury* to 1343 BM

Banebiria 1146 (c. 1225) RegAntiquiss, *Baneberiam cum castro* 1149 (c. 1225) RegAntiquiss, *Banebir'* 1203 Pat, *Banebirye, Banebure* 1285 *Ass*

Bannesbiri 1220 FF

Baynebyry 1285 *Ass*

Banbury 1285 *Ass, Banburgh* 1364 Cl

'*Ban(n)a's burh.' The same personal name is found in Ban-
ningham Nf, and from the forms available for both names it is
difficult to tell whether -n- or -nn- is earlier.

NOTE. BRIDGE ST is *Brydge stret* 1551–2 *Survey*, *Bridgstrete* c. 1605
Survey. BROAD ST was earlier *Colberstreete* 1556 *Bodl*, *Cobarstreete* c. 1605
Survey, *Colebar St* 1634–5 *Bodl*, *Colebarr St* 1639 *Bodl*. GEORGE ST was
Fish St until 1924, and earlier *Scaldinglane* 1551–2 *Survey*, 1716 *Bodl*:
Herbert (*v. infra*) suggests that the last name is due to a soap-boiler, who
used to turn his hot waste water into a stream near by, but the name is
evidently older than Herbert realised, and may refer to the treatment of
animals' carcasses with boiling liquid. HIGH ST is *High Streete* 1556 *Bodl*,
Shoprowe or le Highstreete c. 1605 *Survey*, *High St or Houlting St* 1656 *Bodl*.
HORSE FAIR is *le Horsefaire* c. 1605 *Survey*. Cf. *Horse shewe* 1551–2 *Survey*.
MONUMENT ST is so named from an obelisk erected in the late 18th to mark
the site of the South Bar, which was then taken down: the obelisk was removed in 1845. NEWLAND RD takes name from *La Neuelande* 1285 *Ass*,
Newleland 1551–2 *Survey*. NORTH BAR ST, SOUTH BAR ST take name from
Northbar', *Suthbar'* 1268 *Ass*. The former is *Northbarstreete* c. 1605 *Survey*:
v. barre. OLD PARR RD was named from a murderer hanged on this site in
1747. ST JOHN'S RD. Cf. *Seynt Jones streate* 1551–2 *Survey*, *St John Strete*
c. 1605 *Survey*.

Other names which appear in early records are: *Barkehille* 1551–2
Survey, *Barkhillstrete* c. 1605 *Survey*, *Lebark(e)hill*, *Barkehill St* 1647 *Bodl*
(perhaps 'tanners' hill,' from ME *barkere*, cf. PN ERY 300); *Beaste markett
St* 1621 *Bodl*, *Beast market St* 1672 *Bodl*; *Broadyate* 1638 *Bodl*, *Broadgate
Street* 1696 *Bodl*; *Cornemarkettstreete* c. 1605 *Survey*, *Corn Hill* 1709 *Bodl*;
Flaxcheaping 1638 *Bodl* ('flax market'); *Frogelane* 1551–2 *Survey*; *Parsons
Lane* 1551–2 *Survey*, *Parson's Lane* 1692, 1766 *Bodl*; *Procession Waye*
1551–2 *Survey*, *the Procession Way* c. 1605 *Survey* (referring to the beating of
the parish bounds); *Sugarbarre streate* c. 1605 *Survey* (sceācere, 'robber,'
is the first element in the name of Sugarswell Fm in Shenington and is
found in the field-names of Banbury; it may be in this name also).

The origin of a number of comparatively modern names, such as Bath Rd,
Beargarden Rd (formerly *Cork Lane*), Hightown Rd, The Leys, is discussed
in *Banbury Through One Hundred Years*, W. Potts, Banbury 1942. A number
of others, not listed here, are carried back to the early 19th by their inclusion
in the perambulation of Banbury in *Shoemaker's Window*, George Herbert,
Oxford 1948. This book also contains a map of Banbury in 1825.

BERRYMOOR FM (6″). Cf. *Burye more meade* 1551–2 *Survey*, *Berrie
more meade* c. 1605 *Survey*. *v.* burh, mōr.

BRETCH FM (6″) and *The Bretch* in North Newington. Cf. *le Breche*
15th AD, *v.* breche.

CALTHORPE HO (6″) [kɔˑlθɔˑp or kælθɔˑp] takes name from *Cotthrop*
1278–9 RH, *Cortthrope*, *Cothrope* 1285 *Ass*, *Colthrop* 1285 *Ass*(p), 1354,

1435 AD, *Codthropp* 1394 AD, *Cowthrop* c. 1605 *Survey*. The original form of the name may have been col-þrop, the first element being col, 'charcoal.' Souldern, which is from OE *sulh-þorn*, appears as *Sowthorne* 1514 Blo.

CROUCH HILL FM (6″), CROUCH HILL, FM take name from *spinetum de Cruk* 1215 Ch, *boscum q.v. Cruche* 1268 *Ass*, *spinetum de Cruche* 1278–9 RH, *spinetum de Croyche* 1278–9 Eynsh, *le Crouche* c. 1605 *Survey*. British *crouco-, 'hill.'

EASINGTON is *Hisenden*' 1278–9 RH, *Esendon* 1435 AD, *Easingden Feilds* c. 1605 *Survey*. '*Ēsa*'s hill or valley,' *v.* dūn, denu. Cf. Easington 125.

GRIMSBURY, OLD GRIMSBURY (formerly in Nth) are *Grimberie* 1086 DB, *Grimesberi* 1198 P, *Grimesbury* 1301 Blo, *Grimmesbury* 1316 Blo. *v.* burh. Cf. also Grimsbury (PN Nth 63). *Grim* in this combination is a name for a supernatural power, probably Woden. It is related to OE *grīma*, 'a mask,' and refers (like the ON name *Grímr*, which is used of *Óðinn*) to the god's habit of appearing in disguise. The burh must have been a prehistoric earth-work, which is not now visible. Banbury Lane runs by the place to Hunsbury Camp above Northampton. Cf. Grim's Ditch *supra* 5.

HARDWICK FM takes name from *Herdwyke* 1224 FF *et freq* with variant spellings *Herdwike*, *Herdwich*, *Herdwyk* to 1370 AD, *Herdewich* 1239 Eynsh *et freq* with variant spellings *Herdewich*', *Herdewyk(e)* to 1449 Eynsh, *Hardwicke* 1535 Eynsh. *v.* heordewīc.

HUSCOTE Ho and NETHERCOTE: *v.* PN Nth 63.

NEITHROP

> *Ethrop* 1224 FF, 1285 *Ass*
> *Nethrop* 1278–9 RH, 1435 AD, *Nethropp* 1316 FA, *Nethorp* 1385 Cl, *Netrup* 1675 Ogilby
> *Hethethrop* 1285 *Ass*
> *Northrop(e)* 1285 *Ass*
> *Neithrup* early 18th ParColl

v. þrop: the first element is uncertain. The 1285 *Ass* forms for this county are mostly to be ignored, but the form from 1224 FF also suggests hǽþ. The rest of the forms suggest 'nether.'

WYKHAM FM (6″), MILL, PARK take name from *Wicham* 1086 DB *et freq* with variant spelling *Wycham* to 1346 FA, *Wicheham* 1159–62 Eynsh, c. 1160 RegAntiquiss, *Wykam* 1208–13 (c. 1300) Fees, *Wikam*, 1218 FF, *Wykham* 1238 Eynsh *et freq* with variant spelling *Wikham*,

Wikeham 1428 FA, *Wicam* 1524 AD, *Wickham* 1797 Davis. *v.* wichām.

SPRINGFIELDS and VINEYARD NURSERY (both 6"). Cf. *Spring Close* and *The Vineyards* c. 1840 *TA*.

FIELD-NAMES[1]

(*a*) In c. 1840 (*TA*) Blue Barn Meadow, Castle Meadow (*Castell meade* 1551–2, *Castlemeade* c. 1605, 1608–9, *v.* mǣd), Dry Close, Durdens (*Derdene* 1278–9 RH, *Durden* 1435 AD, *Dordene* 1551–2, *Durdane* c. 1605, *Durdan* 1608–9, *Durdaine holde* 1685 (c. 1700) *BodlT*; 'animal valley,' from *dēor* and denu), Little Enshams (*greate and little Evensham* 1551–2, *Great and Little Emsham* c. 1605), The Fullock (*great and little Fullacke* 1551–2, *Great and Little Fullake* c. 1605, *Great Fullaker, Little Fulloke* 1608–9, *v.* fullock), Gartridge Close, Hirons Meadow (*v.* 240), Hook Meadow, Hopyard Meadow, Hovel Close, Lady Grove Close (*v.* Lady), Lodge Hill (cf. *Lodge close* c. 1605, 1608–9), Lousy Bush (*v.* lūs), Mayfield, Parkwall Ground, Parsons Meadow, Pest House Ground (*v.* pest-house), The Ridings (*v.* ryding), the Roundabouts (*v.* Des), Rye ground, Shoulder of Mutton piece (*v.* Des), Short Shugmuster Piece (*Sugmyster* 1608–9), Smoak Acres (*v.* smoke), Thorney Close, Turnpike Close, Wadd Ground (the same name occurs about four miles north-west, *v.* PN Nth 52; the first element is 'woad'), Windmill Close (cf. *Wyndemylne felde* 1551–2, *Winmill feilde* c. 1605, *Wynmyll feilde* 1608–9), Wing Ground.

(*b*) In 1608–9 *Gadresse* (*Gaderesse* 1551–2, *Gadresse* c. 1605), *Swynslowe* (*Swyneslowe* 1551–2, *Swinslowe* c. 1605, probably 'pigs' wallow,' second element slōh). In 15th (AD) *Ellestobfurlonge* ('elder stub furlong'), *Heywey* (*v.* hēg, weg), *Houndefeld, Myddulchirstowe* (*v.* middel, cirice, stōw). In 1268 (*Ass*) *Schukersfed* (this looks like another occurrence of the element scēacere, 'robber,' found in Sugarswell Fm in Shenington, *v.* PN Wa 285: the final element should probably be feld). In c. 1265 (RegAntiquiss) *Eylesham* ('*Ǣgel*'s hamm,' for the personal name *v.* 324).

2. Bourton

GREAT BOURTON [bəˑtən is commoner than bɔˑtən]

Burton' 1209–12, 1208–13 (both 1300) Fees, *Magna Burton'* c. 1265 RegAntiquiss, *Burtona major* 1278–9 RH, *Mucheleburton* 1323 Ipm, *Magna Burton* 1328, 1346 FA
Bortone, Bordene 1285 *Ass*
Bourton Magna 1316 FA

[1] Except where otherwise stated, the forms are from *Survey*.

LITTLE BOURTON

> *Burton Parvum* 1278–9 RH, *Parva Burton* 1328, 1346 FA
> *Bourton Parva* 1316 FA, *Bourton* 1317 AD
>
> v. burhtūn.

SLATE MILL (6″) is *Sclattemylle* 1482, 1509, 16, 17, *Sclatemylle*, *Sclattmylle* 1521, *Sclat myll* 1531, *Slate myll* 1595, *Slatt mylne* 1601, *Slatt mill* 1628, 33, *Slatmill* 1633. These forms are from deeds in the possession of Dr T. Loveday. The modern name gives the correct etymology: Dr Loveday informs us that the slate roof of the building has only recently been removed.

LITTLEGOOD FM (6″). Cf. *Little Good* 1723 Loveday, v. Fan.

FIELD-NAMES

(a) In 1778 (*EnclA*) the Dirt House, Foxden Way (so named 1723 *Loveday*), the Greensword Ground, Hills Close and Land, Long Croft Closes (cf. *Longcroftfurlong* 1323 Cl), the Meadow Way, New Closes, Pursland Leys (*Pursland* 1723 *Loveday*), Sow bridge (*Sowbridge, Southbridge* 1551–2 *Survey*, probably 'south bridge'; it was evidently on the boundary between Bourton and Cropredy). In 1671 (*Loveday*) Adder furlong, Battle, Blackmore Gogges (cf. *Blakemorehill* 1710 *Loveday*, for Gogges v. gog), Blackland, Breach (cf. *Brechfurlong* 1323 Cl, v. breche), Bryars Leighs, Bryfurlong, Butt furlong (v. butts), Farthing (v. fēorðing), Hester furlong, Ryfurlong, Sowscroft, Ten Lands. In 1723 (*Loveday*) Baggleye's Meadow, Cowswell, Elderstubb, Hadley, Holland's Hook, Matthew Ennock's Pike (v. picked), Over Leys, Pitts, Swanns. In 1710 (*Loveday*) Berrow, Broad Corner, Catbrainhill (v. catsbrain), Hawkhill, Holloway's End, Lousehill land (v. Fan), River's Piece, Sharpland, Stonhill. In 1668 (*Loveday*) Cockmorehill, Deadman, Langehill, Langland (v. lang), Woolland (v. wōh).

(b) In 1551–2 (*Survey*) Conyngtrewaye (v. conygree), *Hilles hedge*, *Truseclose*. In 1323 (Cl) *Grascroft* (v. gærs), *Honymede* (v. honey), *Hullefurlong*, *Hullese* ('hill furlong and lǣs'), *Lonecroftfurlong* or *Lovecroftfurlong*, *Yatfurlong* (v. geat).

3. Charlbury

CHARLBURY [tʃɔ·lberi]

> *Ceorlingburh, Ceorlingcburh* c. 1000 Saints
> *Cherleberiam* 1109 Eynsh *et passim* with variant spellings *Cherleberi(a), Cherlebury, Cherleburi(a), Cherlebir(y), Cherlebur', Cherlebyr', Cherlebir', Cherlebure, Cherlebery, Cherlebyri* to 1325 Eynsh
> *Cerlebiriam* 1159–62 Eynsh, *Cerlebiria* c. 1160 RegAntiquiss
> *Churlebiry* 1197–1208 Eynsh
> *Chelebyr'* 1268 Ass

Chirlebir' 1278–9 RH
Charlebury 1320 Eynsh, *Charleburye* 1575 AD
Scherlusbury 1375 Dean
Chorlebury 1428 FA *et freq* with variant spellings *Chorlebery*,
    Chorleburye to 1572 AD
Chorlbury 1429 Dean, 1471 Eynsh
Charilbury 1526 LS

'*Ceorl*'s burh,' with connective -ing-.

BAYWELL GATE (6″) is *Baywelle* 1271–2 *For*. Perhaps '*Bǣga*'s stream,' cf. Bayford (PN Herts 214) which is spelt *Bayford* 1251 Ch. *v.* w(i)elle.

COATHOUSE FM (6″) is *Cotes* 1268 *Ass et freq* to 1359 Eynsh, *Cote* 1390 Eynsh, *Coat House* 1805 *EnclA*. Cf. *the Coate field* 1608–9 *Survey*. *v.* cot(e).

DUSTFIELD FM takes name from *Dustesfeld* 1298 Eynsh, *Dustlesfeld* 1300 Wych, *Dustfield* 1608–9 *Survey*. The first element is probably the common word *dust*, in spite of the -s- in the earliest forms. This element occurs in Duston in Nth and in some minor names in that county, *v.* PN Nth 82.

HUNDLEY ROAD (6″). Cf. *cultura nuncupata Hundeley* 1363 Eynsh. Perhaps '*Hunda's clearing,' *v.* lē(a)h.

NORMAN'S GROVE is *Normannes groue*, *Normanesgrove* 1305 Eynsh: 'Norman's grove.'

RUSHEY BANK (6″). Cf. *Ruschemere* 1363 Eynsh, which is said to be "tendens in Ryschemereslade," *Rushmore*, *Rushmore coppice* 1608–9 *Survey*. 'Rush lake,' to which (ge)lād, 'watercourse,' has been added in the second of the 1363 forms. *v.* rysc, mere.

WALCOT

> *Walecote* c. 1130 *Bodl* (p) *et passim* with variant spellings *Walecota*,
>   *Walecot'*, *Walekot(e)* to 1301 Cl
> *Walcot'* 1230 P (p), *Walcote* 1349 Ipm *et freq* with variant spelling
>   *Walcot(t)*, *Walcott Farm* 1571 AD, *Wallcott* 1575 AD

Probably 'cot(e) of the serfs or Britons,' *v.* w(e)ala.

LEE PLACE, LEE'S FM. Sir Henry Lee, "Ditchley's first owner of note…Knight of the Garter and a favourite of Queen Elizabeth who visited him here[1]," is mentioned 1608–9 *Survey* in connection with

---

[1] Miss R. M. Marshall, *Oxfordshire By-Ways*, 76.

a "fair house" called *Lees*. *v.* E. K. Chambers, *Sir Henry Lee*, O.U.P. 1936.

BANBURY HILL (6″) is so named c. 1840 *TA*. Charlbury is some distance from Banbury, but in Banbury Hundred. CLARKE'S BOTTOM and THE WILDERNESS are so named c. 1840 *TA*. CONYGREE FM may be named from *the Connygree* 1608–9 *Survey*, *v.* conygree. PINTLE BARN (6″). Cf. *Pinckle hill* 1608–9 *Survey*, *v.* pightel.

FIELD-NAMES

(*a*) In c. 1840 (*TA*) Aggrave or Aggrove, Ashley Close, Aubridge Bottom (*Abridge* 1608–9 *Survey*), Badger Bury, Banslade (probably 'bean valley'), Bar Acre, Beggars Bush, Blue Gate Yard, Bobwell, Brogborough Field, Brockwell Corner, Bullham Corner (*v.* hamm), Castle Head Close, Cockpit, Cra(y)borough, Dead Lands (*Dedelonde* 1363 Eynsh), Devils piece, Dry Close, Farthing Field (*v.* fēorðing), Gallows Piece, Gilling Piece, Handing-post piece (*v.* handing post), Hatch Yatt Piece (*v.* hæcc-geat), Hunting Bridge Meadow, Lambell Ground, Lank Yeat (*v.* lanket), Little Leason, Leason Hill, Leasow (*v.* lǣs), Further and Hither Loft Closes, Longcut (*v.* cut), Mackrelshire (*Makerelshauwe* 1363 Eynsh: the second element is *sceaga*, 'copse,' but it is difficult to account for the presence of the mackerel unless it be a personal name; the word occurs from the 15th to the 17th with the meaning 'bawd'[1]), Marebridge, Marsham, May Acre Pits (? *Myngeputtes* 1363 Eynsh), Nuns Close, Nurzley Pits, Penny Land (*v.* penny), Pest (*v.* pest-house), Picked Piece (*v.* picked), Playing Close, Rainbow Acre (*v.* Des), Green Riding piece (*v.* ryding), The Sart (*v.* sart), The Side Land (*v.* sideland), Sidnam Meadow and Hades (*Sedenham, Sedenhamhegge* 1363 Eynsh, '(at the) wide hamm,' identical with Sydenham 114–15: hecg has been added to one form), Sling (*v.* sling), Smock Acre (*Smokacre* ? 1272 (c. 1280) S, *v.* smoke), Spires Lake, Spring Ground, Sturt (*v.* steort), Swan Lane Close, Tandross Field and Meadow, Thrift (probably from fyrhþ(e)), Ticknel(l), Tillason, Twenty Bushel piece, Volgar Assarts (*v.* sart), Winter Slade Bottom (cf. *Winter Slade coppice* 1608–9 *Survey*, *v.* slæd).

(*b*) In 1608–9 (*Survey*) *Horsman Walles coppice, Horseman Walles* (*Horsemanwalle* 1363 Eynsh, second element probably wælle, *v.* under w(i)elle; *horseman* may be used as a personal name), *London Sart coppice* (*Londonesart'* 1363 Eynsh, *v.* sart), *Mayet Sarte coppice, Styquarter coppice* (*Styequarteron* 1363 Eynsh, first element either stigu, 'sty,' or stīg, 'path'). In 1363 (Eynsh) *Ankusdene* (second element denu), *Blountescroice, Croiceryding* and *Portrude* (cf. *Cristesmel* c. 1160 Eynsh, *Crucacre* ? 1272 (c. 1280) S: these names all contain words for 'cross,' *croice* is French, *Cristesmel* is OE *cristelmæl*, 'crucifix,' *-rude* is OE *rōd*, and *Cruc-* is OE *crūc*: for the other elements *v.* ryding and port: *Blount* is probably a surname), *Efurlong* (*v.* ēa), *Four-*

---

[1] Charlton Mackrell (So) takes its suffix from a family named *Makerel* (DEPN). The surname is recorded as early as the 13th century (C. W. Bardsley, *Dictionary of English and Welsh Surnames*, Oxford 1901).

lourhemhache ('gate of the people of Fawler,' *v.* hǣme, hæcc), *Hemelonde* (*v.* heme), *Meredene* (*v.* mere, denu), *le Merske* (*v.* mersc), *Putteslane*, *Shepecroftfurlong*, *Whytefurlong*, *Wythylonde* (*v.* wīðig). In ?1272 (c. 1280) (S) *le Benlonde* (*v.* bēan), *Blakelonde* (*v.* blæc, land), *Bradacre* (*v.* brād), *Cawesmor'* (perhaps '*Cawe*'s marsh,' *v.* mōr), *Cortileshulle* (*v.* hyll), *le Gerstone* (*v.* gærs-tūn), *Hasel(w)iyde* ('hasel wood,' with *widu*, old form of wudu, as second element), *Heylonge*, *Misfurlong*, *Pundfold'* ('pinfold'), *Pykedeston* (*v.* picked), *Russacre* (*v.* rysc), *Sorchemdene* ('valley of the people of Shorthampton,' *v.* hǣme, denu), *Sortebrode* ('short broad'), *Waledenehulle* (*v.* denu, hyll, first element identical with that of Walcot).

4. Claydon with Clattercote

CLAYDON

> *Cleindona* 1109 Eynsh, *Claindona* 1159–62 Eynsh, c. 1160 Reg-Antiquiss, *Claendon* 1208–13 (c. 1300) Fees, *Cleindone* 1221–6 Os, *Clayndone* 1241, 7 FF
> *Claydon* 1215 Cl, *Claydon'* 1268 *Ass*, 1278–9 RH, *Cleydon* 1216 Cl *et freq* with variant spellings *Cleydon(e)*, *Cleydon'*, *Cleidone*, *Cleidona* to 1428 FA
> *Cheindon'*, *Cheyndon* 1268 *Ass*
> *Cladon* 1346 FA

'Clayey hill,' OE (dative) *clǣgigan dūne*. The first part of the name appears in (*on*) *Clǣihǣma* (*broc*) 956 (c. 1200) BCS 947: *v.* hǣme. The same name occurs in Bk (PN Bk 53) and Sf (DEPN).

CLATTERCOTE

> *Claterecota* 1167 P
> *Clatercota* 1168 P, *Clatercot* 1235 Cl *et passim* with variant spelling *Clatercote* to early 18th ParColl, *Clattercote* 1526 LS
> *Clatrecot* 1204 P (p)
> *Cladercot* 1797 Davis

Ekwall (DEPN) suggests that this is 'cot(e) by a clatter,' and that the dialect word *clatter*, meaning 'debris, loose stones,' may be old, although it is not recorded till the 19th century. The same element is apparently found in Clatterford Wt and Clater He.

GLEBE FM. Cf. *Glebe Allotment* 1837 *Plan*[1]. LAWN HILL is so named 1775 *EnclA*. CLAYDON HAY, HAY BRIDGE (6"). Cf. *Hay Field Quarter*, *Hay Stone and Ford* 1776 *EnclA*: a *Clatercotehey*, *Clatercote Haye* appears 1551–2 *Survey* in the bounds of Cropredy: the suffix of this and of Claydon Hay is probably (ge)hæg.

---

[1] See the field-names for this document.

FIELD-NAMES

(a) Modern names (supplied by Mr R. Hillier) Barn Ground, Bridge Meadow, Dove-house Close (possibly the dove-cote of the Gilbertian Priory of Clattercote), Plant Meadow, Stone-pit ground. In 1837 (supplied by Mr R. H. A. Holbech from a Reference to the Plan of the Manor and Township of Claydon made by the Lord of the Manor) Gulliver's Ground, Hill Fields (*Hill Field Quarter* 1776 *EnclA*), The Home Ground, Home Leys (*v.* home), Homeward Land, The Knowle, The Pike (*v.* picked), The Poors Allotment, Sweet Pot, Three Fields, Town Close, Vicar's Piece, Well Field (also 1776 *EnclA*). In 1776 (*EnclA*) Brook Furlong, Green Furlong, Loan Stone and Ford, Little Meadow Furlong (*Lutlemede* 1239 Eynsh, *v.* lȳtel, mǣd), Urchin Furlong (*urchin* is a dialect term for a hedgehog), Warden Way, Withybeds, Upper Withy Beds (*v.* wīðig).

(b) In 1278–9 (RH) *Pinkeworde* (*Pinkewroche* 1239 Eynsh, first element the personal name *Pinca*; the second might be worþ). In 1239 (Eynsh) *Sutbreche*, *Westbreche* (*v.* breche, to which 'south' and 'west' have been prefixed), *Caldewellefurlong* (*v.* c(e)ald, w(i)elle), *Costowe* (*v.* cot-stōw), *Gorebrugge* (*v.* gāra, brycg), *Hildebaldeshamme* ('*Hildebeald*'s hamm'), *Sepesbrugge* (second element brycg).

5. Cropredy

CROPREDY [krɔprədi or krɔpərdi]

Cropelie 1086 DB
Cropperi(a) 1109 Eynsh *et passim* with variant spellings *Cropper'*, *Croppery*, *Cropperie*, *Cropperey(e)*, *Cropperri* to 1367 Cl, *Croperia* 1159–62 Eynsh *et passim* with variant spellings *Croperi(e)*, *Croper(y)e*, *Croper'* to 1390 Eynsh
Cropri c. 1180 Madox, 1285 *Ass*, *Cropry* 1285 *Ass*, *Cropprye* 1297 Cl
Coppri early 13th AD (p)
Croprithi c. 1275 (c. 1450) Godstow (p)
Crorpery 1285 *Ass*
Cropurthe 1316 FA
Cropredy 1390 Eynsh, *Croppridy* 1428 FA, *Cropidy* 1449 Eynsh, *Croprydy al. Cropprydy* 1472 BM, *Croperedy* 1526 LS
Cropredy otherwise Croperdy 1777 *Loveday*, *Cropedy* 1783 *Loveday*
CROPREDY MILL (6″) is so named 1778 *EnclA*.

The second element is rīðig, 'small stream.' The first may be a weak form *Croppa* of the strong personal name found in Cropston Lei.

Ekwall (DEPN) suggests that it is OE *cropp*, referring in this case to plants, perhaps water plants.

OATHILL FM takes name from *Hothulle* 1239 Eynsh. The etymology is probably that suggested by the modern form.

OXEY HILL, FM take name from *Oxeye* 1239 Eynsh: cf. *Oxhey Close* 1788 *Loveday*. 'Ox enclosure,' *v.* (ge)hæg.

CROPREDY LAWN. Cf. *Lawn Hill Close and Meadow* c. 1840 *TA*.

FIELD-NAMES

(*a*) Modern names (supplied by Mr R. W. Cross, Mr C. Lambert, Mr R. Roberts, Mr J. Whitaker and Dr T. Loveday) Bretch (*v.* breche), Brickhill (this is a dialect form of *brick-kiln*), Little Bullmoor (*Boulmore* 1551–2 *Survey*, *v.* mōr), Corn Ground, the Cup and Saucer field (the remnants of Cropredy Cross stand here, and the base is hollowed), Fenny Lake (*Venylake* 1551–2 *Survey*, 'muddy stream,' *v.* lacu), Flick Piece, Ham Ground (*v.* hamm), Upper Harble, Ladymoor (so named 1775 *EnclA*, *v.* Lady), Landmere (*Londymere, Landmore* 1551–2 *Survey*; the first form looks like OE *landgemǣre*, 'boundary,' and this form occurs in a list of the bounds of Cropredy), Moat Meadow (named from the moat of the manor house), The Moor, Olan Ground, Rushford (*Rushford Close* 1788 *Loveday*), School Leys (behind the building which was once a school, founded by Walter Calcott in 1574), Stone Stile Ground, Tale (cf. *Thale Plank* 1775 *EnclA*, *v.* plank), Big and Little Townhill, Turnpike Ground, Withy Holt (*Withey Holt* c. 1840 *TA*, *v.* wiðig). In c. 1840 (*TA*) Dry Moor (so named 1797 *Loveday*), Madcroft (so named 1797 *Loveday*, *v.* mǣd), The Nursery Close, Ram Close (so named 1797 *Loveday*). In 1788 (*Loveday*, from a Sale Catalogue) Ainsmoor Close, Austins Knobb, Bin Furlong Close, The Bogg Meadow, Canal Meadow, Deep Furrow Close, Hale Meadow (*v.* h(e)alh), Hall Meadow, Home Close (*v.* home), Howland Close (*Howland Quarter* 1775 *EnclA*), Moorstone Close (*Moor Stone* 1775 *EnclA*), Upper and Lower Sandymoor Close, Stone Pit Close, Windmill Close, Wyatt's Park. In 1775 (*EnclA*) Ast or Alst Mead, Broadway Road (*Bradeweye* 1239 Eynsh, *Brodwaye* 1551–2 *Survey*, *v.* brād, weg), Calves Close, Common Bush Leys, Field End Quarters, Hackthorn or Haikthorn Quarter (*Haghorne* 1551–2 *Survey*; *hag* is a dialect form of *haw*, and *hag-thorn* is given in EDD for the hawthorn tree), Hayway Quarter, Hillington Cross Furlong (cf. *Yllenden* 1551–2 *Survey*), West Meadow Acres (*Westmeade* 1551–2 *Survey*).

(*b*) In 1551–2 (*Survey*) *Alege*, (*bridge called*) *Boottam*, *le Foxhole* (*v.* foxhole), *Gulmore* (*v.* mōr), *Helborysham, Landhille, Sydkynges* (probably an error for *Sydlynges*, *v.* sideling). In 1239 (Eynsh) *Hundesgore* (second element gāra, first the personal name *Hund), *Voxhulleforlonge* ('fox hill furlong'), *Walecote* (*v.* weala, cot(e)), *Watereshulle* (*v.* hyll), *Wodehulle* (*v.* wudu, hyll), *Wolforlong*).

6. Epwell

EPWELL

(*on*) *Eoppan wyllan* (*broc*) 956 (c. 1200) BCS 964, (*of*) *Eoppan wyllan* (*broc*) 956 (18th) BCS 967, (*on*) *Eoppan welles* (*stream*) 956 (c. 1200) BCS 966, (*on*) *Eoppan wylles* (*stream*) 956 (c. 1250) BCS 966[1]

(*of*) *Coppan wyllan* (*broc*) 956 (c. 1200) BCS 964

Epewella 1185 P, *Eppewella* 1187 P *et passim* with variant spellings *Eppewell*(*e*), *Eppewell*' to 1506 AD, *Eppuwelle* 1199 FF

Uppewelle 1213–28 Eynsh, c. 1240 Os, *Uppewell* 1285 Cl

Ippewelle c. 1260 Os *et freq* with variant spellings *Ippewell*, *Yppewell*(*e*) to c. 1300 Thame

Ipwell 1482, 4 AD, 1509–10 Os

Eppwell 1537 AD

'*Eoppa*'s spring,' *v*. w(i)elle.

7. Fawler

FAWLER

Fauflor 1205 OblR *et passim* with variant spellings *Fauflore*, *Fauflur* to 1251 Eynsh

Fauylor 1213–28 Eynsh, *Fauilore* c. 1230 (c. 1425) Frid

Faulore c. 1230 AD, 1349 Cl, 1385, 90 Eynsh, 1428 FA

Fauelore c. 1230 (c. 1425) Frid *et freq* with variant spelling *Fauelor* to 1428 FA, *Fauelaure* 1428 FA

Fan(*n*)*eflur* 1268 Ass, *Faneflore* 1278–9 RH

Favelore 1275 Cl

The name is identical with the phrase (*to*) *fāgan flōran*, which occurs in the boundaries of Water Eaton in 904 (BCS 607). It means 'variegated floor,' i.e. 'tesselated pavement.' *v*. fāg, flōr. The pavement at Fawler was one of those in a Romano-British house in a meadow on the north bank of the Evenlode. One was opened up in 1865, but covered in again, and another was destroyed in making the railway line. The same name occurs in Berks. Cf. also *Beowulf* 725 (*on fāgne flōr*) and PN Nth 82.

LEESREST FM. Cf. E. K. Chambers, *Sir Henry Lee*, p. 209: "The court spent most of September at Woodstock and from here the King and Queen...went to visit Lee at a lodge three miles away, which was probably Lee's Rest." The reference is to the year 1603. For Sir

[1] v.r. *Eow anwelles* (18th).

Henry Lee *v.* 416. *Lees Rest House, Light and Wood* are mentioned
c. 1840 *TA*, and the wood appears also 1822 O.S. For *light v.* 346.
For *rest* in this sense cf. NED sb¹ 5.

HILLBARN FM is so named 1822 O.S.

FIELD-NAMES

(*a*) In c. 1840 (*TA*) Ashey Close, Beadley field, Bury Close (cf. *Berry
barne* 1656 *Bodl, v.* burh), Little Coldshore, Dagtail piece (*v.* church),
Eldern Lane piece, Harrell Poll piece, Kings Acre field, Ladbury, Moor
Mead, Parsonage Linces (*v.* hlinc), Parsons piece, Old Pound, Red Stone
Quarry Lane, Reed Hill field and Quarry, Sweeten Tree piece (a *sweeting*
is 'a small, sweet early apple').

(*b*) In 1608–9 (*Survey*) Nettleden (*Netleden* 1300 Wych, 'nettle valley,'
v. denu). In 1363 (Eynsh) *Gylberdescroft* ('Gilbert's croft'), *Horsseley* ('horse
pasture'), *Henleden, Lurttesse, Ordeweygrove* (cf. *Ordwyeswode* 1270 Eynsh,
Ordeweygraue 1271–2 *For, v.* weg, grāf(a), wudu: the first element might be
ord, 'point,' cf. PN Ca 79), *cultura S. Andree, le Slade* (*v.* slæd), *Strittehuppe-
breche* (*v.* breche, to which 'straight up' has been prefixed). In 1270 (Eynsh)
Roggeresrudinge ('Roger's clearing,' *v.* ryding).

8. Finstock

FINSTOCK

Finestochia 1135–50 Eynsh *et passim* with variant spellings
  Finestoches, Finestok', Finestok(e), Finestroc, Fynestok', Fynestoke
  to 1300 Wych
Fines-stokes 1191–1205 Eynsh
Finstoke 1208 Eynsh *et freq* with variant spellings *Finstok,
  Fynstok(e)*
Foystoke 1285 *Ass*

'stoc frequented by woodpeckers,' *v.* fina.

DUNFORD COPSE (6″) takes name from *Derneford* ?1272 (c. 1280) S:
cf. *Dunforde meade* 1656 *Bodl, Dunford Coppice and Meadow* c. 1840
TA. 'Hidden ford,' *v.* d(i)erne. The same name occurs again rather
less than six miles away, *v.* Lower and Upper Dornford Fm in
Wootton 293. Places called *darneforde* and *darnecrofte* are mentioned
1490 *Bodl*, probably with reference to this place.

ILLCOTT COPSE (6″) takes name from *Hyldecott'* 1363 Eynsh, *Hillcott*
1608–9 *Survey*. Cf. *Illcotts Coppice, Long Illcott* c. 1840 *TA*.
'Cottage(s) on a slope,' *v.* h(i)elde, cot(e).

PATCH RIDING (6″), PATCH HILL GATE (Cornbury Park 6″), PATCH HILL (Wychwood). Cf. *Pachesdiche* 1268–81 Eynsh. *v.* dīc: the first element is the personal name **Pæcc(i)*. *v.* PN Sx 249.

TOPPLES LANE, WOOD (both 6″) take name from *Teppewelle* 1215–23 Eynsh, *Cappewelle* 1270 Eynsh, *Tamewelle* 1285 Eynsh, *Tappewelle* 1285 Eynsh, 1316 FA, 1349 Cl, 1355 Ch. The wood is *Tapples Wood* 1821 O.S. '**Tæppa*'s spring,' *v.* w(i)elle. For the personal name cf. PN Bk 231–2 and PN Wo 114.

DOWNFIELD COPSE and WALLBOROUGH GROVE (both 6″). Cf. *Downe Field* and *Wadbury* 1608–9 *Survey*, *Down field Coppice* and *Walborough Grove* c. 1840 *TA*. LADY GROVE (6″) is so named c. 1840 *TA* (*v.* Lady). STOCKFIELD BRAKE (6″) is *Stockfield Coppice* c. 1840 *TA*.

FIELD-NAMES

(a) In c. 1840 (*TA*) The Breach (cf. *Iamesbrech le ridere* 1270 Eynsh, *v.* breche: *ridere* looks like an agent noun from the unrecorded OE verb *ryddan*, 'to clear land,' in which case James would be the man who cleared the newly cultivated strip of forest; but he may simply have been known as 'the rider' or 'the knight' (*rīdere* occurs in OE as the equivalent of *miles*): the construction is a common one in ME, cf. the phrase *Piers berne þe plowman*, i.e. 'the barn of Piers the Plowman,' *Piers Plowman* xix, 354), Buckhorn (the word is a dialect term for clubmoss, *Lycopodium clavatum*), Damask Lays (*Domase Leaze* 1608–9 *Survey*; *domase* is an obsolete form of *damask*, but the meaning here is obscure: there is a Damaskfield Copse on the 6″ map in Hampstead Norris Berks: *v.* lǣs), Gaddle Hill (cf. *Gattwell* 1608–9 *Survey*), Lurton Ground (*Lurteden*' 1268–81 Eynsh, *Lurden field* 1608–9 *Survey*, 1641 Wych, *v.* denu: a personal name *Lorta* is found in *Lortan hlæw* BCS 705, and Ekwall (RN 259–60) assumes an OE **lort*, 'dirt,' which might be the source of the personal name; either would be a possible first element here), Peaked Piece and Lane (*v.* picked), The Pound, Wall Ground.

(b) In 1608–9 (*Survey*) Benninge, *Lymepitt field* (*Lymeputtes* 1268–81 Eynsh, *v.* pytt, first element 'lime'), *Squire piece*. In 1270 (Eynsh) *Sireford*, *Taylardescroft* (*v.* croft; the first element is probably a surname). In 1268–81 (Eynsh) *Houterodeweye* (second element **rod*, 'clearing,' final element weg; the prefix is probably 'out': the word *roadway* is not recorded before 1600), *la Ritterode*.

9. Prescote

PRESCOTE MANOR

Prestecote c. 1196 Os (p) *et passim* with variant spellings *Prestecot*, *Prestekot*, *Prestecot*' to 1278–9 RH, *Prestekote alias Prestecot* 1251 Ipm (p)

Prestcote 1235–6 Fees, 1227–8 WellsR, 1346 FA, *Prestcot* 1428 FA
Prustecote 1285 *Ass*
Prescote 1316 FA, *Prescote Manor* 1797 Davis, *Prescott Manor* 1802 *Loveday*

UPPER PRESCOTE (6″)

Over Prescot 1797 Davis, *Upper Prescott* 1802 *Loveday*

'Priests' cottage,' *v.* prēost, cot(e).

FIELD-NAMES[1]

(*a*) Modern names (supplied by Mrs McDougall) Big Ground, Bradmere Meadow (see below), Coggy Meadow (*Gagg Meadow* 1797, *Gogg Meadow* 1802, c. 1840 *TA*, *v.* gog), Dairy Ground (cf. *South Middle Field or Dairy Ground* 1802), Duck Meadow (so named 1797), Freeman's Holme (*Freeman's Ham* 1797: this name is connected with the legend of St Fremund (? earlier *Friþumund*), for which *v.* Canon Wood's articles in *The Antiquary* for 1893, and F. N. Macnamara's *Memorials of the Danvers Family*, London 1895, p. 257 ff.: Canon Wood traces the legend back as far as the early 13th, but most of the details relevant to the Prescote name are found in a 15th-century poem by Lydgate: after the saint's death and first burial his body was removed to a place between the Cherwell and Bradmere; here it was found by a pilgrim who was told in a dream to look for it, one of the signs being that he would see a milk-white sow at the place with thirteen piglets; the body was found and removed to Dunstable: there is evidence for the former existence of a shrine of St Fremund in Cropredy church, and at Prescote House, embedded in the interior, there is a sculptured stone of a sow with two pigs, which Canon Wood was told had long since been brought from Freeman's Holme), The Fuzzens (cf. *Homeward and Further Furzey Field* 1797), Lag Meadow (*v.* lag), Old Woman's Meadow (so named 1797), Pikey Ground (*v.* picked), Rushy Close (cf. *Rushey Ground* 1797), Square Hayes (*Square Hey* 1797, *Square Hay* 1802, *v.* (ge)hæg), White Ban Field (middle element probably bēan). In c. 1840 (*TA*) The Banks (*the Bank* 1802), Bridge Bit (cf. *Bridge Lane* 1797), Buttermilk Hall (so named 1797), Haddocks Hoof (*Addocks Hooks* 1797) Middle and Upper Spellow, Lower Spillow (*Spellow* 18th; formally the name could be identical with that of Spellow in Nth, which means 'speech hill' and is used of a hundred meeting place; but the forms are too late to be used with confidence). In 1802 Bushy Ground, Cabin Ground (*Cabbin Ground* 1797), Corn Close (also 1797), The Grove or Rookery (also 1797), Homeward and Little and Long Hay (*Homeward and Little and Long Hey* 1797, *v.* (ge)hæg), Horse Close (also 1797), The Mill Holme (also 1797, *v.* holme), Old Orchard (also 1797).

[1] Except where otherwise stated, the forms are from *Loveday*; those for 1802 and 1797 are from Sale Catalogues.

10. Shutford

SHUTFORD, EAST AND WEST

Schiteford' c. 1160 (c. 1225) RegAntiquiss
Su(i)telesford' 1168 P
Setelesford' 1169 P
Setteford' 1209–12 (c. 1300) Fees
Schutford 1240–1 Ass, *Schuttford* 1483 AD
Sutteford (bis) 1246–7 Ass
Schutteforde c. 1250 AD, *Schutteford* 1278–9 RH
Shutteford 1252 FF
Shetteford 1283 Ch
Shitford 1285 Ass, *Shitforde* 1526 LS
Sitford 1285 Ass
Shiutford 1316 FA
Southeford 1346 FA
Sciteford' 1392 RegAntiquiss
Shuthford 1428 RegAntiquiss
Shetford 1676 Plot

The two 12th-century Pipe Roll forms suggest that the first element is the personal name *Scyttel* found in Shillington Beds (PN BedsHu 174) and Shitlington WRY and Nb. The other forms accord better with the etymology '*Scytta*'s ford,' *Scytta* being the name of which *Scyttel* is a diminutive.

FIELD-NAMES

(a) In 1766 (*EnclA*) Alices Meadow, Barnhill furlong, Crabtree Balk, Deans Meadow, the Ham, the long Ham (*v.* hamm), Meadow Lane, Picked Meadow (*v.* picked), the Spinney, the two Stile(d) Meadow, the Tythe piece.

(b) In 1278–9 (RH) *la Hide* (*v.* hīd).

11. Swalcliffe

SWALCLIFFE [sweiklif *olim* sweikli]

Sualewclive c. 1166 Madox, *Sualewecliue* 1189–91 Os
Swaleclive c. 1190 (c. 1280) S (p) *et freq* with variant spelling
    Swaleclyve to 1382 Cl, *Swallecleffe* 1483 AD
Swaleueclive 1194 Cur (p), *Swaleweclif* c. 1200 AD (p), *Swaleweclyve* 1327, 8 Ch

Suaneclive 1200 P

Sualecliue 1208–13 Fees, c. 1240 Os (p), *Sualeclive* (bis) 1278–9 RH (p)

Swawecliue c. 1217, 1218–21 Os (p), *Swaweclive* 1278–9 RH (p)

Swaulecliue 1240–1 *Ass*

Swalweclyue 1252 FF

Swalclyf 1266 FF *et passim* with variant spellings *Swalclive*, *Swalcleve, Swalclyve, Swalcliff*

Suthelewceclive 1275–6 RH (p)

Swalocliue 1285 *FF*

Swaltclyve 1428 FA

Swakeley 1546 AD

Swacliff 1526 LS, 1797 Davis, *Swakliffe* 1589 AD

'Swallow cliff'; *v.* clif, and cf. the same name PN W 192–3, in the form Swallowcliffe.

UPPER AND LOWER LEA FMS (6″). Cf. *la Le* 1278–9 RH, *la Lee* 1316 FA (p), *la Legh* 1346 FA (p), *v.* lē(a)h.

MADMARSTON HILL is *Mad Marton, a hill call'd* early 18th ParColl. This is perhaps a corrupt version of the name of the adjacent parish of Tadmarton.

LANGLEY HILL (6″). Cf. *Langley Ground* c. 1840 *TA.* ROW BARROW is *the Roberrow* 1676 (c. 1700) *BodlT*: 'rough tumulus,' *v.* rūh, be(o)rg: a round barrow was opened in 1854 (VCH O II, 347). STOUR WELL is so named 1797 Davis: the river Stour rises here.

OLD GRANGE FM (6″). Cf. (grange of) *Olewelle* late 12th *AOMB*, *Holewelle* c. 1166 Madox, (grange of) *Holewelle* 1278–9 RH. The early name means 'spring in a hollow,' *v.* holh, w(i)elle. There is a spring in Hill Bottom a little to the south. For other occurrences of the name, *v. supra* 325.

FIELD-NAMES

(*a*) In 1939 (VCH O I, 308) Blacklands or Blakelands (so called from a considerable depth of discoloured earth, indicating Romano-British habitation). In c. 1840 (*TA*) Dovehouse Home close (*v.* home), The Park, Ram Close.

(*b*) In c. 1166 (Madox) *Hetdic* (*v.* hǣp, dīc), *Litlewald* (*v.* w(e)ald, first element 'little').

12. Wardington

WARDINGTON

Wardinton c. 1180 Madox *et freq* with variant spellings *Wardintona*,
Wardinton', *Wardynton(e)* to 1370 AD

Wardington' (bis) 1268 *Ass et passim* with variant spellings
Wardyngton(e), *Wardington*

Wordinton' 1268 *Ass*

Ardyngtone (bis) 1285 *Ass*

'*Wearda's farm,' *v.* ingtūn. Ekwall (DEPN) suggests, however,
that there may have been an OE word *wearde or *wearda corresponding to ON *varða*, *varði*, 'beacon, cairn,' and this, not an
unrecorded personal name, may be the first element of *Weardan hyll*
BCS 663 and of Wardington.

BELL LAND (6″) is *Allotment of the Trustees of the Curfew Bell* 1760
EnclA. Dr T. Loveday informs us that the Cropredy Bell Land
Trust was instituted 1512–13 by Roger Lupton, Vicar of Cropredy,
for the keeping of the church clock and ringing of the curfew and
day bell. The rent is applied to this purpose.

COTON FM. Cf. *Cothamhul* early Hy 3 *AOMB*, *Cotes* 1316 FA,
Cottes alias Cotton 1551–2 *Survey*. *Coton alias Cotes* appears frequently in the 17th *Bodl*. The modern name is from *cotum*, the
dative plural of cot(e).

FERNHILL FM. Cf. *Verne hille* 1551–2 *Survey*, *Fern Hill* 1797 Davis.
'Fern hill.'

WILLIAMSCOT [wilzkɔt]

Williamescote 1166 (c. 1203) LN *et passim* with variant spellings
Willamescot', *Wil(l)amescot*, *Wyl(l)amescote*, *Willameskote* to
1346 FA, *Willamuscote* 1285 *Ass*, *Willamscote* 1316 FA

Walmescote 1166 (c. 1280) RBE, 1208–13 (c. 1300) Fees

Willescot', *Willescota* c. 1240 *AOMB*, *Willescote* c. 1270 AD (p)

Willemecote 1253 Cl

Willelmescote 1254–68 Os (p)

Williamescote c. 1275 AD (p) *et passim* with variant spellings
Wyllyamescote, *Williamescot*, *Willyamescote* to 1428 FA, *Wil-
liamscote* 1334 Cl

Wilhamescot 1284–5 FA, *Wylhamescote* 1285 *Ass*, *Wilhamescote*
1332 Eynsh (p)

Willemescote 1304–5 AD (p), 1328 Eynsh (p), *Willemmescote*
c. 1304–5 AD (p)
Willyonscote, Willonscot 1428 FA (p)

'William's cot(e).' It is interesting to note that the shortened form represented by the modern pronunciation is found in the 13th century.

HAY'S BRIDGE is *Hayes Bridge* 1760 *EnclA*. REDLUNCH BARN (6″) takes name from *Red Lunch* 1761 Loveday, *v.* lunch. WILLIAMSCOT HILL. Dr Loveday informs us that this is known locally as *Kala-bergo's Hill* after an Italian travelling jeweller who was murdered there by his nephew in 1852. The story is told in *Shoemaker's Window* by George Herbert (Oxford 1948), p. 88.

FIELD-NAMES[1]

(a) Modern names (supplied by Dr T. Loveday) Ash ground (*Ash Quarter* 1760 *EnclA, Ash Tree Ground* 1857: this is said in Beesley's *History of Banbury*, 360, to be the place where Charles I dined under an ash-tree on the day of the skirmish at Cropredy Bridge), Banky, Barn Pit, Barley Close, Beggar Bush, Berry or Bury Ham (cf. *Buryclose* 1551–2 *Survey, Berry Close* 1775 *EnclA, v.* hamm, first element burh: Dr Loveday tells us there is a local theory that soldiers killed at Cropredy Bridge are buried here), Black-land, Bourne mouth, Bridge Meadow (*Bury Ham Bridge Meadow* 1777, 1857), Broad Meadow (so named 1760 *EnclA*; Dr Loveday informs us that it is part of a low-lying tract of land known as Br(o)adimore; cf. the field-names of Prescott, and Broadmoor Bridge and Spinney in the 6″ map), Bushill (*Bishill* 1745, *Bissell's furlong* 1760 *EnclA*), Bull's Piece (owned by William *Bull* 1702), Bush Ground, Bunyards, Butchers Meadow (so named in the 17th), Canathan Hill (*Canathon Hill* 18th), Catsbrain (so named 1745, *v.* catsbrain), Carpenter Hill, Cheek Brook, Chapel Close, Church Ground, Clump Ground, Cotsmore Hill, Cowpen (cf. *Cow Close* 1633, *Cow Pen Close* c. 1840 *TA*), Cub Ground (*cub* is used in dialect for 'a crib for cattle or horses to eat from' and for 'a wide sweep in a road'), Dibdale (*Depedale* 1551–2 *Survey, Deepdale* 1777, 83, 'deep dale'), Dorkings, Dry Ground, Elias Piece, Fern Flat, Fellow, Fidlers Ground (cf. *Fidlers Corner* 1796), French's Ham (*v.* hamm; an Edmund *French* has land 1760 *EnclA*, and the surname is common in the district), Gogs, Pigeon Gogs (*v.* gog), Great Hill (so named 1633), Grinstead, Heritage's (Thomas *Heritage* was a yeoman in Coton in 1777), Hirons Hill (*v.* 240), Holloway Lane (*Holywell Lane* 1760 *EnclA*, but the earlier form is probably incorrect; the road has steep banks), Kirby Close, Lady Furlong (so named 1702, cf. *Lady Meadowe* 1633, *v.* Lady), Leighs, Lord's Ground (cf. *The Lord's Meadowe, The Lord's Lott* 1633),

[1] Forms for which no references are given are from documents in the possession of Dr T. Loveday. We are also indebted to him for the Enclosure Award forms, and for information about landowners etc.

Madam's Hill and Hedge (the latter is *Mrs Denton's Hedge* 1760 *EnclA*: Mrs Denton was one of the Chamberlaynes who owned the Manor House in the 18th), Marches (cf. *grounds in the parish of Chalcombe called Marches* 1760 *EnclA*; Chalcombe is in Nth), May Furlong, Moor Hill (so named 1745, 50; cf. *The Moore* 1702, *v.* mōr), Over Leys, Over Hays (*v.* (ge)hæg), The Osiers (cf. *The Witheys* 1745, 50, *v.* wīðig), Pear Meadow (*Paremeade* 1745, 50), Pettifer Hill (*Pettifer* is a not uncommon surname in the district), Pikes (*v.* picked), Pits, Plain, Pond Ground, Pratt's Sales (so named 1796, *v.* PN Nth 157 on the word *sale*), Puds House Ground, Pump Ground, Raven Hill, Sand fine, Sandlands (so named 1702), Sand Pit, Slinket (*v.* slinket), Snailscroft (*Snail's Croft* 1760 *EnclA*), Spellen (*Short Spelham* 1702, *Long Spelham* 1745, *Spelham Quarter* 1760 *EnclA*), Steel's Hill (owned by J. *Steel* in 1819), Stone Close, Stone Pit, Swans Close (*close called Forsworne* 1551–2 *Survey*, *Sworn Close* 1750: the meaning is obscure, but there was a *Forswornewod* in Nt (PN Nt 134)), Ten Leys, Thistle Ground, Three Thorns, Tinkers (*Tinkers House* 1760 *EnclA*), Toll Gate, Townsend (there are a number of fields in the *EnclA* the names of which consist of Townsend and a prefix or suffix), Wad Ground (cf. the field-names of Banbury), Wade Meadow, Whitnell (so named 1702), Windmill Ground (the windmill, now vanished, is mentioned in the *EnclA*).

(*b*) In 1857 *Cross Leys* (*Cross Lease* 17th), *Smart's Leasow* (also 1633, *v.* lǣs). In c. 1840 (*TA*) *Little Bit, Corn Close, Farm Homestall, Homeward Dairy Ground*. In 1799 *Cherry Pitt Way* (also 1702). In 1798 (*Loveday*, from a Sale Catalogue) *Thatchum Ground and Meadow* (cf. *Thakam hills* 1551–2 *Survey*, *v.* þæc-hamm). In 1796 *Shoulder of Mutton* (*v.* Des). In 1777 *Meerhedge Quarter* (*Meerhedge* 1702). In 1768 *The Overys* (*Overes* t. Hy 6 (Dr Loveday, from a Lincoln Rental), *the Over Reye* 1551–2 *Survey*, 'over the river,' cf. Overy 152). In 1760 (*EnclA*) *Pale Meadow Leys, Pasture Lane, Shepherd's Bench* (*v.* bench), *Standard Gap*. In 1750 *Berry Hill* (also 1702), *Blakemore* (also 1745, *v.* blæc, mōr), *Hamditch* (also 1745, *v.* hamm), *Short Holland* (also 1745), *Longham Leys, Somer Leys* (also 1702), *Wheatsmall* (also 1745). In 1745 *Haywell Leys*. In 1711 *Hopyard*. In 1702 *Flexfurlong* (*v.* fleax). In 1551–2 (*Survey*) *Chalkefeld* ('chalk field'), *les Hames* (*Hammis* t. Hy 6 (Dr Loveday, from a Lincoln Rental), *v.* hamm), *le Horstone* (Morton, *The Natural History of Northamptonshire*, 1712, mentions a *Horestone*, apparently on the border of the two counties; *v.* PN Nth 34 for the quotation, *v.* hār, stān), *Meryhouse, Moryhome* (the first element of both names might be the name of a kind of cherry, which occurs also in Broadwell fields), *Stakamford* (*v.* ford: first element an oblique case of staca, 'stake'). In 1466–7 (*Rental*) *Emore* (*v.* mōr), *le Morefe, Oldwelslade* (*v.* (e)ald, w(i)elle, slæd), *Sungrascroft* (*v.* gærs, croft). In early Hy 3 (*AOMB*) *Horsepoleshale* ('horse pool,' to which h(e)alh has been added), *Rodmoor* (*v.* hrēod, mōr).

THE ELEMENTS, APART FROM PERSONAL NAMES, FOUND IN OXFORDSHIRE PLACE-NAMES

Under some of the elements the examples are arranged in three categories. (*a*) Uncompounded elements and examples in which the first element is a significant word or another place-name, not a personal name, (*b*) those in which the first element is a personal name, (*c*) those in which the character of the first element is uncertain. Where no statement is made it may be assumed that the examples belong to type (*a*). Names for which no forms earlier than 1500 have been found are only included if they are of special interest.

āc, OE, 'oak tree.' Oakley (2), Fiveoak Copse, Noke, Roke, Shakenoak, Smalloaks Copse. Also in field-names.

æcer, OE, 'cultivated piece of land,' later used to denote a measure of land. Sparacre Lane, Twelve Acre Fm. *passim* in field-names.

æsc, OE, 'ash tree.' Ashford Bridge. Also in field-names.

æw(i)elm, OE, 'river-spring.' Ewelme, *Ewelme Pill*.

āte, OE, 'oats.' Oathill Fm, Oatleyhill Fm. Also in field-names, where there are two more examples of 'oats hill,' in Stratton Audley (1412–13) and Milton under Wychwood (1160–80).

bake, beak. *v.* PN W 450–1, where this is explained as a dialect word meaning 'to chop up with a mattock the rough surface of land to be reclaimed, afterwards burning the parings.' This word and the compound *burn-bake* are used substantively to denote ploughed land reclaimed in this way. In Oxfordshire *burn-bake* occurs as a field-name in Bensington, Northmoor and Pyrton, and *the Beake* occurs in Piddington.

bakke, ME, 'bat,' may be the first element of the stream-name *Back Brook*, which occurs four times in the county.

balle, ME, 'a landmark of earth set up as a boundary mark' (*v.* PN W 422) occurs occasionally in field and minor names. There are probable early examples in Chinnor (Ballfield Shaw takes name from *Le Balle* 1296), Pyrton (*Ballond* 1300), Weston on the Green (*Ballethorne* 1241) and Aston Rowant (*Ballhill* 1487). The modern name *Ball(s)* occurs in Ascot under Wychwood, Baldon, Caversfield and Garsington.

barre, ME, 'a barrier closing the entrance into a city,' afterwards applied to the gate by which these were replaced, occurs several times in the street-names of Banbury.

Bayard, a stock French name for a bay horse. Bayard's Green, Bays-water Brook. Cf. also *Bayerdes leyes* (1551–2), a field-name in Bruern, and *Bayard Furlong* (1777) in Blackthorn.

bēam, OE, 'tree, beam.' Bampton.

bēan, OE, 'bean,' is common in field-names, **bēan-land**, which gives *Bandland* in modern names, being especially frequent. The element occurs in several lost stream-names, for which *v.* 13.

bēce, OE, 'beech tree.' Beech Fm (2), Beech Wood (2). Also in field-names.

bedd, OE, 'place where plants grow.' Nettlebed. Also in field-names, an early example being *riscbed*, 956 in Tadmarton: cf. wīðig *infra*.

benc, OE. *v.* PN W 423, where it is suggested that this word was used in place-names in a similar way to Anglo-Scandinavian *banke* to mean 'slope.' There is one early example in Oxfordshire (*Benchfurlung* c. 1240 in Sibford Gower) and the modern field-names *The Benches*, *Green Benches*, *Binchcroft* occur in Spelsbury, Chadlington and Baldon respectively. *Shepherds Bench* occurs in Shipton under Wychwood and Wardington.

beonet, OE, 'bent-grass.' Binfield. Also in field-names.

be(o)rg, OE, 'hill, barrow.' (*a*) Burwell Fm (?), Roughborough Copse, *Spelberwe*, *Spelburghe*, *Thornbury*, Warborough; (*b*) Hand-borough, *Kenners Barrow*. Frequent in field-names, where there are references to groups of barrows, cf. *crofta trium Bergarum* c. 1200 in Oxford, *Trembergh* c. 1190 in Rollright, *Tuamberewe* late 12th in Fifield, *Fifburghe* c. 1260 in Hook Norton and *Fifberwe* late 12th in Fifield. An interesting use of the word is seen in the field-name *Maydeneberewe*, c. 1270 in Hook Norton, where it denotes a prehistoric camp: *burh* or *castel* are the usual words in names of this type, *v.* PN Cu 255–6.

be(o)rht, OE, 'shining, clear, bright.' Brightwell Baldwin. Cf. also *Brictewelle*, c. 1240 in Steeple Barton.

beorn, OE, 'man, prince, warrior.' Bicester (?).

***berd**, a mutated form of OE *bord*, corresponding to ON *byrði*, has been postulated as the first element of Beard Mill.

bere, OE, 'barley.' Barford. Fairly frequent in field-names, where it gives the modern forms *Bear*, *Beer* and *Bare*. Cf. beretūn, berewīc.

beretūn, OE, literally 'barley farm,' later denoting 'a grange situated in an outlying part of a manor, where the lord's crop was stored.' 'Outlying grange' is perhaps the usual meaning of the common place-name Barton. In Oxfordshire the name occurs in Barton in Headington, and in the group of names, Middle, Steeple and Westcot Barton, in Wootton Hundred. Westcot Barton appears as

Bærtune 1050–2 (13th) KCD 950 (p), and this may indicate that the names in Wootton Hundred have as their source the unrecorded OE *bærtūn*, of identical meaning, which has been postulated to explain the early forms for some Bartons.

berewīc, OE, identical in meaning with the preceding element. Berrick Prior, Berrick Salome.

biscop, OE, 'bishop,' occurs in the following early field-names: *Biscopesmor, bisshopisheyte*, 1124–30 and c. 1270 in Oxford, *Bissopeswode*, 1278–9 in Witney, *Bisschopesden'*, 1300 in North Leigh. Also in Bishop's Court and Bishopsland Fm, for which the forms are late.

blæc, OE, 'black.' Blacklands Plantation, Black Leys. The element is common in field-names, especially in the name 'black land(s),' which has been noted fourteen times. 'Black stream' (with second element w(i)elle) occurs some six times.

***blæcþorn**, OE, 'blackthorn.' Blackthorn.

blind, OE, 'blind,' applied to streams in the sense 'hidden by vegetation.' Blindwell appears twice on the modern map (in Crawley and Eynsham) and five times in field and lost stream-names.

boga, OE, 'bow, arch.' *Denchworth Bow*, Standbow Bridge.

bold, OE, 'building.' Bould. Cf. also *Boldecroftes*, 1442 in Eynsham.

box, OE, 'box tree.' Box Wood. Cf. also *Boxden*, 1300 in Spelsbury. Cf. ***byxe** *infra*.

brād, OE, 'broad.' Bradmore Road, Broadmoor Barn, Broadwell. Frequent in field-names, where there are several more examples of 'broad marsh,' with second element **mōr**.

breche, ME, from OE **bræc**, 'land newly taken into cultivation.' Breach Barn, Fm (2), Wood, Bretch Fm, Furzy Breach. *passim* in field-names, where it frequently gives the modern forms *Breach* and *Bretch*, and occasionally the form *Bratch*.

brōc, OE, 'brook.' (*a*) Brookend Ho, Brookfurlong Fm, Brookhampton, Broughton (2), *Cumbe Brok*, Danes Brook, Fulbrook, *Humble Brook*, Lashbrook, Madley Brook, Northbrook, *Sandbrook*, Swinbrook; (*b*) Begbroke, *Roppan broces*. *passim* in lost stream-names. In field-names **brōc-furlang**, 'furlong by the brook,' occurs some fourteen times.

broken, ME and ModE, occurs in *Broken Hays* and in three occurrences in field-names of the common name *Brokeneberge*, modern Brokenbury, which may denote a tumulus which has been broken into by robbers. Cf. also *Brokenemed'*, 1278–9 in Chesterton.

bruiere, OFr, 'heath.' Bruern.

brycg, OE, 'bridge.' (*a*) *Brugeset*, Gosford Bridge, Heyford Bridge, Hythe Bridge, *Knights Bridge*, Knightsbridge Fm, Quaking Bridge;

(*b*) Curbridge. Frequent in field-names, where the metathesised form *burge* occurs several times. With the two examples of Knightsbridge cf. *Sildenebrige* (c. 1200 in Warborough).

bula, OE, 'bull.' Bolney Court, Bullingdon (?), Bulstake Bridge. This word or a formally identical personal name occurs occasionally in field-names.

burh, OE, 'fortified place, town, manor house,' sometimes used of a prehistoric earthwork. (*a*) Barleyfields, Burdrop, Burford, Burleigh Fm, Burroway Bridge, Burwell Fm (?), Cornbury Park, Grimsbury, Howbery Park, Ilbury, *Kingsbury*, Mixbury; (*b*) Adderbury, Banbury, Charlbury, Idbury, Loughborough, Spelsbury, Wendlebury; (*c*) Albury. **burh** has been noted several times as a second element in early field-names, once with a personal name (*Bicanbyrig*, 1005 in Shipton on Cherwell) and once in another example of 'king's manor' (*Kyngesbur'*, 1270 in Newington). In the sense 'manor house' it may be the source of the element *Berry-, Bury-*, which occurs *passim* in such modern field-names as *Berry Field, Bury Croft, Berry Close*, but where the forms are late it is impossible to distinguish between **burh** and **be(o)rg**.

burhtūn, OE, either 'tūn (*v. infra*) by a **burh**' or 'enclosed settlement with a **burh** as its nucleus.' Bourton, Black Bourton.

burna, OE, 'stream.' *Hetheneburnde*, Shirburn, *Shitbarn Lane* (?). Occasionally in lost stream-names.

butere, OE, 'butter,' used in place-names to describe rich pasturage. Butter Hill. The element occurs also in several field-names, *Botereden* (c. 1278) in Enstone, and *Butter Bush, Croft* and *Field* in Pyrton, Curbridge and Bix, and in a lost stream-name, *Butterwell* in Bourton. Cf. also *Buttermilk Hall*, in the Prescote Tithe Award and Buttermilk Fm in Barford (*Butter Milk Hall* in 1797).

butts occurs *passim* in field-names. It is from ME **butte**, and is used of strips of ground abutting on a boundary, often at right angles to other ridges in the field. The forms date from the early 13th century onwards.

byrgen, OE, 'burying place.' Berins Hill (?), Berring's Wood.

bytme, OE, 'bottom,' occurs as a field-name in Aston Bampton, Aston Rowant (1411–12), Chinnor (1278), Eye and Dunsden (early 17th), South Stoke (1220–7) and Standlake. It gives modern *Bittham, Bettham, Bittam, Betam*.

*byxe, OE, 'box tree.' Bix. ***byxen**, an adjective formed from this, is the first element of Bixmoor Wood. ***byxe** occurs also in the field-name *Byxemor*, 1363 in Rollright.

cærse, OE, 'cress.' *Karshille* (early name of Bayswater Hill). **cærse-w(i)elle**, 'stream where water cress grows,' occurs nine times as a lost stream-name. ***cærsen**, an adjective formed from **cærse**, is the first element of Cassington. In OE the word was used for all cresses, not exclusively for water cress.

camp, OE, used in place-names with the probable meaning 'an enclosed piece of land.' Campsfield.

castel, OE from OFr, 'castle.' Castle, Castle Mill, Deddington Castle. Also in the following field-names: *Casteldych'*, 1315 in Hailey, *Castelfurlong*, 1328 in Ducklington, *Castell meade*, 1551–2 in Banbury.

catsbrain, the name of a coarse soil consisting of rough clay mixed with stones, occurs in Catsbrain Hill and is very frequent in field-names. *v.* PN Ca 315 for a discussion of the term, the origin of which has not been satisfactorily explained. It can only mean what it says.

catt, ME, 'cat.' Catsham Lane, *Cattesham* (2), Cat Street. Fairly frequent in field-names.

c(e)alc, OE, 'chalk, limestone.' Chalford (2), Chalgrove, Chalk Wood. Also in field-names.

c(e)ald, OE, 'cold.' Caulcott, Coldwell Brook, Cordle Bushes. 'Cold stream,' second element w(i)elle, occurs ten times as a lost stream-name.

ceastel, OE, probably used of a prehistoric camp. Chastleton.

ceaster, OE, 'city or walled town, ancient fort.' Chesterton, Alchester, Bicester, Dorchester. Cf. *Chestreweye, Chasterewye*, c. 1240 in Sandford on Thames.

ceole, OE, 'throat,' which may occur in place-names in the sense 'gully,' is possibly the first element of Chilmore Bridge and Shilcott Wood. Cf. also the field-names *Chelle* 1271–2, *Chille* 1278–9 (Holton), *Chelhurst* c. 1216 (Watlington), *Chelfelde* a. 1211 (Stoke Talmage).

ceorl, OE, 'free peasant.' Charlton on Otmoor. The precise sense of this common name (from OE *ceorlatūn* or *ceorlenatūn*) is uncertain. It may denote simply a place where peasants lived, or it may have some technical sense. ceorla, 'of the ceorls,' occurs also in the field-names *ceorla graf* (956 in Wheatley) and *Churlegrave* (c. 1180 in Mapledurham), 'peasants' grove,' *Cherleia* (t. Hy 2 in Sandford on Thames), 'peasants' island,' *ceorla pytte* (11th in Pyrton), 'peasants' pit,' and *Cherlefeld* (1349 in Henley).

ceosol, cisel, OE, 'gravel, shingle.' Chislehampton. Occasionally in field-names.

church. Land the rent of which was used for the upkeep of church equipment is known by names indicating the purpose to which it was applied. *Lamplands* occurs in Broughton Poggs, Lower Heyford (1606) and Wroxton, and *Lamp acre* in Churchill, Hook Norton, Watlington and Wootton. Cf. *Vestry Light* in Bruern.

Bell Piece occurs in Crowmarsh and Salford, and *Bell Butts* in Dorchester: cf. also Bell Land in Wardington. *Rope Ham* in Oxford, *Rope Croft* in Berrick Salome and *Rope Acre* in Wootton may refer to the upkeep of church bell-ropes, and *Dagtail piece* in Fawler was probably used to supply the tufted ends of the church bell-ropes (*v.* EDD). There are two references to a chantry, *Chantry Piece* (1825) in Chadlington and *Chauntry lands* (1679) in Rotherfield Greys, and four references under various names to the chancel—*Chauncell close* (1608–9) in Watlington, *Seyntuary Close* (t. Hy 8) in Oxford, *le Quere* (c. 1290) in Baldon and *the Quire* (1776) in Broadwell.

cīeping, OE, 'market.'[1] Chipping Norton, *Chepyngstret* (a lost street-name in Deddington), *Flaxcheaping* (a lost street-name in Banbury).

cild, OE, 'young nobleman.' Chilson. Cf. also *Childeslond*, 1366 in the field-names of Goring.

cipp, OE, 'log, trunk.' Chipping Fm.

cirice, OE, 'church.' Church Enstone, Churchill (?), Sarsden (?), Whitchurch. It is a frequent first element in field-names.

*cisen, OE, 'gravelly.' Chisnell Fm.

clǣg, OE, 'clay.' Clare, Clearsale. **clǣgig**, OE, 'clayey.' Claydon. **clǣg** occurs *passim* in field-names, where there are also two examples of an unrecorded OE *clǣgiht*, 'clayey' (*Cleyteforlonge*, c. 1275 in Black Bourton, and *Cleitlanda*, 1160–80 in Milton under Wychwood).

clǣne, OE, 'clean, clear, open.' Clanfield. Cf. also *clǣnandune*, 11th century in Pyrton.

clatter, dialect word for 'a heap of stones' first recorded in 1865 but probably much older. Clattercote.

clif, OE, 'cliff, slope, bank of a river.' Cleeve, The Cleeve, The Cleeves (2), Cleveley, Clifton (2), Swalcliffe. Also in field-names.

close, ME, 'enclosure' occurs *passim* in field-names.

cniht, OE, 'boy, youth, servant' and then 'servant of some military superior such as the king.' Knightsbridge Fm, *Knights Bridge*.

cocksho(o)t, ME, 'glade in a wood through which woodcocks might dart or "shoot," so as to be caught by nets stretched across the opening.' Cockshot Copse, Cockshoot Corner, Cockshoothill Copse. Also in the field-names of Holton, Minster Lovell and Stonesfield.

*cogg, OE, identical with ME and modern *cog*, 'cog of a wheel,' here used to mean 'hill.' Cogges.

col, OE, 'charcoal.' Calthorpe Ho (?), Colwell Brook, Coll Well.

colt, OE, 'colt.' Coldron Brook.

common, modern English, 'the undivided land belonging to the members of a local community,' hence often used of the patch of

---

[1] *v.* F. E. Harmer, 'Chipping and Market: A Lexicographical Investigation,' in *The Early Cultures of North-West Europe*, Cambridge 1950, pp. 335–60.

unenclosed or 'waste' land which remains to represent this, is
frequent in field-names.

conygree, 'rabbit warren,' from ME *conynger(e)* ultimately from OFr.
Coneygar Pond, Coneygar Copse, Coneygear Wood, Coneygre
Fm, Coneygree Wood, Conygree Fm, Conygree Terrace. The
forms are late. The ME form is represented by *Cuninger*, 1679 in
the forms for Coneygre Fm in Cottisford, and Coneygear Wood
in Nuffield is *Corngrey* in 1624. The element is frequent in field-
names, where the word *warren* also occurs *passim*.

copp, OE, 'top, summit.' Cobditch Hill, Adwell Cop. Occasionally
in field-names.

coppede, OE, recorded in OE charters of trees with the probable
meaning 'having the top cut off, pollarded,' and in ME with the
meaning 'rising to a top or head, peaked.' The element is fairly
frequent in field-names, but the meaning is not always clear.
Coppedeþorn, c. 1280 in Watlington, *Coppedethorne*, c. 1220–30 in
Chinnor, *Copthorne*, 1647 in Kidlington, and *Copythorn* in Dorchester and Hailey can be translated 'pollarded thorn-tree': cf. also
Copid Bush in Rousham. *Copt Hall* in Great Haseley and Caversfield probably means 'hall with a peaked roof': the name occurs
several times in Essex and Middlesex with early forms, v. PN
Ess 24. *Coppedelynche*, 1326 in Goring, *Coppydburye*, late 16th in
Warborough, and *Coppied hill* in Kidlington could mean either
'peaked hill' or 'hill with a flat top,' but the former is perhaps
more likely. The meaning of *Copped Lands* in Enstone and of
Coppede more, c. 1260 in Little Tew, *Coppidmore*, t. Hy 8 in
Shipton under Wychwood, *Copped* or *Coppied Moors* in Upper
Heyford, is obscure. v. PN Nth 267–8. There are several occurrences of *Coppedemor* in that county, and it is suggested there that
the meaning may be 'pollarded,' with reference to the reed-thickets
having been cut.

corbin, ME from OFr, 'raven.' Corble Fm.

*****corn**, OE, metathesised form of **cron, cran**, 'crane,' or, as in modern
dialect 'heron.' Cornbury Park, Cornwell. Perhaps also in *Corne-
heyte*, c. 1300 in Cassington fields, *Corndiche*, 1297 in Oxford,
Cornewelelond', early 13th in Kirtlington. *cran* occurs in Cranehill
Copse, *Cranemeare* (earlier name of Highfurlong Brook), Cranmoor
Plantation, *Cranweye*, c. 1290 in Baldon fields, and possibly
Cranwell close, 1545–6 in Oxford fields.

cot(e), OE, 'cottage.' (*a*) Coates Copse, Coathouse Fm, Cote, *Cote*,
Coton Fm, Ascott (2), Caulcott, Clattercote, Draycot, Fencot,
Fewcot, Illcott Copse, Murcot, Nethercote (2)[1], Nethercott,
Prescote, Rycote, Sescut Fm, Shilcott Wood, Upcott Fm, Walcot,

---

[1] These two names have different first elements.

Westcot Barton, Woodcote; (*b*) Alvescot, Arncott, Balscott, Berncote Lodge, Bodicote, Bromscott, Burcot, Kelmscott, Kencott, Pemscott, *Uffcot*, Williamscot; (*c*) Cop Court, Radcot. *Lambcot* and *sheepcot* occur frequently in field-names, cf. e.g. *Lambecotefurlonge*, c. 1195 in Charlton on Otmoor.

cot-stōw and cot-steall, OE, both meaning 'cottage site,' appear to have been fairly common as minor place-names. Occurrences in other volumes are Costal Wood (PN Sr 77), Costow Ho (PN Nth 55), Costow Fm (PN W 279), and probably Coster Pits (PN Bk 12) and Castor Fm (PN D 508). The two compounds are probably the source of the following modern Oxfordshire field-names: *Costal(l)s* (Asthall), *Costell* (Hailey and Tackley), *Costars, Costall, Costhall* (Standlake), *Costoll, Costall* (1606 in Warborough), *Corstall* (Great Haseley), *Costar* (Spelsbury), *Costers* (Rousham), *Castar* (Ewelme), *Costard* (Horspath), *Custard* (Dorchester), *Cositer* (1685 in Culham), *Coestowe hille* (1606–7 in Wootton). cot-stōw also occurs in the following early names: *Costowe* (1239 in Claydon, 1412–13 in Stratton Audley), *Cotstowe* (c. 1197 in Tetsworth, 1200–19 in Merton), *Costowa* (1268 in Great Tew). Only in Great Tew have modern and early forms been found in the same parish, but there the development of *Costowa* to *Castors* in 1761 may be compared with *Castors* in 1815 for Costow Fm in W (PN W 279).

cotman, ME, 'tenant of a cottage,' occurs some ten times in field- and minor names, the earliest forms being *Cotmanemor*, 1185–6 in Sydenham, and *Cotman forlonge*, c. 1139 in Bletchingdon.

courte, ME from OFr, applied to a manorial house. Bishop's Court, Blounts Court, Moor Court, Phyllis Court. Common in field-names, *Court Close* being particularly frequent. An early example is *court of laurens*, c. 1240 in Bletchingdon.

crāwe, OE, 'crow,' Crawley, Crowmarsh, Crowell, *Crowell*. Also in field-names, cf. *Croowelle*, 1278–9 in Headington, and *Crowellemore*, 1217–30 in Shipton on Cherwell.

crocc(a), OE, 'pot, vessel.' Crockerend Common (?), Crockwell.

croft, OE, 'small enclosure.' (*a*) Highcroft Lodge; (*c*) Haycroft Wood, Heycroft Shaw, Lycroft's Shaw. *passim* in field-names.

crouche, ME from OFr, 'cross.' Crutchmore Plantation. Occasionally in field-names.

*crouco-, British, 'heap, barrow, hill' especially 'a round hill or hillock.' Churchill (?), Crouch Hill. This word may be the source of a 17th-century field-name in Eye and Dunsden.

crundel, OE, possibly meaning 'chalk pit' or 'hollow,' occurs in the field-names of Brize Norton (1187), Crowmarsh (966) and Goring (c. 1245).

crypel, OE, 'narrow passage, burrow, drain.' Cripley Road.

cuckoo pen has been noted as a field-name in Beckley, Broadwell, Crowell, Eynsham, Idbury, Kirtlington, Shorthampton, Souldern, Sydenham and Westwell. J. E. Field, *The Myth of the Pent Cuckoo*, London 1913, states that there are also places with this name in Bensington, Checkendon, Clifton Hampden, Crowmarsh, Ewelme, Ipsden, Lewknor, Shirburn, Swyncombe and Warborough. The term is recorded in EDD with the meanings (i) a swing-gate in a V-shaped enclosure, and (ii) a small enclosure. In the first sense *cuckoo-gate* is an alternative term, and this occurs in Eynsham in the form *Cookoyate* in 1481–3, probably corresponding to the name *Cuckoo Pen* in 1858. Apart from this all the forms are 19th century. The name obviously suggests a connection with the story of the attempt to pen the cuckoo and so prevent the summer passing which is told of the men of Gotham (cf. Cuckoo Bush PN Nt 247). It may be that the place-names contain a direct allusion to this story, or that the story lies behind the dialect uses of the term *cuckoo pen* recorded in EDD.

cumb, OE, 'valley, coomb.' (*a*) Combe, Coombe End Fm, Coombe Wood, Harcomb Fm, Holcombe, Huntercombe End, Milcombe, Swyncombe, Watcombe Manor, Withycombe, Withycoombe Fm; (*b*) Warmscombe; (*c*) Postcombe. Fairly frequent in field-names.

cunestable, ME from OFr, probably in the sense 'an officer of a parish or township appointed to act as conservator of the peace and to perform a number of public administration duties in his district,' occurs in field-names, presumably applied to land which belonged to the holder of this office. There is one early occurrence, *Cunstableland*, 1229 in Goring. The word is first recorded in English a. 1240, and not in the above sense till 1328: *v.* NED *s.v.* *constable* for the senses one of which it might have had in 1229. It occurs in modern field-names in Churchill, Duns Tew (1634), North Newington, Rousham, Spelsbury and Standlake.

cut. This word has been noted as a field-name element in PN Sr 368 and PN Herts 262, where it is suggested that it represents OE cot(e). It is frequent in Oxfordshire field-names, and its use there definitely suggests that it is a term for a piece of land. Cf. *Longcut(t)* in Brize Norton, Charlbury and Hook Norton, *Broadcutt* in Aston Bampton and the set of names in Ipsden—*Bradcutt*, *Crabcut*, *Heathcutt*, *Kingcut* and *Smithcutt*. *v.* EDD sb[1] 12 and 13 for possible meanings, but EDD sb[2], 'lot,' is perhaps a more probable source, in which case this is a term similar to *set* in the field-names of Churchill (345) and lot (*v. infra*), used of land assigned by lot. All the forms are modern.

cutted, ME, a form of the past participle of the verb *cut*. Cut Mill, Cutmill Fm.

cuttele, ME, a stream-name of obscure origin, to which there are German parallels, occurs five times in the county. *v.* 7.

cwēn, OE, 'woman.' Queensford Mill.

cyning, OE, 'king.' *Kingsbury*, King's End, Kingsey, King's Mill, Kingstanding Fm, Kingston Blount, King's Wood, Kingwood Common. Fairly frequent in early field-names, where there are two more occurrences of 'king's wood' (1235 in Ewelme and 1263 in Checkendon), three of 'king's hill' with second element dūn (1363 in Eynsham, 1379–80 in Warborough, 1498–9 in Westwell) and one with second element hyll (1411–12 in Aston Rowant), three of 'king's mead' (c. 1605 in Bensington, 1363 in Henley, c. 1115 in Oxford), two of 'king's pool' (c. 1325 in Bicester, c. 1139 in Bletchingdon), a 'king's weir' (c. 1182 in Wolvercot), 'king's ditch' (1352 in Henley), 'king's manor' (1270 in Newington), 'king's way' (c. 1280 in Cassington), 'king's tree' (c. 1230 in Hook Norton) and 'king's gate' (1388 in Gosford). The earliest example is *cynges steorte*, 969 in Crawley. The element may sometimes be a surname, but there is probably a reference to royal ownership in most of these examples.

dēad, OE, dede, ME, 'dead,' is a fairly frequent field-name element. 'Dead Land' occurs in Charlbury (1363), Eynsham (1442) and Rollright (1363). Cf. also *Thedede Claye*, 1273 in Marston, *Dedeyerdene*, 1490 in Chinnor, and the modern field-names *Dead Mead* (Baldon), *Dead Croft* (South Stoke), *Dead Moor* (Glympton), *Deadsands* (Sandford St Martin) and *Dead Knowle* (Aston Bampton). *dead man*, noted in other counties as occurring in field-names, perhaps with reference to the finding of human bones, occurs in Bensington, Bourton (1668), Crowell, Dorchester, Eynsham (*Deadmanes buriall* 1615), Ewelme, Kencott (1634) and Spelsbury (1608–9). There is an early example of the field-name *dedecherle* (c. 1300 in Cassington), noted also PN Nth 275.

denu, OE, 'valley.' (*a*) Dane Hill (2), Danes Bottom, Danes Brook, Dean, Dean Clump, Dean Fm, Delly Pool and End, Denton, Evenden Copse, Green Dean Wood, Harpsden, Hollandtide Bottom, Ramsden, *Sanden*; (*b*) Checkendon, Dunsden, Gangsdown Hill, *Hildesden*, Ipsden, *Sukedene*; (*c*) Assendon, Bullingdon, Sarsden. Frequent in field-names.

dēop, OE, 'deep,' occurs occasionally in field-names, five times in combination with denu, as in the earliest form for Danes Bottom. The other 'deep valleys' are in Chinnor (c. 1230–40), Chipping Norton (c. 1280), Forest Hill (1271–2) and Shipton under Wychwood (1160–80).

Des. The commonest descriptive field-name referring to shape is *Shoulder of Mutton*, which occurs in Banbury, Bix, Cuddesdon, Henley, North Newington, Shirburn, Tetsworth, Wheatley and

Wroxton. Other names of this type are *Moonpiece* in Forest Hill, *Moon Croft* in South Stoke, *Moon Slade* in Swerford, *The Half Moon* in Henley, *Cock up hat* and *Milking Pan* in Aston Bampton, Cockedhat Copse in Filkins, *Saddle Back Field* in Tackley, *Kidney Plantation* in Nuneham Courtney, *Buttock Hill* in Bensington, *Elbow Furlong* in Warborough and *Cats Tail*, *Snakes Tail Piece* and *Bulls tail* in Deddington, Tackley and Milton under Wychwood. *Roundabout(s)*, a term for a field surrounded by a wood or with a clump of trees in the middle, occurs in Aston Rowant, Banbury, Churchill, Mapledurham, Newton Purcell and Oxford. *Rainbow Acre* and *Rainbow Piece* in Charlbury and Hailey describe fields ploughed 'rainbow,' i.e. parallel to the sides of a curving field. *Straits* in Swyncombe and Shipton on Cherwell, *Streights* in Cornbury Park and *The Shanks* in Chelgrove presumably describe long, narrow strips of land (cf. PN Cu 468–9). *Duck(s) Puddle* occurs in Aston Bampton, Culham, Dorchester, Forest Hill, Grafton, Merton and Waterperry, *Duck Pool(s)* in Warborough and Wychwood (1641), and *Duck Marsh* in Clanfield. Another reference to wet land is presumably contained in *Frog Lane*, found in Banbury, Chalgrove, Handborough, Milton under Wychwood and Rollright. *Wilderness* occurs in Burford (1551–2), and a number of other parishes. *Dairy Ground* has been noted as a field-name in some twenty parishes. *Breakneck Hill* in Tetsworth, *Wet Foot* in Idbury and *Drinkwater Mead* in Shenington are self-explanatory.

dīc, OE, 'ditch, dike.' (a) Dike Hills, Ditchley, Cobditch Hill, *Greenditch*, Grim's Ditch, Reddish Fm; (b) *Pachesdiche*; (c) *Canditch*. Frequent in field-names.

d(i)erne, OE, 'hidden, secret.' Dornford, Dunford Copse. Cf. also *Derneford'*, c. 1200 in the field-names of Sandford on Thames.

diggin. This element occurs in *Newedyggyns* (1551–2) in Blackthorn, *The Diggons* in Bicester, *The Diggins* in Hardwick with Tusmore and Diggings Wood in Finmere. It is probably a form of *digging*, used perhaps of a quarry. These names are all in the north-east of the county. Cf. NED s.v. *digging*, where there is a quotation from 1538, "on the South side...ys a goodly quarre of Stone, wher appere great Diggyns."

docce, OE, 'sorrel.' Dogslade Bottom. Possibly also in *Docfurlong*, c. 1240 in Sibford Gower.

dole, ME, from OE dāl, 'portion or share of land' especially of the common field, is very frequent in early field-names. Cf. *Smededel* (c. 1185 in Hook Norton, 'smooth dole'), *Mideldol* (c. 1250 in Bletchingdon), *Winterdole* (c. 1220–30 in Aston Rowant).

*dræg, OE, a common place-name element for which the meanings 'portage' (i.e. a place where boats are dragged over a narrow piece of land or past an obstruction in a river) and 'steep slope' (i.e. a place where more than ordinary effort is required) have been conjectured (*v.* DEPN s.n. Drayton). Draycot, Drayton, Drayton St Leonard. *v.* E. Ekwall, *Namn och Bygd* xx, 46–70.

drift and drove, and *driftway, driftroad, droveway,* used in the sense 'a lane or road along which horses or cattle are driven,' are very frequent in field-names. drift is more common in modern names, the earliest example being *Heards drift,* 1662 in Rollright. There are several examples of drove from the 13th and 14th centuries. Cf. *Foredrift* (c. 1840 in Shipton under Wychwood), *fordroue* (c. 1250 in Bletchingdon), *Fordrowe waye* (1606 in Lower Heyford).

dru(i)e, drie, ME, dry, ModE, is frequent in field-names. Early examples are *drygean broc* (956 in Horspath), *Driuhurst* (c. 1200 in Middleton Stoney), *Druihurst* (c. 1215–30 in Bicester) and *Drienhulle* (c. 1270 in Weston on the Green). Modern names are *Dry Close* (Banbury, Charlbury, Chinnor, Goddington, Rousham), *Dry Ground* (Bruern, Enstone, Hardwick with Tusmore, Wardington), *Dry Leys* (Henley, Souldern, South Newington), *Dry Piece* (Piddington), *Dry Moor* (Cropredy), *Dry Hill* (Wigginton), *Dry Well* (Steeple Aston).

dūn, OE, 'hill.' (*a*) Downhill Fm, Dunthorp (?), Claydon, Elvendon Fm, Little Faringdon, Garsington, Gilton Hill, Grindon Lane, Haddon Fm, Hayden Fm, Shenington, Underdowns; (*b*) Ambrosden, Attington, Baldon, Bletchingdon, Bromsden Fm, Cuddesdon, Easington (2), Godington, Headington, Horsendon Hill, Oddington, Primsdown Fm, Tiddington; (*c*) Lobbersdown Fm. Frequent in field-names.

dūst, OE, 'dust.' Dustfield Fm.

ēa, OE, 'river.' *Aldee,* Overy, Ray, Isle of Rhea, Water Eaton, Woodeaton. Also in several lost stream-names. *Ray Meadow* (from OE *æt þǣre ēa,* cf. Ray *supra* 9), occurs as a field-name in Milton under Wychwood, Nuneham Courtney, Rollright (1363), Shiplake and Spelsbury: and ēa-furlang, 'furlong by the river,' has been noted in Charlbury (1363), Cowley (1220), Hampton (c. 1195), Great Haseley (c. 1200), Hensington (c. 1190–1200), South Leigh (early 13th) and Merton (1200–19). Cf. brōc-furlang *supra.*

(e)ald, OE, 'old.' Albury (?), *Aldee, Aldweir,* Northfield House. Also in field-names: 'old (or possibly *Ealda*'s) burh' occurs also in Checkendon (1312), Chinnor (1312), Crowmarsh (966), Ewelme (1235) and Shipton under Wychwood (1551–2). For lost stream-names with this first element *v.* 13.

ēast, OE, 'east.' Ascott (2), Asthall, Aston Bampton, Aston Rowant, Aston Leys Fm, Middle, North and Steeple Aston, Astrop, Eastend, Eastfield (2). Also in field and lost stream-names. ēasterra, 'eastern,' is the first element of Asterleigh, and occurs occasionally in field-names.

ecg, OE, 'edge.' (c) Roustage.

ef(e)n, OE, 'equal, level.' Evenden Copse. Cf. also *Evenle*, c. 1230–40 in Chinnor.

elle(r)n, OE, elder(n), ModE, 'elder tree,' probably occurs in Sescut Fm and is very common indeed in field-names, particularly with *stubb* or *stump*, the former word being usual in early and the latter in modern names. Early examples are *le Ellerverstobbe* (1300 in Wychwood), *Elrenest(r)ubbe* (c. 1270 in Cuxham), *Ellestobfurlonge* (15th in Banbury) and *Eldernstubbe* (1449 in Chinnor), and there are modern examples of the term in Bourton, Burford, Deddington, Eynsham, Forest Hill, Rousham, Wheatley and Wigginton.

ende, OE, 'end' or 'district.' Brookend Ho, Coombe End Fm, Crockerend Common, Eastend, King's End, Market End, West End. Also in field-names.

eorþburh, OE, 'earthwork,' occurs in the early forms for Ash Bank, and in early field-names in Curbridge (969) and Ardley (995). It may be the source of the modern field-names *Arbour* in Shorthampton and *Harbours Hill* in Deddington. *Ardyche*, 1551–2 in Dorchester, may represent OE *eorþdīc*.

eyt, ME, 'small island.' Cripley Road, Port Meadow (earlier *Portmaneyt*). Frequent in field-names. v. (ī)eg *infra*.

fæst, OE, 'firm, stiff, dense.' Faws Grove.

fāg, OE, 'variegated.' Fawler. The same phrase, meaning 'tesselated pavement,' occurs also in (*to*) *fagan floran*, 904 in Gosford.

fal(o)d, OE, 'fold.' (c) Wyfold Court. Cf. also *Derefolde*, c. 1220 in the field-names of Cowley, *hindfaldan*, 983 in Arncott.

Fan. The most frequent type of fanciful field and minor name is that which refers to the infertility of the land. *Beggars Bush* occurs in Asthall, Bensington (1606–7), Charlbury, Mollington, Wardington, Wroxton, and possibly Hethe (*Bakers bush*, c. 1575): cf. also *Beggar Ground* (Shifford), *Beggars Piece* (Drayton by Banbury), *Beggars Lane* (Churchill), *Beggars Bridge* (1634 *et seq*, Fringford). *Jews Bush Furlong* (Little Milton) is perhaps analogous. *Cold Harbour* (v. PN Sr 406–10) occurs as a minor name in North Aston, Crowmarsh, Goring, Lower Heyford, Mixbury, Oxford, Rotherfield Greys, Shifford, Stadhampton and Little Tew. *Littleworth* has been noted in Bensington, Bletchingdon, Swyncombe and Wheatley, and there is a Littlegood Fm in Bourton. *Small Gains* occurs in Aston Bampton and Chadlington, *Small Profit* in Watlington, *Starveall* in Fifield, Hailey and Holton, *Hungerhill* in Launton and Minster Lovell, *Hungryhill* and *Hunger Brook* in Shirburn, and *Purgatory* in Steeple Barton and Forest Hill. Cf.

also *Jobs Balk* (Tackley), *Job's Close* (North Aston), *Job's Copse* (Hailey), *Jobs Piddle* (Eye and Dunsden), *Hang-dog Leys* (Wigginton), *Breakback, Broken Back, Idler Piece* (Wroxton), *Lifeless Close* (Minster Lovell), *Work Hards* (Drayton St Leonard), *Rotten Plot* (Bensington), *Rotton Lays* (Crowmarsh), *Break Heart Hill* (Ewelme), *Spiteful Yards* and *Sullen field* (Ipsden), *Ragged Farm* (Whitchurch), *Cold Comfort Farm* (Heythrop), *meagre hill* (South Newington), *Greedy Guts* (Pyrton, perhaps needing a lot of manure), *Lousy Lot* (Nuneham Courtney), *Lousehill* (Bourton), *Louseham* (Alvescot) and *Louse Hall* (Gosford).

Complimentary nicknames are *Paradise* (Hailey, Milcombe, Swerford, Swinbrook, Wychwood), *Fatting Ground* (Chastleton, Drayton St Leonard, Waterperry), *Fatting Field* (Rollright), *Fat Field* (Lewknor), *Fatting Fence* (Horton), *Philbarn Hill* (Bix), *Fill Barn Furlong* (Steeple Aston), *Sweet Pot* (Claydon), *Sweetmowe* (1662 Rollright), *Banquetting field* (Henley), *Easy Furlong* (Chadlington), *Mount Pleasant* (Kingham, and a number on the 6″ O.S. maps), *Thanky furlong* (Milton under Wychwood), *Long Loved Ground* (Shirburn), *Merry piece* (Bladon), *Noble Furlong* (Eynsham), *Goodley Croft* (Swyncombe), *Richland* (Standlake) and the early *Richfurlongo* (a. 1211 Stoke Talmage) and *Rychiforlong* (1338 in Iffley). Cf. also **butere** *supra*.

Names of foreign places are frequent as field and minor names, sometimes with reference to a battle[1]. Cf. *Paris* (c. 1220) and *Rome* (1498) (both in Oxford), *Newfoundland* (Chadlington, Crowmarsh), *Botany Bay* (Checkendon, Eye and Dunsden, Lewknor), *Waterloo* (Ascott under Wychwood, Fringford), Little Blenheim Fm (Northmoor), Nineveh Fm (Newnham Courtney), *New Zealand* (Waterperry), *America Field* (Ewelme), *America's Head or Hill* (Idbury), *Calys* (1476 in Nuffield), Gibraltar (Bletchingdon, Hook Norton), Porto Bello (Shirburn), Jericho Fm (Cassington), *Port Mahon Garden* (Oxford), *Spioncop* (Wheatley) and probably *Maida Hill* (Nuneham Courtney, cf. PN Mx 133). Less remote references are contained in *Londonesart'* (1363 in Charlbury), *Little London* (Drayton by Banbury, Churchill), *London Dean* (Crowmarsh), Pimlico Fm (Hardwick with Tusmore), *The Isle of Man* (Bletchingdon) and Isle of Wight Bridge (Bampton).

Sarcastic references to the size of the land are found in *Handkerchief piece* (Tackley), *The Handkerchief Ground* (Hailey), *Tiney Hand field* (Henley). Cf. also **shovelbrode** *infra*.

Remote position is indicated in *The Worlds End* (Curbridge), *the Lands ends* (Wroxton) and Lonesome Fm (Crowmarsh).

---

[1] *Waterloo*, Blenheim, Porto Bello, *Spioncop* and *Maida Hill* must refer to the battles of 1815, 1704, 1739, 1900 and 1806.

The precise significance of the following names is not clear: *Gingerbread Hill* (Bix), *Ginger Bread Close* (Pyrton), *Sweetbread Lane* (1657 in Rotherfield Greys), *Cupboards* (Lewknor[1]), *Cupboard Hill* (Warborough), *Frendly Hill* (Tetsworth), *Puppy's Parlour* (Tackley), *Toothlesse hedland* (1605 Cowley), *Bear Garden* (Rotherfield Peppard), *Mooneshine gate* (1629 Elsfield), *Eight o'clock Gate* (Swinbrook), *Fiery Mountain* (Tiddington), *Bacon and Bean Meadow*, *Aunt Sally* (both in Waterperry), *Welcome Meadow* (Fifield), *Cock and Hen Woods* (Wychwood), *Dronkenhill* (1551–2 Dorchester), *Doctors Gift* (South Stoke), *China Mead* (Whitchurch), *Crooked Elbow* (Churchill), *Angel Meadow* (Oxford).

fearn, OE, 'fern.' Little Faringdon, Fernhill Copse, Fernhill Fm. Also in field-names, where there is another example of the compound with **dūn** (*Farendone*, 1271–2 in Wychwood), and several of the compound with **hyll**.

fēawe, OE, 'few.' Fewcot.

feld, OE, 'open country.' (*a*) Barleyfields, Binfield, Campsfield, Clanfield, Dustfield Fm, Eastfield (2), Greenfield, Hayfield Shaws, Leafield, Northfield Fm, Northfield Ho, Nuffield, Rotherfield, Southfield Barn, Upperfield Fm, Westfield Fm, Wheatfield; (*b*) Caversfield, Elsfield, Stonesfield. *passim* in field-names, where it probably has the modern sense 'enclosed piece of ground.'

felg, OE, 'felly.' *Felley.*

fenn, OE, 'fen, marsh.' Fencot, The Carvens, Chipping Fm. Fairly frequent in field-names, where the adjective **fennig** also occurs, cf. *Fenniforde*, c. 1240 Sibford Gower.

fēorðan dǣl, OE (accusative), 'fourth part,' recorded from 1542 in the sense 'the fourth part of an acre; a rood,' occurs in the field-names of Bampton, Clanfield (c. 1240), Enstone (1315), Fulbrook (1551–2) and Upper Heyford. The terms *farndel* and *farundell* are frequently used as nouns in 17th-century Oxfordshire terriers in the Bodleian. **fēorðing**, OE, 'fourth,' recorded as a term for various measures of land (*v.* NED *s.v. farthing* sb. 4), occurs in the field-names of Bourton, Charlbury, Chinnor (1296), Ipsden, Mapledurham, Little Milton, Shipton under Wychwood (1551–2), Stanton St John, Waterperry and Wychwood.

fēþa, OE, 'foot-soldier, band of foot-soldiers, warfare, battle.' *Fethelee.*

fīf, OE, 'five.' Fifield (2), Fiveoak Copse. Cf. *Fifberwe* (late 12th in Fifield), *Fifburghe* (c. 1260 in Hook Norton), *Fifþornesfurlunche* (1160–80 in Milton under Wychwood), *Fyfeldes* (1551–2 in Adderbury) and *Fifacre* (c. 1220 in Thomley).

---

[1] This is probably identical with the *Cupboard Hill, Little and Great Cupboards* which occur in the *TA* for Stokenchurch in Bk.

*fildena, OE, the genitive plural of a noun formed from **feld** and meaning 'dweller in open land,' occurs in the road-names discussed under the heading FIELDEN WAY. *v.* Tengstrand 99–104 for a full discussion of the element.

filiþe, OE, 'hay,' *filiþu (plural), ? 'hayfield.' Phyllis Court.

fina, OE, 'woodpecker.' Finmere, Finstock.

fleax, OE, 'flax,' occurs frequently in field-names, cf. e.g. *Flexfurlong*, c. 1180 in Pyrton, *Flexhulle*, c. 1260 in Hook Norton. An adjective *fleaxen may be the first element of Flexney Fm.

flēot, OE, 'stream,' occurs in field and lost stream-names, cf. *fleotan,* 11th century in Pyrton. It gives *Flit*(*t*) in modern names.

fliten, ME past participle, 'disputed,' occurs in the field-names *Flitenhulle* (c. 1230–40 in Chinnor) and *Flitenlonde* (c. 1218 in Hampton). Cf. also *Disputforlang'* (c. 1200–10 in Thomley) and the field-name in Eynsham which probably goes back to OE *wroht-(ī)eg*, 'debate island.'

flōr, OE, 'floor.' Fawler. Cf. fāg *supra*.

folly, a name for an extravagant or foolish building (*v.* PN Wa 382–5), occurs in Folly Bridge, Folly Cottages, Folly Fm (3), The Folly (5) and in the field-names of Curbridge, Dorchester, Enstone, Kiddington, Kingham, Standlake (1551–2) and Steeple Aston (where it refers to a mock ruin built in the 18th century).

ford, OE, 'ford.' (*a*) Fordwells, Barford, Burford, Chalford (2), Dornford, Dunford Copse, Fringford, Gosford, *Harpsford*, Hazelford (2), Heyford, Langford (2), *Langeford*, Latchford, Milford Bridge, Queensford Mill, Radford, Rayford Lane, Salford, Sandford (2), Shifford, Shillingford, *Somerford*, Stowford Fm, Swerford, Swinford Bridge, Twyford, Washford Pits, Widford; (*b*) Cottisford, Rofford, Shutford, Sibford, Stonesfield Ford (earlier *Stuntesford*), Yelford. Frequent in field-names.

*forst, OE, used in place-names of a ridge-like hill, postulated by Tengstrand (*Studia Neophilologica* vi, 100–1). Forest Hill.

forþ, OE, 'in front,' occurs in field-names, most frequently in the combination with (ī)eg, noted in other counties, which gives *Forty* in modern names. This occurs in Crowmarsh (1303), Elsfield, Handborough (1608–9), Harpsden, Horspath, Great Milton, Sydenham and Warborough (1606–7). It is used of an island or peninsula of land standing out from surrounding marshy or comparatively low ground (cf. PN Wo 202–4). Cf. also *Forthamm* (1239 in Bampton), *Forteforlong* (1312 in Chinnor), *Forthoesdich* (c. 1275 in Kirtlington), *Fortfurlung'* (c. 1225 in Bicester) and *forthebiri* (c. 1310 in Rollright). The forms for the last name, which is used of a space in front of a town, show alternation with OE *fore*, also meaning 'in front.'

forthshetere, ME. This term, which has not been noted in other counties and is not in the dictionaries, occurs in the field-names of Aston Rowant (1510), Bicester (c. 1325), Chalgrove (c. 1225), Dorchester (c. 1200), Elsfield (1273), Garsington (c. 1240), Goring (1345), Hook Norton (c. 1270), South Stoke (1220–7 and Tackley (1605). It means literally 'forward shooter,' and is evidently descriptive of the shape or position of the land. The Bicester and Chalgrove names (*For(e)schetere*) may have as first element OE *fore*, which often alternates with forþ.

fox, OE, 'fox.' Foxhill Fm, Foxley Fm, Foxtowns End Fm. Also in field-names. fox-cot(e), OE, 'foxes' earth.' Foscot. fox-hole, ME, identical in sense with the preceding compound, occurs in Fox Hill and in field-names.

freeboard, a modern dialect term which can mean (i) a strip of land lying beyond the boundaries of an estate, over which the owner possesses certain rights, (ii) the pasture edges of an arable field, (iii) a right of way (*v.* PN Nth 273), occurs as a modern field-name in some fifteen parishes.

freht, fyrht, firht, OE, 'augury.' Fritwell.

fūl, OE, 'foul, dirty.' Fulbrook, Fulwell (2). Also in a number of lost stream-names (*v.* 14) and in field-names, where 'foul slough' occurs several times.

fullock. This term has been noted in the field-names of Banbury (*Fullacke* 1551–2, *Fullake* c. 1605, *Fullaker, Fulloke* 1608–9, *Fullock* c. 1840), Fringford (*Fullake, Fallake* 1634, *Fullick* 1685) and Sonning in Berks (*Greate Fullaker, Little Fulloke* 1603–4 *Survey*). *Fulleacre*, 1436 in Great Tew, may be the same name. The meaning is unknown.

furlang, OE, 'furlong.' Brookfurlong Fm. *passim* in field-names.

furze and furzy, ModE, and dialect fursen, occur *passim* in field-names.

fyrhþ(e), OE, 'woodland.' The Thrift. Occasionally in field-names.

gædeling, OE, 'kinsman, comrade.' Gagingwell.

*gærsen, OE, 'grassy.' Garsington. gærs-tūn, OE, 'grassy enclosure,' Garson's Copse, Garsons Fm. *passim* in field-names, where it gives the ME forms *Garston(e), Gerston(e)* and the modern forms *Garson(s), Gasson, Gaston(e), Gussan.*

gāra, OE, 'triangular piece of land,' used in later field-names of a wedge-shaped strip, might be the first element of Goring and occurs *passim* in field-names. *v.* gorebrode *infra.*

gāt, OE, 'goat.' Gatehampton (?).

g(e)alga, OE, 'gallows.' Gallos Brook. *gallows* occurs in a considerable number of field and minor names for which the forms are mostly modern. Cf. *Gallows Close* (Cowley, Broadwell, Handborough),

Gallows Piece (Charlbury, Rousham), *Gallows Tree Common* (Rotherfield Peppard), *Gallows Stile and Hill* (Horley and Hornton), *Gallow Furze Leys* (Milcombe), *Gallows Corner* (Wroxton), *Gallows Leaze* (Bensington), *Gallows Furlong* (Charlton on Otmoor, Glympton), *Gallowes wood* (1606–7 in Combe) and *Gallow feld* (1493 in Mapledurham). The last name may be an early example of the term *gallows-field*, recorded in EDD for a field with a transverse upper portion. There is a Hangman's Bridge on the 1″ map in Little Milton, and a Hangman's Hill in Sandford St Martin. Cf. also *Peloribarne*, 1492–3 in Great Haseley, and *Pellery Barne*, 1522–3 in Watlington.

geat, OE, 'gate.' Barnard Gate. Cf. also the gates of Oxford (44). Occasionally in field-names, where it sometimes gives the modern forms *Yat(t)*, *Yate*. *clap-gate*, a modern dialect term for 'a gate which shuts on either of two posts joined with bars to a third post; a small hunting gate wide enough for a horse to pass,' occurs in Souldern and the field-names of Bicester and Kiddington, and OE *hlīepgeat*, 'a low gate in a fence that can be leaped by deer, while keeping sheep from straying,' occurs once in the field-names of Enstone. *v.* also hæcc-geat *infra*.

geolu, OE, 'yellow.' Ilbury Fm.

gibitz, MHG, 'plover.' An OE word cognate with this may be the first element of Iffley.

glebe, 'a portion of land assigned to a clergyman as part of his benefice,' is frequent in modern field-names. Cf. *Glebe Piece* (Burford, Lower Heyford, Little Tew) and *Glebe Land* (Horspath, Islip, Kencott).

gog, dialect word for 'a bog, swamp,' occurs in the field-names of Bourton, Milton under Wychwood, Prescott, Shiplake, Steeple Aston and Wardington. The compound *gog-mire* occurs in Stanton St John and *gog-moor* in Merton.

golde, OE, 'marigold.' Golder, Goldwell Spinney, Gorville St (earlier *Goldwell street*). The compound with w(i)elle, in which the meaning is probably 'marsh marigold,' occurs also in a lost stream-name in Beckley (*goldwyllan* 1005–12), and there is a *Goldebroc* in Hampton (c. 1195). golde is also found in the following early field-names: *Goldeberge* (1187 in Bampton), *Goldforlong* (c. 1325 in Bicester), *Goldhulle* (c. 1185 in Hampton), *Goldclyf* (1315 in Witney). The word *gylde, identical in meaning, assumed by Ekwall (DEPN) as the first element of Guildford Sr, occurs in *Guldiche* (1208–9 in Great Haseley) and *Guldefurlong* (1312 in Checkendon).

gorebrode, ME, denoting a broad strip of land tapering to a point, occurs in the field-names of Ascott under Wychwood (early 15th),

Asthall (no date), Cuxham (c. 1230), Goring (1349) and Iffley. *Broad Gore(s)* occurs several times in modern names.

gōs, OE, 'goose.' Goose Eye Cottage, Gosford, Gossway Cottage. Also in field-names.

gospel in field-names refers to a place where a halt was made and a passage from scripture read during the Rogation ceremony of 'beating the bounds.' *Gospel Oak* occurs in Handborough (1608–9) and Wychwood, *Gospel Ash* in Kirtlington, *Gospel Bush* in Alvescott and *Gospel furlong* in Drayton by Banbury.

græf, OE, 'pit.' Chalgrove.

grǣg, OE, 'gray.' Greyhone Wood.

grāf(a), OE, 'grove, copse.' (*a*) Grafton, Graven Hill, *Grove*, The Grove (2), Grove Ash Fms, Groveridge Wood, Barton Grove, Faws Grove, Hen's Grove, Maidensgrove, Nor Grove, Priest Grove, Silgrove Wood, Warpsgrove; (*b*) Norman's Grove. Also in field-names, cf. *Bastardesgrove*, 1338 in Beckley.

grange, ME from OFr, 'grange.' Grange Fm, Stoke Grange, Sydenham Grange.

grēne, OE, 'green.' Green Dean Wood, *Greenditch*, Greenfield, Greenmore Hill, Grindon Lane. In Greenmore Hill the word is used as a noun, and *The Green* is frequent in late field-names. 'Green way' is frequent in field-names, the forms dating from the 10th century onwards, and *Greensward* occurs in the modern names of some six parishes.

grubbed, a modern term presumably denoting land which has been cleared of trees, weeds, and the like, occurs in the field-names of Bix, Ducklington, Harpsden, Shiplake, Shirburn, South Stoke, Watlington. *Grubbing* occurs in Bix, Ipsden, Pyrton, and *Grub* in Bix, Henley, Pyrton, Watlington.

gylden, OE, 'golden,' used of places in the sense 'rich, productive, splendid' (*v.* PN Ca 61–2), Gill Mill, Gilton Hill. In the latter name the reference may be to golden flowers (cf. golde *supra*), and in the following field-names the element may mean 'productive' or 'golden with flowers': *la Gildenacre* (c. 1210 in Stoke Talmage), *Gilden acre* (1412–13 in Stratton Audley), *Gilton Acre* (Milton under Wychwood and Warborough), *Gilton Piece* (Chadlington), *Guldenedene* (1363 in Henley). Cf. also the modern names *Golden end* (Shenington), *Golden Ground* (Wroxton), *Golden Furlong* (Crowell and Eynsham), *Gold Pitts* (Tetsworth), *Golden Bottom* (Horspath).

gyr(u), OE, 'mud, marsh.' *The Carvens.*

hades, plural of *hade* from OE hēafod, 'head,' used of a 'head-land, unploughed land at the end of the arable where the plough turns,' is very frequent in field-names. The usual form is *hades*, but cf.

hudes in Aston Rowant, Bensington and Crowmarsh, and *hawdes* (1606–7) in Bensington. The singular occurs occasionally, cf. *Hade* in Charlton on Otmoor and Headington. The earlier hēafod occurs *passim* in charters, often in the dative plural.

hæcc, OE, 'gate.' Playhatch (the meaning here is probably 'flood-gate'). Also in field-names, where it gives modern *Hatch*. The compound hæcc-geat is common in field-names. It gives ME *Hecket* (p. 1212 in Baldon), *Hachet* (c. 1200 in Thame), *Hacche yate* (1470–1 in Kirtlington), and modern *Hatchet* (Crowmarsh, Kingham, Shorthampton, Weston on the Green), *Hatch Yatt* (Charlbury), *Hatch Gate* (Bampton, Stanton Harcourt), and possibly *Hecate* (Fencott and Murcott).

(ge)hæg, OE, 'hedge, enclosure.' (*a*) Claydon Hay, Gossway Copse, Oxey Hill, Oxey Mead, Stockey Bottom; (*c*) Pinsey Bridge. Fairly frequent in field-names, where it is the source of the common elements *hay, hays, heyes*.

hǣme (nominative plural). For a full discussion of this term, *v. Crawford Charters*, ed. Napier and Stevenson, Oxford 1895, pp. 116–17. It is a mutated derivative of hām, and means 'the people of.' It is usually compounded in the genitive plural (hǣma) with the first part of a place-name, and the compound followed by a word such as (ge)mǣre, 'boundary': but cf. *Fourlourhemhache*, 1363 in Charlbury, where the whole place-name is apparently used. The occurrences of hǣme in the charters suggest that it was often employed in the naming of places on boundaries, and in the Oxfordshire parishes where it occurs in field-names the first part of the compound generally refers to an adjoining parish. The element occurs in charter boundaries with reference to Aston Bampton, Toot Baldon, Claydon, Culham, Cuxham and Ingham, and has been noted with later forms in the following field-names: *Buchamwey* (c. 1325 in Bicester), *Burthemeleye* (c. 1240 in Black Bourton), *Caldhememere* (early 13th in Lower Heyford), *Drey-hemeweye* (c. 1290 in Baldon), *Garshamestred* (c. 1240 in Sandford on Thames), *Glimhemwode* (1278–9 in Glympton), *Horhemewode* (1278–9 in Beckley), *Kudishamweye* (c. 1200 in Sandford on Thames), *Mershemebrugg'* (1278–9 in Garsington), *Rolhememere* (late 13th in Hook Norton), *Sippeme Ware* (1261 in Hampton), *Sorchemdene* (? 1272 in Charlbury), *Wychemestrete* (c. 1270 in Hook Norton).

hǣminga, evidently an equivalent term to hǣma (*v.* ingas *infra*), has been noted once in a charter boundary with reference to Nuneham Courtney. *Copinghemewey*, c. 1230 in Aston Rowant, probably contains a combination of hǣma with the connective particle ing.

hæsel, OE, 'hazel.' Great Haseley, Hazelford Bridge, Hazelford Mill, Hazel Wood. Also in field-names.

hǣþ, OE, 'heath, uncultivated land.' Haddon Fm, Heath Bridge, Heath End, Little Heath, Hethe, Neithrop (?), Goring Heath, Pyrton Heath, Rollright Heath Fm. Frequent in field-names.

haga, OE, 'enclosure.' Haw Fm. Also in field-names. An unrecorded derivative of *haga* may lie behind the names discussed under Hained-in Wood.

hālig, OE, 'holy.' Holwell, Holywell, Holy Well. There are three more early examples of this compound among unidentified streamnames, *v.* 14, and cf. also the modern field-names *Holey Well* in Middle Aston and *Holywell Field* in Aston Bampton.

hām, OE, 'village, estate, manor, homestead.' (*a*) Lyneham (?), Mapledurham, Newnham Murren, Nuneham Courtney; (*b*) Bloxham, Ipenham (?), Rousham, Worsham (?); (*c*) Ingham. hāmst(e)all occurs in Armstalls and in the field-name *depanhamsteal*, 11th century in Pyrton; and hāmstede in Hampstead Fm. It is impossible to determine the precise sense of such compounds, but it is possible that they both refer to the actual site of the chief house of the farm or manor. hāmtūn, which may denote 'the village proper' in contradistinction to outlying parts, occurs in Hampton Gay and Poyle, Brookhampton, Gatehampton and Shorthampton.

hamel, ME from OFr, 'hamlet.' The Hamel.

hamm, OE, 'enclosed plot, meadow, low-lying meadow by a stream, land in the bend of a river.' (*a*) Ham Court, Hammer Lane, Catsham Lane, *Cattesham* (2), Lyneham (?), Millham Ford, Norham Manor, Northam, Stadhampton, Sydenham; (*b*) Culham, Cuxham, Eynsham, Ipenham (?), Worsham (?). *passim* in fieldnames.

hān, OE, 'stone.' Greyhone Wood.

handing post, dialect term for 'sign post,' occurs in the field-names of Charlbury and Northmoor. hand post has been noted in Broughton Poggs, Drayton by Banbury, Mollington and Wroxton, and *Hand and Post* occurs in Upton and Signet.

hangende, hanginde in early ME field-names, hanging in modern names, is used of land on a slope. The element is very common both by itself (cf. *le Hangynde*, 1273 in Elsfield, and *Hanging(s) passim*) and in combination with other elements, of which land is the most frequent. Cf. also *Hanging of the Hill* in Ducklington, Merton, Warborough, and *Hanging on the Hill* in Rousham.

hangra, OE, hanger, ModE, 'wood on a slope,' occurs in the earlier name of Beech Fm (*Appelhangre*), and in the field-names of Chinnor (1350), Elsfield, Forest Hill (1271–2), Goring (c. 1307), Horton cum Studley (1634), Stonesfield, Watlington and Woodeaton (c. 1366).

hār, OE, 'grey, hoar,' which can mean 'boundary' in place-names from its use in the compound hār-stān. Harcomb Fm, Hoarstone Spinney, Hoar Stone (2). Other occurrences of OE hār-stān, ModE *hoarstone*, 'boundary stone,' have been noted in the field-names of Broughton Poggs (1685), Cassington (c. 1244), Iffley, Oxford (1358), Shifford (c. 1360), Shipton under Wychwood (1591), Sibford Gower (c. 1240), Taynton (1059), Little Tew and Wardington (1551–2).

hēafod, OE, 'head, headland.' *v.* **hades** *supra.*

hē(a)h, OE, 'high.' Hailey (2), Hailey Wood, Hempton, Henley, Henton, Heythrop, Chislehampton. Also in field-names: there are other examples with lē(a)h in Crawley (969) and Chinnor (c. 1220–30).

h(e)alh, OE, 'corner, secret place, recess.' (*a*) Hale Fm, Holton, Asthall, Westhall Hill, Wroxhills Wood; (*b*) Boynall Copse, Brasswell Corner, Hempton Wainhill, Ledall, Padnell's Wood. Frequent in field-names.

h(e)all, OE, 'hall,' hence 'manor-house.' Downhill Fm.

hecg, OE, 'hedge.' Rumerhedge Wood. Frequent in field-names.

hechinge, ME, hitching, modern dialect, 'part of a field ploughed and sown during the year in which the rest of the field lies fallow.' For a detailed discussion of the term *v.* PN W 435. It is common in Oxfordshire field-names. The usual modern form is *Hitching*, but *Itchen, Itchin, Hutchings* and *Hitchen* have also been noted. **inhoke** is a synonymous term which occurs in Elsfield (1273), Eynsham (1473–4) and Great Tew, and *Inhechinges* occurs in Ducklington (1280). Cf. also *Hitch* in Whitchurch and *Hitch Croft* (1603–4) in Eye and Dunsden.

hēg, OE, 'hay.' Hailey, Haycroft Wood, Hayden Fm, Hayfield Shaws, Hayway Lane, Heycroft Shaw, Heycroft Wood, Heyford. Also in field-names, where there are several more examples of 'hay way.'

hege, OE, 'hedge.' *Broken Hays.*

heme, ME, 'border of a piece of land.' Hen's Grove. Also in the following Oxfordshire field-names: *Hememede* (1302 in Chipping Norton, c. 1230 in Garsington, c. 1195 in Hampton), *Hememed* (a. 1185 in Hook Norton), *Hemede* (c. 1260 in Little Tew), *Hemelond* (1363 in Charlbury), *Hemeland'* (c. 1150–60 in Garsington), *Hemland(e)* (c. 1366 in Woodeaton), *Hemehoke* (t. Ed 3 in Shirburn), *Hemehurst* (1281 in Eynsham), *Hemecroft* (c. 1190 in Thame), *Hemedon* (1331 in Warborough). Cf. also *Hemestreme* (c. 1230–40 in Thomley). The form recorded in OE is *hemm*, and -*mm*- occurs in most of the spellings in NED (*hem* sb[1]), but the names quoted above point to a ME form *heme*. The word was noted as a field-name element in PN Wo 390, where line 1648 of the

Alliterative Morte Arthure (Hovande one þe hye waye by þe holte hemmes), which appears in EDD to illustrate the use of *hem* in this sense in modern dialect, is quoted from NED. *Morte Arthure* also uses *wod(d)e-hemmes* at 1359, 2219, 2825. Cf. also DEPN *s.n.* The Hem (Sa), and B. G. Charles, *Non-Celtic Place-Names in Wales* 187, 194 (London Mediæval Studies, 1938). *v.* liii.

henn, OE, 'hen,' probably used in place-names with the meaning 'wild bird,' is fairly frequent as a first element in field-names: cf. e.g. *Henne acre*, 1326 in Ipsden, *Hennfield*, c. 1454 in Mapledurham, *Henfeld*, 1424 in Henley, *Henforlonge*, 1490 in Chinnor.

heordewīc, OE, a compound of *heord*, 'flock,' and wīc (*v. infra*), 'dwelling-place for flocks.' Ekwall (DEPN) translates it 'sheep farm.' Hardwick (4).

herepæþ, OE, 'army road.' *Harpesford.*

hīd, OE, 'land adequate for the support of one household.' Hyde Fm, Hyde Shaw, Fifield (2). Fairly frequent in field-names.

h(i)elde, OE, 'slope.' Illcott Copse. Fairly frequent in field-names, cf. *Helde*, c. 1280 in Enstone, c. 1230–40 in Chinnor.

hīwan, genitive plural hīgna, OE, 'members of a family' and especially of a religious community, occurs in the following field-names: (*on*) *hina gemæro* (956 in Horspath), *Hynacre* (c. 1325 in Bicester), *Hynecroft* (c. 1230–40 in Chinnor), *Hinecroft* (early 13th in Kirtlington), *Hynewrthe* (c. 1250 in Goring).

hlāw, OE, 'hill, mound, tumulus.' (*a*) Himley Fm, Ploughley, Shenlow Hill; (*b*) Cutslow, *Shoteslaw*. hlǣw, identical in meaning. Lew, Whittles Fm. hlāw is common in field-names, often with a personal name as first element, but cf. *langan hlawe* (1004 in Shipton on Cherwell), *Nordlangelawe* (c. 1210 in Steeple Barton), *Anelaw* (c. 1260 in Little Tew), *Rowelowe* (c. 1325 in Bicester) and *Twysdelowe* (1358 in Wolvercot). hlǣw occurs in the field-names of Ardley (995), Curbridge (969 and 1004), Cuxham (995), Hook Norton (c. 1250), Great Tew (c. 1260). Both terms usually refer to a tumulus.

hlinc, OE, 'bank, rising ground,' later used in various technical senses such as 'an unploughed strip serving as a boundary between fields.' (*a*) The Lince, Lince Lane, Linch Hill, The Linsh; (*c*) Battle Edge. Common in field-names, where it gives ME *linch*, *lynch(e)*, modern *linch*, *lynch*, *lince*.

hliþ, OE, 'slope,' occurs in field-names: cf. *hlið weg*, 956 in Horspath. *Lithinghill*, 1614 in Shiplake, probably has the dative plural as first element.

hlȳde, an OE stream-name derived from *hlūd*, 'loud.' Ledwell, Ludwell Fm. Cf. also *hlydan* (956 in Holton) and possibly *Ludeswellehulle* (c. 1242–3 in Wroxton) and *Ludewelle* (c. 1230 in Hook Norton).

hōc, OE, 'hook,' probably used in place-names in various senses, such as 'bend, projecting corner, spur of hill,' is fairly frequent in field-names, cf. *hochylle* (1054) in Nuneham Courtney and *Hook hill* in Warborough.

*hōd, OE, 'shelter.' Monk's Wood.

hōh, OE, 'projecting ridge of land.' Howe Hill, Howbery Park, Nuffield, *Piriho Wood*. Also in field-names.

holegn, OE, 'holly.' Holme Copse, Holmes's Fm and Wood. Cf. also *Holinthorne*, 1366 in South Stoke.

holh, hol, OE, noun and adjective, 'hollow.' Holcombe, Hollandtide Bottom, Homer Fm, Old Grange Fm (earlier *Holewelle*), Horsalls. The element occurs in a number of lost stream-names, three times with brōc and seven times with w(i)elle.

holm(e), dialect word for 'a flat low-lying piece of land by a stream,' occurs in the modern field-names of some twelve parishes, the earliest example being *Milne Holme*, 1605 in Cowley.

home, used of land in the immediate neighbourhood of a farm, is very common in field-names, the most usual compounds being *Home Close* and *Home Ground*. The earliest example is *Hom(e)felde*, c. 1275 in Crowmarsh. This use of the word *home* is first recorded in NED in 1662, but earlier examples have been noted in other counties (cf. PN Herts 262). The terms *homer* and *fielder* occur several times: cf. *the homerhay, the fielder hay*, 1685 in Fringford.

honey, used in field-names with reference to sticky soil, is frequent, the earliest examples being *Honymede*, 1323 in Bourton, and *honyforlonge*, 1388 in Oxford. Cf. also the modern field-names *Puden hedge piece* in Middle Aston and *Pudding Bush Furlong* in Adderbury. *Honey Pot* has been noted once, in Bensington.

hord, OE, 'hoard, treasure.' Hordley Fm. Cf. also *Drakenhord* (175).

horh, OE, 'filth.' Horton. Cf. also *horwyllan*, 904 in Gosford.

*horna, OE, 'corner, bend, tongue of land.' Horley, Hornton. Cf. also *horninga mære*, 969 in Curbridge, *Hornle*, 1271–2 in Forest Hill, *Horneputte*, c. 1230 in Garsington, *Hornforlong*, c. 1270 in Wendlebury.

hors, OE, 'horse.' Horsalls, Horspath. Also in field-names.

hrāgra, OE, 'heron.' Rayford Lane.

hramsa, OE, 'wild garlic, *Allium ursinum*.' Ramsden, Ramsey Fm.

hrēod, OE, 'reed.' Radcot. Also in field-names.

hrycg, OE, 'ridge.' (*a*) Groveridge Wood, Lankridge Copse, Notteridge Copse, Shambridge Wood, Standridge Copse, Witheridge Hill; (*b*) Badgemore (earlier *Baggeridge*); (*c*) Kildridge Wood. There are many occurrences of hrycg-weg, for which *v*. 3. hrycg is frequent in field-names, where it gives modern *Ridge, Rudge*.

hrȳðer, OE, 'cattle.' Rotherfield, Ruddy Well. Cf. also *hryþera forda*, 956 in Cuddesdon, *ryðeraford*, 1059 in Northmoor.

*huntera, OE, 'of the huntsmen.' Huntercombe End.

hwǣte, OE, 'wheat.' Watcombe Manor, Wheatley. Also in field-names.

hwīt, OE, 'white.' Wheatfield, Whitchurch, White Hill, Whitehill (3), Whitley Hill, Whittles Fm. There is another 'white hill' in the field-names of Watlington (1317), and another 'white lē(a)h' in Chinnor (c. 1250–60).

hyll, OE, 'hill.' (*a*) *Hulwerk*, Broadstonehill, Butter Hill, Chastleton Hill, Chisnell Fm, Cockshoothill Copse, Fernhill Fm, Forest Hill, Foxhill Fm, Graven Hill, *Karshille*, Langley Hall, Millhill Barn, Oathill Fm, Oatleyhill Fm, Pishill, Port Hill Ho, Sainthill Copse, *Shippenhull*, Stapnall's Fm, Summershill Shaw, Whitchurch Hill, White Hill, Whitehill (4)[1]; (*b*) Beanhill Barn, Bignell Ho, Bucknell, Coursehill Fm, Pound Hill, Snakeshall Clump; (*c*) Churchill. *passim* in field-names.

hymele, OE, a plant-name which may refer to the wild hop or to bryony or bindweed. Himley Fm(?), *Humble Brook* (earlier name of Baldon Brook). Cf. also *Hemeleforlong*, c. 1200–10 in the field-names of Thomley.

hyrne, OE, 'corner.' Coldron Brook. Also in field-names, cf. *dichehurne*, c. 1235 in Milcombe.

hyrst, OE, 'hillock, bank, wooded eminence, wood.' (*b*) Chipping-hurst. Frequent in field-names.

hȳþ, OE, 'landing place.' Highcroft Lodge, Hythe Bridge, Bolney.

(ī)eg, OE, 'island,' used in place-names of land surrounded by streams or marsh. (*a*) Andersey Island, Flexney Fm, Goose Eye Cottage, Kingsey, *Langney*, Litney Fm, Medley, Otney, Ramsey Fm, Rye Fm, Rushy Weir, Sonning Eye, Wally Corner; (*b*) Green Benny, Binsey, Chimney, Edgerley Fm, Osney, Pixey Mead, Sparsey Bridge, Witney. Fairly frequent in field-names. In the forms for *Langney* and Medley (ī)eg alternates with eyt.

(i)elfen, OE, 'elf, fairy.' Elvendon Fm. Cf. *Elfwelle*, *Elfwellegrene*, c. 1240 in Garsington, 'elf stream.'

in. Compounds with in and ūt as first element occur in field-names, denoting fields etc. attached to the home estate and occupied by the owner or cultivated for his use, and outlying parts of an estate or manor which were granted to tenants. *inland* occurs in six parishes, the earliest example being c. 1240 in Garsington. *inmǣd*, modern *In(n)mead*, has been noted some eight times, the earliest being c. 1190–1200 in Hensington. Cf. also *Inneclose* (1606–7 in Bladon), *Infelde* and *Ingreen* (1551–2 and modern in Bruern), *In*

[1] Whitehill in Tackley has a different first element from the other three names.

Coombe (Ascott under Wychwood). There are two compounds with *out* where it has obviously the sense given above, *Outlands* (1685 in Broughton Poggs and *Outmead* in Aston Bampton, where *In Medowe* and *Oute Medowe* are mentioned 1551–2. *Outwood*, which may mean a wood lying just outside a park or demesne, or the outer border of a wood or forest (PN Sr 286), occurs in Eynsham and Kiddington. There are also five examples of *utfurlang*, the earliest being c. 1139 in Bletchingdon, and *Utlongelonde*, late 12th in Fifield.

-ing-, OE, is used as a middle element in place-names of which the first element is a personal name. The personal name + ing has much the same sense as the personal name in the genitive case, the particle indicating that the object referred to in the final element of the place-name is connected with the person referred to in the first element. ingtūn, '...'s farm,' occurs in Alkerton, Bainton, Bensington, Brighthampton, Chadlington, Deddington, Ducklington (?), Emmington, Kiddington, Kidlington, Kirtlington, Piddington, *Saxinton*, Wardington, Watlington and Yarnton. -ingcot(e), '...'s cottage(s),' occurs in Arncott, Bodicote, Kencott, Pudlicote, Wilcote and Wolvercot. Charlbury contains -ingburh, '...'s fortified settlement.' The particle is also used with w(i)elle in Mongewell, **weg** in *Tidgeon Way* and **ford** in *tidreding ford* (969 in Witney).

-ingas, OE, nominative plural, meaning 'the people of ...' when compounded with a personal name, and 'the dwellers at ...' when compounded with a topographical term, is probably combined with a personal name in Filkins and Goring. -inga-, the genitive plural, is used as a middle element in place-names. It occurs with a personal name and a topographical term in *englingadene* (11th century in Pyrton, 'the valley of *Engel*'s people'), Fringford, Shillingford and *wylfinga ford* (940 in Culham). With a personal name and a word for a settlement it occurs in Kingham. With another place-name or a topographical term as first element it occurs in Astall Leigh ('woodland of the people of Asthall'), *Foulwellingemere* (c. 1278 in Enstone), Hornton ('village of the *Horningas*, or people in a fork of land'), *horninga mære* (969 in Curbridge), *Horsepathingeston*' (c. 1240 in Garsington) and *Witefeldingefeld*' (1211 in Stoke Talmage). In this last group of names, the use of the element may be compared with that of **hǣme** *supra*, which, however, is usually added to the first element of a place-name, not the whole name.

inninges, ME, 'land taken into cultivation,' occurs in the field-names of Eye and Dunsden (early 17th), Lewknor and Watlington.

kitchen occurs in seven parishes as a modern field-name element. It probably refers to land the produce of which was used mainly for domestic purposes. Cf. also *Kitching* in Ardley.

lache, leche, ME, 'stream flowing through boggy land.' Lashbrook, Latchford, Latchfordhole.

lacu, OE, 'stream, watercourse.' (*a*) Marlake Ho, Shiplake, *Shirelake*, Standlake; (*b*) Bablock Hythe. Also in a number of unidentified stream-names.

(ge)lād, OE, 'road, water-course.' Occasionally in lost stream-names. In *hafocgelad* in Great Haseley the second element is **gelād**, in the sense 'water crossing.'

Lady occurs frequently in field-names, with various second elements, early examples being *Leuediescroft*, c. 1225 in Tetsworth, and *Ladydiche*, 1440 in Bensington. The element occurs more frequently in modern than in early names. In PN Wa 335 it was suggested that such names were given to pieces of land dedicated to the service of Our Lady. Cf. also *Mariecrofta*, 1209–18 in Great Haseley, *Seynte Marye Parrocke*, 15th in Mapledurham[1].

læs, OE, dative singular **læswe,** occurs *passim* in field-names, and is the usual source of the modern elements *lease, leaze,* though these may sometimes go back to the plural of **lē(a)h.** **læswe** has given the field-name elements *leasow, lesewe* (1366), *lesowe* (c. 1360), *leasowes, leazow, leason(s), lezzer.*

lag, dialect word for 'a long, narrow, marshy meadow, usually by the side of a stream,' occurs in the field-names of Littlemore and Prescote, and *leg,* 'a long narrow meadow, generally one which runs out of a larger piece of land,' occurs in Chalgrove.

lain, ME, may denote land which is periodically allowed to lie fallow by being sown in regular *laines* or divisions, *v.* PN W 439. It occurs in Oxfordshire field-names in the following forms: *leyn(e)* (1422 in Deddington, 1506–7 in South Newington), *laynys* (1517 in Goring), *layen* (1538–9 in Waterstock), *laynes* (1606–7 in Warborough), *leyon* (late 16th in Warborough), *lains* (Aston Bampton, Baldon), *laines* (Broadwell), *Leynes* (1599 in Burford) and possibly *lion* (Bensington) and *lyons* (Swerford).

Lammas is a common field-name element, applied to land which was under particular cultivation till harvest and reverted to common pasturage at Lammastide (August 1st), remaining as such till the following spring. The earliest examples in Oxfordshire are *Lammas Close,* 1650 in Eynsham, *Lammas ground* 1621 in South Leigh. Cf. also *Michaelmas Grounds* in Alvescot.

land, OE, 'earth, soil, landed property, estate.' Blacklands Plantation, Longlands Spinney, Newland Ho, Newland Road, Red Lane. *passim* in field-names, where it may have the technical sense 'strip of land in an open field,' *v.* **blæc** *supra* and **lang** *infra.*

---

[1] Cf. the name *Lady Lande vel St Marie Land vel Ladie meade* 1575 *SpecCom* in Painswick, Gl, which refers to land attached to a Chapel of St Mary.

landew. This term has been noted in the following field-names: *the Landewes* (1329 in Mapledurham), *Laundewes* (c. 1360 in Shifford), *le Landew* (1365–6 in Deddington), *le Landewe* (no date in Asthall, represented by *Land-dues* 1814), *Land Ewes* (c. 1840 in Minster Lovell). No etymology can be suggested.

landriht, OE, in the sense 'property,' may be the second element of Rollright.

lang, OE, 'long, tall.' *Langeford*, Langford (2), Lankridge Copse, Langley (2), *Langney*, Langree, Launton, Longlands Spinney. Common in field-names, where there are about a dozen more examples of 'long land(s).' *lang furlang* is also common, and gives modern *Lancke Furlong* (early 17th in Wheatley), *Lanck Furlong* (Sandford St Martin), *Lank Furlong* (Deddington, Fritwell, Middleton Stoney, Noke, Stadhampton, South Weston) and *Lang Furlong* (Rousham, Duns Tew, Wroxton).

lanket or **langet,** a dialect term for a long, narrow field, occurs in modern field-names in the following forms: *Lanket(t)* (Crawley, Ducklington, Enstone, Eynsham, Hailey, Minster Lovell, Waterperry, Wootton), *Lancot(t)* (Islip, Leafield, Northmoor, Shifford, Yarnton), *Langcott* (Eynsham, Kiddington), *Langett* (Alvescot), *Langate* (Chastleton), *Lank Yeat* (Charlbury). Cf. also Langhat Ditch in Alvescot.

launde, ME from OFr, 'open space in woodland, glade, pasture.' South Lawn. Occasionally in field-names.

lē(a)h, OE, 'wood, open place in a wood, meadow, pasture land.' (*a*) Lea Fm, North and South Leigh, Asterleigh, Asthall Leigh, Barleyfields, Black Leys, Burleigh Fm, Cleveley, Corble Fm, Crawley, Delly End, *Felley*, *Fethelee*, Foxley Fm, Hailey (3), Great Haseley, Henley, Hordley Fm, Horley, Iffley, Langley, *Linley*, Oakley (2), Sidlings Copse, Stockley Copse, Studley (2), Tangley Hall, Thomley, Weavely Fm, Wheatley, Whitley Hill, Great Wichelo Shaw, Widley Copse, Woodleys; (*b*) Ardley, Barleypark, Beckley, Cookley Fm, Cowley, Crowsley Park, Hundley Road, Huntley Wood, Kemsley Barn, Madley Brook, *Otley*, Pinsley Wood, Tilgarsley. *passim* in field-names, where in modern forms the plural cannot be distinguished with certainty from lǣs. lē(a)h is probably the usual source of *Leys* and *Lays* in modern names, however.

leet, which occurs in the names *le Longelete* (1363 in Eynsham), *Flexlete* (1363 in Rollright), *The Old Mill Leat* (1844 in Great Milton), *Broadway Leets* (1776 in Rousham) and *the leete feild* (1679 in Hethe), is probably the dialect word meaning 'an artificial channel for water' (*v.* EDD *s.v. leat*).

lῑn, OE, 'flax.' *Linley*, Lyneham. Frequent in field-names, where the compound lῑn-tūn, 'flax enclosure,' occurs several times.

lok, ME, 'barrier on a river.' Hartslock Wood.

lot. This is a frequent field-name element, used of common land the shares in which were assigned by lot. *Lot Mead(ow)* is particularly common. The forms are 16th century or later.

lunch occurs in Redlunch Barn, The Lunches and *Lunch Furlong* in the field-names of Fritwell. It has been noted as a field-name element in Sr and Wa, and in PN Sr 369 it is suggested that it is a topographical use of *lunch*, 'lump, thick piece.'

lūs, OE, 'louse.' *v.* Forsberg 182–9 for a full discussion of this element in place-names. *(to) lusan þorne* and *lusþorn(e)* occur in charter boundaries, and Forsberg suggests that the reference is to a thorn-tree infested with plant-lice, and compares the two Oxfordshire field-names *Lusythoren* (1285 in Goring) and *the lowsy thorn*' (1388 in Godstow). There are also three Oxfordshire minor names in which a similar first element is combined with grāf(a), 'grove': *Losnegrave*, *Losengraue* (13th in Wychwood, represented by *Lowzie Grove* 1617), *Losyng Grove* (1545–6 in Hailey) and *Lowsing Grove* (1538–9 in Fulbrook). *Lowsie bush* occurs early 17th in Wheatley, and *Lousy Bush* as a modern field-name in Banbury, Ipsden, Shirburn. The precise relationship of these forms to each other and to OE lūs is difficult, but Forsberg's suggestion that the OE names refer to trees or bushes infested with plant-lice gives a satisfactory sense for all the O names.

lȳtel, OE, 'little.' Litney Fm, Littlegate Street, Little Heath, Little Minster, Littlemore, Littlestoke Fm. Fairly frequent in field-names, where there are two other examples with mōr, c. 1195 in Oddington and c. 1280 in Brize Norton.

mǣd dative singular mǣdwe OE, *mead* and *meadow* ModE, occur *passim* in field-names. mǣd frequently gives modern *Mad-*, as in *Madcroft*, which occurs in Cowley, Cropredy, South Leigh, Piddington, Pyrton, Stanton St John, Stratton Audley and Tackley. In Cowley and Stanton St John there are early forms with *Med(e)*- and later forms with *Mad-*, but *Mad-* is sometimes early, as in *Madfurlong*, c. 1185 in Hampton.

(ge)mǣne, OE, 'common.' Maidensgrove, *Meaning Way*, Menmarsh Fm. Also in field-names.

(ge)mǣre, OE, 'boundary.' *Mallewell*, Manual Spring, Marlake Ho, *Marlakes Ditch*, Cold Harbour (probably identical with *Caldhememere*), Hockmore. Also in a number of unidentified stream-names, for which *v.* 14. As a field-name element it is common in charters, but in later names frequently impossible to distinguish from mere.

mangthorn, presumably a plant-name, occurs in Mangthorn Wood (*Mangthorne* 1679) and in the field-names *Ma(n)gethorn* c. 1325, *Mangethorne* 1634, *Mangton* c. 1840, in Fringford, and *Margh*

Thornes, 1739 in Alvescot. No trace of the term has been found in the dictionaries.

mapuldor, OE, 'maple-tree.' Mapledurham. Occasionally in field-names.

mēos, OE, 'moss.' Muswell Hill. Also in *meoslege*, 1005–12 in Beckley.

mere, OE, 'pool.' (*a*) Merton, *Cranemeare* (early name of High-furlong Brook), Cranmoor Plantation, Finmere, Greenmoor Hill, Homer Fm, Roomer's Spinney, Rumerhedge Wood, Rushey Bank, Tadmarton; (*b*) Colmore Fm; (*c*) Tusmore, Uxmore Fm. Probably fairly frequent in field-names, where it is difficult to distinguish from (ge)mǣre. In minor names in the Chilterns it is probable that *-more* and *-moor*, which appear frequently on the 6″ map, often represent earlier **mere**: pools, formed where there are patches of clay on top of the chalk, are a noticeable feature of the topography of the area.

mersc, OE, 'marsh.' Marsh Baldon, Marsh Haddon Fm, Marston, Cowley Marsh, Crowmarsh, Menmarsh Fm. Frequent in field-names. The form **merisc** occurs in May's Fm.

middel, OE, 'middle.' Medley, Middle Aston, Middle Barton, Middleton Stoney, Milcombe, Milton (3). Also in field-names.

mixen, OE, 'dung-heap,' Mixbury. Cf. also the field-names *Blake-mixerne* (1315 in Enstone), *Uselenemixene* (c. 1218 in Hampton) and *Long Miskin* (c. 1840 in Curbridge).

mōr, OE, 'fen.' (*a*) Moor Court, Moreton, Moorton, Murcot, Brad-more Road, Crutchmore Plantation, Littlemore, Newton Morell, Northmoor, Pilmoor Arch, Priest's Moor; (*b*) Badgemore, Cottes-more Fm, Cotmore Fm, Ot Moor. *passim* in field-names.

munuc, OE, 'monk.' Monk's Wood. Cf. also *Monekenelake*, c. 1260 in Hook Norton, *Monkene lane*, 1504–5 in Watlington.

mycel, OE, 'great,' occurs frequently in field-names. Cf. also *Mucheleburton*, 1323 in the forms for Great Bourton.

myln, OE, 'mill.' (*a*) Millham Ford, Millhill Barn, Beard Mill, *Castle Mill*, Churchill Mill, Cutt Mill, Cutmill Fm, *Doders Mill*, Eynsham Mills, King's Mill, *Shitpilchmill*, Slate Mill, Trill Mill Stream; (*b*) *Boymill*, *Hulk Mill*; (*c*) *Wygon Mill*. Frequent in field-names, where *Millham* (*v.* **hamm**) and *Millway* are particularly common.

mynecenu, OE, 'nun.' Minchen's Barn, Minchery Fm, Minchin-court Fm, Minchin Recreation Ground.

mynster, OE, 'monastery.' Minster Lovell.

*næt, OE, 'wet.' Notteridge Copse.

nattock, ME, noted as a field-name in other counties, occurs in Cowley (1207) and Little Tew (c. 1240). It may also occur in Notoaks Wood and Nutoaks Copse, for which the forms are late. The origin of the term is unknown, but *v.* PN Nth lii, where it is stated that in modern Nth field-names it is applied to little patches of higher ground in the marshes.

neoðera, OE, 'lower.' Neithrop (?), Nethercott.

netel, OE, 'nettle.' Nettlebed. This compound occurs also as a field-name in Milcombe and Woodeaton (c. 1366): cf. *Netleden*, 1300 in Fawler.

nīwe, OE, 'new.' Newington (3), Newland Ho, Newland Road, New Street, Newton Purcell, Newnham Murren, Nuneham Courtney. Some of these names contain the weak dative singular, nīwan. Also in field-names.

no man's... in field-names, refers to land on a boundary. Cf. *Nomannyscroft* (c. 1300 in Sydenham), *Noe mans pleacke* (1611 in Horley), *No mans gapp* (1629 in Elsfield), and the modern field-names *No mans plot* (Aston Bampton), *No mans patch* (Northmoor), *No Mans Gore* (Drayton St Leonard). There is a No Man's Land on the 6″ map in Sarsden, and a No Man's Hill on the 1″ in Badgemore.

norþ, OE, 'north.' Norham Manor, Nor Grove, Northam, North Aston, North Bar St, Northbrook, Northfield Fm, North Leigh, Northmoor, North Newington, North Weston, Brize Norton, Chipping Norton, Over Norton. Also in field-names.

ofer, OE, 'over.' Over Norton, Overy. The last name occurs again in the field-names of Wardington.

ōfer, OE, 'border, river-bank.' Ashford Bridge, Shotover (the forms show confusion with ōra).

ōra, OE, 'border, bank, shore,' in place-names often 'hill slope.' (*a*) Worton, Bixmoor Wood, Chalk Wood (earlier *Chalcore*), Clare, Golder, *Radnor*, Shotover (alternating with ōfer), Stonor; (*b*) Chinnor, Launder's Fm, Lewknor. In some of these names there is confusion with ōfer.

ōðer, OE, 'other.' Nethercote.

oxa, OE, 'ox.' Oxey Hill, Oxey Mead, Oxford. Also in field-names.

pæþ, OE, 'path.' Horspath. Occasionally in field-names.

parke, ME from OFr, 'enclosure for beasts.' Cornbury Park.

parting occurs in the following field-names: *Parting Close* (Denton, Kingham, Northmoor), *Partingmeade* (1606–7 in Wootton), *Parting mead*, *Part lot mead* (Noke), *Parting Acre* (Oxford). The reference could be either to land which can be divided, or to land which forms a boundary. *Part lot mead* suggests the former.

pearroc, OE, 'enclosure.' Park Wood.

penny. Field-names which refer to the rent of the land are common, *penny* being the most frequent amount. The earliest occurrence is in Eye and Dunsden, where there is a 13th-century form *Pendenemed*, from the rare OE form *pending*. There is a *Threepenny Copse* in

Wychwood, and *Sixpenny close*, *Ham and Mead* occur in Tiddington, Shifford and Spelsbury. Cf. also *Tenne penny leaze* (1647
in Kidlington), *Tenpenylande* and *le fore Shillinges acre* (1551–2 in
Dorchester), *The 5 pound piece* (c. 1840 in Rotherfield Greys) and
Tippenny Meadow (1802 in Bloxham).

peose, OE, 'pea.' Pishill. Fairly frequent in field-names, where there
is another example with **hyll**, *Pushil*, c. 1225 in Rollright.

pest-house occurs in the field-names of Banbury, Bicester, Chipping
Norton, Deddington and Steeple Aston. It refers to the former
existence of lazarettos for plague-stricken persons. Cf. also *Pest*,
a field-name in Charlbury.

picked, from ME **piked**, is the commonest and the earliest of the
terms describing an angular piece of land, which are very frequent
in Oxfordshire field-names. The earliest example noted is *ate-
pikedelonde*, c. 1300 in Denton, represented by *The Picken* c. 1840.
piked, **picket(t)**, **pikey**, **peaked** also occur in modern names, and
pikes and **picks** (occasionally **pix**), **pike** and **pick** are alternative
modern terms.

pightel, early ModE from ME *pigtel*, *pictel*, is common in field-names.
The earliest example is in Cowley, where there are 13th- and 14th-
century forms. Forms of the nasalised variant **pingle** occur in
Pinkhill Barn in Stanton Harcourt and Pintle Barn in Charlbury,
and the field-names *Pinkle* in Upper Heyford and *Pingle's Field* in
Hanwell. The variant **piddle** occurs in some seven parishes, the
earliest example being *Piddle pittes*, 1572–3 in Swyncombe.

pirige, OE, 'pear-tree.' *Piriho Wood*, Purwell Fm, Pyrton, Waterperry, Woodperry. Also in field-names.

plank occurs in the following modern field-names: *Ash plank meadow*
(Charlton on Otmoor), *Marton Plank meadow* (Fencott, probably the
same meadow as the two parishes are contiguous), *Plank Meadow*
(Deddington and Swerford), *plank pitts* (Great Tew), *Thale Plank*
(Cropredy), *Witell planck* (1591 in Kirtlington). The term is
recorded of 'a piece of cultivated land longer than broad, a strip
of land between two open furrows; a more or less definite measure
of land.'

plat, a dialect word meaning 'a piece of ground,' is fairly frequent in
field-names, the earliest example noted being *Greneplatte*, 1551–2
in Piddington. It is not evidenced in the NED till the 16th century,
but it is recorded in the 13th century in field-names, *v*. PN Wo 311.

plek, ME, 'a small piece of ground,' occurs in field-names in the
following forms: *pleck* (Brize Norton, Crowell, Lewknor), *plek'*
(1366 in South Stoke), *plek* (1412–13 in Stratton Audley), *pleacke*
(1611 in Horley), *plack* (1601 in Newton Purcell) and *plext*, *plex*
(1685 and 1806 in Wigginton).

pohhede, OE, 'baggy.' Ploughley.

poor(s) is a frequent first element in field-names, presumably denoting land which was used for charitable purposes. *Poor(s) Allotment*, *Poors Common*, *Poor(s) Ground*, *Poors Close*, *Poor Folks Closes*, *Poors Furlong*, *Labouring Poors Allotment* have been noted, and also *Charity Farm and Mead*, *Charity School and Land*, *Charity Pightle*. *Poeresham* (no date in Lyneham) may be a somewhat earlier example of this type of name.

port, OE, 'town.' Port Hill. For the numerous occurrences of port-weg in the county, *v.* 2–3.

portmann, OE, 'townsman, burgess.' *Portmaneyt* (earlier name of Port Meadow).

prēost, OE, 'priest.' Prescote, Priest Grove, Priest Hill, Priests' Moor, Crowmarsh Preston. A fairly common first element in field-names.

pūca, OE, 'goblin.' Poppets Hill. This name, with second element pytt, occurs again in *Pukkespytte*, c. 1470–80 in Newington and *Powkputte*, 1435–6 in Burford. Cf. also the field-names *Poukwelle-forlong*, c. 1325 in Bicester, *Poukebrugge*, 1406 in Eynsham, and the street-name Puck Lane in Eynsham and Witney, which may contain pūca though the forms are late. Similar names are *Shucke-lawe* (first element *scucca*, 'demon') and *Demnesweye*, c. 1215 in Steeple Barton.

pyll, OE, probably used in place-names of any small stream, occurs in The Pills, Pilmoor Arch and the following field-names: *Pilford* (1634 in Shipton on Cherwell), *pyll dyche and furlonge* (15th in Mapledurham), *Pill Meadow* (Tackley), *Pill Furlong* (1605 in Cowley), *Pillands* (Crowmarsh), *Pil Leys* (Adderbury). Cf. also Ashton Pill Bridge in Grafton.

pytt, OE, 'pit.' (*a*) *Putts*, Poppets Hill, Redpitsmanor Fm, Slatepits Copse; (*c*) Mogpits Wood. Common in field-names.

quar(r), 'stone quarry,' an abbreviation of *quarry* which survives in dialect, is fairly frequent in field-names. Cf. *Quarr furlonge*, 1635 in Cornwell.

rack, south-western dialect word for 'a narrow path or track' (*v.* NED sb[1] 4) from ME *rakke*. The Rakke, Rack End. The earliest form for the first name is somewhat earlier than the ME example quoted in NED. There are several field-names which may contain this word, but *rack* has other dialect meanings for which *v.* EDD.

rād, OE, 'riding.' Radford.

rǣw, OE, 'row.' Shiplake Row, Stoke Row. This word and rāw, identical in meaning, both occur in field-names.

rēad, OE, 'red.' Radcot (?), *Radnor*, Reddish Fm, Red Lane. Also in field-names.

Recreation is frequently referred to in modern field-names, the commonest names of this type being *Revel(s) Mead* (seven, of which one in Cornwell is dated 1614: there is also a *Burcote Revel* in Clifton Hampden) and *Pleasure Ground(s)* (eight). *Footeball close* occurs 1608–9 in Wootton, *Football Ground* in North Newington and Hailey, and *Lower and Upper Football* in Churchill. *Gamfelde* also occurs 1608–9 in Wootton. Cf. also *Playing Close* (Charlbury), *Play-close Lane* (Chadlington), *Play Close* (Rousham), *The Running Close* (Leafield), *The Race Course* (Curbridge), *Race Ground Common* (Bicester), *Recreation Ground* (Great Milton, Milton under Wychwood), *Wrestling close* (Milcombe), *Wrestling Grounds* (Eynsham), *May Pole Ground* (Whitchurch), *Bowling Alley* (Deddington, Great Milton, Piddington, Waterstock (1609), South Weston), *Bowling Green* (Checkendon and Goring). The two occurrences of 'holliday hill' (17th century in Marston and Westwell) may belong here.

refham occurs in field-names in the following forms: *Refham* (c. 1210 in Churchill, 1268–81 in Eynsham, c. 1190–1200 in Headington, 1278–9 in North Leigh, 1412–13 in Stratton Audley), *Refhamme* (1315 in Chinnor), *Reeveham*, *Rifeham* (1768, 1774 in Adderbury), *Reefham* (1799 in Kelmscott). There are two examples in PN W 433, *Refham* 1327 and *Reveshum* 1420. The meaning is probably, as is implied there, 'reeve's *hamm*,' with reference to tenure by a local official. The NED *s.v. reeve* sb[1] 3 quotes from a 13th-century Somerset source in which "ii hammes prati...que vocantur Refhammes" occurs in the same context as *Reflond* and *Refmede*. It is curious that the compound with hamm should occur eight times in Oxfordshire, where the only other compound of *geréfa* noted is *Reveton'*, 1278–9 in Great Tew.

ríðig, OE, 'small stream.' Cropredy. Also in unidentified stream-names.

rod, OE, 'clearing in a forest,' occurs occasionally in early field-names. Cf. *Estur(e)broderode*, 'eastern broad clearing,' c. 1230–40 in Thomley, *ealdan Rode*, 958 in Ducklington.

rod, ModE, probably means 'osier' in such compounds as *Rod Eyott* (noted in six parishes), *Rod Ham* (in five parishes), *Rod Moor* (Bicester), *Rod(s) Close* (Baldon and Enstone). NED gives the following quotation dated 1883 *s.v. rod* sb[1] 12, "From here a quarter of a mile of crooked stream, bordered with rodhams, brings us to Shillingford Bridge."

rúh, OE, 'rough.' Roomer's Spinney, Roughborough Copse, Row Barrow, Rumerhedge Wood. Fairly common in field-names—there is another example of 'rough barrow' in Ramsden.

ryding, OE, 'clearing, cleared land.' The Riding, Deadman's Riding,

Lower Riding Fm, Minster Riding, Rudgings Plantation. Fairly common in field-names.

ryge, OE, 'rye.' Rycote. Frequent in field-names.

rysc, OE, 'rush.' Rushey Bank, Rushy Weir. Also in field-names.

*sænget, OE, 'land cleared by burning.' Signet, Singe Wood. Occasionally in field-names, cf. *sænet hylle*, 11th in Pyrton, *Syngett*, 1522 in Stanton St John.

sainfoin, *Onobrychis sativa*, is very frequently referred to in modern field-names. The spellings *Saint Foin, St Foin, Saintfoin, Sanfoin, Sainfoin, Sandfoin* have been noted, those with -*t*- being due to identification of the first syllable with *saint*, 'holy,' common in French in the 16th and in English in the 17th century (NED). The word is probably made up of French *sain*, 'health-giving' and *foin*, 'hay.'

sand, OE, 'sand.' Sainthill Copse, *Sandbrook*, Sandford (2), Sand Hill, Shambridge Wood, Soundess Ho. There is another *sandford*, 956 in the field-names of Tadmarton.

sart or assart, ME from OFr, the legal name for a clearing or settlement where the land had formerly been waste. Assarts Cottage, Field Assarts, Glympton Assarts Fm. Fairly common in field-names.

sceācere, OE, 'robber.' *Sugarbarre streate* (?), Sugarswell Fm. Cf. also *Shokereswey*, 1435–6 in Watlington.

sceād, OE, 'boundary.' Shadwell Spring. This compound with w(i)elle also occurs five times as an unidentified stream-name (*v.* 14), and there is a *Shad Brook* in Milton under Wychwood.

scē(a)p, OE, 'sheep.' Shifford, Shiplake, Shipton (2). Also in field-names.

*scēot, OE, 'steep slope.' Shotover.

sc(ī)ene, OE, 'beautiful, bright.' Shenington, Shenlow Hill.

scipen, OE, 'cattle-shed.' *Shippenhull, Bolles Shipton*. Occasionally in field-names.

scīr, OE, 'bright, shining.' Shirburn. Cf. also *Shyremere*, c. 1294 in Thomley, *Schirewellefeld'*, c. 1240 in Garsington.

scīr, OE, 'shire.' *Shirelake*.

sclate, ME from OFr, 'slate.' Slate Mill, Slatepits Copse. Also in field-names.

scort, OE, 'short.' Shorthampton. Fairly frequent in field-names.

scylf, OE, 'rock, crag,' probably also 'ledge' and 'bank of a river.' Shilton. Cf. also *scylfhrycg*, 887 in Brightwell Baldwin.

s(e)alt, OE, 'salt.' Salford. For the occurrences of s(e)alt-weg in the county *v.* 3.

seofon, OE, 'seven.' Showell Covert, Showell Fm. This compound with w(i)elle is probably also the source of Showells Spring in

Crawley and the field-names *Showels* (Wheatley) and *Showels Mead* (Aston Bampton).

(ge)set, OE, 'dwelling, place of residence' also 'fold for animals,' is probably the second element of *Brugeset*.

several, referring to land in private ownership or over which a person has a particular right, especially enclosed land as opposed to common land, occurs occasionally in modern field-names, cf. *The Several* in Broughton Poggs, *Severel* in Lewknor.

shovelbrode, ME, 'shovel broad,' occurs in the field-names of Milcombe (*shouelbrode* c. 1235), and there is a variant of the name in Great Tew (*Shulebrede* ? c. 1240, with second element **brǣd**, 'breadth'). Cf. also the comparatively modern names *Broad Shovel Furlong*, no date in Warborough, and *Short Shouell furlong* (early 17th in Wheatley). This is a widespread contemptuous nickname for a small field. *v.* PN Wa 322 for other examples, to which may be added *Sholebreade*, t. Ed 6 in Welford Gl (Gray 88) and *Schuilbraidis*, 1599 in Eymouth Berwickshire (Gray 163).

sīc, OE, 'small stream,' occurs in field-names and in lost stream-names, cf. (*on* þ') *eastre sic*, 956 in Tadmarton, *Sichefurlange*, 1207 in Cowley.

sīd, OE, 'wide.' Sidlings Copse, Sydenham. In field-names there are six more examples of names from OE (*æt þām*) *sīdan hamme*, 'at the wide river-meadow,' and a similar formation is found in *Sidenhal*, c. 1325 in Bicester, with second element h(e)alh.

sideland(s) refers to the headlands of a ploughed field, where the plough has been turned. It is a common element in modern field-names, and there is a probable early example in *Brodesedland*, c. 1230 in Garsington.

sideling(s), 'a strip of land which runs along an edge (of a stream etc.),' is fairly frequent in field-names, with forms dating from the 13th century onwards. There is possibly confusion with sideland(s) in the field-names of Oxford and Spelsbury, though it may be that both the names occur in these parishes. In Spelsbury there are the forms *Sidelong Mead* (1743), *Sideland Meadow* (1779), *Sid(e)-lings*, *Sidelands* (modern). *the Sidelong* occurs also in Stonesfield.

*s(i)ele, OE, an unrecorded derivative of *sealh*, 'willow,' conjectured by Ekwall (DEPN) as the first element of Silchester Ha, Silton Do, Selby WRY and Selham Sx, may be the first element of Silgrove Wood.

slæd, OE, 'valley, dell.' (*a*) Slade Fm (2), Dogslade Bottom, Waterside Ho; (*b*) Exlade Street. Frequent in field-names.

slǣp, OE, probably 'slippery place,' perhaps also 'place where goods are dragged across a river.' Slape Bridge, Islip. *occan slæw*, 1044 in Ducklington, should probably be *occan slæp*.

sling, dialect term for 'a long narrow field; a strip of land,' occurs in the field-names of Charlbury, Elsfield, Headington (*The Slenge or Slinge* 1805), Oxford and Souldern (1693). slinket, dialect term for 'a long narrow strip of ground, a narrow wood,' occurs in the field-names of North Newington, Thame and Wardington.

slipe, slip are common as field-names for a long narrow strip of land. All the forms are modern. *Slipes* occurs in Rotherfield Greys.

slōh, OE, 'slough, mire,' is fairly common in field-names. Cf. *fuleslo*, c. 1270 in Cassington, *fulanslo* 11th in Pyrton, *Fouleslowe*, 1606 in Benson, with fūl as first element.

smæl, OE, 'small, narrow, slender.' *Small Bridge*, Smalloaks Copse, Smallstones Fm. Also in field-names, and a number of unidentified stream-names, for which *v.* 15. 'Narrow way,' from smæl and weg, is common in field-names.

smēðe, OE, 'smooth,' occurs occasionally as a first element in field-names, cf. *Smythemers*, 1299 in Churchill, *Smythforlong*, 1312 in Chinnor. An oblique case is represented in *Smythene hille*, 1506–7 in North Newington, and *Smithen green*, 1676 in North Leigh. *Smethe*, late 13th in Garsington, is the ME word used as a noun meaning 'level space,' a use which is not recorded till c. 1440.

smoke is a common field-name element, the significance of which was discussed in PN W 446. It is suggested there that it should be associated with the terms *smoke-silver* and *smoke-penny*, used of a household tax, levied for various reasons. The exact relationship of land called *Smokacre, Smocacre, Smoke Acre, Smock Acre, Smock Furlong* etc. to a household tax is, however, not clear. The forms for these field-names date from the 13th century onwards.

snǣd, OE, occurs in Corble Fm (earlier *Corbynesnedle*). The word is only found in charters, and its meaning is uncertain: 'piece of land, clearing, piece of woodland' have been suggested.

spearwe, OE, 'sparrow.' Sparacre Lane.

spell, OE, 'speech.' *Spelberwe, Spelburghe.*

spring, spryng, OE, 'spring,' is frequent in field and minor names. The compound *spring-well*, first recorded a. 1300, occurs in modern names in Bletchingdon, Chesterton, Fritwell, Iffley and Little Tew, and in one early name (*Sprungwelle*, c. 1241 in Clanfield). *Well Spring* occurs in Asthall, Shipton on Cherwell and Little Tew, and *Springfontain* in Hanwell.

staca, OE, 'stake.' Bullstake Bridge. Cf. also *Stakamford*, 1551–2 in Wardington.

stæniht, OE, 'stony.' *Stony Way.*

stān, OE, 'stone.' (*a*) Standbow Bridge, Standlake, Standridge Copse, Stanton (2), Stonor, Stowford Fm, Stowood, Hoar Stone (2),

Hoarstone Spinney, Smallstones Fm, Wroxton; (*b*) Enstone, Lidstone; (*c*) Broadstone, Taston. Also in field-names, *v.* hār *supra*.

stān-(ge)delf, OE, 'stone quarry.' Standhill. Occurs about a dozen times as a field-name.

stēap, OE, 'steep.' Stapnall's Fm. This phrase ('at the steep hill') occurs also in field-names, cf. *Stapenhulle*, c. 1270 in Hook Norton, *Stapenhilmede*, 1377 in Aston Rowant, *Stepehyl*, c. 1139 in Bletchingdon. Cf. also *steapancnollesseyd*, 11th century in Pyrton with *cnoll*, 'knoll,' as second element, and Steep Hill, a modern minor name in Steeple Barton.

stede, OE, 'place, position, site,' occurs occasionally in field-names, but in major names only in the compound hāmstede (*supra*).

steort, OE, 'tail,' used in place-names of a tongue of land. Sturt Fm, Sturt Copse and Fm, Sturt Copse. Frequent in field-names.

stiche is a field-name element of uncertain origin. Cf. the Oxford-shire field-names *nine styches* 1517, *Nine Steeches* c. 1840 (Denton), *Stiches* (1676 in Mapledurham), *Stache* (1605 in Marston), *Steach* (Aston Bampton), *Stuchfield* (Piddington). These forms suggest association with NED *stitch* sb[3] 2, 'a ridge or balk of land.' Cf. however PN W 447, where it is stated that the Wiltshire names in *stic(c)he*, *styche* must go back to an OE **sticce* (not OE *stycce*, 'piece'), and doubt is expressed as to a connection with the word for 'a ridge or balk,' which is considered to be an East Anglian term. The term *stitching*, which occurs in the field-name *Stitchings* in Spelsbury, was noted several times in Wiltshire. No meaning can be suggested for this.

stīepel, OE, 'steeple.' Steeple Aston, Steeple Barton.

stīg, OE, 'narrow path,' occurs occasionally in field-names, cf. *le Grenesty*, 1498–9 in Black Bourton.

stigel, OE, 'stile,' occurs in the early forms for Hart's Lock (*Locstigle* 1181 etc.), and occasionally in field-names.

stoc, OE, 'place' (*v.* DEPN for a discussion of the possible meanings in place-names). Stoke Lyne, Stoke Row, Stoke Talmage, Fin-stock, Littlestoke Fm, North Stoke, South Stoke, Waterstock, Woodstock.

stocc, OE, 'tree-stump.' Stockey Bottom, Stockley Copse, *Stock Well*. Also in field-names.

stocking, ME, 'clearing' (i.e. 'place cleared of stocks'). Stocken Corner Covert, Stocking Barn, Stockings Fm, Stockings Planta-tion, Stockings Shaw.

stōd, OE, 'stud, herd of horses.' Stadhampton, Studley (2). **stōd-fal(o)d**, 'stud-fold,' occurs occasionally in field-names.

stōw, OE, '(holy) place.' Godstow. Occasionally in field-names.

strǣt, OE, 'street, Roman road.' Stratford Bridge, Stratton Audley, Street Hill, Akeman Street. For occurrences of **port-strǣt** and **s(e)alt-strǣt** v. 2–3, 3–4. Occasionally in field-names. ME *strete* occurs frequently in the street-names of Oxford.

string(s), used of a long narrow strip of land, often woodland, especially in a valley by a stream, occurs in Parkstrings Wood and in several modern field-names.

sulh, OE, 'furrow, gully.' Souldern.

sumor, OE, 'summer.' *Somerford*, Somerton, Summershill Shaw. A common first element in field-names; there is another *Sumerford* (1005 in Standlake), a *Somerwelle* (1412–13 in Stratton Audley) and a *Somersmore* (? c. 1240 in Great Tew). *Somerlesa*, 1146 in Thame, is an early example of a name which occurs frequently in modern field-names as *Summer Leys* or *Leaze*. The reference is to a field used for pasture in summer, and *Summer Eating Ground*, *Summer Ground*, *Summer Hays*, *Summer Field* also occur. Cf. also *Midsummer Plot* (Garsington), *June common* (1674 in Northmoor), *whitson Leaes* (1605 in Iffley), *Whitson moore* (1605 in Tackley), the precise significance of which is uncertain.

sūr, OE, 'sour,' later used of land in the sense 'cold and wet,' is a fairly common field-name element. Cf. *Sourehul*, c. 1260 in Thomley, *Sureforlong*, *Sureland*, late 13th in Shirburn. **sweet** occurs occasionally in modern names, cf. *Sour and Sweet Middle Ground* in Pyrton.

sūþ, OE, 'south.' Sescut Fm, South Bar Street, Southfield Barn, South Leigh, South Newington, Southrop, South Stoke, South Weston, Sutton. Also in field-names.

swath occurs occasionally as a modern field-name element, and probably denotes a measure of grass-land. It is used in the plural, and appears in the forms *swaths* (Elsfield and Stanton St John), *swathes* (Northmoor), *swarths* (Kingham and Wheatfield).

swealwe, OE, 'swallow.' Swalcliffe.

swēora, OE, 'col.' Swerford. Cf. also *Swire Furlong* in the field-names of Churchill.

swift, OE, 'swift,' occurs in several lost stream-names, with second element lacu.

swīn, OE, 'pig.' Swinbrook, Swinford, Swyncombe. Also in field-names.

tāde, OE, 'toad.' Tadmarton.

taen, Welsh, 'a sprinkling.' A river-name related to this is the first element of Taynton.

þæc-hamm, OE, 'river-meadow where reeds for thatching are obtained,' is the source of about a dozen medieval and modern field-names. The earliest form is *Thecham*, c. 1200 in Lower Heyford and c. 1215–30 in Bicester. There is also a modern name *Thatch Ground* in Ardley.

þorn, OE, 'thorn-bush.' *Thornebury*, Souldern. Frequent in field-names.

þrop, OE, 'farm, hamlet.' (*a*) Thrupp, Astrop Fm, Burdrop, Dun-thorp, Heythrop, Southrop, Tythrop Ho; (*c*) Calthorpe Ho, Cokethorpe Park, Neithrop.

þyrne, OE, 'thorn-bush.' Thorngreen Copse. Occasionally in field-names.

tite, dialect word for 'a fountain of water; a small rivulet or rill dammed across to collect water for family use,' occurs in Tyte End and several times in field-names, cf. *Tite End* in Chipping Norton (*Tytend* 1659).

tōte, ME, 'look-out hill.' Toot Baldon. Occasionally in field-names, cf. *Toot hill Butts* in Headington.

trench, ME from OFr, 'a path or track cut through a wood or forest; an alley; a hollow walk.' Trench Green.

trēo(w), OE, 'tree.' *Treton*, Langtree. Also in field-names, cf. *Kingestreu*, c. 1230 in Hook Norton.

*trill, *tryll, OE, a word meaning 'brook' postulated by Ekwall (RN 418) to explain the river-names Trill, Trull. Trill Mill Stream.

tūn, OE, 'enclosed piece of ground, homestead, village.' (*a*) Aston Bampton, Aston Leys Fm, Aston Rowant, Middle, North and Steeple Aston, Bampton, Brookhampton, Broughton, Broughton Poggs, Cassington, Charlton on Otmoor, Chastleton, Chesterton, Chilson, Chislehampton, Clifton, Clifton Hampden, Denton, Drayton, Drayton St Leonard, Foxtowns End Fm, Garsington[1], Glympton, Grafton, Hempton, Henton, Holton, Hornton, Horton, Kingston Blount, Launton, Marston, Merton, Middleton Stoney, Milton, Great and Little Milton, Milton under Wychwood, Moorton, Moreton, Newington, North Newington, South Newington, Newton Purcell, Brize Norton, Chipping Norton, Over Norton, Pyrton, Shilton, Shipton on Cherwell, Shipton under Wychwood, Somerton, Stanton Harcourt, Stanton St John, Stratton Audley, Sutton, Tadmarton, Taynton, *Treton*, Upton, Walton, Water Eaton, Weston on the Green, North Weston, South Weston, Woodeaton, Wootton, Worton (2)[2]; (*b*) Wigginton, Willaston; (*c*) Hensington, Hook Norton. *v.* also -ing- and -inga- *supra*. Occasionally in early field-names, where the compounds tūn-furlang and līn-tūn ('flax enclosure') both occur several times. In modern field-names *town* occurs *passim*, in such compounds as

---

[1] Replacing earlier dūn.
[2] These two names have different first elements.

Town Furlong, Town End, Town Side, Town Land, Town Quarter, Town Green.

twī-, OE, 'double.' Twyford Wharf, Tythrop.

twicene, OE, 'a fork in a road, a forked way,' occurs frequently in lost street-names in Oxford, and survives in Kybald Twitchen, the name of a house in Kybald Place.

twisled, OE, 'forked,' occurs in the following field-names: *Tvyseledeweye* (c. 1280 in Watlington), *Twyseledwey* (c. 1325 in Bicester), *Cueseledelake* (1324 in Enstone), *Twysdelowe* (1358 in Wolvercot), *Twiseldene* (1412–13 in Stratton Audley).

under, OE and ModE. Underdowns.

upp-, OE, 'higher.' Upcott Fm, Upperfield Fm, Upton. Cf. also *Opfelde*, 1334 in Northmoor, and the early forms for Holcombe, some of which have upp- prefixed.

ūtan, OE, 'on the outside.' Otney.

vente, ME, 'opening, outlet.' Vent Fm.

wād, OE, 'woad,' occurs in field-names, cf. *Wadbrech*, c. 1230 in Hook Norton, *Wadbreche*, c. 1240 in Steeple Barton.

(ge)wæsc, OE, 'overflow of water.' Washford Pits.

wæter, OE, 'water.' Water Eaton, Waterperry, Waterside Ho, Waterstock. The word is very frequent as a first element in medieval and modern field-names, where it is evidently the usual opposite of *dry* (*v. supra*), though ME *wet* occasionally occurs. The adjective *watery* occurs in *Waterilond* (c. 1230–40 in Thomley), and in modern names in such compounds as *Watery Lane*: and wæter sometimes occurs as a second element, presumably meaning 'stream' or 'pool,' cf. *Newerewater* and *Northlongwater*, 1275 in Bampton.

wash-way, recorded in NED in the 17th century for 'a portion of a road crossed by a shallow stream,' occurs in the field-names of Marston (*Wassh Waye* 1552) and Westwell (1770). There is a possible ME occurrence in Tetsworth (*Waissiewaieshende* c. 1225).

w(e)ala, OE, 'of the British.' Walcot. Cf. also *Walecote*, 1239 in the field-names of Cropredy, *Walecotesborwe*, c. 1230 in Oxford.

w(e)ald, OE, 'forest land,' later 'open country.' Weald, Claywell Fm. Cf. *Litlewald*, c. 1166 in Swalcliff, and the early forms for Burford.

w(e)all, OE, 'wall.' Walton.

weard, OE, 'watch.' Warborough. Also in *wearddun*, 966 in the field-names of Crowmarsh, *weardstige*, 1005 in Eynsham, and possibly in *Warboro' Bank*, a modern field-name in Idbury.

weg, OE, 'way.' (*a*) Burroway Bridge, *Fielden Way*, Hayway Lane, *Meaning Way, Stony Way*, Woodway Fm (2); (*b*) Hanwell, *Tidgeon Way*. *passim* in field-names, cf. *Euerlongwey* (c. 1360 in Shifford),

Harperes Weye (c. 1270 in Weston on the Green), *Chepmanneweye* (a. 1279 in Baldon).

(ge)weorc, OE, 'fort, defensive work.' *Hulwerk*.

wer, OE, 'weir.' *Aldweir*, King's Weir. Frequent in field-names.

west, OE and ModE. Westcot Barton, Westend, West End, Westfield Fm, Westhall Hill, Weston on the Green, North Weston, South Weston, Westwell. Also in field-names. There is another 'west end' 1551–2 in Adderbury.

wīc, OE, 'village, dairy farm.' (*a*) Wick Fm, East Wick Fm, *The Wyke*; (*b*) Wretchwick. Occasionally in field-names. wīchām, a compound of wīc and hām (*supra*), the precise sense of which it is impossible to determine, occurs in Wykham Fm and in the field-names *wicham* (969 in Hailey) and *Wycham* (c. 1250 in South Newington).

wice, OE, 'wych-elm.' Great Wichelo Shaw.

w(i)elle, OE, 'spring, stream.' (*a*) Wellground Shaw, Blindwell Wood, Brightwell Baldwin, Broadwell, Burwell Fm, Col Well, Colwell Brook, Cordle Bushes, Cornwell, Crockwell, Crowell, Fritwell, Fulwell (2), Gagingwell, Goldwell Spinney, Hanwell (replacing *weg*), Hawkwell, *Holewell* (earlier name of Old Grange Fm), Holwell, Holywell, Holy Well, Ledwell, Ludwell Fm, Mongewell, Muswell Hill, Newton Morell, Purwell Fm, Ruddy Well, Showell Covert, Showell Fm, Sugarswell Fm, Westwell; (*b*) Adwell, Baywell Gate, Cadwell, Daddles Close Spinney, Digger's Well, Epwell, Poffley End, Topples Lane, Shelswell; (*c*) Britwell, Caswell Ho, Cherwell, Pinnel Spring, Sedgehill Spring, Tomwell Fm. *passim* in field-names and lost stream-names. wælle, an Anglian variant of w(i)elle, occurs in Wally Corner, *Benseual*, some of the forms for Cadwell, and occasionally in field-names and lost stream-names, e.g. *Chreswal* (1302–3 in Hampton).

*w(i)erpels, OE, 'path.' Warpsgrove.

wiht, OE, 'bend.' Whitehill.

winter, OE and ModE, is a fairly common field-name element. It occurs in three lost stream-names (*v.* 15), where the reference is presumably to streams dry in summer. In the early field-names *Wintercombe* (c. 1200 in Rollright) and *Wynt'dole*, *Wenterdole* (c. 1225, 1415 in Aston Rowant), and the modern names *Winter Slade* (1608–9 in Charlbury), *Winter Hill* (1679 in Middleton Stoney), *Winter Furlong* (Cuxham and Tackley), *Winter Close* (Ramsden), *Winter Croft* (Crowell), *Winter Thorn* (Spelsbury), the meaning is uncertain. *winter* is used of autumn-sown crops that stand through the winter, and there is a *Winter Beer Furlong* ('winter barley') in Spelsbury. Cf. also sumor *supra*.

wiðig, OE, 'willow.' Weavely Fm, Widford, Widley Copse,

Witheridge Hill, Withycombe Fm, Withycoombe Fm, Wood-leys (?). Frequent in field-names, where there are three more examples of the compound with cumb, in Kingham, Rollright (c. 1190) and Sibford Gower (c. 1240). OE wīðig-bedd, ModE *withy bed*, is a fairly frequent field-name, the forms dating from the 13th century. Cf. also *Sally Bed* in Chastleton and Enstone.

wōh, OE, 'crooked,' occurs in several unidentified stream-names (*v.* 15), and is fairly frequent in field-names, where it is the probable first element of the names *Woolland, Wollands, Wooland*, which occur in some six parishes. *Wochemulne*, c. 1190 in Wat-lington, is reminiscent of the nursery rhyme about the crooked man who had a crooked mill.

worþ, weorþ, wyrþ, OE, 'enclosure, homestead.' (*a*) *Sullyngworthe*; (*b*) Chilworth, Tetsworth. Fairly common in field-names, where there is one occurrence of the expanded form *worðig* (*Francwordy*, c. 1270 in Cassington).

*wrocc, OE, 'buzzard.' Wroxhills Wood, Wroxton.

wudu, OE, 'wood.' Woodcote, Woodeaton, Wood Fm, Woodperry, Woodstock, Woodway Fm (2), Wootton, Beech Wood, Box Wood, Green Dean Wood, Hazel Wood, Kingwood Common, Stowood, Westwood Manor Fm, Wychwood. widu, the earlier form of the word, is represented in some of the forms for Wootton and in the field-name *Hasel(w)iyde* (? 1272 in Charlbury). wudu occurs *passim* in field-names, where wudu-weg and wudu-ford, ModE *Woodway* and *Woodford*, are particularly common.

wyrt, OE, 'vegetable.' Worton.

PRE-CELTIC AND CELTIC NAMES

Crouch Hill, Icknield Way and the river-names *Bladene*, *Giht*, Glyme, Thame, Thames, Windrush. Tangley Hall and Taynton have a pre-English river-name as first element, and the first elements of Alchester and Dorchester are of similar origin.

FRENCH NAMES

Beaumont, *Beamondelond* (1492–3 in Tetsworth), Bruern, Carfax, Collice Street and Field, Grandpont, *Pettypont*, Rewley.

NOTES ON THE DISTRIBUTION OF THESE ELEMENTS

be(o)rg is considerably less frequent than **hyll**, as is the case in Bk, Nth, Wa and Wo.

bold occurs in Bould, in the extreme west of the county, and possibly in a field-name in Eynsham. This is the only form of the element recorded in Wo (3) and Wa (4): it is generally regarded as the Mercian form. **bōtl**, regarded as Northumbrian rather than Mercian in origin, is the only form recorded in Bk (2), but both forms occur in Nth (5).

brōc is fairly frequent in major names, as in neighbouring counties, and very frequent in field and lost stream-names. It is less common than **w(i)elle**, however.

burh is about as frequent as in Bk, Wo and Nth, and the proportion of examples in which the first element is a personal name is roughly similar. Of the nineteen certain examples, eleven are mentioned in DB or earlier. The element is rather less frequent in Wa. **burhtūn** occurs occasionally in all these counties.

burna is rare. There are five occurrences in lost stream-names to be added to the three in the list of elements. It is similarly very or rather rare in Bk, Wo, Nth and Wa.

ceaster occurs but is rare, as in neighbouring counties. Of the four examples, Dorchester is first recorded c. 730, Chesterton 1005 and Bicester 1086.

cot(e) is frequent, as in the neighbouring counties, less frequent than in Wa and a good deal more frequent than in Bk. Of the forty-five examples in the list of elements, eighteen have a personal name as first element. Only seventeen are recorded before 1100. There are a few more examples in early field-names (excluding the examples of cot-stōw and 'lambcot' and 'sheepcot'), but none with a personal name, or for which the forms are very early.

cumb is fairly frequent in major names and early field-names, but less frequent in both than **denu**.

The stream-name *Cuttele* is apparently specially common in, though not confined to, this part of the country. It has been noted five times in O, nine times in Wa and five times in Nth.

dæl. The only early examples of this word noted in the county are *Langedale*, c. 1152 in Piddington and 1213–28 in Eynsham: cf. also *Depedale*, 1551–2 in Wardington. The element was only noted once in Bk, in a field-name. There are three examples in major names in Wo and one in Wa, where, however, it has been noted several times in field-names. This or the corresponding Scandinavian element is more frequent in Nth.

denu is roughly as frequent in major names as in Bk. It is considerably less common in major names in Nth, Wa and Wo, though in Wa it is a common field-name element.

dūn is frequent in major names, as in neighbouring counties. Of the twenty-seven examples in the list of elements, fourteen are recorded before 1100. In early field-names it is less frequent than hyll but more common than be(o)rg.

ēa is apparently more common in O than in the neighbouring counties, but it is impossible to be sure without a detailed survey of the field-names in the latter.

feld is fairly common in major names, as in neighbouring counties, but so far as one can judge most of the names are late: only six appear in DB.

grāfa appears to be rather more frequent in O than in neighbouring counties.

(ge)hæg is less common in major names in O than in Nth, Wa and Wo, but slightly more common than in Bk.

-hǣme, which is characteristic of this part of the country, is frequently used in the formation of minor names in O.

hām. The frequency of the element in O is similar to that in Wa, Wo and Nth. It is considerably more frequent in Bk. Of the seven certain examples in O, four are in the south-east of the county, three of these (Nuneham Courtney, Newnham Murren and Mapledurham) being on the Thames, and the other (Ingham) on the line of the Icknield Way. These names are first recorded in 940, 966, 1086 and 887 respectively. The remaining three names are Kingham, Rousham and Bloxham, all mentioned in DB: Rousham is on the Cherwell and Kingham on the Evenlode.

(ī)eg is more frequent than in Bk, Nth, Wa and Wo.

-inga- is fairly frequent, but a considerable proportion of the names have a topographical term or another place-name as first element.

lacu is rather more common than in Bk, Nth, Wa and Wo.

lē(a)h is very frequent as in neighbouring counties. Of the fifty-one names in the list of elements, only fifteen are recorded before 1100.

mere. This element is fairly frequent, as in neighbouring counties. In lost names and in those which survive it is noticeably more frequent in the south-east than in the rest of O, v. supra 459.

mōr is much the commonest word for a marsh, as in Bk, Nth, Wa and Wo. fenn is rare both in major names and field-names. mersc is rather rare in major names but more frequent in fields.

ōra is evidently specially characteristic of the Chilterns. Of the eleven examples in the list of elements, nine are in the south-east, and of four examples in early field-names three are in that area. The six examples noted in Bk are in the Chiltern Hundreds. ōra does not occur in Wa or Nth, and there is only one example in PN Wo. In these three counties there are several examples of ōfer, which is not recorded in Bk and rare in O. In the country as a whole, ōra is distinctively a south country suffix: in the west it has been noted as far north as Pershore in Wo, but in the east it has only been noted in Mx and counties south of Mx.

rīðig. This rare element occurs in Cropredy and in three lost stream-names. There is one example in PN Nth and two in PN Wa. It has not been noted in Bk or Wo.

slæd. As in neighbouring counties, this element is rather rare in major names but frequent in field-names.

stān is considerably more frequent in O than in Bk, Nth, Wa or Wo.

stede has been noted five times in early field-names, twice with tūn as first element. It has not been noted in Bk or Wo, but is rather more frequent in Wa and considerably more frequent in Nth.

stoc is rather more common in O and Bk than in Nth, Wa or Wo. Of the nine examples given in the list of elements, six are in the south-east of the county, and seven appear in DB. No examples have been noted in early field-names.

þrop is more common than in Wa or Wo, and much more common in the north of the county than in the south. Of the ten examples, all are north of Bampton and six north of Chipping Norton. The distribution of the seven examples in Bk is similar, these being with two exceptions in the northern half of the county: it is noteworthy also that the three examples in Wa are in the east of the county, and that in Nth, where it is difficult to distinguish this element from Scandinavian þorp, the names likely to contain the OE word are mostly in the south-west, on the borders of O, Bk and Wa. Five of the O names appear in DB.

tūn is very frequent, as in neighbouring counties. Of the eighty-nine names in which it occurs, seventy are recorded in DB or earlier. It is much the most frequent second element among the names in DB.

w(e)ald is rare: there is only one example in an early field-name to add to the two in the list of elements. It is similarly rare in Bk and Wo, but more common in Nth and Wa.

wīc is not very common: there are some six examples in early field-names. It is not frequent in Bk, Nth or Wa, but much more common in Wo.

w(i)elle is very common. In major names more examples have been noted than in Nth, where it is also frequent, and considerably more than in Bk, Wa and Wo.

worþ is rare in major names, but rather frequent in early field-names, where some fifteen examples have been noted. A similar situation was observed in PN Bk. The element is rare in major names in Wo, but more common in Nth and Wa. In O a considerable majority of the examples noted are in the southern half of the county. For a single example of *worðig*, *v. supra* 472.

PERSONAL NAMES COMPOUNDED IN OXFORDSHIRE PLACE-NAMES

Names not found in independent use are marked with an asterisk. The date and the parish are given where the place-name in which the personal name occurs is a field-name.

A. OLD ENGLISH

Aba (*Abenacre*, no date in Asthall), *Abba* (*Abban wylle*, 996 in Bensington), **Āceman* (Akeman Street), *Ācwulf* (*Aculfes dene*, 996 in Bensington), **Ægel* (Yelford, *Ailespiteshille*, c. 1260 in Little Tew, *Eylesham*, c. 1265 in Banbury), **Ægen* (Eynsham (?)), *Ælfgifu* (f) (*Aluyuedene*, 1257 in Wootton), *Ælfhēah* (Alvescot, *Aluesmore*, c. 1366 in Woodeaton), *Ælfrēd* (*ælfredes denn*, 1059 in Taynton, *Alfradesham*, c. 1240 in Bletchingdon), *Ælfweard* (*Aluedesham*, c. 1230 in Hook Norton, *Alewardescumbe*, c. 1280 in Hampton), *Ælfwīg* (*Alweyesham*, 1231 in Brize Norton), *Ælfwine* (*Alwinescrofte*, c. 1240 in Sibford Gower), *Ælfwynn* (f) (*Aluinelond*, 1244 in Stanton Harcourt), *Æðelhēah* (*æðelheges gemære*, 887 in Brightwell Baldwin), *Æðelheard* (*Aylardeslonde*, 1388 in Oxford), *Æðelrīc* (*Ailrikesmor(e)*, a. 1152 in Thame, *Heilricamore*, 1170–85 in Rollright, *Ailricheswelle*, c. 1210 in Steeple Barton), *Æðelstān* (*Athestaneshamm*, 1239 in Bampton), *Æðelweald* (*Æðeluuoldes lea*, 995 in Ardley), *Æðelwynn* (f) (*Athelynneham* t. Edw. 2 in Shirburn), **Ambre* (Ambrosden), **Assa* (Assendon[1]), *Babba* (Bablock Hythe), *Bada* (Bainton, *badandene*, 11th in Pyrton), *Bæcga* (Badgemore), *Bæga* (Baywell Gate), **Bæll* (Balscott), **Bætti* (*Batesham*, ? c. 1240 in Great Tew), **Ban(n)a* (Banbury), **Bata* (*Batemore*, a. 1152 in Cassington), *Bealda* (Baldon, *Baldeburne*, c. 1250–60 in Enstone), **Bearda* (*Bardenhulle*, c. 1240 in Sibford Gower), *Becca* (Beckley, Begbroke), **Benesa* (Bensington), *Benna* (Green Benny), *Beorhtfriþ* (*Brifordeswell*, 1315 in Enstone), *Beorhthelm* (Brighthampton), *Beorhtstān* (Brasswell), *Beorhtwulfing* or *Beorhtwulf* (*berhtulfing yge*, 1069 in Aston Bampton), *Beorna* (Bicester (?), Barleypark Fm, Berncote Lodge), *Beornmǣr* (Bromscott, *Bermersdene*, early 15th in Ascott under Wychwood), *Bēowa* (Beanhill Barn), *Bica* (*Bicanbyrig*, 1005 in Shipton on Cherwell, *Bikehegge*, 1220–7 in South Stoke, *Bikeweyesforlunge*, 1257 in Wootton), *Biga*

---

[1] The element could be the common noun meaning 'ass.'

(Bignell Ho), *Billa* (*Billebergam*, c. 1200 in Watlington, *Bilawella*, 1209–18 in Great Haseley), *Biscop* (*Bisepesmer*, 1239 in Cropredy), **Blæcci* (Bletchingdon), **Blæcci* or *Blæcca* (*Bleccan ford, Blecces forda*, 1012 in Whitchurch), *Blæcman* (*Blakemanesdoune*, 1308 in Goring, *Blakemanacre*, c. 1250 in Wendlebury), **Blocc* (Bloxham), *Boda* (Bodicote), *Bode* (*Bodesle*, 1280 in Gosford), *Boia* (Boynal Copse, *Boyham*, c. 1165 in Wolvercot, *Boywellefurlong*, 1340 in Beckley, *Boywere*, 1440 in Warborough, *Boymill*), *Botta* (*Bottethorne*, c. 1185 in Hampton), **Bottede* (*Bottededich*, c. 1260 in Hook Norton), *Brāda* (Broadstone[1]), *Brūn* (Bromsden Fm, *Brunesmere*, c. 1190 in Oddington), **Brȳda* (Burcot, *bryda beorh*, 996 in Bensington), *Bucca* (Bucknell), *Bugga* (*Buggan broc*, early name of Limb Brook), **Bul(l)a* (Bullingdon[2]), *Byni* (Binsey, *Bunse(s)loke*, 1278–9 in Nuneham Courtney), *Cada* (Cadwell, *Kadewrthe*, 1240 in Clanfield, *Cadeford*, c. 1325 in Bicester, *Cademersshe*, 1412–13 in Watlington), **Cǣga* (Kingham), **Cāfhere* (Caversfield, Caswell Ho (?), *Chavereshull*, 1231 in Handborough), *Cana* (*Caneneye*, c. 1300 in Brize Norton), *Cāsere* (*Cayseriswere*, 1405 in Oxford), **Catta* (*Cattan ege*, 966 in Crowmarsh), *Cawe* (*Cawesmor*,' ?1272 in Charlbury), **Ceacca* (Checkendon), *Ceadda* (*Chad(d)egrove*, c. 1235 in Hampton), **Ceadela* (Chadlington), **Ceahha* (*ceahhan mere*, 969 in Curbridge), **Ceattuc* (*Chettuchesham*, a. 1192 in Standlake), *Cēola* (Chilworth), *Cēolwulf* (*ceolwulfes treowe*, 887 in Brightwell Baldwin), **Cēomma* (Chimney), **Cēonna* (Chinnor), *Ceorl* (Charlbury), **Cibba* (Chippinghurst), **Cobba* (Cobbler's Bottom), **Cocca* (Cokethorpe Park[3]), **Cōd* (*Codesacre*, t. Ed 3 in Watlington), *Cǣna* (Kencott), *Cænhelm* (Kelmscott, Kemsley Barn), *Cola* (Colmore Fm, *Coleworthe, Collowe, Colewey, Colewelle, Colebroc*, 12th and 13th century in Hampton, *Colewrþe*, 1268–81 in Eynsham, *colnoran*, 11th in Pyrton, *Colneyshacch*', 1300 in Crawley, *Colnham*, 1278–9 in Combe), *Coppa, Cuba* or **Cobba* (one of these may be the first element of Cop Court), **Cott* (Cottisford, *Cottesmore*), *Creoda* (Curbridge), **Croppa* (Cropredy (?)), **Crypsa* (*crypsan hylle*, 11th in Pyrton), **Cuc* (*Cuxham*), **Cuca* (Cookley Fm), *Cuda* (*cudan hlæwe*, 995 in Cuxham, *Cudendone*, c. 1220 in Watlington), *Cufa* (Cowley), **Cūla* (Culham), *Cūþrēd* (Coursehill), *Cūþwine* or **Cūþen* (Cuddesdon, Cutslow), *Cwēnburh* (f) (*Queneburgheye*, 1238 in Bampton, *uuenburge byrgge*, 958 in Ducklington), *Cwichelm* (*Cwicelmes hlæw*, 995 in Ardley), **Cycga* (*cycgan stan*, 1044 in Hailey), *Cydda* (Kiddington), **Cydela* (Kidlington), *Cynelāf* (*Cynlafes stan*, 1005 in Shifford), *Cyneweard* (*Kenners Barrow*), *Cynewine* (*Kenewines treow*, 1005 in Shifford), **Cynewynn* (f) (*Cynewynne wylle*, 995 in Ardley),

---

[1] The element could be the adjective meaning 'broad.'
[2] The element could be the noun meaning 'bull.'
[3] The element could be the noun 'cock.'

Cyrtla (Kirtlington), *Dǣda* (Deddington), *Dēora* (*Derenslade*, 1412–13 in Stratton Audley), *Dicen* (Digger's Well), *Dodd* (*Doddesuelle*, 1187 in Brize Norton), *Dod(d)a* (Daddles Close Spinney, *Doddendene*, c. 1200 in Steeple Barton, *Doddeleye*, 1264–8 in Woodeaton, *Dodegrove*, c. 1220–30 in Chinnor), *Ducel* (Ducklington), *Duda* (*dudemede*, ? c. 1240 in Great Tew), *Dunn* (Duns Tew), *Dunna* (Dunthorp (?)) *Dunstān* (*Dunestaneswelle*, c. 1200 in Charlbury), *Dyne* (Dunsden), *Ēadburh* (f) (Adderbury), *Ead(d)a* (Adwell, *Addehurst*, c. 1360 in Shifford), *Ēadlāf* (*eadlanes ac*, 1005–12 in Beckley), *Ēadrīc* (*Edricheslonde*, c. 1230 in Cuxham), *Ēadweard* (*eadwardes mylne*, 956 in Tadmarton, *eadweardes ge mǣre*, 958 in Wootton), *Ēadwine* (*Edwinesweye*, c. 1240 in Sibford Gower), *Ealda* (*Eldindon*, 1273 in Elsfield), *Ealdrēd* (*Aldradeslade*, c. 1270 in Cassington), *Ealhhere* (Alkerton), *Eama* (Emmington), *Ēanfriþ* (*eanferþes hlau*, 956 in Horspath), *Earda* (Yarnton), *Eardwulf* (Ardley), *Earn* (Arncott), *Eatta* (Attington), *Eccel* (*Echelesdene*, 1306 in Watlington), *Ecga* (*Eggemede*, c. 1190–1200 in Rollright), *Ecgbeald* (*Egbaldiche*, 1213–20 in South Stoke), *Ecgfriþ* (*ecgfriðes gemǣre*, 887 in Brightwell Baldwin), *Ecgheard* (Edgerly Fm, *ecgerdes hel*, 969 in Hailey), *Ecghild* (f) (*Eggildeham*, late 13th in Goring), *Ecgi* (Exlade Street, *Eggesdown*, 1522–3 in Watlington), *Egsa* (*egsaforda, egsan ford*, 887 and 995 in Brightwell Baldwin), *Elsa* (Elsfield), *Engel* (*englingadene*, 11th in Pyrton), *Enna* (Enstone), *Eoppa* (Epwell), *Ēsa* (Easington (2)), *Fēra* (Fringford), *Filica* (Filkins (?)), *Focca* (*Fokeneye*, c. 1241 in Clanfield), *Franca* (*francanslo*, 1005–12 in Beckley, *Francwordy*, c. 1270 in Cassington), *Friðugils* (*friðeles stane*, 1059 in Wychwood), *Gāra* (Goring), *Gīsl* (*gisles bæce*, 887 in Brightwell Baldwin), *God* (*Godesthornefurlong*, 1328 in Ducklington), *God* or *Goding* (*Godesland, Godingeslonde*, c. 1233 and c. 1280 in Enstone), *Gōda* (Godington), *Godesman* (*Godesmannesfurlong*, late 13th in Garsington), *Gōdrīc* (*Godrichescroft*, 1199 in Headington), *Gōdwine* (*Godwinesthorne*, c. 1250 in Thame), *Gōsa* (*Gosenhelle*, 1206 in Bensington), *Grīm* (*Grimesmede, Grimeshevedesden'*, 1300 in Witney), *Hægel* (Clearsale), *Hægelweard* (*Hailwordesheie*, c. 1190 in Finmere), *Hæsting* (*hastinges lace*, 958 in Ducklington), *Hætta* (*Hattemerse* c. 1220, *Hattecumbe* c. 1170, in Watlington), *Hafoc* (*hafoces hlewe*, 969 in Curbridge), *Hagena* (Handborough), *Hana* (Hanwell, *Hanewerd*, c. 1220–30 in Chinnor), *Haneca* (*Hanechulle*, c. 1200 in Cowley), *Headda* (*headdan stigele*, 1012 in Whitchurch), *Hedena* (Headington), *Hengest* (*hengestes ige*, 969 in Witney), *Heoruweard* (*Huruardesberewe*, c. 1230–40 in Churchill), *Herebeorht* (*Hereberdesho*, c. 1270 in Wendlebury), *Hereman* (*Heremoneslede*, c. 1200 in Chastleton), *Heremōd* (*H'modeshey'*, 1315 in Witney), *Hering* (*Heryngesham*, c. 1165 in Wolvercot, *heryngeborow*, ? c. 1240 in Great Tew, *Haringisden*, early 13th in Kirtlington), *Hild*

(*Hildesden*), *Hild* (f) (*Hildeden'*, c. 1250 in Bletchingdon), *Hildebeald* (*Hildebaldeshamme*, 1239 in Claydon), **Hocc* (Hawkwell), *Hocca* (Hook Norton (?)), **Hod* (*Hodesham*, c. 1220 in Bicester, *Hodesacre*, ? late 14th in South Weston), *Horsa* (Horsendon Hill), *Hringstān* (*Ringstoneswelle*, 1239 in Cropredy), **Hrōc* (*roces æcere*, 1005–12 in Beckley), **Hrolla* (Rollright (?)), **Hroppa* (Rofford), *Hrōþwulf* (Rousham), *Hūda* (*Hudenhill*, c. 1225 in Rollright, *hodelowe*, c. 1230 in Oxford, *Hodleye*, 1300 in Wychwood), *Hūnbeorht* (*Humbrestreu*, c. 1200 in Kirtlington), **Hūnburh* (f) (*hun burhge leage*, 956 in Tadmarton), **Hund* (*Hundeshulle*, c. 1180 in Chastleton, *Hundesgore*, 1239 in Cropredy, *Hundeswell'*, 1278–9 in Chalgrove, *Hundescrofte*, 1311 in South Stoke), **Hunda* (Hundley Road), *Hunta* (Huntley Wood, *Huntemede*, 1267–84 in Black Bourton), *Ida* (Idbury), **Ippe* (Ipsden), **Ippa* (Ipenham), *Ladda* (*Ladenacre*, 1219 in Hampton), *Lāfa* (Launder's Fm), **Lahha* (*lahhan mere*, 956 in Cuddesdon), **Lēoda* (Ledall Cottage), *Lēodwine* (Lidstone), *Lēofeca* (Lewknor), *Lēofnōþ* (*Leuednodeswelle*, c. 1260 in Little Tew), *Lēofrīc* (*Liveruchesdich*, c. 1325 in Bicester), *Lēofrūn* (f) (*Leofrune gemære*, 1012 in Whitchurch), **Lēofsa* (*Levesendone*, a. 1296 in Checkendon), *Lēofstān* (*Leofstanes bricge*, 1044 in Curbridge), *Luca* (*Lukenden*, 1240 in Bloxham), *Luda* (*Ludemere*, 1241–64 in Eynsham), *Lufa* (Loughborough, *Lufan mere*, 11th in Pyrton), *Luh(h)a* (*luhanþirne*, 1005–12 in Beckley), *Lull* (*Lullesden*, c. 1325 in Bicester), **Luttoc* (*Luttokeslake*, 1241 in Oddington), **Māda* (Madley Brook), **Mægenhild* (f) (*magnhilde beorh*, 1059 in Taynton), *Mann* (*Mannesdene*, 1300 in Enstone), *Manna* (*la Manne mede*, 1240 in Bloxham), **Matt* (*Matteshey*, c. 1240–9 in Iffley), *Mildburh* (f) (*Mildburges slade*, c. 1260 in Hook Norton), *Muca* (*Mokedone*, c. 1366 in Woodeaton), **Mucga* (Mogpits Wood (?)), *Munda* (Mongewell), *Occa* (*occan slæw*, 1044 in Ducklington, *Occhestowe*, c. 1250 in Warborough), *Ōsa* (Osney), **Ot(t)a* (Oddington), **Otta* (Ot Moor, *Otley*), **Pæcc(i)* (Patch Riding), *Peada* (Padnell's Wood), **Peohtmund* (Pemscott), **Pappa* (*Pappelane*, 1228 in Eye and Dunsden), **Pāwa* (Pound Hill), **Pearta* (*Pertenhulle*, 1412–13 in Stratton Audley), **Pecg* (*Pegeshey*, 1317 in Britwell, *Pekgesheth*, 1300 in Watlington), *Pīc* (Pixey Mead), *Pīcel* (*Pykelespathe*, 1412–13 in Stratton Audley), *Pin* (Pinsley Wood), *Pinca* (*Pinkeworde*, 1278–9 in Claydon), **Pinna* (Pinnel Spring (?)), *Podda* (*Poddeleye*, 1300 in Wootton), *Pohha* (Poffley End, *Pochwele*, 1300 in Wychwood, *Pockelegh'*, 1240–1 in Nuneham Courtney), *Prēn* (Primsdown Fm), **Pudel* (Pudlicote), **Pult* (*Pultesweie*, 1189 in Checkendon), **Pulta* (*Pultecrofte*, 1228 in Eye and Dunsden), **Pyda* (Piddington), **Pyppa* (*pippan lege*, 983 in Arncott, *Puppelowe*, c. 1240 in Cowley), **Pytta* (Puttenee, c. 1240 in Hampton), **Rica* (*Rikedone*, 1220–7 in South Stoke), *Rippe* (*Ripesfeld*, 1195 in Witney), *Sǣflǣd* (f) (*Sefledethorne*, c. 1240 in

Sibford Gower), *Sǣwine* (*Sauuinesueie*, c. 1210 in Steeple Barton, *Sewynes dich*, c. 1260 in Hook Norton), **Sc(e)obba* (*Sobeford*, c. 1170 in Watlington), *Sc(i)eld* (Shelswell, *Sceldeshlaw*, c. 1250 in Sydenham), *Sciella (Shillingford, *Sullyngworthe*), *Scot* (*scottes healh*, 958 in Ducklington, *Scotislake*, c. 1244 in Cassington), *Scytta (*scyttan mere*, 11th in Pyrton, *Shyttenham*, 1299 in Churchill), *Scytta or *Scyttel (Shutford), *Seaxa* (*Saxinton*), *Secg (Sedgehill Spring[1]), *Selewīg* (*Selewiswell*, c. 1250 in Thame), *Seofeca* (*Sewkeford*), *Sibba* (Sibford), *Sidelāc (*Sidelakesham*, 1213–28 in Eynsham), *Sigehere* (*Sideresfelde*, c. 1200 in Watlington), *Sigerēd* or *Sigeweard* (*Sigardesthorn'*, 1300 in North Leigh), *Sigeweard* (*Sywardeseyth*, 1252 in Great Haseley), *Snell* (*Snelleseye*, 1224 in Oxford), *Snoc (Snakeshall Clump), *Sol* (*Soleshill'*, c. 1200–10 in Clifton Hampden), *Spearwe (Sparsey Bridge), *Spēol (Spelsbury), *Sprott* (*Sprottesfurlong*, 1325 in Ipsden), *Stoppa (*Stoppewelle*, c. 1220–30 in Chinnor), *Stunt (Stonesfield), *Sunta* (*Suntendone*, 1252–9 in Stoke Talmage), *Swǣffriþ (*swæferðes wylles heafdon*, 995 in Cuxham), *Tæcca (Tackley (?)), *Tæppa (Topples Lane), *Tætel (Tetsworth), *Tica* (*tycan pyt*, 969 in Curbridge), *Tīda* (*Tidenwelle*, c. 1240 in Sibford Gower), *Tīdrēd* (*Tidreding ford*, 969 in Witney), *Tilgār (*Tilgarsley*), *Tud(d)a* (*Tidgeon Way*), *Tulla* (*Tulldenden'*, c. 1275 in Kirtlington), *Tytta (Tiddington), *Uffa* (*Uffcot*, *Uffewylle*, 995 in Ardley), *Wæcel (Watlington), *Wændla (Wendlebury), *Wǣrmōd (Warmscombe[2]), *Wearda (Wardington), *Wicga* (Wigginton, *wicgan dic*, 1002 in Great Haseley, *Wyggestubbe*, c. 1210–20 in Thomley, *Wyggeleuam*, c. 1250 in Hook Norton, *Wigenham*, 1278–9 in Combe), *Wifel (Wilcote, *Wifeles lace*, 904 in Marston, *Wyueles ho*, 1005–12 in Beckley), *Wīghere* (*Wyresh(e)y*, 1228–39 in Cassington), *Wīglāf* (Willaston, *Wilausdene*, c. 1210 in Steeple Barton), *Wīgmund* (*Wymundesplace*, 1380 in Clanfield), *Wilbeald* (*wilbaldes ecge*, 956 in Tadmarton), *Wilheard* (*Wilardesfordeshulle*, c. 1240 in Bletchingdon), *Willa* (Hempton Wainhill (?)), *Wina* (*Wynemere*, c. 1360 in Shifford), *Wine* (*Wynestorn*, c. 1190 in Watlington, *Winsimor*, 1220 in Cowley), *Wineca (*Winecalea*, 11th in Pyrton), *Witta* (Witney), *Wittel (*Whetleswey*, c. 1240 in Sandford on Thames, *Whittleston*, 1246 in Forest Hill), *Wraca* (*Wrag(g)enhurst*, ? c. 1300 in Tetsworth), *Wulf* (*wylfinga ford*, 940 in Culham), *Wulfgār* (Wolvercot, *Wolgesham* c. 1366 in Woodeaton, *Wlgaresham*, c. 1180–97 in Chadlington), *Wulfhēah* (*Wolfeyesle*, 1270 in South Stoke), *Wulfheard* or *Wulfweard* (*Wlfardeswell*, c. 1225 in Tetsworth), *Wulfhūn* (*wulfunes treow*, 904 in Gosford), *Wulfmǣr* (Worsham Mill, *Wolmersham*, ? c. 1240 in Great Tew), *Wulfrūn* (f) (*Wluerunescroft*, c. 1219 in Crowmarsh, *Woluernedene*, 1366 in South Stoke), *Wulfsige* (*Wolshamforlong*,

---

[1] The element might be the noun 'sedge.'
[2] The forms show confusion with *Wǣrmund*.

c. 1225 in Hampton, *Wolsieslond*, c. 1240 in Bletchingdon, *Wlsies Welle*, c. 1270 in Hook Norton), *Wulfstān* (*Wolstane crofta*, c. 1260 in Hook Norton), *Wulfweard* (*Wlwardeshulle*, 1151–4 in Chesterton), *Wulfwine* (*Wluinesforlong*', 1198 in Stoke Lyne), *Wynsige* (*Winsisheche*, c. 1180 in Shiplake), *Wynstān* (*Wynstanes ham*, 996 in Bensington).

B. OLD NORSE AND ANGLO-SCANDINAVIAN

Clac(c) (OE from ON *Klakkr*) (*Claxhurste*, c. 1360 in Shifford, *Claxhurst*, 1363 in Eynsham, *Claces wadlande* and *Clakkesle*, 11th century and 1387 in Pyrton), *Crōc* (OE from ON *Krókr*) (Crowsley Park), *Cytel* (OE from ON *Kettill*) (*Kutelesmore*, 1235 in Stanton Harcourt), *Fareman* (ME from ON *Farmann*) (*litelfaremmanysdone*, c. 1270 in Great Tew), *Gunna* (*Gonnecroft*, 1331 in Goring), *Gunnhildr* (f) (*Gunnildegrove*, 1251 in Wychwood), *Norþman* (Norman's Grove), *Ólāf(r)* (*Bereford Olaui*, 1194 in the early forms for Barford St Michael, *Olaveshide*, 1195–9 in Stanton St John), *Thurcytel* (*Thurkeldeshide*, 1232 in Handborough).

C. MIDDLE ENGLISH AND CONTINENTAL

Alice (f) (Collice Street, Dame Alice Fm), *Bernard* (*Barnardesland*, 1449 in Stanton St John), *David* (Great David's), *Dickon* (diminutive of *Richard*) (*Diconesmede*, 1328 in Baldon), *Elizabeth* (f) (*Elizabeth ham*, 1498–9 in Westwell), *Everard* (*Euerardeshamdelond*, c. 1240 in Garsington, *Euerardeshulle*, 1412–13 in Pishill), *Gerard* (*Gerardeslake*, c. 1260 in Hook Norton), *Gilbert* (*Gilberdeshegge*, c. 1230–40 in Thomley, *Gileberdescroft*, 1339 in South Stoke, *Gylberdescroft*, 1363 in Fawler), *Haukyn* (diminutive of *Hal*, a pet form of *Henry* (*Hawkynescroft*, 1306 in South Stoke), *Helen* (f) (*Helenesmede*, c. 1325 in Bicester), *Jame(s)* (*Iamesbrech*, 1270 in Finstock), *Laurence* (*Court of Laurence*, c. 1250 in Bletchingdon), *Martin* (*Martinacre*, c. 1235 in Hampton), *Mirabel* (f) (*Mirabelescroft*, 1300 in North Leigh), *Ne(a)le* (*Nelesbrech*, c. 1220 in Cowley), *Patric* (*Patrikesfearn*, 1170–85 in Rollright, *Patrichesmede*, 1363 in Eynsham), *Phelippe* (*Phelippesgrof* and *Phelippeslith*, c. 1285 and 1359 in Goring), *Randolph* (*Randolfsbrigge*, 1302–3 in Hampton), *Roger* (*Roggeresrudinge*, 1270 in Fawler), *Walcelin* (*le holeredacre Waukelini*, c. 1196 in Wendlebury), *William* Williamscot).

FEUDAL AND MANORIAL NAMES

Manorial holder's name added: Ascot Earl, Ascot d'Oyley, Aston Rowant, Berrick Prior, Berrick Salome, Brightwell Baldwin, Britwell Prior, Britwell Salome, Broughton Poggs, Crowmarsh Battle, Crowmarsh Gifford, Hampton Gay, Hampton Poyle, Kingston Blount, Minster Lovell, Newnham Murren, Newton Purcell, Rotherfield Greys, Rotherfield Peppard, Stanton Harcourt, Stanton St John, Stoke Lyne, Stoke Talmage, Stratton Audley. Many manorial additions which appear in early forms of place-names, as Abbot (of Eynsham) 156, have not survived.

Manorial holder's name prefixed: *Bolles Shipton*, Brize Norton (?), Duns Tew, Sesswell's Barton, Temple Cowley.

Other manorial names: Ashbys, Bardolph's Wood, Blounts Court, Boy's Wood, Camoise Court, Chazey Fm, Chestlion Fm, Cottesmore Fm, Doyley Wood, English Fm, Greys Court, Mankorn's Fm, Merrimouth Inn, Merriscourt Fm, The Moors, Satwell, Turnerscourt Fm, Westwood Manor Fm.

SAINTS' NAMES

St Aldate 43, St Andrew 151, St Fremund 424. *v.* also Index 509–10 *infra*.

APPENDIX

BOUNDARIES OF OXFORDSHIRE CHARTERS

As the names from these boundaries have not been treated in the volumes in the order in which they occur in the Charters, the boundaries are given here, with the page on which each name is discussed indicated in brackets after the name. The bounds of Pyrton are not repeated, as they are quoted on pp. 87–9. The texts of the following boundaries have been taken from BCS and KCD, except for the Beckley and Taynton charters, the Bampton boundaries of 1069 (taken from OSFacs), and the St Frideswide and Eynsham foundation charters, which last two surveys are taken from Frid and Eynsh. The text of the Beckley charter is taken from the Red Book of Thorney in Cambridge University Library, and that of the Taynton grant from a photograph of the charter (which is in the Archives Nationales, Paris), supplied by the late Professor L. V. D. Owen. This last charter has recently been printed in Appendix II to Miss F. E. Harmer's *Anglo-Saxon Writs*, pp. 538–9, Manchester 1952.

ARDLEY, 995 KCD 1289. Ærest of ðare greatan dic (5) ðæt to Æðeluuoldes lea (197) to ðan landgemære (197); of ðan gemære swa æfter dene (197) in sexig broc (203); of sexig broce ðæt into Uffewylle broce (17); of ðan broce ðæt on ða grenan dic (197); of ðære dic be suðan ðære eorðbyrg (197) ðæt on Cwicelmes hlæw (197); of ðan hlawe ðæt on ða portstræte (3); of ðære portstræte ðæt wið lytle Ciltene (197) an æcer bræde; ðæt on ðæne grenan weg (197) ðe scyt to hegforda (220); æfter ðan grenan wege ðæt foran ongen Cyne-wynne wylle (17); of ðære wylle ðæt into ðære greatan dic; andlang ðære dic ðæt into bunon (197n); andlang bunan ðæt to ðan ealdan forda (197); of ðan forda ðæt into Eardulfes lea (196); of ðan lea ðæt eft to ðære greatan dic.

ARNCOTT, 983 KCD 1279. Ærest of ðan ealdan slæpe (222) up andlang Giht (9); of Giht on ðæt riðig; andlang riðies on ðone mere; of ðan mere eft on ðæt riðig; andlang riðiges to ðan hindfaldan (162); of ðan hindfaldan on ðone swinhege (162); of ðan swinhege on pippan lege (162); of pippan lege eft on ðone swinhege; andlang swin-heges innan easthealas (162); swa be wyrtuualen (162) innan ðone smalan weg (162); andlang smalan weges ðæt eft on Giht to ðan ealdan slæpe ær hit ær ongan.

BAMPTON, 1069 OSFacs. Ærest þær ceoman lace (302) ut scytt. andlang ceoman lace þ hit cymeð on temese (11). anlang temese westward. swa westsexena gemære is ꝺ myrcena. þ hit cymeð up to ðamgemyðan. þonne went hit on ða norðeran ea. ꝥ hit cymeð to anre lace. betwix berhtulfing yge (303). ⁊ hrisyge (304) ꝥ on ða norþ ea. ꝥ anlang þære ea. ꝥ hit cymeð eft to ceoman lace. ⁊ ꝥ land æt cyngbrycge norð andlang broces. ꝥ hit cymð þær holanbroc ut scytt. andlang broces up to þam wege be norðan cynstanes treowe. andlang weges to fulan broces heafdon. andlang broces on þa stanbricge. of þære stanbricge andlang weges on burgdyc. andlang dyc on þone broc. andlang broces eft on cyngbricge.

The second half of the survey, the bounds of the land at *cyngbrycge*, presumably relates to Oxfordshire, but none of the places mentioned has been identified. The charter also gives boundaries of a piece of land at Holcombe in Dawlish (PN D 492).

BECKLEY, 1005–12 (c. 1325–50) *Thorney*[1]. of scipwege (167) into meoslege (167). of meoslege into Westlege (167). of Westlege into holowege (166). of holowege into mærbroce (14). of mærbroce into francanslo (166). of francanslo into miclandic (167). of myclandic into þere ealden ea (13). up of þere ealdenea into ottanmere (208). of ottanmere þuyrs ouer bugenroda (242). of bugeroda into mær-mere (166). of mærmere on mer þorn (166). of mærþorn to eadlanes oc (166). of eadlanes ac to luhanþirne (166). of luhanþyrne on þone ealdan mærweg (166) into wude. andlang þes ealdan mereweges into hildesdene (179). of hildesdene into Wyueles ho (167) to roces æcere (167). of roces æcere to þolege (167). of þolege to goldwillan (16). of goldwyllan to grenewege (166) into scipwege.

Bynsingtun land (119n), 996 (13th) KCD 1292. Ærest of smalan wylle (15) east be heafdan (119) be ðan gemære ðæt hit cymð innan cealcseaðes weg (119); and swa andlang weges innan Aculfes dene (119); andlang dene ðæt on fildena wuduweg (1–2); andlang weges ðæt on bryda beorh (119); middeweardne of ðan beorge andlang dene on waddene (119); andlang waddene on wyrðe (119); of wyrðe and-lang weges to hean lincan (119), to rugan hegcan (119); swa andlang hegeræwe (119) on Abban wylle (16); ðannon eft on smalan wylle. Ðis sind ðas wudes gemæra ðe to ðam lande gebyriað. Ðæt, is ærest andlang æcerweges (119) on hreodslæd (119); andlang slædes on gegan dene; andlang dene ðæt on gegan lege, eastewearde of ðære lege andlang burhslædes (119) on burhwege (119); ðanon on hageweg (119) ut on ðæne feld; and swa þwyres ofer fernfeld (119) on Wynstanes ham (119); of ðan hamme a be wurtruman (119) ðæt eft on ðone æcerweg.

BRIGHTWELL BALDWIN, 887 (11th) BCS 547. —from teolulfes treowe (122) ond long longanhylles (122) on fildena weg (1–2) þonan

---

[1] For this charter, *v.* Introduction xxiv–xxv.

on holandene (133) up on cadandune (121) to æðelheges gemære (122) þonan to ecgfriðes gemære (122) þonne a big ecgfriðes gemære to cuces hæma gemære (125) ꝥ to incghæma gemære (96) ꝥ swa ondlong incghæma gemære suð þurh east leh (122) ꝥ to gisles bæce (122) ꝥ ondlong gisles bæce ꝥ eft to ceolwulfes treowe (122). ⁊ ꝥ mæð lond be betweonum egsafordā (122) ⁊ strætforda (122) be norðan broce ⁊ þone wudu þærto þe scylfhrycg (122) is haten.

COWLEY, 1004 (t. Ed 2) Frid. of cere willa bricga (35) andg lang stræmer on þa riþig, wid hacelinges crofte (32) andglang rightes estward ꝥ hit comæ into ofranfurlange, ꝥ scyt vpp nordwerd to hwet furlanges heafde (29), of þam hefde on þat riþig east weard to mer higte, of þam hwge in to þam broce, of dam broce to den acere, of þam aceron into hocce mære (28), of þam mere in to Gifetelea (32), of gifetelea into þam broce, of þam broce eft into cere willan.

CUDDESDON, 956 (contemporary) BCS 945. [of] hryþera forda (168) on holan ford (168). of holan forde on lahhan mere (168) ⁊lang riþiges on bradan mædwa (170). þæt swa norð ⁊lang fura on set þorn (170). of set þorne on fulan riþig (14) on anne pyt. of þam pytte ⁊lang riþiges on þæt heafod lond (168). of þam heafodon ⁊lang fura. on pric þorn (170) on foreweardne eanferþes hlau (170). of eanferþes hlawe ⁊lang fure. þæt on an riþig. ⁊lang riþiges ꝥ on ane dic. ⁊lang dices on drygean broc (169). þæt swa ⁊lang dices on mærwelle broc. ⁊lang broces on mærwelle (9). of mærwelle. on þæt heafod long on gerihte to stræt. þonne east ⁊lang stræte. oþ þæra stræta gelæto (168). þ[on]an rihte norþ ondlong weges oþ þa heafdo ꝥ on mær weg (194). ⁊long mær weges ꝥ onbutan ceorla graf (194). on fost broc (172). of fost broce on þone hlið weg (177). ⁊long þeges on hina gemæro (177). ⁊long hina gemæres on þa hlydan (16). ꝥ of þær hlydan on þa stan bricge (189). ⁊long healhtunes gemæres (176) on risc dene (177). þæt of risc dene on gerihte on þæt þri ex (177). of þan þri exe on þa stræt (177). ⁊long stræte on holan broc (14). ⁊long broces on herpaþ ford (142) on tame (10–11) ⁊long tame ꝥ eft on hryþera ford.

CULHAM, 940 (c. 1200) BCS 760. Ærest on wylfing ford (151) on Temese (11). ꝥ of wylfinga ford ⁊lang anre smale dic to niwan hæminga londgemære (183) on ða heafdo (151). ꝥ forð be ðon heafodon on fippel beorgas (151). of fippel beorgon on Culanhema dic (151). ⁊lang dic on æppelford (Appleford, Berks). of æppelforda ⁊lang þære richt temese onbutan utan ege (151) þæt eft on wylfing ford.

CUTSLOW, 1004 (t. Ed 2) Frid. erest of þere portestrete (3) on trilwille (11) of ðere wille on þet riþig, of þam riðie to þes biscopesge meron (268), of þem gemarun in to wifeleslace (181) on þed flad, of þam slade on wyfeleshille (181), of þare hille on hyne.

CUXHAM, 995 (10th) KCD 691. Ærest of cudan hlæwe (126) on fildena weg (1–2). andlang weges ꝥ on ðone ealdan egsan ford (122). of ðam forda andlang hweowelriðiges (87) ꝥ on swæferðes wylles heafdon (16). of ðæs wylles heafdon. on þone æsc (126). of ðam æsce. eft on hweowelriðig. of ðam riðige. on þa ealdan dic (126). of þære dice. ꝥ on þa wudu wíc (126) æt wylleres seaðon (126).

DUCKLINGTON, 958 (c. 1250) BCS 1036. Þis sindon þa land gemæro to Duclingtune (317). xiiii. hida ꝺ þa ealdan cyricean æt æstlea (*v. infra*) ꝺ þær to. xl. æcera. ꝺ byrnan lea (317) eal into Duclingtune. Ærest of duclingtune on weric (11–12) ꝺ lang wenrices on þone byge (319) of þam byge on þa ealdan lace (13). ꝺ lang lace on þa norð ea (18) ꝺ lang streames on folgor hyrste (319) neoþewearde þonon on þa ealdan dic (319). ꝺ lang dic ꝥ suð eft on wænric up on gean stream on þone ealdan ford (319). of þone forda up on þa Riþe an furlang wið svþan þa cyrican ꝺ lang Riþe on þa wurtwalan (319) ꝥ ut þurh þone hagan on burh dic (319) ufeuuearde. of þære dic on þa ealdan Rode (319) of þære rode on scottes healh (319) of þam heale on uuen-burge byrgge (319) of þæra brucge on þa dic. ꝺ lang dices on east hæma gemære (302) on þone bige to þan heafdan (319) on gate þyrnan (319). of þære þyrnan on blace þyrnan (319) on þa dic of þære þyrnan to uurt walan to þan furan ꝺ lang fura on þa ealdan dic to þan ellere (319) ꝺ lang dices to þan oþern ellene (319). of þan ellene to þære apoldre (319) ðanon to æglesuullan broce (324) up on gean stream on stanford (319) of þan forda on fugelslæd (319) of þam slæde on coluul-lan broc (6) ꝺ lang broces on swyllan healas (319). of þan healan on hastinges lace (18) ꝺ lang lace on þone ea stream. ꝺ twegan hammas æt loppede þorne (319) hyrað in to Duclingdune.

æstlea (*v.* east, lē(a)h) has not been identified: it may, like *byrnan lea*, have been in the parish of Ducklington.

EYNSHAM, 1005 (late 12th) Eynsh. ærest of ruganlace (17) on Buggan broc (8). andlang broces on Tilgares dic (260). of þære dic on weardstige (264). of þam stige on Winburge stoc (264). of þam stocce to þrim acon (264). andlang weges on þæt gemær treow (264). þonne andlang weges on þa port stræt (3). of þære stræte on swana croft (264). þanon on hæðfeld (264) on þa ealdan dic (264). þanon rihte on mærbroc (14). andlang broces innon Bladene (7). andlang Bladene into Temese (11).

LITTLE HASELEY, 1002 (13th) KCD 1296. Ærest on roppan forda (123); ðæt andlang wicgan dic (131) ðæt hit sticað on wearra ford

(143); swa andlang mores oð ðene bradan herepað (131, 142); ðæt
on ðæra æcera heafada (131) ðæt hit sticað on Humbra (15); andlang
Humbra ðæt on roppan broc (123) foron ongean stangedelf (90);
andlang ropan broces on hafocgelad (131); eft andlang roppan broces
ðæt hit cimð on roppan ford ðær hit ær onfeng.

Newnham Murren 966 (contemporary) BCS 1176. Cattan ege (50)
into niwan ham (49) of þam hæþnan birigelsan (51) up ꝺlang dic
innan mær wege (51) up ꝺlang mær wege þæt up on wearddune (51)
þær þæt cristel mæl (51) stod of þan up on þa readan slo (51) oþ þære
ealdan byrig (51) of þære readan slo on þæt crundel (51) þær se haga
(51) utligeþ. Of þan crundelle innan mid slæde (51) ꝺlang mid
slædes on þa grægan hane (48) of þære grægan hane ꝺlang hearp dene
(72) on cealfa leage (51) neoþe wearde of cealfa leage a be hagen ꝺ be
þan ealdan wege (51) in on þ bec siþþan ꝺlang beces on tæmese (11)
ꝺlang ea on cattan ege.

Sandford on Thames, 1054 (c. 1200) KCD 800 (the same bounds
occur also in KCD 793). Ærest of stubbucwere (187); swa norð
æfter ðære Temese (11) be healfan streme into Sandfordes læce; swa
andlang ðære lace into Sandforda (186); of Sandforda east andlang
ðære lace up to fernniges heafdon (180); [of ferniges heafdon] up
þurh ðone mor east into ðære stræt; and swa suð andlang ðære
stræt into bealdanhema gemære (163); and swa west andlang gemæres
into niwanhæma gemære (183); and swa andlang gemæres on suðe-
wearde hochylle (184); of hochylle swa west on gerihte eft on
stubbucwere.

Shifford, 1005 (late 12th) Eynsh. ærest of Temese (11) on Ceomina
laca (302). of þare lace on þone weg. andlang weges on Cynlafes
stan (328). of þam stane andlang weges on Kenewines treow (328).
of þam treowe andlang weges on þa lace. andlang lace þ eft on
Sumerford (331). 11. weras. oþer bufan þære lade. oþer beneoðan.

Shipton on Cherwell, 1005 (late 12th) Eynsh. of Cearwylle (6)
on Humbran (15). andlang Humbran on þ slæd. þanon on þa stræt.
of þære stræte on Bradewyllon (17) on þone ealdan garan (282). of
þam ealdan garan andlang þæs wudu weges (282) on þa heh stræte
(282). of þære strætte on þone weg þe scyt to Bladene (7). þonne
andlang weges to þam hagan. of þam hagan to Bicanbyrig (281). of
Bicanbyrig on þa ealdan dic (282). of þære dic on þone weg. andlang weges to wiðigleas gemæro (286). andlang mores on langan
hlæw (282). of langan hlæwe. andlang we[ge]s to þam eoldan Cristelmæle (282). of þam Cristelmæle on Cyrwylle (6). andlang Cyrwylle
eft on Humbran.

TADMARTON, 956 (c. 1200) BCS 964. Ærest of coppan wyllan broc (421) þonne ða blacan wyllan (13) þ of blacan wyllan on ðone heafod æcer (407). of þan æcere ᵹlang gemæres on hesl burh (397) midde wearde. of hæselbyrg on hæsl ford (397) ᵹlang streames on þone ealdan ford (407). of þan forde a be gemære þ on ða stræt of þære stræt on þone læg acer (407). of þan læg æcere a be mære þ on þone hrigc weg (3). of þan hric wege be gemære þ on þa ealdan dic (407) ᵹlang dices on lang dices brigce (407). of þære brigce on gean stream þ on gres wyllan broc (13) of þam broce on fule wyllan (14) of þam wylle be gemære on scearpannesse (407) a be gemære þ on ðone steort (407) of þan steorte on ða stræt ᵹlang streate on hun burhge leah (407) of þære leahe þ eft on eoppan wyllan broc (420).

Another version of these bounds occurs in BCS 967, in a charter of the same date, of which the copy is 18th century. Ærest of eoppan wyllan broc þ on ða blacane wyllan þ of blacan wyllan on ðone heafodæcre. of ðan æcre ᵹ lang gemærrees on hæslburh middeweardre of hæslbyrg on hæslford ᵹ lang streames on ðone ealdan ford of ðan forda a be gemære þ on ða stræt of ðære stræt on ðone læg æcer of ðam læg æcer a be gemære þ on ðone hrigc weg. of ðam hric wege be gemære þ on ða ealdan dic ᵹ lang dices on landgares brigce of ðære brigce ongean stream þ on cærswyllan broc of ðam broce on fule wyllan of ðam wille be gemære on scearpannæsse a be gemære þ on ðone steort. of ðam steort on ða stræt ᵹ lang stræt on hunburg leah of ðære leah þ eft on eoppan willan broc.

TADMARTON, 956 (contemporary) BCS 965 (a somewhat shortened version of these bounds occurs in BCS 967). Ærest of eadwardes mylne (407) þ on ða ealdan dic (407) of ðære dic on mær broc (14) of mærbroce on þ eastre sic (14) of ðam sice on mær stan (407) of mær stane on ðane ealdan garan (407) of ðan garan a be heafdan (407) a be heafdan (sic) þ on ðone broc of ðam broce ongean stream þ on þ riscbed (407) of ðam riscbedde þ on ðone weg. þ suð ᵹlang weges þ on þ slæd þ of ðan slæde up on þa ecge þ ᵹlang ecge on heort wyllan (18) of heort wyllan on ða ealdan styge (407) þ ᵹlang styge on ðone mær pyt (407) of ðam pytte on wilbaldes ecge (407) of wilbaldes ecge þ eft on eadwardes mylne.

TADMARTON, 956 (18th) BCS 966 (these bounds occur also in BCS 967). ærest on halhford (407) þ andlang wo burnan (15) þ on eow anwelles stream (420) þ up ongean stream an sandford (407). of sandforda a be gemære þ on ða heafod stoccas (407). of ðan stoccan on ðone mær stan (407). of ðan stane a be gemære þ on landgares bricge (407).

TAYNTON, 1059 (11th) *St Denis.* ærest of þam readan clife (385) on ælfredes denn (385). ᵹ of þam denne. on þone haranstan (385).

ꝛ of þam stane on mægnhilde beorh (385). ꝛ of þam beorge on risc wille (118). ꝛ of þære wylle. on þa rugaðyrna (385). ꝛ of þara ðyrne on þon holan broch (14). ꝛ of þam broche. on hæselford (385). ꝛ of þam forde andlangc weges on þone stapel (385). ꝛ of þam stapele on dryge pytt (385). ꝛ of þam pytte. on fulla wille (14). ꝛ of þære wylle. on cobban hyll (353). ꝛ of þære hylle. on cobbanbroc (353). ꝛ of þam broche andlang streames inne wenric (11–12). ꝛ swa to þam readan clyfe. Þis is þ gemære to þam more (366) þe þider inn toligð. þ is of dic lace (18) a wilstede (367). ꝛ of wilstede on ryðera ford (367). ꝛ of þam forde. on wireneges þorn (367). ꝛ of þam þorne. andlang wenric (11–12) on beafolces ears (367). ꝛ of beafolces earse andlang temese (11) be healfan streame eft inne dic lace. Þis is þ gemære to þam wuda þider inn. þ is ærest of friðeles stane (389) on þone stanian weigg (4). ꝛ of þam wege on fæste graf (384). ꝛ of þam grafe andlang weges on wiðilea (384). ꝛ of þære lea swa eft on þone stan.

Water Eaton, 904 (11th) BCS 607. ærest from wifeles lace (181–2) þ swa up andlang riðiges þ hit cymð to fagan floran (268) ꝛ þonne swa andlang slædes be þam twam lytlan beorgan þ hit cymð to wulfunes treow stealle will (268). an suna þ swa þwyres ofer þ furlang þ on þa þyrnan (268) westewarde þær se mycla þorn (268) stod þ swa on fugelmere (17) þ þonne a ondlang dices oð þ hit cymeð to horwyllan (17) þ swa ondlang riðies þ hit cymð to cearwyllan (6) þonne mæreð hit cerwelle seoððan.

Whitehill, 1004 (t. Ed II) Frid. of ealdon hensing' lade (271) ofer þe clyf on þam stennithtanwege (4), of þan wege on langan hlawe (282), of þam hlaewe on þa porte strete (3), of þare strete on cere willam stream (6), swa æfter streame þ hit scyt eft into hensing lade.

Witney, 969 (12th) BCS 1230. Ærest of hafoces hlewe (316) on wenrisc (11–2) on þa wiðig rewe (315) on hnut clyf (366). of þam clyfe on hean leage (314). þ on lungan leage weg (315). and lang weges. þonne on swon leage (314) þonne on swon weg. ꝛlang weges þ hit sticað on norðe weardum cynges steorte (315). Ða non on suga rode (315). and lang rode on huntena weg (323). ꝛlang weges þ hit sticað æt wic ham (323). ða non a be wyrt wale (323) on ofling æcer (323). þo non on ealdan weg (323) ꝛlang weges on cycgan stan (323). of þam stane on þane grenan weg (323). and lang weges. þonne on yccenes feld (323). of yccenes felda on ða hege rewe (323). ꝛlang hege rewe on met sinc (323) and lang met sinces on ecgerdes hel (323) ufeweardne æfter wyrt walan on wenric and lang wenricces on fulan yge (334) easteweardne. þo non æfter ge mære on tidreding ford

(334). ða non on occan slæw (319). þa non on wittan mor (333) suðe
wearðne þo non on colwullan broc (6) of þam broce on þa ealdan dic
(319). of ðære dic on fugel sled (319) of þam slede on þa stan bricge
(319). æfter broce on þane ealdan weg of þam wege on horninga
mære (316) ða non on wæredan hlinc (316) suðeweardne þonan and
lang slædes on tycan pyt (316) and lang broces on ða myþy (316) of
þas gemyþon on ceahhan mere (18). Ða non on lythlan eorþ beorg
(316) of þære byrig on þa on heafda (316) of þas on heafdon on cytel
wylle (316) of ðas wylle on þa stret. ꝥlang strete on hafoces hlew of
þam hlewe eft on hnut clif ðer hit ær aras.

ꝥ ðis is þæt med land þe þar to ge byrad æt hengestes ige (334) an
ꝥ twentig æcra.

WITNEY, 1044 (c. 1150) KCD 775. Ærest andlang ðæs streames on
ðone mædham ðe hyrnð into Scylftune (319); and fram Scylftune
andlang streames ðæt it cymð to ðam mylewere ðe hyrnð into
duceling dune (317); of ðæm wære ofær ðone wegean mor (319) into
hocslew (319); ðanon on ða niwan dic (319); of ðære dic on horninga
mære (316); of horninga mære andlang ðæs gemæres to hlæwan slæde
(316); of ðam slæde into dufan doppe (9) and swa andlang gemæres
into Leofstanes bricge (316); of Leofestanes bricge into kytelaceras
(316); of kytelacæras innon ða wudestret (316); andlang ðære strete
into hafoces hlæwe (316); of halfoces hlewæ innon wænric (11–2); of
wenric to swondæne (314); æfter swondæne to ðære haran apeldran
(315); of ðære apeldran andlang gemæres innan swonlege (314); of
swonleage upp to ðam heafdam (315); of ðam heafdan andlang surode
(315) innan huntenan weg (323); andlang huntenan wege into Wicham
(323); of Wicham a be ðare wyrtruman (323) ðæt hit cymð on sceapa
weg (323); of sceapa wege andlang rihtes gemæres innan æcenes feld
(323); of æcenes felda andlang rihtes gemæres on kicgestan (323);
of kicgestane into æceres felda; of æcenes felda ðær ða cnihtas licgað;
and fram ham ðe ða cnihtas licgað on mætseg (323); andlang metseg
into wenric.

WOOTTON, 958 (12th) BCS 1042. Ærest æt meolforda (294) upp and
lang streames oþ ramma ford (249) of þam forda and lang ramma dæne
(249–50) to eadweardes ge mære (295) of eadweardæs ge mære to
glim (7). ꝥ lang glim adune on þone stream oþ hit cymþ to þam stream
þæ scyt fram meolcforda up and lang þæs streames þæt hit cymþ æft
to meolcforda.

INDEX

OF SOME WORDS OF WHICH THE HISTORY IS ILLUSTRATED IN THIS VOLUME

INDEX

OF PLACE-NAMES IN OXFORDSHIRE

Where a name is mentioned on several pages, the primary reference or references are given first in clarendon type. Field-names have not in general been indexed, nor have the Notes on the Dialect and the Lists of Elements and Personal Names. The Addenda and Corrigenda to *The Place-Names of Oxfordshire* have been indexed, but not those to other volumes.

INDEX

OF PLACE-NAMES IN COUNTIES OTHER THAN OXFORDSHIRE